HISTORY OF THE
33D IOWA INFANTRY
VOLUNTEER REGIMENT

The Civil War in the West

Series Editors: Anne J. Bailey and Daniel E. Sutherland

HISTORY OF THE

33D IOWA INFANTRY

VOLUNTEER REGIMENT

1863–6

BY A. F. SPERRY

*Edited by Gregory J. W. Urwin
and Cathy Kunzinger Urwin*

THE UNIVERSITY OF ARKANSAS PRESS, FAYETTEVILLE 1999

03 02 01 00 99   5 4 3 2 1

Designed by Ellen Beeler

This project is supported in part by a grant from the Arkansas Humanities
Council and the National Endowment for the Humanities.

⊗ The paper used in this publication meets the minimum requirements of the
American National Standard for Permanence of Paper for Printed Library
Materials Z39.48-1984.

Library of Congress Cataloging-in-Publication Data

Sperry, A. F. (Andrew F.), 1839–1911.
    History of the 33d Iowa Infantry Regiment, 1863–6 / by A. F. Sperry; edited
by Gregory J. W. Urwin and Cathy Kunzinger Urwin.
       p. cm.
    Includes bibliographical references (p.) and index.
    ISBN 1-55728-576-4 (cloth: alk. paper)—ISBN 1-55728-577-2 (pbk.: alk. paper)
    1. United States. Army. Iowa Infantry Regiment, 33rd (1862–1865) 2. United
States—History—Civil War, 1861–1865—Regimental histories. 3. Iowa—
History—Civil War, 1861–1865—Regimental histories.   I. Urwin, Gregory J. W.,
1955–   II. Urwin, Cathy Kunziner, 1954–   III. Title

E507.5 33rd .S64 1999
973.7'477—dc21   99-047807

To Edward,

Our light and our love.

CONTENTS

ILLUSTRATIONS

SERIES EDITORS' PREFACE

The Civil War in the West has a single goal: To promote historical writing about the war in the western states and territories. It focuses most particularly on the Trans-Mississippi theater, which consisted of Missouri, Arkansas, Texas, most of Louisiana (west of the Mississippi River), Indian Territory (modern day Oklahoma), and Arizona Territory (two-fifths of modern day Arizona and New Mexico), but it also encompasses adjacent states, such as Kansas, Tennessee, and Mississippi, that directly influenced the Trans-Mississippi war. It is a wide swath, to be sure, but one too often ignored by historians and, consequently, too little understood and appreciated.

Topically, the series embraces all aspects of the wartime story. Military history in its many guises, from the strategies of generals to the daily lives of common soldiers, forms an important part of that story, but so, too, do the numerous and complex political, economic, social, and diplomatic dimensions of the war. The series also provides a variety of perspectives on these topics. Most importantly, it offers the best in modern scholarship, with thoughtful, challenging monographs. Secondly, it presents new editions of important books that have gone out of print. And thirdly, it premieres expertly edited correspondence, diaries, reminiscences, and other writings by witnesses to the war.

It is a formidable undertaking, but we believe that The Civil War in the West, by focusing on some of the least familiar dimensions of the conflict, significantly broadens understanding of that dramatic story.

Andrew F. Sperry, born in 1839, was a New Englander who came of age in Iowa. He joined the Thirty-third Iowa Infantry in August 1862 and served with the regiment until it was disbanded three years later. The following year, Sperry published his *History of the 33rd Iowa Infantry Volunteer Regiment*. Thus, unlike the authors of most Civil War regimental histories, some eight hundred of which were published in the sixty years following the war, Sperry wrote his book with the conflict still fresh in his mind. Evidence also suggests that his memory was assisted by a diary he kept during the war. The result is a lively, honest, and detailed account of the regiment's movements and actions from the time it was organized through the end of the war. The Thirty-third Iowa served in Kentucky, Mississippi, Texas, Alabama, and, most importantly, Arkansas, where it spent most of its time. These Hawkeyes played an especially conspicuous role in the Camden campaign, the Arkansas phase of the Union's larger, but ill-fated, Red River campaign in the spring of 1864.

Sperry served first as a regimental fifer and eventually as chief musician, which gave him a unusual perspective on the war and the activities of his comrades. Along with the regimental drummers and other fifers, Sperry sounded the duty calls that regulated a soldier's day from reveille to taps. In combat, he stood directly behind the firing line to play "fight songs" that bolstered regimental morale. But like any good historian of the war, Sperry devotes as much attention to life on the march and in camp—where soldiers spent the vast majority of their time—as he does to the battles. He adds to our knowledge and understanding of those momentous days, weeks, and months with a perceptive narrative of army life. Sperry is also remarkably candid. He exhibits tremendous pride in his regiment's accomplishments, but he also chronicles the hard side of war with unflinching depictions of looting, resistance to orders, and the "extermination" of Confederate guerrillas.

Scholars have long considered Sperry's work a classic among regimental histories. Allan Nevins, Bell I. Wiley, Edwin Bearss, James I. Robertson Jr., and Ludwell H. Johnson have all sung its praises. Johnson, in his own impressive book about the Red River campaign, describes Sperry's work as "an unpretentious memoir, pleasingly written, and one of the few unofficial sources for the campaigns in Arkansas." With only a handful of the original books having survived, this republication in a scholarly edition, edited and annotated by Gregory J. W. Urwin and Cathy Kunzinger Urwin, only enhances its value and should delight all students of the war.

Anne J. Bailey
Daniel E. Sutherland

ACKNOWLEDGMENTS

In editing this new edition of A. F. Sperry's history of the 33d Iowa Infantry, we received invaluable assistance from our own regiment of supporters. We would like to take this opportunity to express our deepest thanks to them.

We begin at our home base, the University of Central Arkansas. George W. Schuyler, chair of the Department of History, gave us unlimited access to the department's Microtek scanner, which allowed us to transfer most of Sperry's book to computer disks without typing it ourselves. Departmental secretaries Donna Johnson and Judy Huff typed and proofread those parts of the text that the scanner could not read. Graduate assistants Karren Lee, Sheri Moore, Carel Osborne, and Calvin White Jr. checked the scanned version of Sperry's book against the original. They also proofread our introduction and annotations. James W. Brodman, our colleague in the History Department, and his wife, Marian M. Brodman, chair of UCA's Department of Foreign Languages, helped us identify the Roman poet Horace as the source of a Latin proverb quoted by Sperry. Jimmy Bryant, director of the UCA Archives, and two of his subordinates, Betty Osborn and Evon Sonderlick, were tireless in tracking down references to obscure Arkansas places and personages. Lisa Murphy, head of interlibrary loan in UCA's Torreyson Library, worked wonders in obtaining rare books and copies of articles essential for our annotations.

This project owes its inception to the urging of Kevin Brock, acquisitions editor at University of Arkansas Press, who remained a source of constant encouragement.

Mark K. Christ, the special projects coordinator at the Arkansas Historic Preservation Project and a major force in the preservation and interpretation of the state's Civil War heritage, reviewed our manuscript and saved us from making several factual errors. Other historians who assisted us in various ways were Craig L. Symonds, U.S. Naval Academy; Wolfgang Hochbruck, University of Stuttgart; William L. Shea, University of Arkansas at Monticello; Carl H. Moneyhon,

University of Arkansas at Little Rock; Anne J. Bailey, Georgia College
and State University; Daniel E. Sutherland, University of Arkansas;
James E. McMillan, Central College; Mark Lause, University of
Cincinnati; Norman A. Nicholson, Blakeley State Park; Ronnie A.
Nichols, the former director of the Old State House Museum; and John
T. Hubbell, director of Kent State University Press and editor of *Civil
War History.*

Budge Weidman of the National Archives speedily answered our
repeated requests for the military service and pension records belonging to several 33d Iowa personnel. Rob Dillard of the College Relations
Office, Central College, in Sperry's hometown of Pella, Iowa, searched
the school archives to confirm that Sperry attended that institution
before going off to the Civil War. Muriel Kooi, co-archivist of the Pella
Historical Society, and Iris Vander Wal, the society's business manager,
supplied information on Drummer Tommy Cox, the pride of Company G
and one of Sperry's prize recruits. Ms. Kooi also provided the image of
Cox that appears elsewhere in this book.

Many 33d Iowa descendants, descendants of other Civil War soldiers,
and private collectors enriched this volume by permitting us to make
use of letters, diaries, memoirs, photographs, and other historical relics
in their possession. These include: Jeff Brodrick, Clarks Summit, Penn-
sylvania; Dave Powers, Omaha, Nebraska; Larry Pearson, Anchorage,
Alaska; Richard S. Warner, Tulsa, Oklahoma; Robert C. Burke, Altus,
Oklahoma; Charles Swanson, Lawton, Michigan; Richard L. Clift, Lake
Forest, California; Corwin Trinkle, Marshalltown, Iowa; Renee Brittain,
Broken Arrow, Oklahoma; Richard Merritt, Little Rock, Arkansas;
Frances Thompson, Clarksville, Arkansas; M. D. Hutcheson, Camden,
Arkansas; Mark Warren, Bloomfield, Iowa; Roger Davis, Keokuk, Iowa;
Rick Fish, St. Joseph, Michigan; James W. Combs II, The Dalles,
Oregon; Jodi Eichelberger, Portland, Oregon; Ruth E. Rogers, Daly
City, California; Sandy Rasmussen, Rock Springs, Wyoming; John
Petzold, Houston, Texas; Townsend Mosley, Camden, Arkansas; and
Ernie Huff, Little Rock, Arkansas.

Finally, we dedicate this book to our ten-year-old son, Edward
Gregory Urwin. We have received many blessings since moving to
Arkansas in 1984, but he stands first and foremost among them. Though
determined to become a restaurateur, he has inherited his parents' passion for the past. He accompanied his mother on research trips to the

Arkansas History Commission and UCA Archives, and helped unearth some of the information that appears in this book. It has been a memorable experience to walk in A. F. Sperry's footsteps across Arkansas and other parts of the old Confederacy. Having Edward at our side has made the journey even more meaningful and enjoyable.

Gregory J. W. Urwin
Cathy Kunzinger Urwin

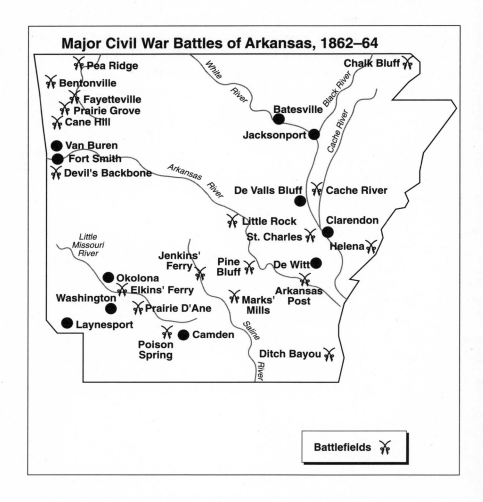

Major Civil War Battles of Arkansas, 1862–64

Pea Ridge
Bentonville
Fayetteville
Prairie Grove
Cane Hill
Van Buren
Fort Smith
Devil's Backbone

White River

Chalk Bluff
Black River
Batesville
Cache River
Jacksonport

Arkansas River

De Valls Bluff
Cache River
Little Rock
Clarendon
St. Charles
Helena

Little Missouri River

Jenkins' Ferry
Pine Bluff
De Witt
Okolona
Elkins' Ferry
Arkansas Post
Washington
Prairie D'Ane
Marks' Mills
Laynesport
Poison Spring
Camden
Saline River
Ditch Bayou

Battlefields

Map by Steve Scallion. *Courtesy Arkansas Historic Preservation Program.*

EDITORS' INTRODUCTION

On August 5, 1862, Andrew Fuller Sperry, a twenty-three-year-old schoolteacher, entered the recruiting station in his hometown of Pella, Iowa, and enlisted in Company G of the 33d Iowa Volunteer Infantry Regiment. Capt. Lauriston W. Whipple and 1st Lt. George R. Ledyard, the two officers who enrolled Sperry in Company G, noted that their newest recruit had hazel eyes, dark hair, a dark complexion, and measured six feet in height. For agreeing to risk life and limb on behalf of his divided country, Sperry received twenty-five dollars in cash—an advance on the one-hundred-dollar bounty that the federal government offered at that time to any man who voluntarily joined the Union army.[1]

It was in this quiet, businesslike way that Andrew Sperry went off to the American Civil War. That conflict, the bloodiest to ravage American soil, also turned out to be the grandest adventure in Sperry's life. During his three years in uniform, the impressionable teacher tasted all the monotony, hardship, and danger that soldiering had to offer. He traveled hundreds of miles in cramped discomfort in steamboats up and down the Mississippi Valley and across the Gulf of Mexico. He marched through the dust and mud of seven different states. He participated in two pitched battles in Arkansas and a formal siege in Alabama. He saw men die instantly in combat or suffer long, agonizing deaths from wounds or disease. He savored the ecstatic joy of liberated slaves and gazed into the faces of civilians victimized by both Union and Confederate troops. He witnessed feats of valor and watched heroes succumb to vice in camp and garrison. No one can experience such things and come away unaffected.

With the resumption of peace in 1865, most newly discharged Union veterans preferred to forget the war and its horrors, but Sperry was not one of them. He could not put aside his memories as easily as he stored away his faded blue uniform. He knew that he and his comrades had done something of historic importance, and he felt driven to preserve their experiences on paper. In the eight months following his departure from the army, Sperry wrote a complete history of his regiment and rushed it into print.[2]

Americans living on the brink of the twenty-first century belong to an egocentric culture, and they may think it odd that Sperry wrote about the 33d Iowa rather than himself. It bears noting, however, that Sperry and other survivors of the Civil War viewed life through a different lens. They were a highly mobile people, like their descendants, but they possessed a stronger sense of community, which influenced everything they did—even how they made war.[3]

The regiment functioned as the basic tactical and administrative unit in the armies created by both the North and the South. Sperry's 33d Iowa was just one of 1,696 volunteer infantry regiments raised for the Union army between 1861 and 1865. These units were ordinarily formed on the state level and then turned over to federal authorities for active service. The men in any regiment came primarily from the same part of their state. Where population was dense, a regiment might consist of residents of the same city or county. In the more rural parts of the North, regiments drew their recruits from two or more adjacent counties. This localized approach to manpower mobilization endowed Civil War regiments with tremendous unit cohesion—even before their members underwent the bonding of training and combat.[4]

As Michael P. Musick, the chief caretaker for the regimental records at the National Archives, has observed: "For the Civil War generation, a regimental designation was not merely a military convenience. In truth, the regiment was the primary object of identification for the men who fought the war. For the most part, a unit meant neighbors, friends, and in many cases . . . blood relatives. To speak the name of a unit was often to summon up a host of associations within a particular state and community."[5]

Failure to appreciate the pivotal place the regiment occupied in the life of Billy Yank and Johnny Reb results in an imperfect understanding of the conduct of the Civil War. Fortunately for students of that era, Andrew Sperry and many of his contemporaries left vivid testimonials that explain what their regiments meant to them. Between 1865 and 1925, Civil War veterans published approximately eight hundred regimental histories, the majority about Union commands. Just as the regiment was the main "building block" for Union and Confederate armies, the regimental history is indispensable to historians seeking to reconstruct battles and campaigns or the everyday life of the Civil War soldier.[6]

The late Stephen Z. Starr, one of the conflict's more prolific historians, called the regimental history "the characteristic literary by-product of the Civil War" and "a peculiar literary species with its own canons and, above all, its own special flavor."[7] "There is a considerable variation in content from one regimental history to another," Starr admitted, "but as a group, they cover every conceivable aspect of the lives of the two million troopers, gunners and foot soldiers in the Union army, over a period of four years: their trials and tribulations, successes and defeats, joys, and pleasures, virtues and misdeeds, feelings and opinions, in short, all their experiences from the most meaningful to the most trivial."[8]

By publishing his *History of the 33d Iowa Infantry Volunteer Regiment, 1863–6*, so soon after the war, Sperry became a pioneer in an important historical genre. That proved to be his misfortune, but a boon to subsequent generations. As noted earlier, most Union veterans returned home determined to put the Civil War behind them. They did not want to relive the sufferings they had known in the South, and they doubted Northern civilians could understand what had really happened to their boys in blue. Likewise, noncombatants desired no reminders of the national catastrophe that had taken the lives of so many of their loved ones. Blind to this antipathy, publishers who brought out the first wave of Civil War books in 1866 saw sales lag far behind expectations.[9]

It was not until 1880 that public interest in the Civil War showed signs of reviving. By then, the nation's psychological scars had begun to heal and veterans were growing nostalgic. More than half of the regimental histories penned by Civil War soldiers appeared between 1885 and 1910, a period that Stephen Starr dubbed the genre's Golden Age. One hundred more regimental histories came out between 1910 and 1925.[10]

Although there is no question of their value to scholars, reenactors, and other Civil War buffs, the greater number of regimental histories published after 1885 exude a stuffy formality that can deter all but the most dedicated readers. By the time these books were written, the typical Union veteran had matured into a solid citizen in his forties, fifties, or sixties. He and his comrades now had reputations to protect, and they wanted to be regarded as models of civic virtue by their children and society at large. Consequently, the regimental histories of the Golden

Age tended to present a sanitized picture of the Civil War and especially of the parts played by the regiments they covered. These accounts contained little or no mention of the grisly side of combat, Union cruelty to Confederate civilians and runaway slaves, or offenses against Sunday-school morality or military discipline. To judge from these works, every Union regiment was officered by gallant gentlemen who never made tactical mistakes or issued unjust orders, and the rank and file consisted of simple, patriotic boys who cheerfully did whatever was asked of them. Some of the later regimental histories were produced by committees, which only added to their stultifying, self-conscious character.[11]

Composed in the immediate aftermath of the Civil War with the sheer enthusiasm of a man harboring no hidden agenda, Sperry's book on the 33d Iowa brims with an unrehearsed freshness and candor which set it apart from the ponderous treatises that followed it decades later. Sperry took pride in his regiment and its exploits, but he did not attempt to transform himself and his comrades into living monuments. He admitted that campaigning in Dixie hardened his fellow Iowans, and he chronicled instances of looting, resistance to objectionable orders, and his own desire to exterminate Confederate guerrillas. He did not hesitate to criticize blunders committed by his superiors, and he clearly enjoyed teasing the 33d's officers for their attachment to the privileges of rank. Fortunately, Sperry was a good-humored man with a strong sense of compassion, and his acknowledgment of the negative aspects of soldiering never degenerated into full-blown diatribes.

Sperry's history of the 33d Iowa may not have found a large audience in 1866, but the surviving copies have attracted the notice and respect of various Civil War historians. Michael Mullins and Rowena Reed thought highly enough of Sperry's effort to include it among the 246 titles featured in their *Union Bookshelf*, the first annotated guide to the best books "about the Civil War from the Union perspective." Only 97 other regimental histories made their list. Years earlier, three giants in Civil War studies—Allan Nevins, James I. Robertson Jr., and Bell I. Wiley—singled out Sperry for special praise in their magisterial *Civil War Books: A Critical Bibliography.* "Written without pretense or exaggeration," they decreed, "this is an excellent source for the campaigns in Arkansas."[12] Armed with such impressive endorsements, Sperry's little volume continues to pop up in the bibliographies of some of the best examinations of the Civil War in the trans-Mississippi theater. It is hoped that this new edition will bring Sperry the wider readership he has long deserved.[13]

Andrew Sperry was born on June 21, 1839, in Troy, New Hampshire. His parents hailed from Massachusetts, and his father, at least, shared the wanderlust that infected multitudes of Americans in the nineteenth century. Andrew later revealed that his family lived in "numerous places" until 1855, when it set down roots in Pella, a promising agricultural community in Marion County, Iowa. The place Sperry would call home for the next seven years had been founded in 1847 by religious dissenters loyal to Dominie Henry P. Scholte, a resolute cleric who broke with the Dutch Reformed Church in his native Netherlands in 1834.[14]

The industrious Hollanders who followed Scholte to the Iowa prairies built a prosperous colony that attracted many American-born settlers. The Baptist Church Organization of Iowa opened Central University (today Central College) in Pella two years before the Sperrys arrived, and the presence of that institution stimulated the local economy and population growth. According to records housed in the college archives, Andrew Sperry attended a preparatory school operated by Central during the 1857–58 academic year. In the fall of 1859, he enrolled as a freshman in the university's Science Department. It is not known if he ever graduated, but the instructors at Central helped hone Sperry's literary skills by exposing him to Latin and the writings of Washington Irving and other prominent American authors of the day.[15]

Sperry also developed some musical talent in his youth. When he joined the 33d Iowa in August 1862, he was named Company G's fifer. Along with his company drummer and the drummers and fifers from the regiment's nine other companies, Sperry was responsible for sounding the duty calls that regulated a soldier's day: reveille, breakfast call ("Peas on a Trencher"), sick call, fatigue call, guard mount, dinner call ("Roast Beef"), assembly, troop, adjutant's call, supper call, tattoo, and taps. Regimental field musicians provided the appropriate martial airs for such dignified exercises as dress parade and grand reviews. Their tunes helped the rank and file keep the proper marching cadence whenever the regiment moved. In combat, the fifers and drummers stood right behind the firing line and played "fight songs" to bolster unit morale. A regiment's field music also assisted with battlefield communications, sounding command signals that could be heard over the gunfire and other clamor more easily than the hoarse orders shouted by officers.[16]

Sperry's fifing and his background as a teacher evidently impressed his superiors. When the 33d Iowa was mustered into federal service on October 1, 1862, Sperry's dark blue coat sported the sky blue chevrons of a fife major, one of the six slots authorized for a volunteer infantry regiment's noncommissioned staff. Sperry's new position put him in charge of training and conducting the music of the 33d's ten fifers, some of whom were mere boys. Sperry had every reason to be pleased with himself, but he soon suffered a decline in status. While the 33d Iowa was in the process of moving south, Sperry came down with smallpox and had to be confined in the post hospital at Cairo, Illinois, from December 22, 1862, to January 10, 1863. The disease marked his skin with a few faint scars. He quickly rejoined his regiment at Helena, Arkansas, where he was promptly assigned to post headquarters as a clerk from January 16–22, no doubt to spare him from arduous duties until he was fully recovered. With the expiration of his temporary desk job, however, Sperry did not resume his place as fife major, but returned to Company G as a common fifer.[17]

The reasons for Sperry's demotion remain a mystery, but whatever he did wrong was soon forgotten. On May 1, 1863, Sperry was appointed the regiment's sole principal musician, which gave him authority over not only the 33d's fifers, but its ten drummers as well. He would hold that rank until the 33d Iowa disbanded in August 1865, and he never missed another day of duty. Naturally, Sperry's regimental history makes frequent references to the role music played in Civil War military life, as well as allusions to the author's performance as principal musician. He was a firm taskmaster, and not everyone appreciated his high standards. One soldier who considered Sperry overly demanding was Pvt. John N. Shepherd of Company I. "In the Summer of 1864," Shepherd related, "I was detailed as Fifer I Stayed with the Band two months and because the Leader [Sperry] tried to run over me I resigned, and had the Col. [colonel] to return me to my company."[18]

One of the most popular fife tunes in the Union army was "The Girl I Left Behind Me." That song spoke with a special poignancy to Sperry because he fell in love with a girl before he marched off to war. Her name was Hannah Bassett, and she was two years his junior. Sperry's sweetheart waited for him, and the two pledged their vows before Rev. E. H. Scarff on September 10, 1865, a month after Andrew's final discharge from the 33d. As his wedding approached, the stolid veteran became every bit the eager bridegroom. Two days before the ceremony, he noted in his diary: "Now I am anxiously awaiting for my darling Han to come. Every noise sounds like the stage[coach] to me." The day after his nuptials, a contented Sperry wrote: "By the mercy and blessing of God I sit here with *my wife* alone, in peace and health and hope, and more of happiness than I ever dreamed to have."[19]

Sperry's marriage lasted nearly fifty years. By all accounts, he and Hannah remained devoted to each other until separated by death. The couple had two sons, Arthur, born on October 5, 1866, and Paul, born on January 11, 1879. As an adult, Arthur made his home in Pittsburgh, Pennsylvania. Paul studied for the ministry at Cambridge, Massachusetts, and went on to head congregations in Bath, Maine, and Brockton, Massachusetts.[20]

Marital bliss failed to cure Andrew Sperry of the wandering ways he learned as a child. He and Hannah began their life together in Panora, Iowa, where he worked for a newspaper. After a little more than a year, Sperry moved his wife and baby Arthur to Knoxville, Iowa, residing there until the fall of 1871. Following a short stay in Dubuque, Iowa, and a few months in Dorset, Ohio, the Sperrys relocated to Ashtabula, another Ohio town, in 1873. Paul was born there six years later. Sperry kept his family at Ashtabula until late 1881 or early 1882, when he changed his address once again to Washington, D.C. The national capital would be home to Sperry for the twenty-nine remaining years of his life. One reason why he stayed so long was that he landed a good, steady job as a clerk in the United States Post Office Department.[21]

On July 30, 1904, Sperry applied to the Department of the Interior for a veteran's pension. He claimed to be "suffering from a disability of a permanent character" that made it increasingly difficult to support himself "by manual labor." On an accompanying questionnaire, the sixty-five-year-old government employee reported his weight as "About 150 lbs.," his eyes as "faded hazel," and his hair color as "Very dark, turning grey." The Pension Bureau approved Sperry's application, and he began receiving monthly payments of eight dollars.[22]

By 1907, Sperry's health was showing sure signs of deterioration. He requested an increase in his pension and had it raised to fifteen dollars per month.[23] On July 26, he drew up this straightforward will:

It is my desire and purpose that all property, real or personal, of which I may be possessed, shall at my death become the sole and full property of my true and faithful wife, Hannah B. Sperry, if she be then living, and that she shall be the sole executor and administrator of my estate, if any executor or administrator be needed; and that if she be not then living, said property shall be inherited in full and equally by my two sons.[24]

The dreaded event anticipated by all wills came into view in the summer of 1910 when Sperry suffered two serious physical setbacks. He was immobilized from the waist down by paraplegia and diagnosed with arteriosclerosis. Despite the care of Dr. D'Arcy Magee, Sperry's condition worsened steadily. The old soldier's straining heart finally stopped beating at 5:00 A.M., March 15, 1911, in the family home at 1437 Q Street N.W. Andrew F. Sperry had lived seventy-one years, eight months, and twenty-one days. Now left without any visible means of support, Hannah Sperry applied for a widow's pension on March 16 and buried Andrew in Arlington National Cemetery the next day. Hannah outlived her husband by twelve years, dying on May 4, 1923.[25]

The Iowa that Andrew Sperry knew on the eve of the Civil War was a young, frontier state that had been part of the Union only since 1846. The state's population stood at 674,913 in 1860, and most adult white Iowans had been born someplace else—a fact that jumps out from the 33d Iowa's personnel records. They were a sturdy lot, these early "Hawkeyes," and they faced the world with a sense of hard-earned accomplishment. Farmers and farm laborers made up 62 percent of the state's work force. Iowa ranked seventh in the nation in corn production and eighth in wheat.[26]

A majority of the 192,214 people who settled in Iowa by 1850 came from the southern Ohio River Valley and tended to vote Democrat. Consistent with their Jacksonian principles, they drafted a constitution and several laws aimed at banning African Americans from living or voting in their midst. In the decade preceding the Civil War, however, Iowa experienced a dramatic influx of emigrants from the Midwest, New England, and the Mid-Atlantic states. The tone of state politics reflected this marked change in demographics. When Southern extremists turned to political fraud, physical intimidation, and violence after 1854 in an ill-fated effort to force slavery on Kansas Territory, more and more Iowa voters adopted the example of other Northerners and aligned themselves with the newborn Republican Party. Iowans signified their shift in political loyalties by giving a strong plurality in 1856 to John C. Fremont, the first Republican presidential candidate. Four years later, Iowa went for Abraham Lincoln by a wide margin, helping to make him the first Republican to occupy the White House, a political turnover that immediately triggered the secession crisis.[27]

Despite all the tensions stirred up by "Bleeding Kansas" and other sectional controversies of the 1850s, the dissolution of the Union and the outbreak of civil war caught most Iowans by surprise. On account of its youth and a paucity of Indian troubles, the state had little or no military tradition. Iowa organized no regiments to fight in the Mexican War, and the only militia in existence consisted of a handful of neglected volunteer companies headquartered in such towns as Dubuque, Davenport, Iowa City, Ottumwa, Council Bluffs, Dyersville, Mount Pleasant, Burlington, Keokuk, Washington, and Columbus City. Andrew J. Comstock, a future captain in the 33d Iowa, was the only man in Mahaska County credited with Mexican War service, and he had enlisted in a Tennessee regiment after the fighting had ended. Military weapons were even scarcer in Iowa than veterans. When Confederate gunners forced the surrender of Fort Sumter on April 14, 1861, President Lincoln responded the next day with a call for 75,000 militia from the loyal states to restore order in the South—including a 780-man regiment from little Iowa. Upon receiving Lincoln's summons, a worried Governor Samuel J. Kirkwood blurted to a member of Iowa's congressional delegation: "The President wants a whole regiment of men! Do you suppose . . . I can raise that many?"[28]

Kirkwood need not have worried. Iowa was brimming with patriots eager to rush to arms. The state not only met its first troop quota with impressive speed, but it raised 19,105 soldiers before the close of 1861, enough to field sixteen infantry regiments, four cavalry regiments, and three light artillery batteries. By the time the Civil War ended, Iowa would have given more than 76,000 of its sons to the Union army, nearly half of its males of military age. Except for 4,000 draftees, these men enlisted voluntarily, and 7,202 Iowa veterans reenlisted to see the war through to the finish. The overwhelming majority of Iowa soldiers were white, and they went into forty infantry regiments, five smaller infantry battalions, nine cavalry regiments, and four light batteries. State authorities also scraped together 440 men from Iowa's tiny African American community to organize an infantry regiment for the United States Colored Troops.[29]

A total of 13,001 Iowa soldiers died in the Civil War, the third highest death rate among all the Northern states. Of these, 3,540 sustained fatal wounds in combat; 8,498 succumbed to disease in Union hospitals; 515 more died from abuse or neglect as prisoners of war; and 448 died as a result of accident or other nonbattle causes. Another 8,500 Hawkeyes survived wounds. Altogether, nearly 16 percent of Iowa's soldiers became battlefield casualties over the course of the war. Iowa may have been small and off the beaten track, but there is no doubt it did more than its fair share in preserving the Union.[30]

Before permitting Principal Musician Sperry to get on with his story, it seems appropriate to offer a few observations on the men who served beside him. Sperry and his comrades were a more realistic sort than the "Boys of '61," who flocked to the colors expecting a quick and easy war full of fun and glory. The soldiers of the 33d Iowa did not step forward until the war was well into its second year, and they had more than an inkling of the dangers and privations that awaited them. John Shepherd, a carpenter from Marion County, described the inner anguish that accompanied his decision to sign up: "I Studied over it and prayed about it I hated to leave my wife and four Children, but I finaly concluded it was my duty to go. One of my Friends said he would take care of my Family if I would go as he thought he could not go So I enlisted on August 15th 1862 in company I 33d Iowa Infantry."[31]

There were more than just personal considerations for men like Shepherd to ponder. The 33d Iowa came to life in the summer and fall of 1862, a particularly low point for the Union war effort. In the eastern theater, the incomparable Robert E. Lee had thwarted two Northern attempts to capture the Confederate capital at Richmond, Virginia, and then went on the offensive by invading Maryland. Blue forces had made substantial headway in areas west of the Appalachians, but each success exacted heavy losses and Southern resistance showed no sign of weakening. The Union army urgently needed new regiments at the front, and the older regiments needed replacements to replenish their depleted ranks.

On July 2, 1862, President Lincoln issued a call for 300,000 fresh volunteers to serve for three years. The War Department fixed Iowa's quota at 10,570 men. Governor Kirkwood put out an impassioned proclamation urging his male constituents to flock to the recruiting officers: "The preservation of the Union, the perpetuity of our government, the honor of our State demand that this requisition should be promptly met.

... The necessity is urgent. Our national existence is at stake. The more promptly the President is furnished the needed troops the more speedily will this unholy rebellion be crushed, and the blessings of peace again visit our land."[32]

Despite Kirkwood's florid rhetoric, enlistments lagged through July. The governor thought the problem a temporary one. "Our harvesting prevents rapid recruiting just now," he wired Lincoln on July 5. "Iowa will do her duty." But Lincoln would not settle for optimistic promises. On August 4, the War Department ordered a draft of three hundred thousand militia for nine months' service in the Union army. The real purpose of this coercive move was not to draft short-term troops, but to stimulate volunteering. Under the new policy, any three-year man enlisted by a state above its July quota would count as four militiamen. Anyone who waited to be drafted, however, would not receive the one-hundred-dollar federal bounty reserved for volunteers. It must also be remembered that conscription was seen as a stain on a man's honor in mid-nineteenth-century America—better to freely enlist than to be dragged into the army like a slave or a common criminal.[33]

The carrot-and-stick approach served the Lincoln administration well. Under the calls of July and August 1862, the Union army enjoyed a much-needed infusion of 421,465 three-year volunteers and 90,000 nine-month men. From Iowa on August 20, a jubilant Kirkwood telegraphed Secretary of War Edwin M. Stanton: "There are companies now full and that will be full by the 23d to fill eighteen to twenty regiments. Our whole State appears to be volunteering. . . . The companies are now coming into rendezvous as rapidly as I can furnish blankets for them." Iowa ended up enlisting 24,438 volunteers before Christmas, organizing them into twenty-two new infantry regiments, the 19th through 40th Iowa. One of these outfits was the 33d Iowa Volunteer Infantry, which mustered into federal service at 980 strong.[34]

In addition to cold, clear-headed patriotism, a strong religious streak permeated the 33d Iowa. The letters, diaries, and memoirs of the regiment's members contain affirmations of faith and frequent mention of church services and other spiritual matters. Languishing in a military hospital at St. Louis, Pvt. Allan McNeal directed this appeal to his father on January 15, 1863: "Remember me at the thron of grace that I may be brought into the ful covenant of grace as it is in Jesus Christ is my prayer." "I carried a Testament with me the whole three years," claimed Pvt. John Shepherd of Company I. "I read it t[h]rough by course four times while in the Army." When a backsliding comrade declared that "War and Religion don't agree," Shepherd shot back: "The Lord has not forsaken me yet and I wont forsake Him." On another occasion, the first sergeant of Shepherd's company asked Pvt. James A. Newman why he was always so cheerful. "Well," Newman answered, "I resolved when I enlisted I would strive to obey my superiors and do my duty as a soldier, and honor the Christ I recognized as my Savior and friend that was able to keep me."[35]

The officers of the 33d Iowa took special care in selecting a regimental chaplain, narrowing their choices to Rev. Robert A. McAyeal, the pastor of Oskaloosa's First United Presbyterian Church since 1856, and Rev. Francis M. Slusser, the pastor of the First Methodist Episcopal Church in the same city. McAyeal was a graduate of West Geneva College and Allegheny Theological Seminary, his candidacy had the backing of the United Presbyterian Presbytery, and he was three years younger than the thirty-eight-year-old Slusser. In an election held on September 23, 1862, the officers awarded McAyeal the chaplaincy by nineteen votes to fourteen.[36]

No matter how impeccable, peacetime credentials are no guarantee that a man will take to soldiering. Southern heat and remittent fever sapped McAyeal of his strength and prevented him from bringing much comfort to his flock. On June 9, 1863, the ailing McAyeal obtained a certificate from Assistant Surgeon William M. Scott, who recommended that the chaplain be granted an extended rest, as "a Change in Climite is necessary to save life." Two days later, McAyeal headed north on a twenty-day sick leave. His health recovered, but not his spirits. On June 28, McAyeal tendered his immediate and unconditional resignation. It was accepted by order of Maj. Gen. Ulysses S. Grant on July 24.[37]

The rank and file of the 33d Iowa went less than half a year without a chaplain before they acted to safeguard their spiritual welfare. In the winter of 1863–64, enlisted men from the 33d and from the 29th Iowa (another regiment deserted by its chaplain) established a religious society called the "Earnest Christian Band." The Earnest Christian Band held lively nighttime revivals for the large Union garrison at Little Rock, Arkansas. "We had some wonderful meetings," testified Pvt. John Shepherd, the group's leader. "There were many conversions."[38]

As Sperry's history will show, not everyone in the 33d Iowa qualified for sainthood. For the most part, however, the regiment's moral lapses were minor in character. No man in the 33d could judge his comrades more harshly than Pvt. George Washington Towne of Company G, the son of a Baptist minister, and this was the worst that he had to say: "I am so sorry that the company is getting to play cards & swear & every wickedness that soldiers are liable to fall into. From having the name of being the best company in the regt it has the name now of being the most abandoned. Young men who at home belonged to the church & were moral young men now play cards & use the name of God in vain. I hope I never shall become so wicked."[39]

Even the strongest faith cannot protect a soldier against bullets and disease. Private Towne fell mortally wounded at the Battle of Jenkins' Ferry, Arkansas, on April 30, 1864, and spent his final days in enemy hands. He was not the only member of the 33d Iowa to find a Southern grave. Counting the replacements recruited for the regiment after its creation, 1,194 men served in the 33d Iowa over the course of its existence. Twenty-five enlisted men were killed in action, 4 officers and 37 men were mortally wounded, 1 officer and 166 men died of sickness, 3 men drowned, and another perished in an accident, raising the regimental death toll to 237. Eight officers and 166 other ranks suffered battle wounds but recovered, as did 2 men badly injured in accidents. The 33d reported 1 officer and 73 men captured by the enemy, and listed 7 other men as missing. The regiment granted early discharges to 109 men for disability and released 2 officers and 34 men for "cause unknown." When the 33d Iowa formed up for the last time on August 8, 1865, only 430 sun-baked veterans were in good enough shape to fall in and dress on the colors.[40]

The 33d Iowa is not one of the more celebrated regiments of the Civil War. It did not hold a length of stone wall against Pickett's charge, delay Confederate pursuers at Chickamauga, scale enemy earthworks at Spotsylvania, or watch Lee's tattered survivors surrender at Appomattox. The 33d Iowa served out its time in the war's backwater sectors in Kentucky, Mississippi, Arkansas, Alabama, and Texas, and its battles are largely forgotten. Be that as it may, the 33d did its duty by helping to restore Union authority in some of the farthest corners of the Confederacy. Along with hundreds of other reliable, workhorse regiments, it applied the sustained pressure that did as much in breaking the South's will to resist as the war's big battles.

Statistics alone cannot begin to do justice to the 33d Iowa's story. That requires abundant detail, and such detail is to be found in the words of Andrew F. Sperry, a careful and reliable eyewitness. Sperry's text is reprinted here as it first appeared in 1866, complete with occasional misspellings and eccentric punctuation. In the case of misspelled proper names, the correct versions are to be found in the editors' notes.

HISTORY

OF THE

33ᴰ IOWA INFANTRY

VOLUNTEER REGIMENT

1863–6

—————

BY A. F. SPERRY

PREFATORY.

In presenting this history of our Regiment to my fellow-soldiers of the 33d Iowa Infantry, I hope their memories while reading, may be as warm and pleasant as have been mine while writing it.

For what of omission or error it contains, I have only to say, that the whole was written amidst the very press of editorial and many other duties, and a very great part of it after nine o'clock at night. The work is as well as I could make it under the circumstances.

Much of monotony may be ascribed to the sameness of the events to be described; and many omissions may be accounted for by lack of data which others should have furnished, as requested, and as they promised to do.

And hoping this volume may but bring more vividly to memory, the times we have passed together in our noble old Regiment, I am,

Very Respectfully,

A. F. SPERRY.

PANORA, IOWA, April 24th, 1866.

CHAPTER I.

FROM HOME TO ST. LOUIS

The 33d Iowa Infantry Regiment was organized under the Presidential call of June, 1862, for additional volunteers to aid in putting down the Great Rebellion. The number and place of rendezvous of the regiment were designated, with those of other regiments from the State under the same call, by proclamation of GOVERNOR KIRKWOOD;[1] and after some uncertainty, SAMUEL A. RICE, of Oskaloosa, then Attorney General of the State, was appointed its colonel.[2]

The mean date of the filling up and organization of the companies was about the 20th of August. The companies which, some time after reaching rendezvous, were lettered as A, I and G, were from Marion County; B, F and H from Keokuk County, and C, D, E and K from Mahaska County.[3] The roll of the regiment in full, will be found in the Appendix.

The manner of organizing the companies was much like that used for other regiments. Persons more than ordinarily patriotic or ambitious, obtained recruiting commissions from the Governor, and by personal solicitation among their acquaintances and others, obtained the requisite number of enlistments. Public meetings were held; and the already deep and intense patriotic excitement was fanned and strengthened by speeches, songs, martial music, and all other available and proper means. But a brief effort was required. In most cases, those who had recruited the companies received, by common consent, the first positions, and the remaining company-officers were filled by election.[4]

The Fair Grounds just north-west of the city of Oskaloosa,[5] were selected as the place of rendezvous, and named Camp Tuttle, in honor of Brigadier-General J. M. TUTTLE, of Iowa.[6] Within the first week of September all the companies arrived there; and in a few

Col. Samuel A. Rice, 33d Iowa Infantry. A self-made lawyer who helped found Iowa's Republican Party, Rice accepted command of the 33d Iowa after he lost bids for the governorship and the U.S. Congress. He turned out to be a born soldier. *Photo courtesy of U.S. Army Military History Institute.*

days each of them had erected its own barracks, from lumber furnished by the Government. The barracks were of uniform style:— square, or nearly so; of rough boards, unpainted, without floors, windows or chimnies, and lined around the inside with tiers of bunks. Each barrack contained one company.[7]

The first duty of the regiment was to learn to drill. With no previous military experience, Colonel Rice applied himself to the study of the regulations and tactics with such intense and unremitting attention that he soon made himself an excellent drill-master; and he always gave his personal care and effort to the instruction of the regiment. From four to eight hours a day were devoted to this; and it was not long till the result was apparent in the discipline and proficiency of the command.

Meanwhile, there were frequent parties of visitors to camp—the relatives and friends of the regiment; and the good cheer and delicacies that so abounded then were remembered many a time afterward, when the perils and privations of a soldier's life were no more prospective, but present realties. There was very naturally, much grumbling at the fare and circumstances in Camp Tuttle; but after the regiment had seen a year or two of active service, and knew what hardships really were, it was a common remark among us that if we were only back at Camp Tuttle, we would make ourselves comfortable as clams at high tide.

Late in the afternoon of the 4th day of October,[8] our regiment was mustered into the United States service, by Lieutenant Chas. J. Ball, of the Regular Army.[9] It was an impressive scene. The day was clear and beautiful; and as the mellow rays of sun approached more nearly to the horizon, the men were drawn up in long double lines in camp, and the necessary examinations followed. Several who were now rejected, were nevertheless determined to go with us; and did go with us, and made as good and efficient soldiers as any of the rest. The examination over, the clear and ringing voice of Lieutenant Ball pronounced the oath of enlistment, the upraised hands fell to the position of "attention;" and the 33d Iowa Infantry, was part of the great United States Army.[10]

As speedily as possible the regiment was supplied with clothing, arms and equipments. The guns first furnished were the smoothbore muskets, which some months afterward were exchanged for

Enfield rifles.[11] A brass band, under the leadership of acting Drum-Major A. L. Ellis,[12] was organized and put on drill; and it continued to play, upon occasion, until the commencement of the Yazoo Pass Expedition, when it failed entirely; and from that time all attempts to revive it, or to organize another, proved utterly unsuccessful—or rather, there was never much earnest effort made in that direction. Our dress-parades in Camp Tuttle were frequently attended by crowds of spectators;[13] and often the line of the battalion itself would be so long there was not room for it inside the campground. Greatly in contrast with this was the thinned and shortened line which remained to us after three years of service.

On Thursday morning, the 20th of November, we left Camp Tuttle, under orders "for active service in the field." A large concourse of relatives and friends had gathered to say good-bye. Such partings come but once in a life-time,

> "Who could guess
> If evermore should meet those mutual eyes?"

But cheerfully, buoyantly, the regiment marched away, strong in the consciousness of a great and noble cause. If they should return, this day would yet be re-called with pride and pleasure; if they should fall—but that they left to Him who guides the destinies of nations and of men.[14]

The march to Eddyville, ten miles, over a muddy road, under knapsacks which bore down heavily on unaccustomed shoulders, was one of the hardest we ever had. Taking the cars at Eddyville we reached Keokuk that evening;[15] and at about ten P. M., to the music of our brass band playing on the deck of the steamer *Northerner,* we bade adieu to Iowa.[16] Now came our first experience of that stowing away of soldiers like freight in a boat, which afterward became so familiar that nothing better was expected. Yet that very stowing and packing away of human beings in this manner, even leaving entirely out of view the greatly increased risk of accident, has caused more suffering and death than many a hard-fought battle.

Passing down the river without any very remarkable incidents, we reached St. Louis in the night of the 21st.[17] Colonel Rice reported to Major-General Curtis, then in command there;[18] and

First Lt. Henry B. Myers, 33d Iowa Infantry. Myers was
the 33d Iowa's first quartermaster. He resigned his
commission on March 16, 1864. Here he strikes a
Napoleonic pose in his company officer's frock coat and
the crimson waist sash that U.S. army regulations
required officers to wear on duty. *Photo courtesy of Rance
Hulshart and U.S. Army Military History Institute.*

next morning we marched through town up to Schofield Barracks, near Fremont's residence, on Chateau Avenue.[19] Accustomed to the manifestations of interest at Oskaloosa, we were somewhat vexed that there was almost no appearance of welcome for us in St. Louis. But General Curtis, as we marched past him in cadenced step of regular rythmic fall, complimented the appearance of the regiment very highly.

For want of room, Companies G and B were separated from the rest, and assigned to quarters two or three squares distant. Company H was detailed on provost-duty; and the remainder of the regiment was put on guard at the Gratiot Street and Myrtle Street Military Prisons, under the general supervision of Colonel Rice.[20] The duty was rather hard for raw soldiers; and soon there was much sickness in the regiment. The condition of the barracks— which, heated up at night, grew cold and chilly before morning— was undoubtedly one of the causes of disease.[21]

Drills came once in a while, and parade occasionally; but guard-mounting was by far the most important ceremony of the day. The pass system was somewhat strict; but most of us found means, nevertheless, to circulate about town quite freely. There were but few excesses committed, however; and the regiment was much praised, as the most quiet and orderly one that had been in the city. So passed our brief period of "fine soldiering." There was hard duty here, in some respects, but there was "style" and convenience; and the days of really "active service" were yet to come.[22]

First Lt. Eugene W. Rice, 33d Iowa Infantry. A resident of Mahaska County, Rice was appointed as the 33d Iowa's quartermaster sergeant on August 22, 1862, and he succeeded Henry Myers as regimental quartermaster on April 10, 1864. He posed for this photograph in a natty officer's shell jacket following that promotion. *Photo courtesy of U.S. Army Military History Institute.*

Cpl. William M. Blackstone, Company E, 33d Iowa
Infantry. Blackstone enlisted as Company E's sixth
corporal on July 30, 1862. He wears the dark blue frock
coat that was part of the Union infantryman's dress uniform. His chevrons and the piping on his collar and
cuffs are sky blue. *Photo courtesy of U.S.
Army Military History Institute.*

CHAPTER II.

FROM ST. LOUIS TO HELENA.

Saturday night, the 20th of December, we lay down in our bunks to sleep, as usual. Thoughts of the pleasant soldiering in the city, yet in store for us, were common in many minds, as it seemed to be the general opinion that we would remain in St. Louis, for some time. But about mid-night a "change came o'er the spirit of our dreams." There was a general waking-up in the barracks; and the cause of it was an orderly, going the rounds to notify the regiment to "be ready to leave, to-morrow morning at 8 o'clock, for down the river." Active service was coming now. Well, no regiment was more ready or able for it than we.

Next morning hurried letters were written home, ere we left what seemed to us our last hold on civilization; and at 8 A. M. we embarked on board the steamer *Rowena*.[1] In the morning of the 24th, we landed at Columbus, Kentucky.[2] An attack was expected here, and we were to help repel it.[3] Piling overcoats and knapsacks on the levee, we marched out on the "bottom" below town, and formed line of battle. Remaining in line till about the middle of the afternoon, we were ordered to throw up breast-works. At this, our first attempt toward fortification, we worked faithfully till some time in the night, and then tumbled down to sleep, without shelter, as we were.[4]

Things now began to seem, to us green hands, very much like soldiering. To make the case more agreeable, a heavy rain fell during the night; and next morning the ground we slept on was several inches under water. The hydrostatic bed may be a great luxury, but doubtless much depends on the manner in which the principle is applied.

Next day was Christmas. We passed it in waiting for the attack, but no attack came. Mr. Forest seemed to have changed his mind.[5]

In a few days our new wedge tents were erected, and we were therefore better fixed.[6] But on New Year's morning, the regiment was ordered out to Union City Tennessee, to meet an attack expected there. After our arrival there, in the evening, the alarm was sounded, all rushed to arms, and battle seemed imminent, but nothing really happened. Some firing by our own men was the cause.

Union City was a nice little place, and our men remembered it with pleasure. Perhaps, one reason of their liking, was the fact that it abounded with meat, chickens, bread, potatoes and other eatables; and we there took our first lessons in foraging—lessons well learned and fully remembered, to the sorrow of many a sneaking old rebel who was "just as good a Union man as any body."

While there, one of our men accidently shot off the end of his finger; and Doctor Scott, our assistant surgeon, was called on to amputate it.[7] Having none of the customary instruments at hand, the doctor immediately seized a chisel and mallet, and performed the operation at a single blow. Much fun was made of it afterward; but the actual results were apparently as satisfactory as though the amputation had been done in the regular professional way.[8]

Companies A, F and I, were stationed out about a mile from Union City, to guard a bridge, until the 3d of January, 1863, when the whole regiment returned to Columbus. On the 7th we were ordered to leave, and struck tents and got ready. After waiting for some hours, contrary orders were received, the tents were put up again, and we staid till morning.[9]

Then, being stowed away on the steamer *John D. Perry*, we started to follow the general progress of the war, down the river.[10] About noon of Sunday, the 13th, we reached Helena, Arkansas, which place some of the boys profanely denominated "Hell-in-Arkansas"—a name more intimate acquaintance, inclined to justify; and leaving the boat as soon as we could, in mud and discomfort, we pitched our tents on a devastated garden in the center of the town.[11]

Next morning a more suitable place having been found, our camp was moved to the bank of the river, some half-a-mile south of town. Ordered from Columbus to form part of the expedition then organized to move against Arkansas Post, our regiment had arrived

Capt. Paris T. Totten, Company I, 33d Iowa Infantry. Totten
was a forty-four-year-old blacksmith from Knoxville, Iowa,
who enlisted in the 33d Iowa on August 9, 1862. He was
elected captain of Company I on August 12 and posed for this
photograph soon thereafter. Totten received a twenty-
day sick leave on January 28, 1863, and missed the prelimi-
nary phases of the Yazoo Pass expedition. *Photo
courtesy of Corwin Trinkle.*

at Helena behind time; and as the Post was then too nearly stripped of defense,[12] Colonel Bussey, the commandant, detained us there.[13]

Mud and misery were now the order of the day, with rain, snow, cold and discomfort for variations. We wondered if it always stormed at Helena. On the 24th, orders came for us to prepare five day's cooked rations, and hold ourselves in immediate readiness to start for Vicksburg. The next day, Sunday, saw us busily occupied all the time in cooking meat, baking up the flour already issued, and generally getting ready. The boats were there, the order was positive, and we were sure the wishes of many of us to "get into an actual battle and see how it seemed" were likely to be realized. But we never started, some thing or other changed the state of the case, and there we remained.[14]

These were not the most pleasant days in the world, even for soldiers. Though it seemed to rain most of the time, yet the cold was frequently severe; and for want of any better accommodation, we had to go to the woods and gather brickbats, pieces of wood, &c., and make chimneys to our tents. Teams were scarce—for us, at any rate—and we were compelled to go into the cypress swamps, some half-a-mile from camp, and bring up the wet wood on our backs, to burn. The mud was excessive; and as we were not yet provided with rubber blankets,[15] and had not learned, by three years of soldiering, how to do without almost every thing, and "fix up" in any circumstances, we were of course decidedly uncomfortable.

But this state of things was not to last forever. While we were here, General Grant passed down the river to Vicksburg, with a portion of his army.[16] The sight of the fleet loaded with troops, with colors flying, bands playing, and men shouting and cheering, was a new and grand one to us; and to the great displeasure of Colonel Rice, the regiment all broke camp and scattered up and down the levee, to get a better view. Full many a hour of extra duty was the penalty. Some thought this was paying too dearly for the first view of the "pomp and circumstance" of war, when we soon found ourselves on a fleet, and part of an army, and helping too, though distantly, in the reduction of Vicksburg.[17]

CHAPTER III.

CLEARING OUT THE PASS.

By inspection of the map one will see that the Coldwater River of Mississippi, empties into the Tallahatchie, and this into the Yazoo River, which enters the Mississippi, a few miles above Vicksburg. Seven miles below Helena, on the eastern side of the river, there opens from the Mississippi to the Coldwater, a narrow channel, called the Yazoo Pass. Two miles inland it enters a beautiful sheet of water, which from its crescent shape, is named Moon Lake; and apparently passing through the lake, it continues to the river.[1]

The Pass, though very deep, is but about 60 feet wide on an average. Formerly, it is said, very small craft occasionally were run on it, transporting cotton and plantation supplies; but later, the State of Mississippi had cut it off from the Mississippi River by a levee, to prevent its overflowing the low and level country through which it passes.[2] General Grant, finding it necessary to use all means for the reduction of Vicksburg, had determined to attempt to open a communication to the Yazoo River, through this Pass; and for this purpose an expedition was organized.[3]

On the 1st of February, 1863, a small detail from the different regiments at Helena, went down and cut the levee at the head of the Pass.[4] The Mississippi was then very high; and the swift waters rushed through the narrow opening so fiercely as to flood the adjacent swamps. On the 9th of the month, our regiment went down to Moon Lake, on a "mosquito boat" and small transports, to join other troops in clearing out the Pass, that it might be more nearly fit for navigation.[5] The rebels below us had felled trees across and into the channel, to obstruct the expedition as much as possible; and these had all to be taken out.[6] Raftsmen and lumbermen were in demand, and Colonel Rice's previous experience on the river, came in excellent play. Lieutenant-Colonel Wilson, afterward major-general, was the engineer-in-chief, and performed his duties faithfully.[7]

This was now peculiar soldiering. Heavy fatigue-details were made each day, or twice a day. The men had to get at the logs in the channel, cut them in two, or get them apart in some way, and then fasten ropes to them, by which to draw them out.[8] Brigadier-General Washburne, in uniform distinguished from the others, only by the star on his shoulder, gave his general attention to the work, and would at times lay hold on the ropes, and pull with all the power of a two-hundred-pounder.[9]

To counteract the effects of so much hardship and exposure, rations of whisky were occasionally issued. Those of the men who did not drink, gave up their ration to those who did, and thus some of the latter got "gloriously fuddled." This was before the day of rubber blankets with us; and we had to sleep on the ground, or on such flooring of weeds, cornstocks, boards, &c., as we could gather, with only our woolen blankets for shelter. Rain was abundant. But once in two weeks were there twenty-four consecutive hours of dry weather. Under foot was mud and water, and that continually.[10]

Small boats accompanied us, bearing the rations, headquarters, &c. Of these boats, the *Hamilton Belle,* an old Keokuk ferry-boat, seemed most undaunted and serviceable. Her draught was so light, and her power so great, we used to say she could run in a furrow on a heavy dew.[11]

As the work of clearing progressed, we marched further down the Pass, through the woods and swamps. A part of the regiment one night started to move further down, and darkness overtook them in the midst of a swamp. No place could be found, out of water, where a man could lie down; and they had to turn back in the night, tired, wet, and grumbling, and hunt a place to sleep. But even out of discomforts they made fun. Their camp was chosen close to the brink of the Pass. During the night, one of the longest and slimmest men among them, the flag-staff of the regiment in fact, got up, in the dark and before he was well awake walked off into the deep water of the channel. Fortunately a good wetting was all the consequence; and great was the merriment at Jack's unlucky attempt to sound the river.

But the most cheering event that happened was the arrival of the mail. None but those who have been in similar circumstances can imagine how anxiously each one waited to hear his name called when the letters were distributed, or how great was his disappointment at learning there was nothing for him. Words of love and fond remembrance may seem but little to their writers, but to him who is far away from all he loves, and surrounded only by discomfort and dangers, they are doubly dear.

Companies G and B were left behind the regiment for nearly a week, to clear out a particular drift. During this time a detail from these companies went out a short distance after forage, and several of company B were taken prisoners by a small body of rebels hovering near; but all or nearly all of them, were returned to the regiment before the expiration of our term of service.[12]

This part of the country, swampy as most of it is, has some of the richest plantations in the State. We foraged a great deal. Beef was so abundant that sometimes cows were killed for the sake of the liver; for none of us were particularly desirous to be very saving of rebel property.[13] The forwardness of the season seemed odd to us, when we thought of the time of the year. In one of our camps there was a peach tree in full bloom on the 14th of February. Letters we wrote in the midst of budding Spring would reach home a month later, in the snows of mid-Winter.

On the afternoon of the 18th, Companies G and B were ordered a few miles further down the Pass, to Alcorn's plantation, to re-join the regiment, as there was supposed to be some danger of a rebel attack.[14] Reaching Pettit's plantation about dark, they made arrangements to camp for the night, and went to work to cook their suppers; but just as they were about to commence eating, a renewed and more urgent order came, and they had to start off supperless. That was a queer march, in utter darkness, in single file along the narrow top of the levee which was the most practicable road just then; but it ended at last, in General Alcorn's cotton-press, where the rest of the regiment was camped.

Next day we took formal possession of the general's negro-quarters, one company to a hut. Now came a general cleaning-up-time, our first for two weeks; and most of us experienced what is generally considered one of the last stages of poverty—washing our only shirt, and going to bed while it dries. "Hard-tack" had now entirely lost its novelty, and almost any thing else was welcomed instead.[15] An old negress on the plantation had a quantity of meal; and the regiment kept her overwhelmingly busy, baking corn bread, at 25 cents a pone. Frequently the door of her cabin would be crowded three deep by hungry soldiers waiting for their chances to buy.

The old general had a small corn-mill in his cotton-press, rigged to be worked by mule-power. At first, for some cause or other, the mules were not to be found; so the men laid their shoulders to the wheel by turns, and trotted merrily round the track, to grind their corn. It was a hard way of serving the country, however; and when at last the mules were found, they were put at work with little rest or mercy.

The Pass being now cleared out, there was other work before us. After some delay which seemed to us unnecessary, we went on board the *Hamilton Belle* and another small boat, on the morning of the 23d; and before night reach Helena, and entered our old camp there, glad enough to get back to it. But our rest was not long.[16]

CHAPTER IV.

_____

THE YAZOO PASS EXPEDITION.

On the 24th of February, we received two month's pay[1]—the first installment since we were mustered in; and on the evening of the same day we embarked on the fleet that was to convey us down the Pass.[2] Part of the regiment went on the steamer *Citizen,* and the remainder, with head-quarters, on the *Lebanon No. 2.*[3] Brigadier-General Clinton B. Fisk,[4] was in command of the brigade.[5] The fleet consisted of two iron-clad gun-boats, a mortar-boat, and a number of small transports.

As the boats were to be our camp for some time, and we were going through the enemy's country, preparations were made accordingly. Each company was assigned to some definite portion of a boat. One would have the guard of one side of the cabin deck, from the wheel-house to the bow, another the corresponding place on the other side, a third the bow of the boiler deck, and so on, the room being calculated roughly to give the men place merely to lie down. On the hurricane-decks, breast-works of thick plank, were erected, and sharp-shooters daily stationed behind them.[6]

Of course, there was little or no chance for cooking; there almost never is any, for soldiers on a transport. Coffee was made, "cold-pressed," as it was called, by turning on hot water from the engines; and when the boat stopped, or the engineer wanted to show his importance, even that could not be obtained. The meat-ration was cooked by thrusting frying pans full of it, in at the boiler-fires. About meal-times, dozens or more of men stood waiting their turns for this. Some cooked their pork by holding it on sticks over the escape-pipes of the boats. At times, however, the fleet would stop, when the men went ashore to do as much cooking as might be done at once. The officers in the cabin fared at the boat's table, of course; but the men were not permitted to buy their meals there. After a

while the amazing ration of "hard-tack and sow-belly" became
almost unendurable.[7] From so long confinement to the boats, without exercise, the digestion became impaired. Men would sit by a box
of hard tack and gnaw away at it all day, and lie down tired and
hungry at night. Often some poor fellow might be seen looking in at
the cabin door, at dinner-time, and wishing he had been born an
officer, or even a cabin-negro on a steam-boat.

The country through which we passed was mostly swampy, and
at that time overflowed with water; but there were frequent plantations, with negro-quarters, that looked like little villages. Rebel
guerrillas were all around us, though not daring to show themselves much. On some of the boats men were wounded and killed
by shots from the shore, but our regiment fortunately escaped
injury from them.

The Pass and the Coldwater and Tallahatchie rivers are all very
narrow, but deep, like most Southern streams. Our fleet was compelled to go very slowly, on account of the abrupt bends, swift current, and over-arching trees. The average speed made was about
three miles an hour.[8] Perhaps the best pilots in the world could not
have saved the boats from injury; but we thought the pilot of the
Citizen was a rebel and wanted to smash the boat up. Often there
were murmurs about the propriety of shooting him, when, at some
sudden bend, or other danger, we would hear his old, familiar, careless cry—"Give her a turn back, Dan." The *Citizen* was a stern-
wheeler, and somewhat unwieldy; and before the expedition
returned, she had lost most of her "gingerbread-work," and was
otherwise much injured. In fact, nearly or quite all the boats suffered more or less from the "rakes," as they were called, when they
would swing into the current and hit the over-hanging limbs of the
trees on the bank. There were many such "rakes" on the *Citizen*.
One of them tore off a good part of the guard where Company B
was stationed; and soon afterward another one come near "cleaning
out" Company G, on the other side.[9] Hats, knapsacks, guns and
accouterments were left hanging in the tree as we passed. It seems
almost miraculous that no injury was done to life or limb by these
tremendous collisions; but the men soon learned to jump and dodge
quite nimbly.

The Tallahatchie is perhaps the crookedest river in creation.[10] It is so unearthly crooked that, standing on one boat of our fleet and looking at the others, one could not possibly tell whether they were ahead of him or behind him. In one place there was but just one foot width of ground between the Tallahatchie river on one side and the same river on the other, and yet it was perhaps a mile around the bend. Dense cane-brakes occasionally lined the banks, and sometimes the boats would run into them a little, as if bent on crossing. There was occasional wet weather, of course; when those who slept on the hurricane decks had the disadvantage. They could shelter themselves very well, with their new rubber blankets, from the rain itself as it fell; but when enough water had collected on the decks it would run off in streams, and "wash them out." It is not the pleasantest thing in the world to be waked in the middle of a pitch-black night by a stream of cold water running down one's back, and thus to waken from the sweet dreams of home and comfort to find one's self out of doors and in the rain. But they would be young in the army who were not used to much worse things than that.

In the government of the fleet in emergency, a code of signals had been devised. One whistle, sounded from the head-quarters boat, meant "Form line and prepare for action;" two whistles, "Prepare to land and attack the enemy;" and so on. One night, on the way down the Tallahatchie, the fleet had run until it was too dark to go any further, and anchored in the stream, in the midst of an apparently endless and untraversable swamp. During the night there was a heavy storm of rain; and in the midst of it came the one whistle from the head-quarters boat; all was instantly in excitement, some doubted; but most if not all the companies were formed in such line as was practicable on the boats, and stood waiting for further orders. Of course, an attack was expected; and we wondered how it should come, and could not help wishing we had a more comfortable time for it. Soon came the other signal, "Prepare to land and attack the enemy." How to land, was the question. There had been no land in sight when we anchored, and now it was too utterly dark to see any land if there had been any to see. But orders must be obeyed, whether they can be or not. We were duly proceeding to do the best we could toward fulfilling them, when an orderly came on board, with the word that it was a false alarm. The whistle-rope on the head-quarters boat had got wet and shrunk, and so it "whistled itself." Perhaps that was the first time when a steam-whistle, without human agency, ever called a brigade of soldiers to action.

The negroes at the different plantations along the river greeted us with frequently the most extravagant expressions of wonder and joy.[11] Doubtless they thought "Mass'r Linkum's boats" were wonderful affairs, and his men a wonderful army to bring them down there where nothing like the gun-boats had ever been before.

Great quantities of cotton had been hurriedly taken away before our advance, but we captured large amounts of it, notwithstanding.[12] Before long, the rebels found themselves unable to get it away fast enough, and so they commenced burning it. One day our advance gun-boat came so close to a small steamer loaded with cotton-bales which the rebels were endeavoring to take away, that they fired it and left it to its fate. Cotton burns peculiarly, and for a long time. The bales were unfastened, and the burning cotton spread all over the surface of the river. Our part of the fleet passed along there at night; and the appearance was that of a river on fire.[13] It was a strange, wild scene. Indeed, the whole Pass Expedition was a strange scene for us—in a strange country, where every thing seemed odd; and it was a very peculiar kind of soldiering any way.

In the afternoon of the 11th of March, our fleet reached Shell Mound, Miss., a few miles above the confluence of the Tallahatchie and Yulabusha rivers. The plantation had been recently deserted by its owner. It derived its name from a large mound composed entirely of shells, which formerly stood there, but which had been razed to the level, leaving small fragments of shell strewn over the ground. The mound was supposed to have been erected by some aboriginal race. One large mound, in the form of a frustum of a cone, still remained on the plantation, and its top shaded by fruit trees, was a pleasant resting-place.

Landing at Shell Mound, our regiment was immediately ordered out on what many of us supposed to be a march to battle, but which was probably intended for nothing more than a small reconnoissance, and was countermanded almost before it had begun.[14]

Across the narrow strip of land separating the Tallahatchie and Yalabusha rivers, some two or three miles above their junction, the rebels had thrown a defense of earth-work and cotton-bales, which was called Fort Pemberton.[15] This must yield before we could go further. Possibly the object, or one object, of our expedition may have been to draw the rebel force from Vicksburg. On the afternoon of the 11th, there was more exchange of shots between the gunboats and the fort.[16] Our regiment was ordered up the river a short distance, on the *Lebanon No. 2,* as a kind of foraging expedition, on which we twice fired a few shots at a small and rapidly retreating squad of rebels, and burned the plantation on which they were found. We returned to Shell Mound that evening.[17] The fleet lying then in the bend of the river, with lights shining, bands playing and men scattered about, among the close and gloomy southern trees, made a grand, impressive scene.

Owing to the swampy nature of the ground, it was found impracticable to assault the Fort, and therefore there was not much actually accomplished. Regiments were kept out on picket, batteries planted, and other preparations made, but still there seemed to be no good opening for business;[18] and on the morning of the 20th, our fleet started back up the river, on the retreat. That night a boat from Helena, brought us a mail, which came like an angel's visit to us wanderers in a strange land.

While we were on the way up the river, General Ross, who commanded the expedition, was superseded by General Quimby. Turning around immediately, we started back down stream, and reached Shell Mound again, on the 23d.[19] In a day or two, a regular camp was formed—our brigade camping on less space, probably, than ever brigade camped on before. During the night of the 28th, a heavy wind blew down a very large tree, which fell on a tent in the camp of the 47th Indiana, and killed four men and wounded several others.[20] After this there seemed to be among our officers a kind of horror of camping among trees.

General Quimby didn't take Fort Pemberton much more than General Ross did.[21] We were occupied in standing picket, and planting batteries and changing them, until April 4th, when the whole force was ordered up the river again, on the final retreat.[22] No remarkable event happened on the way. One or two plantations— or rather, the buildings and fences on them—were burned, in punishment of occasional shots from the shore near them.[23] The fuel for the boats being now exhausted, landings were occasionally made, and all the rails in the neighborhood brought on board. A kind of rule was adopted in these cases, that whoever went ashore should not return to the boat without a rail; and the General would obey it cheerfully, bringing up the heaviest rail he could get, on his shoulders, though such a proceeding was very much beneath the dignity of some of the petty officers.

Occasionally the men amused themselves by nailing strips of boards, like guide-boards, to the trees, against which the boats were all the time rubbing. On some of them were hung bottles, old clothes, effigies, &c., at which our children may look, perhaps in after years, and wonder how they could have ever been put away up there among the limbs of those tall trees. When our boat reached the Mississippi river, we fired a "grand salute" of all the muskets on board, and the one six-pound brass field-piece on the bow—as a kind of greeting to the noble river. Cramped up as we had been for almost six weeks, on the narrow rivers in the swamps, it gave us a great feeling of relief, to come out again on the broad Mississippi, where there was room enough to breathe. On the afternoon of the 8th of April, we reached Helena; and next day pitched camp on the side of the hill afterward known as Battery A, about a mile north-west of town.

And so ended the expedition. In some respects it was the hardest of our soldiering. Even when men have plenty of the roughest exercise, the army ration as usually issued, is not very well calculated to continue health; and where men are confined so closely on boats, and almost totally deprived of exercise, as we necessarily were, ill consequences must be expected. Diarrhea was universal, almost unanimous. Few of us remained in as good health as usual, and many contracted diseases to whose sad end the lonely grave-yard on the bare Helena hills, within the next few months bore witness.[24]

The whole expedition was peculiar. It was hazardous as can well be imagined. Had the water suddenly subsided while we were down in the swamps, as it soon afterward did, we should have been left at the mercy of a much inferior foe. There was danger all the time, and in many ways. The whole time seemed to us more dream-like and distant, when we re called it to mind, than any other period of our soldiering; and those of us who have been spared to read, in peace and quiet, here at home, these records of our army life and scenes, can hardly retrace, without peculiar feelings, their memories of the Yazoo Pass Expedition.

Capt. John Dillon, Company H, 33d Iowa Infantry. Dillon
helped raise and train Company H, and then he led it
through the Yazoo Pass expedition and the battle of
Helena, only to resign on July 26, 1863.
Photo courtesy of Larry Pearson.

CHAPTER V.

AT HELENA.

In camp again now, in a dry and comparatively healthy situation, we made preparation for a considerable stay. The camp was arranged in as good order as possible, kept thoroughly "policed." Company A was detailed on provost-duty in town, from the 14th of April to the 25th of May. The regiment was put under a thorough course of drill again. Our field-music, which had almost entirely dwindled down to nothing, was started up now in such a way that it did not fail again until near the close of our service. There was a general revival of discipline and drill. On the 16th of April, the welcome countenance of the pay-master appeared, and we received four month's pay.[1] The first time our brigade was ever out in line together, was on Thursday, P. M., the 30th, when Thanksgiving services were held in military order on our drill-ground.[2] General Fisk, commanding the brigade, and Colonel (afterward General) Pyle, made some remarks and offered prayer, which were all our observance of the day.[3]

On the 1st of May there was a slight skirmish between a party of 500 rebel cavalry, of Dobbins' Regiment, which was generally prowling around Helena, and a small portion of the 3d Iowa Cavalry, in which the latter was defeated.[4] Our regiment was immediately ordered out after the rebels; marched out some eight or nine miles west of town; found no rebels, of course; camped over night in a rather pleasant place, and then marched back again.[5] Drills continued, and the usual routine of camp. To aid the field-music in its marked improvement, a large bass drum was bought for the regiment, by contributions from the officers.

On the morning of May 6th, we started out, with two other regiments, a small squad of cavalry, and a section of the 3d Iowa Battery,

Mess 7, Company C, 3d Iowa Cavalry. The 3d Iowa Cavalry
belonged to the Helena garrison in the spring of 1863 and
functioned as the post's early warning system by patrolling
the countryside. The 33d Iowa Infantry marched several miles
into the interior after Confederate irregulars ambushed a
portion of the 3d Iowa Cavalry near La Grange, Arkansas,
on May 1, 1863. *Photo courtesy of Roger Davis.*

for several days of reconnoitering.[6] Colonel Rice had command of the force, and Lieutenant-Colonel Mackey of the regiment.[7] Nothing remarkable happened on the outward march. Moving toward the south-west, we passed through some of the most beautiful prairie that ever was seen, dotted with pleasant groves, and covered with grass and flowers. Frequently our whole train could be seen at once, winding for three miles along the road; and the alternation of white-covered army-wagons and blue-coated soldiers, relieved against the dark-green back-ground of the grove or prairie, was pleasant even to wearied soldiers.

One day there was much fun and excitement over an unsuccessful attempt at capturing a very spirited old white horse which seemed to have the freedom of the prairies. Tired limbs suddenly gained new strength, to join in the chase; but even the officers' horses could make but distant approaches to the spry old nag. Great was the enthusiasm, nevertheless; and one could not but be reminded of Irving's spirited description of "Hunting the Wild Horse," on just such a beautiful prairie.[8] At another time, while we were out on a large prairie covered with small sassafras bushes, there came a report that some rebel cavalry was close upon us. Our skirmishers were speedily sent out, our two pieces of artillery unlimbered, and we were immediately ready for action. But the supposed rebels proved to be only a squad of our own cavalry coming to join us from another road; and so we made much fun afterward, over the "Battle of Sassafras Prairie!"

On the 10th, reaching a large bayou, and without means of crossing, and having by this time accomplished the object of the reconnoissance, we started back to Helena. Tuesday, the 12th, was a hard day for us. Almost entirely out of rations, we had to march very fast, in order to get to town while we had any thing to live on. That night we had little or nothing to eat but parched corn.[9] A rebel lieutenant, whom we had captured, made fun of some of us who seemed to think this hard fare, and said that he had lived solely on parched corn and slippery-elm bark, for months together.

On the 13th, as we started out for the march to town, the command was halted, and three cheers formally called for and loudly given over the first received news of the taking of Richmond![10] Alas! that it wasn't true. But like the story of the wolf, we heard it so

Second Lt. Orlo H. Lyon, 3d Iowa Battery. Two guns from this battery accompanied the 33d Iowa on an eight-day sortie in May 1863 to scatter Confederate irregulars lurking near Helena. *Photo courtesy of Roger Davis.*

much, before we were out of the service, that at last it found no cre-
dence at all.

At Helena again, the old routine returned. Our first brigade-drill
was on the 18th; and battalion-drill, company-drill and skirmish-
drill all the time, with the regular rations of guard- and fatigue-
duty, left little room for idleness.[11] There was an excellent
drill-ground near camp, and we did not let the weeds grow on it. On
the 22d there was a sham battle between the 3d Iowa Battery and
the 5th Kansas Cavalry, which to us, who had never yet known a
real one, was an exciting scene.[12] Next day, Major-General Prentiss
held a grand review of all the troops at Helena.[13] There were on the
field two or three brigades of infantry, three regiments of cavalry,
and one or two batteries. This was the most orderly, sensible and
satisfactory review in which we ever participated. Every thing
seemed to go off according to programme.[14]

About the 1st of June, there began to come rumors of an
approaching attack by the rebels. Occasionally we would have to
stand "at arms" from an early reveille till after sun-rise. One effect
of all this was, that at last we grew to believe there would never be
any attack on the place, and that all the long days of work on the
fortifications, and the false alarms and every thing of the kind,
were but the means adopted by our commanding officers, to keep us
from rusting in rest. The fact was, however, the rebels had even
then commenced moving from Little Rock, against us.[15]

General Fisk having been ordered up the river, Colonel Rice now
succeeded to the command of the brigade; and we never again had
him for our regimental-commander.[16] His life need not be written
here. It is part of the history of our State. But we shall not cease to
remember him as an able, zealous and careful colonel, brave among
the bravest, of good and valued judgment, considerate of the welfare of those under his command, the model of an officer, and proud
of his regiment, as it was proud of him.[17]

On the 15th of June we moved camp to the bank of the river, a
mile north of town. On the 17th, the old muskets we had so long
carried were exchanged for Enfield rifles.[18] The change was made
in good time, as we soon discovered. The weather was now very hot,
and the location supposed to be unhealthy; but we paid full care to
cleanliness in camp, and as much to comfort as possible; and there-

fore got along at least as well as other regiments. And so the days passed, in the endless round of garrison-duty, with its "picket" and "fatigue," "picket" and "fatigue," in almost changless alternation, in the over-powering heat. It was by no means agreeable; but a change was near.

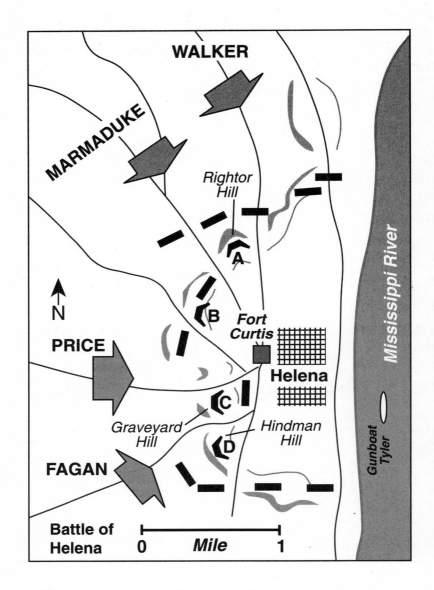

WALKER

MARMADUKE

Rightor
Hill

A

N

PRICE

B

Fort
Curtis

Helena

C

Graveyard
Hill

Hindman
Hill

D

FAGAN

Mississippi River

Gunboat
Tyler

Battle of
Helena

0   Mile   1

Map by Steve Scallion. *Courtesy Arkansas Historic Preservation Program.*

CHAPTER VI.

THE BATTLE OF HELENA.

The progress of the rebels from Little Rock to the attack of Helena seemed to have been well known to our commanders, or if not known, at least well guessed at; and our force at Helena was therefore kept well in readiness.[1] There were frequent camp-rumors of the approaching attack, but few believed them.[2] "Reveille at three o'clock to-morrow morning. Stand at arms till sunrise" became a quite frequent order; but these repeated appearances of alarm only made us believe less in the reality of any cause for them.[3]

But the time came at last. At two o'clock, in the morning of Saturday, the 4th of July, we were called into line and marched down to the vicinity of Fort Curtis, the principal defense of the post, and there stood "at arms" for an hour or more.[4] All was quiet; and though there was evidently "some thing up," many of us did not even then believe the rebels would seriously attack us; and some even doubted that there were any rebels there. In a short time they changed their minds.

Between three and four o'clock, in the misty light of earliest dawn, occasional firing was heard along the picket-line. In a few minutes it increased, and the alarm-gun from Fort Curtis gave the signal for the fight. Our regiment was immediately moved to the support of batteries C and D. The former was a little south-of-west of Fort Curtis, and the latter the most southern point of our western line. On the way to them we met Lieutenant Sharman, of Company G, riding on a horse, wounded, his face covered with blood. He had been in charge of the picket-detail from our regiment, which held the left of the line.[5] A rebel brigade advanced against this feeble squad, and of course our boys fell back on the main line, but not until they had made such a gallant resistance

First Lt. John F. Lacey, Company C, 33d Iowa Infantry.
Lacey was studying law in Samuel Rice's office when he
joined the 3d Iowa Infantry in 1861. Captured in Missouri
and sent home on parole, he became the 33d Iowa's first
sergeant major on August 23, 1862. Lacey was promoted
to first lieutenant on April 16, 1863, and joined Colonel
Rice's staff after the latter received a brigade command.
After the war, Lacey pursued a brilliant legal career and
served eight terms in the House of Representatives.
Photo courtesy of U.S. Army Military History Institute.

that, a year afterward, at the battle of Jenkin's Ferry, some rebel prisoners asked what regiment we were, and upon being told, exclaimed, "O yes, we know you. You're the fellows that fought us so like ——— at Helena."[6]

During a momentary halt, while one or two companies were being detached for a particular station on the line, a sutler of some cavalry regiment, whose stand was near, brought out his stock of bread, cakes and pies, and scattered them among the men. And all day he kept his store open, with all he could supply of bread and water free to every soldier. This was not only a sign of sympathy, but was material and valuable aid; for we went out to the fight without our breakfast, and of course remained fasting most of the day. The greater part of the regiment got a share of the bread and water which were brought up near the line after the battle was over, but many had nothing to eat till night; and it is very uncomfortable fighting on an empty stomach.[7]

The rebels attacked us with about 12,000 men,[8] under Lieutenant-General Homes,[9] Major-General Price[10] and Brigadier-General Marmaduke,[11] striking our ranks with their main force almost at the same instant along our whole line. But their most persevering efforts were directed at our left, which was held mainly by our regiment and the 33d Missouri.[12] On the northern portion of the line, which was attacked by General Marmaduke, the 29th and 36th Iowa held the ground, assisted by a section of the 3d Iowa battery.[13] The fight in this part of the field was not of so long continuance. On the southern portion the attack was repeated again and again, with a bravery amounting to desperation.[14] All along the western side of Helena are abrupt hills, divided by numerous deep and narrow gorges, where in many places a man could only walk with difficulty. The trees that grew there had been cut down, and so disposed as to form the greatest possible obstruction; yet the rebels repeatedly charged over places where, after the battle, we could but slowly clamber in search of the wounded and dead.

For some cause or other, the whole left of the line seemed to be left somewhat to itself. Colonel Rice, in command of the brigade, gave his attention to the northern portion of the field; and upon Lieutenant-Colonel Mackey seemed to devolve the command not only of our regiment but of a good part of the line. Riding constantly from one end to the other, he distributed the companies as seemed most necessary; and so one company would be sometimes at one place, and sometimes at another.[15]

Company C was stationed at battery C when the rebels made a grand charge and succeeded in capturing the battery.[16] After a heavy loss, the company retreated a short distance; but the rebel triumph was of short duration.[17] They attempted to turn our own guns against us, but a well-directed fire from Fort Curtis and battery D soon drove them back with heavy losses.[18] The gunboat *Tyler,* steaming up and down the river and keeping up an incessant fire from her sixty-pounders, gave great assistance by the excellent "moral effect" if not by actual execution.[19] The rebels believed there were several gunboats operating against them.[20]

Under cover of the dense fog of the morning, the rebel sharpshooters had crept up so near our ranks as to be very annoying to us; but when the fog lifted and the sun shone out bright and clear behind us, we soon made them seek a longer and safer range for practice.[21] Our regimental-color was planted in the breast-work where the center companies were first stationed; and there it stood till the battle was over, when it was found riddled with twenty-seven bullet-holes.

In the heat of the battle some of us who were stationed near the colors,[22] upon looking over to battery D, saw a hundred or so of our men go rushing out in a charge. Our hearts went with them as they gallantly advanced. In a little while they returned, bringing with them a crowd of prisoners of three or four times their own number. Oh! how we shouted then! Companies G and B of our regiment were in the charge. A brigade of rebels had advanced down into a deep hollow in front of battery D, and in coming out of it either way, exposed themselves to a raking fire. So our small detachment went and gobbled them.[23]

A battle is generally supposed to be a time not only of carnage and death, but of grim and terrible excitement. But this was not the case in the battle of Helena, at least so far as our regiment was concerned. Our feelings were rather a lack of feeling. We acted and felt apparently just as though we had been in a hard battle every day of our lives. Up in the breast-works men would shoot at rebels as though aiming at buffaloes or deer. Laughing and chatting were abundant as ever. Officers would notice the missing shots of their

Lt. Col. Cyrus H. Mackey, 33d Iowa Infantry. When Colonel Rice became a brigade commander on June 13, 1863, Mackey took over command of the 33d Iowa Infantry, a position he would fill for most of the rest of the war. A lawyer from Sigourney, Iowa, Mackey proved himself as a soldier in the fighting at Helena, July 4, 1863. *Photo courtesy of U.S. Army Military History Institute.*

men, and with all the eagerness of competition insist in trying a few shots themselves. Men would pick the best places for loading and firing behind the breast-works, and laugh at the close misses of the rebel sharp-shooters.[24] Sometimes to get a better shot, they would raise themselves up at full length, thus exposing most of their person to the enemy. In this way private Jacob Miller, of Company G, received his mortal wound.[25]

At the commencement of the battle, when the bullets first began its whiz scatteringly among us, we "bobbed" considerably. This "bobbing" is a purely involuntary motion, like the winking of the eye, when a foreign substance approaches it. Sometimes it seems almost impossible to keep from "bobbing," though every man may laugh at himself meanwhile, for doing it; but when the bullets come thick and fast the motion as involuntary ceases. There seems then to be no room to dodge. "Why don't you stand up straighter?" said one to a man who during a heavy fire of artillery, was crouchingly passing along behind a breast-work. "There isn't room," was the expressive answer. In the hottest of the fire, no one seems to think of dodging, but let the storm of bullets slacken much, and the "bobbing" immediately re-commences.

At one time during the battle there seemed some prospect that the rebels might at least effect an entrance to the town; but soon their advantage was lost in such way as to be worse for them, than to have never gained it.[26] After repeated efforts, they slackened their fire, and finally drew back altogether. By 11 a. m., the battle was over; but our little force could not wisely do otherwise than remain in the defenses and await the renewed assault which all confidently expected. Thirty-five hundred of us would have looked scanty indeed, pursuing twelve thousand in an equal field.[27] We did not know how badly we had beaten them. Had we but known the utter route and demoralization in which they withdrew from the field, we might have driven them to greater losses, or even captured the whole. But while we lay behind our works expecting, and ready for their return, they were rushing away in mad disorder, not even stopping to care for their wounded on the field. We had won a glorious victory; but it was obscured from public view by the still more glorious news from Vicksburg and the east, as moon-light is dimmed by the sun.

Placed in the front of the battle our brigade suffered the heaviest of the loss, and our regiment more than the rest of the brigade. We had 22 killed, 49 wounded, and 16 missing; and a large proportion of the wounded died of their wounds.[28] The names of those who were wounded or fell will be properly designated in the roll of the regiment, herewith appended. Doubtless almost any other regiment, placed as we were, would have done as we did; but it was our fortune in this battle to bear the burden and heat of the day.

In the newspaper reports of the action, much credit was given to a colored regiment which held the left of the works, extending from the bluffs to the river; but the truth was that they were not attacked at all. If they had been, they would doubtless have done their duty bravely, but they deserve no especial credit as it was.[29] The 33d Missouri was immediately with us much of the time; and from this grew a strong liking and cordiality between the two regiments. To pass through danger together is a great aid to mutual esteem. Indeed, it was noticed in the regiment, after the battle, that there was a much better state of feeling among us than before. Things seemed to move on better generally, and there was better discipline with less friction.

After the battle was over, we lay on our arms out in the trenches, to be ready for a repetition of the attack. Bread and water were hauled out from camp; but many of the men got none till well toward evening. The wounded were borne from the field to improvised hospitals, friend and foe alike, and received equal treatment side by side.[30] It was remarked that the prisoners we took had very exaggerated ideas of both their own force and ours, many giving the former at forty thousand, and estimating ours at about half that amount.

One of the many personal incidents worthy of mention, is the adventure of Sergeant Moore, then a private of Company G. At one time during the battle, after an advance of a portion of our force, he suddenly found himself alone, and the rest of the party some distance behind him. Seeking the best route of retreat, he spied a rebel with a flag, and at the same time four other rebels with guns in their hands, who sprang to conceal themselves behind a log. Jumping to a stump, with that quick wit which in sudden danger, seizes the first available expedient for escape, he brought his rifle

Cpl. James H. Sawyer, Company E, 33d Iowa Infantry.
Sawyer enlisted in Company E as a private on July 21,
1862. Wounded in the breast at Helena on July 4, 1863,
he recovered and ended the war as a corporal.
Photo courtesy of Roger Davis.

to bear upon a single rebel—who proved to be a surgeon—and summoned him to surrender himself and the four other men immediately. It was a bold demand, for one man to five; but Moore had the backing of a loaded rifle and full determination, and it didn't take the rebels long to see it. The surgeon surrendered himself and the others, and Moore marched them back to the security of our lines, and delivered them up as his quota of the victory.[31]

We lay in the trenches till noon of the 5th, but no attack came. A few rebel surgeons and nurses came in to attend their wounded. It was remarked that the rebels turned black almost immediately after death. Some supposed this to have been caused by the whisky-and-gunpowder mixture which was furnished them to drink, as remains of it were found in many of the canteens.[32] Their dead were buried on the field; but since then the battle-field has been so changed by barracks and fortification, many of the graves are indistinguishable.[33]

We have spoken thus fully of this battle, because it was our first. There have been many vastly greater conflicts, but never greater victories. Thirty-five hundred men repulsed fifteen thousand, so severely they retreated in a panic, from the effects of which they never recovered. The "moral influence" here gained was of service to us afterward. Had there not been so much greater actions on the same day in other portions of the country, the victory at Helena would have rung through all the North. We would not wish the scene to be repeated; but now it has passed, there is no "celebration of the 4th" to which we look back with so much pride as our 4th of July at Helena.

CHAPTER VII.

THE LITTLE ROCK EXPEDITION.

The welcome the rebels received in the forenoon of the 4th, at Helena, was enough for them, and they did not think it advisable to return; but this we were not aware of at the time, and so an alarm came next day. We were lying in camp, trying to have a Sunday's rest after the battle, when the signal-gun from Fort Curtis, warned us again into line. Now we were mad. If the rebels had but waited a while, and given us some little chance to rest, we would have fought them again quite willingly; but we did not like to be so hurried about it.[1] We made ready however, sulkily determined if the rebels came at us we would give them a worse whipping than before. This time our regiment was sent out just north of Battery A. Skirmishers were deployed, companies posted, and every preparation made for the coming attack; but no attack came, and no sign of any. Our commanders had doubtless happened to remember that "eternal vigilance is the price of liberty." Their caution cost us a very unpleasant night; for a heavy rain came on, and we had to lie in the mud, with only the shelter of our rubber-blankets. Returning to camp next morning, we again received the news of the surrender of Vicksburg, and again greeted it with three hearty cheers.[2]

On the 8th a more formal and less unpleasant "celebration of the 4th," was ordered. All the troops at Helena, numbering perhaps, not far from five thousand, were drawn up *en masse*, at the east side of Fort Curtis, and addressed by Major-General Prentiss, and several minor officers, in terms of the highest congratulation upon their bravery and its glorious result. Just at the proper moment of the General's speech, when he alluded to the roar of the cannon on that day, which should be echoed again in more peaceful times in honor of the day, the guns of the fort and the neighboring batteries opened a fire that brought back the echoes of the recent battle. It may not be unworthy of mention, by the way, that this firing, as well as the cannonading on the 4th, was distinctly heard at Benton, in Saline county, one hundred and forty-five miles away—as we were afterward assured by testimony so concurrent we could not doubt it.[3]

Again on the 10th there came another alarm. The signal-gun was fired, the long-roll beaten, the regiments hurried into line and marched to their appointed places in defense; the "pomp and circumstance" of war was marshalled in all its fullness—and in a little time three negroes were marched within the lines.[4] "*Parturient montes et nascitur*" negro.[5] The poor fellows had come from somewhere out in the country, hiding through the woods, and their sudden appearance at our picket-line was the cause of the alarm.

But finally, the battle and its alarms became an old story, and things settled down into about the usual routine of heavy garrison-duty. In a few days a detail from the different regiments was sent out on a scout; but they returned, with a report only of hard marching and some forage.[6] Occasionally a boat-load of Vicksburg prisoners would pass up the river, looking very much like an animated clay-bank in the unvarying color of dirty-yellow. On account of the heat, the effluvium from the neighboring swamps, and perhaps other causes, our regiment was now reduced to an aggregate of only two hundred and eighty-five effective men. The pleasing presence of the pay-master enlivened us again on the 28th of July, and we were paid for two months.[7] If there is any officer whom, *ex-officio,* soldiers are especially glad to see, it is the pay-master; and if his visits are not quite as welcome as those of angels, they are almost as far between.

About the first of August the rumors of a march across the country to Little Rock began to come in circulation, and frequently hinted at Texas also. In a few days they settled down into the plain facts that General Steele was to command an expedition against Little Rock, and we were to be a part of the expedition.[8] Of course, there must first come a grand review, for which all the troops were formed on our old drill-ground, which was now so overgrown with weeds, that marching on it was extremely difficult. Previous to the march the sick were separated from the regiments; and this proceeding was to some a cause of great anxiety. Many manifested a cheerful willingness to stay. Some were excused by the doctors, who were fully able to go with the regiment, but to offset this, there were many who insisted on sharing the march, though pronounced unable to endure it.[9]

At 2:40 P.M., of the 11th of August, our division, under command of Colonel Rice, took up its line of march.[10] It was a hard beginning of a rather hard time. The heat was overpowering to us, who were unaccustomed to hard exercise in such a climate. Woolen blankets, knapsacks, extra clothing, &c., were soon scattered along the road.[11] One big burly fellow in the regiment, after carrying his heavy knapsack as long as he could, began to haul it over and throw away a part of its contents; and among these he found an old ax-head, which some severe practical joker had slily placed there before we started. In a few days things grew worse; and on the 16th and 17th there was much suffering.[12] The heat and the hard marching together, were too much for any ordinary powers of endurance. Men would fall out of the ranks and tumble down at the side of the road, by dozens and almost by hundreds.[13] All such stragglers would have to come on after us, of course; but that is much easier than marching in ranks. In fact, marching with a regiment is one of the hardest ways in the world of getting along. A man may walk forty miles a day, alone and at his own gait and time, as easily as he can march twenty-five miles a day in the army. And a sick man, who can not march fast enough to keep up with the regiment, is frequently permitted to walk on ahead. This may be called a peripatetic paradox—that a soldier who can not march fast enough to keep up with his regiment, should rest himself by marching on ahead of it, yet such is often the case.

As we approached Clarendon, Arkansas, on the evening of the 14th, some of us, exhausted by the heat and hard marching, had fallen behind the whole column.[14] Resting awhile at the outer picket-post of Davidson's cavalry,[15] who then held the place, we started on again to overtake the regiment. Weak and weary as we were, every mile seemed almost endless, and every minute at least an hour. There are times when even a soldier may have some thing very much like "the blues." The more we marched, the less we seemed to gain; and darkness was fast gathering. Camp must be found that night, or our hard-tack and coffee would never do us any good. Still

Maj. Gen. Frederick Steele. A friend and classmate of
Ulysses S. Grant, Steele arrived at Helena on July 31,
1863, to organize an expedition to capture Little Rock. He
would accomplish his objective in a campaign of masterful
maneuver but fared less well when he invaded southern
Arkansas in the spring of 1864. *Photo courtesy of
Cravens Collection/UALR Archives.*

Col. Thomas Hart Benton Jr., 29th Iowa Infantry. The 33d Iowa served in Benton's 2d Brigade during the Little Rock Campaign. *Photo courtesy of Gregory J. W. Urwin.*

the town seemed no nearer. We began to think of "giving up" generally, and not trying to go any farther, when suddenly the rich tones of a good brass band greeted our ears. Had an angel suddenly stood in the way, we would not have been more surprised or cheered; and we pressed on with renewed vigor. It was dark when we reached the little huddle that bore the name of Clarendon. Davidson's cavalry were all over the place. Our division of infantry had just come in, "and passed on farther" some where, but no one could tell us where. One man would tell of their camping about a mile ahead, and the next would make them two miles distant; and after tramping over those weary miles the first man we met would tell us, carelessly, that the 33d was camped about two miles further on.

At last the camp was reached, but it was a labyrinth of cavalry and confusion. Of all possible places to "get lost" in, a cavalry-camp in the woods at night, is the most inexplicable. You lose your bearings, and there is nothing to show them again. You inquire, and the answer is more bewildering than the ignorance itself. You undertake to go straight across the road, and in three minutes you suddenly find yourself on the same side you started from. Your only resource is to get a darkey to hunt the way for you, or else to wait till day-light. We chose the former alternative; and the sagacious African piloted us through more twists and turnings than Cretan[16] ever dreamed; and at last we reached camp, and soon forgot all present troubles in a cup of the soldier's true comforter, good, substantial coffee.

At Clarendon, General Rice appeared with the star on his shoulders, having received them since we left Helena. Sorry to lose him entirely as a regimental-commander, we were glad to see his sphere of service enlarged, and were proud of his success.[17]

This Clarendon had never been a town, and had been burned some months ago, when General Curtis' army was there; so the little now left of the place was not particularly valuable nor attractive. Perhaps the spirit of the few inhabitants may fairly be judged from the fact, that one night during our stay, a secesh gentleman burned his own house to prevent its being used as a hospital for our sick soldiers.[18]

At Clarendon we remained a week, waiting for orders, or rations, or "some thing to turn up"—we knew not what. There was much

Brig. Gen. Samuel A. Rice. Rice's promotion to brigadier general overtook him at Clarendon, Arkansas, around August 17, 1863, while he was commanding the 3d Division in Steele's "Arkansas Expedition." Rice sat for this portrait in Brown's Gallery at the corner of Little Rock's Main and Markham Streets sometime after the city's capture. *Photo courtesy of Massachusetts Commandery Military Order of the Loyal Legion and U.S. Army Military History Institute.*

sickness, not only in our own regiment, but among all the troops. The march out from Helena, had been too hard for endurance; and beside this, Clarendon was the very home and head-quarters of ague in bulk and quantity. The very air was thick with it. We could almost hew out blocks of it, and splash them into the river. One morning one of the buglers undertook to blow the "sick-call"—a "quinine and whisky," as we usually named it; but before he had sounded a half-dozen notes a sudden ague seized him, and he was shaking vigorously. Another bugler took the horn, and he, too, had to lie down to shake. Lieutenant-Colonel Lofland[19] came to the rescue, but the "sick-call" was too much for him; there was ague in the bugle, and he had to lay it down. At last came one more practiced in blowing, and by great effort he sounded the call; but while the rest went up to the surgeons' tent for their regular rations of quinine and whisky, he went off and spread himself upon the ground and took a shake of unprecedented vigor and duration.[20]

By the way, there used to be a wonderful impartiality in the army some times, in the distribution of medicines. At any rate, the boys used to say it made no difference what a man's ailment might be—diarrhea, constipation, lameness, sore hand, gun-shot wound, or broken leg—the invariable remedy was the "C. C. pills;" and the boys would represent the doctor as occasionally ordering the patient, in his gruff way, to "take one every two hours, or two every one hour, I don't care a d——n which."[21]

And there some how got into circulation the report, that when little Pete H——, stubbed and short as so tough a chap could be, went up to the doctor with some bronchial difficulty, the doctor opened Pete's mouth with no gentle hand, examined him with grim, professional carelessness, and at last gruffly told him that he had "piles or sore throat, d——d if he could tell which."

But to return to our ague: Comparatively speaking the real, genuine "Clarendon shake" is to any ordinary chills and fever, about as a big bull-dog is to a pet poodle. We experienced it in all varieties and degrees; and the worst that any ague can ever do now for us, is to make us think of Clarendon. On Friday night, the 21st of August, the regiment started on, crossing White River on the pontoon. Then came a long stretch of corduroy-road, over which we had to march, in the almost utter darkness, first up, and then down, one foot off, and one on, stumbling and falling, and then scrambling up and tramping on again, till strength and patience were alike exhausted, and we believed that corduroy-road contained the oft-mentioned point "where forbearance ceases to be a virtue." If ever men were pardoned for profanity, surely those teamsters are partially forgiven, who drove their six-mule teams over that worse than road, in the darkness of that dismal night. And how mortal creatures, of limited capacities withal, can drive six indisputable mules hitched to an army-wagon, by a single rein, and wind around safely among stumps, trees and mud-holes, where a man walking must well consider his steps, is a mystery and a wonder.[22]

Morning came at last, and a day of rest; and then we started on again. The country we passed over on the 23d, was so much like Iowa, as to be the theme of constant remark. There was Iowa prairie, and an Iowa breeze blowing over it; and the timber bordering it was like Iowa timber. Several times, in marching through Arkansas, we have found great similarity between the country there and some parts of Iowa, with which we were familiar. Indeed, perhaps, no greater similarity exists between any Northern and Southern States, than that between Iowa and Arkansas.[23]

A little after sun-down, at the close of a hard march on which we had seen some suffering for want of water, we reached Duvall's Bluff, on White River, and went into camp.[24] This was the 23d of August. Here was the terminus of the Little Rock and Duvall's Bluff rail-road, of which the rebels yet held the greater part, and which they had till within a few days been actively using.[25] There had formerly been a few buildings here; but the expedition against Arkansas Post, the previous Spring, had destroyed them.[26]

Here we remained a week in camp.[27] The boats brought supplies up from Helena, and the mails came with tolerable speed.[28] On the 31st of the month the onward march was resumed. Next morning we were informed that twenty miles of prairie lay before us, with no water except what we carried. All the way so far, there had been much difficulty in getting decent water to drink. It was the dry season. Frequently we had to go to the swamps, and skim a thick, green scum from the top of the water we were compelled to use for coffee. So we imagined we had already known what was meant by scarcity of water; but worse was yet to come. The well near us was exhausted, and no creek could be found.[29] So scarce was water now, that to prepare for that twenty-miles march in the heat of a Southern August, many of us had to fill our canteens from a puddle where the hogs had wallowed, and in the bottom of which was a pile of bones.[30]

That day's march was a hard one. The road was high prairie, and the sun shown down unclouded. Before the day was half gone, the "stragglers"—those who, from fatigue and exhaustion, were unable to march in ranks, and had to tumble down at the side of the road, and rest and wait—might be counted almost by hundreds. Many had drank too freely in the morning, and so too much reduced their scanty supply of water for the day. One hardly can imagine what thirst is until he has seen some such time as this, when he begins to have strange, waking dreams of water, and of the happiness of lying down, if only for a minute, on a green bank, and having a river run into his mouth.[31]

It was well toward evening when we marched through the little town of Brownsville, and passed on into the woods near a bayou, to camp.[32] The morrow was a day of rest, which the men improved in washing their clothes. Next morning, September 3d, at six o'clock, our regiment and two others were ordered out, in fighting trim, on a reconnoissance to Bayou Metoe.[33] The weather was exceedingly hot, and the roads dry and dusty. This day's march was always considered in the regiment to be the hardest we ever had. The distance was twenty miles, and we accomplished it a little after noon. But many were compelled to fall out of ranks and wait till night before coming in to camp, or till the ambulance came and took them, if they were absolutely unable to travel.

Arrived at the bridge over the Bayou Metoe, the 33d was deployed as skirmishers. A battery of small howitzers, shelled the woods, but the only enemy was a small squad of rebels apparently on picket. At night, we withdrew, and camped on a beautiful spot, which had evidently been a rebel camp for some time. Ditches, bowers of leaves, portions of banks, rude chairs, straws, remains of garments, old pieces of leather, stoves and broken boxes, were the tokens of recent occupation. The camp had been defended by a breast-work, from which General Davidson's cavalry had driven the rebels in a sharp little skirmish, a few days before. We found here two corpses of Federal soldiers lying in the woods unburied.[34]

Next morning, by a march of less fatigue, we returned to

Brownsville. The object of the movement out to the bayou had been to persuade the rebels that our advance was to be made by that place; and the feint proved fully successful. Sunday morning, September 6th, the regular march re-commenced.[35] A part of the way was over a high and pleasant prairie; and as we marched we asked ourselves what the folks at home, at that hour attending church as usual, away up there in the peaceful North, would think if they were to see us wearily plodding along meanwhile, over those Arkansas prairies. In the evening, as it drew near dark, came one of those times when, as if purely from the innate depravity of things, the train seems to move but a foot at a time and then halt a minute. This is one of the most vexatious of experiences. It is more tiring and disagreeable than twice as much time at hard marching in mud and rain. And to add to the discomforts of the evening, the camping-place assigned our regiment was an old field, completely overgrown with briars, among which we had to pick our way and find room to sleep as best we could. It was a cheerless time; and perhaps the men were pardoned for part of the cursing. But at last the fires were kindled; and the fragrant coffee soothed each weary man to rest.[36]

Next day the march was more agreeable. The road wound for some miles through the woods, where wild vines hung in greater luxuriance and profusion than we had ever seen. Grapes were quite plenty, from the small black frost grape to the rich and juicy muscadine. Emerging from the woods, we marched along the side of a field containing one thousand acres of corn, with a strip of sweet potatoes looking large enough to supply all our army while the season lasted.[37] A New England farmer would scarcely be more surprised at the sight of some Western fields than we were at this, and some other Southern plantations. Here began traces of a contest in our advance, and they continued all the way. Occasionally firing was heard, as our cavalry drove back the rebel out-posts.[38] The end of the journey was at hand.

CHAPTER VIII.

LITTLE ROCK.

The 10th of September was a day worthy of remembrance. The weather was clear and very warm. At about ten in the forenoon we moved out from camp. The train had been posted, guards detailed, and proper dispositions made for the expected contest. But our part of the victory proved very different from what we had anticipated. All day we merely marched along, making frequent halts. One place in the woods, where we stopped to rest a moment, seemed nearer the lower regions, by several notches on the thermometer, than any we had ever tried before. It almost melted the hair on our heads. Occasionally during the day, we could hear the rattle of musketry in the advance, which told us that Davidson's cavalry was still "driving them in." Toward evening the firing grew heavier and more continuous, and was varied by an occasional boom from the artillery. As we neared the ever-moving scene of action, it was with a constant expectation to be soon engaged ourselves; but it was not so to be. The cavalry did the fighting, and the solid columns of infantry steadily marching on, supplied only the requisite "moral support."

Reaching the Arkansas River, we could see how General Steele was flanking the enemy. The cavalry had partially crossed the river and advanced up the southern side. Wounded rebels along the bank were occasionally visible. Still we went marching on; and before sun-down we passed through the outer defenses of Little Rock, which the rebels had just evacuated in considerable hurry. The road was well obstructed, and the earth-works strong enough to command the passage. Here was where the rebels were prepared for us; and had not General Steele so surprised them by the Bayou Metoe feint, and the present flanking-movement, we should certainly have had some difficulty with them here. As it was, the pans and kettles,

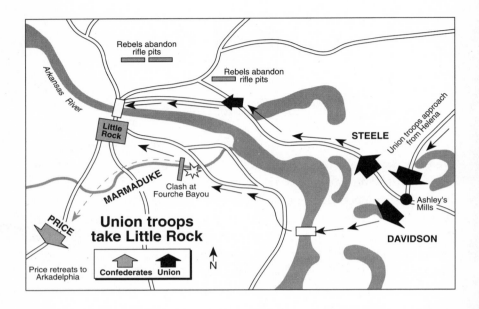

Map by Steve Scallion. *Courtesy Arkansas Historic Preservation Program.*

with victuals yet cooking on the fire, showed how unexpectedly they had discovered the position to be no longer tenable.[1]

All the afternoon, smoke had been seen ascending from the direction of the city. As darkness came on, and we drew near the place, the fires were more distinct. The rebels were burning their cars and steam-boats, and some government buildings.[2] An iron-clad gun-boat had ascended the river some months before, and the fall of the water had left it high and dry on the sand. It was now but a shapeless mass of burning ruins.[3] The wooden pontoon-bridge, however, General Price had not time to destroy, though he made a hasty attempt to do so.

It was almost dark when we arrived opposite the city. The firing on the opposite shore had ceased, and there was a rumor that we were fully victorious. Still we kept marching on. The burning loco-motives stood on the track a little to our left; and some one kept their bells ringing as we passed. Then, as the outlines of the city across the river became dimly discernible through the gloom, a horseman dashed past us, shouting that Little Rock was ours, and Davidson held possession. Loud rose the cheers, and that hour of our arrival opposite Little Rock, with its accompaniment of burning boats and locomotives, bells ringing, bands playing, and regiments cheering as we marched along, was one of the most stirring and poetic of our military life.

There seemed a kind of retaliatory justice in the time. The rebels had left this place, and traveled a month to give us a visit at Helena. We had traveled a month to return the call; but we were more successful than they.[4] Some of our boys, taken prisoners at Helena, had been brought here for confinement; but before we arrived they had been paroled and sent to St. Louis, so we did not have the opportunity, as some had anticipated, of meeting and freeing them at Little Rock.

Camping that night where we first halted, our first business was, as usual, to make ourselves comfortable as might be; but next morning there was leisure for looking around, and wondering how long we should be there. Some sanguine souls flattered themselves with the prospect of a Winter in the city; but the more thoughtful rather expected but a brief rest in the great advance to Texas.[5] So we lay and waited for the order which should let us across the river and into the city. There was much amusement over the story of a rebel surgeon, who had gone to sleep drunk, in the Anthony House, under Confederate rule, and waked to find himself protected by Federal authority, and who growled out his surprise that a man could not even take a little nap at a hotel, without falling out of the Confederacy.[6]

On the morning of Tuesday, the 15th of September, we moved across the river and entered the city.[7] The place assigned for the camp of our brigade was a gravelly and wooded ridge a little south of the arsenal grounds. Room having been allotted to the regiment, our first business was to make it habitable. The ground was covered with a dense under-brush, thickly interspersed with young pine trees. Though immediately contiguous to the capital of the State, it was as much wild land, as any in Arkansas; but it suited our circumstances very well.[8] Our tents and extra clothing having been left at Helena, we now found it necessary to use all our ingenuity in making shelter for ourselves. The ground was cleared off, and large piles of brush were burned. One afternoon there were so

Pvt. Allan McNeal, Company H, 33d Iowa Infantry.
McNeal fell sick during Steele's Little Rock campaign and
was left at the Union hospital established at De Valls
Bluff, Arkansas. He was severely wounded at the battle
of Jenkins' Ferry on April 30, 1864, and died after a long
struggle at his parents' home in South English, Iowa, on
September 24. *Photo courtesy of Larry Pearson.*

many and so hot fires of burning brush that, though the day had previously been perfectly clear, before night a shower came on, evidently caused by the smoke and heat thus raised.

Brush-shelters were now constructed, and laid off by companies as a regular camp. Many of them were no inconsiderable protection. Of course they would not turn rain, but they were very good houses for warm, dry weather. Some of them were erected with much skill and practice. One man of the regiment, who "roomed by himself," kept at work for a week or two in twisting and weaving a kind of kennel in which to stay; and when it was done, and he was in it, the sight was almost equal to a small side-show at a circus.

Supplies were now to be hauled from Duvall's Bluff to Little Rock in wagons, as the railroad had no rolling stock in order.[9] The consequence was, that we were put on quarter-rations; and very scanty living we found it. A great demand sprung up for pieces of tin and sheet-iron, of which to make graters whereon to grate corn. At these home-made graters the men would put in their spare time by turns, until they had meal enough to satisfy hunger for a day or two; and when that was gone the grater was in demand again. One or two small, portable, iron mills were erected, to be worked by two-man-power; and their creaking was heard at almost all hours, monotonous and dreary.

Near our camp was a garden, from which the boys occasionally "drew" sweet potatoes and some few other vegetables; but no body lived too high. Again and again we would run all over Little Rock in search of bread for sale, and find never a loaf. Pies of miserable quality and limited amount, retailed readily at twenty-five cents each; but eatables of any sum and substance, it was frequently impossible to buy.[10] The city seemed quite deserted. Shops and stores were closed, and few citizens could be seen in the streets. Indeed, the ladies had been terrified by all sorts of wild reports about our army, until they dared not remain in sight of us. They got over this after a while, however. One who spent only the last week of our stay in Little Rock with us, could form but a faint idea of the appearance and manners of the city and its people when we entered.[11]

The first part of our stay was by no means agreeable Scanty food, insufficient clothing, and such shelter only as brush-houses

could give, were poor comfort, even after such a march. The nights
were some times so cold we would have to get up before morning
and warm ourselves by the fire. Teams were kept out through the
country after forage, which helped out the provisions considerably;
and some times those of the more fortunate among us could obtain
meals at private houses in town; but altogether, there was not
much in this beginning of our Little-Rock-life to make it's memory
pleasant.

About the last of September, company- and battalion-drills were
commenced again.[12] On the 6th of October we received our tents
and surplus clothing from Helena, and both were very welcome.
The camp was now arranged in more military style, and to better
advantage. The old brush-shelters were remorselessly abandoned
and destroyed, and a general cleaning up ensued. In a few days, Mr.
Scholte, of Marion County, Iowa, arrived, as commissioner to take
the vote of the regiment.[13] The election was held on the 13th, very
quietly, at the Colonel's tent; and resulted in giving forty-six votes
to General Tuttle for Governor, and all the rest to Colonel Stone.[14]
During the Fall, our boys who had been taken prisoners at Helena,
having been paroled and exchanged, returned to the regiment. We
were heartily glad to have them with us again, and the regiment
seemed to them like home. Probably Little Rock seemed more
agreeable to them now, than it did when they were there before.

Cold weather was now coming on, and preparations were made
for Winter. Log-barracks were erected for the companies; and a
great demand arose for brick-bats, sticks and mud, for chimneys.
The town was ransacked for stoves, but with poor success. Only the
Winter before, stoves had sold at one hundred and twenty to one
hundred and fifty dollars; and people seemed to have hardly yet forgotten the old Confederate price-list. But soldiers "draw" things
some times, and buy when they can't avoid it; and so before long
stoves and chimneys began to make the Winter-quarters quite comfortable. We now hoped to remain here quietly during the Winter—
not that we had any desire to shirk duty; but it would have pleased
us much better to have duty come in that way—and things seemed
to indicate that such would be the case.[15] But soon there came an
unexpected, and not wholly delightful change.

CHAPTER IX.

WINTER.

At mid-night of the 25th of October, 1863, we were roused from our slumbers by the never-welcome sound of reveillie. Up and ready for action, was the order understood. Soon it was learned that the rebels had been making a disturbance in the vicinity of Pine Bluff, and we were ordered to Benton, a little town twenty-five miles south of Little Rock, to intersect their retreat.[1] The hour of starting was fixed at two in the morning; and at forty minutes later we were on the move.[2] Stopping about sun-down to take breakfast by the side of the road,[3] we marched on fast and steadily till we reached Benton, at 4 P. M. A small squad of cavalry already held the place, and of course left little to be bought any where around there. But no sooner had we broken ranks, than there was a promiscuous scattering all over town, in search of bread and other eatables.[4] The people must have thought the Union army was almost starved; and just at this particular time the opinion would not have been exceedingly out of the way. But our boys paid for all they obtained at Benton, and left the worthy citizens no cause for grumbling.[5]

One of the "non-commishes" had been unusually successful in gathering provender,[6] and had accumulated quite a pile of corn-cake at his place in camp. One afternoon he went out after more, and on returning he found two men posted as sentinels, walking a beat, arms at a "shoulder" with all due precision and gravity, before his pile of rations. Great was his wonderment, until he was informed that his personal grub had been mistaken for the regimental-commissariat, and this guard placed there in consequence.

On the morning of Thursday, the 29th, the troops started south-west—the 33d only, for a wonder, being left behind. We could only explain, by supposing it to be expected that the attack, if any was made, would be made there. But our detention was quite cheerfully obeyed; and the boys having all the town to themselves, had

room to flourish considerably.[7] The soldier never knows how long he
may stay in any particular place; and experience soon teaches him,
whenever he reaches camp any where, and sees no special probability of going further, to make calculations as if he were to stay a
month. Many of our boys went around and engaged private boarding by the week. At one house where was a rather good looking
young lady, who attempted to play on a somewhat time-worn piano,
and sang rebel songs with such vim as only a female rebel can
exhibit, there were some twenty or thirty blue-coated boarders—
attracted perhaps equally by the cheapness and good quality of the
victuals, the music of the piano, and the undisguised and spirited
rebellion in the looks, words and actions of the black-eyed young
lady.[8]

While the fair weather lasted, it was all very nice to lie there in
camp, and have no fatigue, and not much other duty, to perform;
but on Friday night, while we were all sleeping quietly under our
blankets on the ground, a heavy rain came on, and a hasty rising,
building of fires, and general muttering and discomfort ensued. The
next day, lumber was obtained in some way, and temporary sheds
created for the companies; but of course, this was just too late to do
any good.[9] That night the other regiments returned from their
scout toward Arkadelphia;[10] and on Sunday, November 1st, we
marched back to Little Rock. Very comfortable then seemed the log-
shanties of our old camp, and very glad we were to be back in
them.[11] Now we could learn the truth or falsity of all the big reports
we had been hearing; and they dwindled down to a reality of little,
or nothing at all. Almost always, while we were out on the march,
there would some how get into circulation, vague reports of the taking of Richmond, the defeat of Johnson's army, or some other great
military event; and the truth would generally show no foundation
for them.[12]

Brigade-drills, and all the routine of camp-life, again commenced.
Our brigade as now organized, was composed of the 29th and 33d
Iowa, and the 9th and 28th Wisconsin Infantry. The command of it
devolved upon so many different officers, during the period of its
organization, it would be difficult to name the commander at each
particular time.[13] Occasionally, all the field-music of the brigade
would unite for practice, and on some musters and reviews, played

together thus consolidated. In this way, with from twenty-five to forty fifes and drums, squealing and rattling in unison, a "heap big music" could be made.

November 27th, we were paid off again, and the clothing account for the first year was settled. Some men had considerable money coming to them, while others, having just the same service all around, and apparently dressing no better, found themselves several dollars in debt. Our stay in Winter-quarters had now fairly commenced; and one day was so much like another, that no especial description is necessary.[14] The main events of the day in camp, were guard-mounting and parade, which of course took place regularly, and with all the usual "style." Our part of the picket-line had always to be filled, and the customary camp-guard kept up. Details for fatigue were abundant. There was always some thing to be done. Either freight must be unloaded at the railroad depot, where all our supplies were now received, or there must be a forage-train sent out, or at least a detail to go after wood.

And so the days passed. The men in camp kept warm in the shanties, and amused themselves as best they could. Fiddles and cards were a constant resort. Some played chess, many read, and a few studied.[15] The Library and Reading-Room of the Christian Commission, in town, though some what scantily supplied, were liberally patronized.[16] Our ranks were now noticeably much thinner, than when we left home. Battle had taken some, but disease many. On the 15th of November, a recruiting-party, under Captain Lofland, then acting as lieutenant-colonel, was sent up to Iowa, where it remained till the next April, and obtained a number of recruits for the regiment.[17]

By this time bakeries had been established in town, so that bread could generally, though not always, be obtained. The usual price for a loaf weighing a pound and three-quarters, was twenty-five cents. The army-ration is such intolerable fare for men in camp, that most of our regiment regularly bought a large share of their living, rather than sicken on the unwholesome "hard-tack and sowbelly." Potatoes could generally be had for two dollars per bushel, and butter at sixty cents a pound; and at such figures many a man spent the most of his wages in getting wholesome food. December 7th, Company H was moved out to a tannery, eight miles south of

Pvt. John N. Shepherd, Company I, 33d Iowa Infantry.
Shepherd was a thirty-one-year-old farmer, carpenter, and
father of four when he enlisted at Knoxville, Iowa, in August
1862. During the winter of 1863–64, enlisted personnel from
the 29th and 33d Iowa elected this deeply religious man president of the "Earnest Christian Band," which held frequent
prayer meetings for the Little Rock garrison. Shepherd
received a promotion to corporal on October 14, 1864. *Photo
courtesy of Richard L. Clift.*

Pvts. (l. to r.) Richard P. Shull, Charles M. Shull, and Jacob H. Shull, Company G, 33d Iowa Infantry. The Shull brothers were all born in Jefferson County, in what is today West Virginia. Richard, a farmer, and Jacob, a carpenter, both enlisted at Pella, Iowa, on August 9, 1862. Twenty-year-old Charles waited to enlist until December 14, 1863, after the 33d Iowa sent a recruiting party back home from Little Rock. The three Shulls would survive the war. *Photo courtesy of U.S. Army Military History Institute.*

town, under orders as permanent-guard. They remained there until the 13th of March ensuing, having a very quiet time of it, and of course making some acquaintances among the inhabitants of the neighborhood.[18]

The weather now in its general features, was much like that to which we had been accustomed in Iowa, but on a milder scale. A cold day was not so cold as in Iowa, and a warm day was warmer.[19] The wind seldom blew so much at a time; and a clear evening was more beautifully clear. The moonlight was lovely, flooding camp and wood with a mellow, golden glory that made night more beautiful than day. There was no snow until the season was far advanced. The Winter was mild even for Arkansas. One morning—the 12th of December—we especially noticed as being exactly like one of our finest Spring mornings at home.[20] Going down to the little brook that ran along the north side of camp, we could see fresh, green grass growing, and hear the birds singing in the trees as jubilantly as if Winter were forever gone. The pines looked bright and green; and the warm mist that rested lightly all around, had that languid, balmy, undefinable fragrance which we call "the breath of Spring."

Christmas came this year on the same day of the month as usual; and perhaps for this reason, as much as any, the boys observed it as well as they could. There was nothing public going on, but in camp there seemed an air of general jollification, and much provision of some thing extra to eat. A favorite dish was potatoes boiled and mashed, and heaped up in a plate, with a little butter at the top, "home fashioned;" and as the boys gathered around the rough tables, and saw the savory dish, many a thought went back to the homes we hoped to see before another Christmas should come. A dish of mashed potatoes is a very common matter; but like the Switzer's Ranz des Vaches it may touch a chord of tender memories. Some of the officers celebrated the day by a "treat" to their men. Company G was thus treated to an excellent dinner of roast pig and oysters; and other companies received similar attentions.[21] Among the weary monotonies of life in camp, that Christmas of 1863 will be ever pleasantly remembered.

The 31st of December was such a day as might be chipped out of almost any Iowa Winter—a regular old blustering nor'-wester snow-storm, blowing all day.[22] So the year went out, in cold and storms, and the new year came in, bright, clear and cold, like the eyes of a Northern maiden. There was no celebration of the day in our camp, for Christmas had exhausted the enthusiasm.

On the 8th of January, Charles Dodd was hung at Little Rock as a spy.[23] Details were made from all the infantry, as guards to the execution. The criminal was a young man of scarcely twenty-one years, and had formerly resided only eight miles south of the city. For the last few months before the war, he had attended school at the St. John's College, immediately in front of which he now saw the last of earth.[24] What his thoughts may have been, at this last terrible moment, no tongue can tell; but he bore himself with a bravery and composure that would have done honor to a better cause. This was the only military execution we ever attended. Many of the regiment would not go out to witness this; and the general expression of those who did go, was that they never wanted to see another man hung; yet the same men would walk unmoved, over the bloody horrors of a battlefield.[25]

Company-drills were resumed on the 19th of January, as the weather was now mild and beautiful. Instead of cold and snow, and wind and storms of an Iowa Winter, we had warmth and sun-shine. But things were not all agreeable, by any means. For some cause or other, there came an unprecedented scarcity of rations. For several days about the last of January, not only our regiment, but most of the troops at Little Rock, had actually no rations on hand for several meals before the times of drawing. In our regiment a complaint was made to the lieutenant-colonel commanding, and an extra, or advance-ration was obtained and issued. The mere reading of the abstract statement that men were out of rations for a day or two, may not sound very bad; but the actual reality of going down to the mess-table at noon, and finding nothing to eat but a piece of rusty bacon, and having no means of getting any thing elsewhere, is decidedly a disagreeable matter to a soldier.

Some time in the Winter, a negro family of four persons moved into our camp: an old man, his wife, and two full-grown daughters. The old man built himself a shanty near the "sutler's shebang," and busied himself at whatever work he could find to do; and his wife and the two girls officiated as washer-women for the regiment. They were quiet, sensible, industrious folks; and in a little while a mutual friendship between the regiment and "Uncle Tony and Aunt Lucy," was firmly established. They would talk of us as though we were their brothers; and when the regiment left camp, or returned after a march, there were no truer or warmer words of welcome or parting, than those they gave us. Respecting us and themselves, yet knowing and understanding the differences of color and tastes, they attended unobstrusively to their own business, and were treated as civilly as white folks would have been in the same circumstances. If all negroes were like them, the social problem need never present a difficulty.[26]

"Hard times," in a pecuniary point of view, are no less common in the army than elsewhere. There had now for some time been much stringency in the money market; but it ceased on the 10th of February, when the long-looked for pay-master arrived. General feelings of plethoric contentment pervaded the pockets of light-blue pantaloons; and the folks at home too, who had in many cases needed the customary remittance from absent husbands and fathers in the army, were gladdened by the money as soon thereafter as it could go. Perhaps few regiments equalled, and probably none excelled the 33d Iowa, in respect to the amount of money sent home. It was very common among us for men to thus send off so nearly all their wages, that long before the next pay-day they would have to borrow money to purchase needful food. Some managed to send home more than their wages; but they made the extra money generally by trading watches, or making and selling rings; a few made money by gambling.

On the 20th of March, several recruits arrived for the regiment.[27] Fresh from citizens' life in Iowa, they came just in time to take part in some of the hardest, if not the very worst and hardest, of all our soldiering. It was a rough commencement of army-life for them; but in justice it must be said they bore it bravely and seemed to get along as well as any of the rest. By this time, Spring with us had fairly come, and with it came a break in the monotony of "Winter-quarters." Active movements against the enemy were now the general order of the day, and we were to take part in them. The rest of Winter gave place to the activity and bustle of a Spring campaign.[28]

Pvt. George Washington Towne, Company G, 33d Iowa Infantry. The son of a Baptist minister and a native of Ohio, the eighteen-year-old Towne forsook life as a farmer to enlist on August 9, 1862. His lively letters to his sister illuminate life in the 33d Iowa from its inception to early 1864. He was mortally wounded at Jenkins' Ferry, Arkansas, April 30, 1864, and died in enemy hands on June 11. He is buried in Grave 2372, Section 3, Little Rock National Cemetery. *Photo courtesy of Mark A. Warren.*

CHAPTER X.

THE CAMDEN EXPEDITION.

The 23d of March, 1864, was clear and beautiful. Reveille was sounded at the usual hour; and at 9:40 A. M., with rations packed, knapsacks slung, forty rounds of ammunition in the cartridge-boxes, with all the paraphernalia of a long and dangerous march, to the old, accustomed tune of Yankee Doodle, we marched out of Little Rock—for the last time, we thought—as part of General Steele's column intended to join Banks' army at Shreveport, by way of Camden.[1]

The march seemed harder at first, from our having been in camp so long; but we made the nine miles marked out for the first day without difficulty, and camped at night in an excellent place, on the Benton road. "A good camping-place" means a place where there is plenty of good water convenient for all the men and animals, plenty of rails, or other handy timber for fires, and enough of tolerably smooth ground to sleep on. How we used to hope for all these! and how often to the labors of the day were added much more at night, which might all have been avoided if we could have had a good camping-place! When no water could be obtained within half-a-mile, and no good wood was to be found at all, and the thick brush had to be grubbed away from ground enough to sleep on—all of which some times occurred—there seemed little show for comfort or rest at night. Add to this, mud knee-deep and a steady rain falling, and there is a picture of what soldiers call decidedly uncomfortable.

Next morning our bugle startled the surrounding darkness, and soon the call was answered from all the neighboring fields. Bugles rang as we had never heard them before. If an enemy had been in hearing distance, he must have thought we were at least a hundred thousand men, to raise such a wide-spread din. Finally a brass band, that accompanied the expedition, rang out its mellow tones,

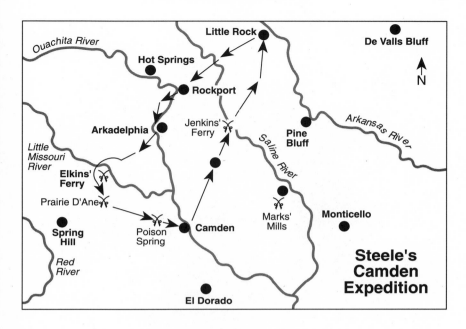

Map by Steve Scallion. *Courtesy Arkansas Historic Preservation Program.*

and the noise of the bugles ceased. The Camden Expedition started out "in style."[2]

On the evening of the second day, camping early in a good place, we drew our first rations for the trip, and learned that during the march, but half-rations would be issued, except that with commendable care and prudence the General had ordered a full allowance of coffee for all the time.[3] For this we always thanked him. Coffee is the soldier's friend. On a cold, wet night, after a hard-day's march, nothing is so eagerly anticipated, and so gratefully welcomed, as the soothing, yet stimulating coffee. Yet the army style of making it would make a woman smile with scorn. If a large amount is to be made, as enough for a company, a doubly-generous quantity of ground coffee is put into an iron camp-kettle, and left to boil till the strength is all out of it; and when this plan is not adopted, each man makes it for himself, on the same principle, but in a little tin can. The liquid in either case looks very much like the water of the Rio Grande, or of the Missouri "on a bender," but its taste is good, and its effects plainly perceptible. It is a thing almost

Brig. Gen. Frederick Salomon. Salomon commanded the
13th Division, XIII Army Corps, which successfully
defended Helena on July 4, 1863, and he led the 3d
Division, VII Army Corps, through Steele's Camden
expedition in the spring of 1864. *Photo courtesy of
Massachusetts Commandery Military Order of the Loyal
Legion and U.S. Army Military History Institute*

indispensable in the army. Necessary as tobacco is generally held to be, and universal as is the use of it, if it were left to the vote of a division of soldiers, whether on the march they should give up their coffee to save their tobacco, the answer would be, after much and painful deliberation, "Let's take the coffee."

Perhaps those who never were in the service, looking at the "regulations" may find that the standard army-ration embraces quite a variety of tolerable food; and they may infer from that that living on half-rations is not so very bad after all. The "army regulations" are all very nice, and the army-ration would do very well for soldiers if they could only get it. But the exact amount of food that was issued to us as half-rations on this expedition was two hard-tacks, a little salt pork, a little salt, and some coffee, to each man per day. And this was not in prison or in camp, but on the march; and on the strength of this men had to tramp through rain or shine, good or bad going, level road or hills, with gun and rig, weighing from twenty to twenty-five pounds, and knapsack, haver-sack and other articles, weighing almost as much more; and this was a fair sample of our fare for months together. Is it any wonder men foraged?[4]

Southern nights and mornings are always cool. The day may be oppressively hot, and the night so cold that the one woolen blanket which the soldier has hardly persuaded himself to carry so far, will not keep him warm enough to sleep. Frequently we had to "tumble up" from our beds on the ground at three or four o'clock, in those cold Spring mornings, and take the remainder of our rest in standing at the fire.

The fifth day of the trip, March 28th, our regiment was taken as train-guard—that is, divided up into squads of a company or less, and stationed along among the wagons. The day for this duty on the march was always counted as a tiresome and disagreeable one with us, for it necessitated slow marching, with an occasional hurry, frequent little stops, much fretting and impatience; some times a good deal of work in getting wagons out of the mud, and always a late coming into camp at night.[5] This day it was about five in the afternoon when we turned off into the brush, as usual, to bivouac for the night. One who has never tried it can not imagine how welcome the camp some times seems to the tired and weary soldier. Of

Sgt. Charles Schroeter, 1st Missouri Cavalry (Union). The 1st
Missouri was one of eleven Union cavalry regiments that
accompanied Steele to Camden. Mounted on inferior horses
and outclassed by their Rebel foes, the Union troopers distinguished themselves on that campaign more as foragers than as
fighters. *Photo courtesy of Roger Davis.*

all fatigue, perhaps that of long marching is the most wearisome. It comes on by such slow, monotonous degrees, and there is so little change or relief about it, that one feels much more worn out after a hard-day's march, than after equal labor in any other way. So this evening, when we were filed off into the brush for the evident purpose of camping, and then had to march and countermarch among the stumps and brush-patches several times before our lines were satisfactorily adjusted, it may be supposed we were not in the very best of humor; and possibly there may have been some very uncomplimentary remarks made concerning the worthy major who commanded us during the march to Camden.[6] But right upon this, adding worse to bad, came the order for our regiment to advance some three miles farther, to hold a bayou, at which there was supposed to be some danger of attack from the rebels. Murmuring rose, not openly but earnest, but of course we had to go; and the rest that night was none the less sweet, when we did get it.

The next day gave us some consolation, in laughing at the sorrows of others. A dirty, ragged old Dutch woman,[7] whose house we were passing, came out obstreperous to us, and with loud words and lamentations, demanded to be directed to the "coornul." Being shown who he was, she besought him sorely that he would help her. Some Dutch cavalry-man in front of the train, had seen a horse in a pasture thereabouts, that was better than his, and had quietly made a trade by changing the saddle and equipments from his own horse to the other, and riding off, leaving the tired cavalry-horse, well pleased with the change. Such little swaps were common in the army, and recognized occasionally by the code of military necessity; but the old woman could not view the matter with our unprejudiced eyes. She wanted Major Gibson to signify authoritatively to the cavalry-man, that she rued the bargain. From a civil stand-point, her position was undoubtedly the correct one, but the major declined to take any definite action in the case; and so the old frau's uncouth rage and lamentation were laughed at by the whole regiment, as we passed. Doubtless she has to this day a very poor opinion of the Yankees.

About three miles from Arkadelphia, we suddenly came to a place, where all the trees, and the brush and grass looked much fresher and greener than any where else. The change was as great and noticeable as though the season had been moved a month forward, while we marched a mile. It had almost the appearance of magic. We never saw a similar appearance elsewhere, and could never account for this. The place itself was like a hundred others we had passed—a low, flat portion of the bottom-lands bordering a bayou, and surrounded by timber. Under ordinary circumstances it would have been pleasant, but then it was delightful.[8]

In the afternoon of March 29th, the sixth day out, we entered camp in the outskirts of the fine village of Arkadelphia—a place which seemed to us much like a Northern town.[9] Situated on the Washita River, and built mostly of good, white frame houses, it presented a very different appearance from many of the dilapidated "huddles" to which we had been more accustomed.[10] Very soon after breaking ranks, our men were pretty well distributed around town, seeing the sights and searching for eatables. There was little, if any foraging done. We paid for nearly all we got; and the women of the place frequently told us, "Yur men treat us better than our own men do." A considerable amount of good ham, corn-meal and molasses was obtained. The town indeed seemed much better provisioned than we had expected, though there was no surplus of food. Many of the citizens were dubious about taking our money, lest after our army had left the place, the rebels should trouble them for having received it.[11]

The regiment was pretty well scattered around town, and not all the men had got their suppers, when at a little before sun-set a most unexpected order came for us to pack up forthwith and march back to the bayou, three miles from town, to camp there as guard for the train, which could not all get across before morning. The order received at regimental head-quarters may or may not have stated this reason for the movement, but the order sent around to the companies said nothing about it. The men could not know the object of the march, or of what length it was to be; all they could learn was, that they were to pack up and move again. Wrath and curses rose loud and thick, but did no good. When we were once started, these ill feelings found better vent in whoops and yells that made the echoes ring. There may have been some need of hurrying, but it was more from a kind of vexation and half-conquered wrath that we struck into a march as fast as we could go, and kept on going faster and faster. The Major's old horse, at the head of the battalion, had to trot all the time to keep out of our way. The first two or three companies marched those three miles in just thirty-five minutes, and turned into camp at a pleasant place near the bayou; but the rear of the regiment was strung out half-way to town.

It is much harder to march in the rear, than in the front of a regiment or column; and of course, when the front marches as fast as it can, the rear must lag behind. But if any regiment can make better time than three miles in thirty-five minutes, in heavy-marching order, we do not know where it is to be found. The next morning it took us just one hour, of good, steady marching, to go back to town. Entering the former camp again, we looked for a rest of two or three days.

There was in Arkadelphia, a pretty good two-story white frame building, used as a seminary for young ladies, and furnished with desks, charts, maps, &c., and a very passable piano. Led on by the very demon of mischief, some of our men, with a number of men from other regiments, ransacked the building from end to end, tore up the maps and papers, destroyed the benches, and smashed the piano into utter ruin. The whole seminary was left a perfect wreck. The guilty parties were not discovered, and so our whole regiment had to bear a share of the odium of this most dastardly and abominable act of wanton destruction; and never before or since, was it concerned in such an abuse of military power.[12]

The rebel General Fagan was reported to be hovering in the vicinity, with a force of about five thousand men. He would never have dared to attack us there and then, of course, but still we had to be ready for him; so our little army went through the farce of standing "at arms," one morning, for a short time.[13]

At 8 A. M., of the 1st of April, we started on again; and at night, after a march of about a dozen miles, the camp was pitched in the woods near a couple of houses, which collectively, were designated in the geography, (if at all) by the romantic name of Hollywood, Arkansas, but by the inhabitants were ordinarily called Spoonville.[14] Next day our regiment was scattered as guard among the train, and part of it was pretty well toward the rear. This was a hard day all round. During a good part of the time, there was skirmishing with a body of rebels, whose number we had no means of knowing.

The field-pieces which accompanied the rear-guard were pretty actively employed with occasional shots "on the wing." Our regiment was not in any of the skirmishing; but two or three of the companies were kept double-quicking a good deal of the time, first to the rear as re-inforcements, and then back to their place in the train again. A part of the afternoon there were great efforts made to "close up the train," which had become badly scattered along the road; and the haste, the bustle, and confusion and fatigue so occasioned, were so nearly like what a stampede or a panic must be, that we hoped never to see any closer imitation.[15]

Nearly all the way was through timber, mostly pine. Some of the time our advance-guard would set the leaves on fire before us, which compelled us at times to march for hours together, through the dense smoke and heated air of the still burning under-brush. This was dangerous business for powder-wagons and caissons, but fortunately there was no explosion.[16] On the 4th of April, as we lay in camp near the Little Missouri River, most of the time under orders to be ready to move at a moment's notice, there was quite a skirmish down on the river, in our plain hearing, for about an hour in the forenoon. General Rice was slightly wounded on the head, several men were killed, and a number of prisoners taken, before the rebels were driven back from the river.[17]

Resuming the march on Wednesday morning, April 6th, we crossed the Little Missouri, on a kind of impromptu bridge, and soon heard the first of that skirmishing in our front, which continued at intervals, more or less all day. The rebels were disputing our advance. At one time nearly our whole force of infantry and artillery was drawn up in battle array on an open place in the woods; and part of the day we marched in line of battle, with skirmishers deployed. There were frequent appearances of an impending battle, but the rebels steadily retreated before our cavalry; and after driving them a few miles, we turned back to a nice place in the woods, near the river, and went into camp. Here we lay until the morning of the 10th. A forage-train was sent out; and as it did not return at the appointed time, there was considerable anxiety lest it had been "gobbled" by the rebels. The seventy-five teams and four hundred men would have been a very good haul for Mr. Price; but he failed to get them that time. They came in all right, after a while, having met with no difficulty.

While we lay here, the long-looked-for and much-talked-of, re-inforcement of "Thayer's command" arrived, from Fort Smith. A nondescript style of re-inforcement it was too, numbering almost every kind of soldiers, including Indians, and accompanied by multitudinous vehicles, of all descriptions, which had been picked up along the road. General Steele toned down this extra trans-portation a good deal before we started again.[18]

On the morning of the 10th, the train commenced moving, but it was one o'clock in the afternoon before it was stretched out enough to allow of our taking the place assigned us. Before long the rebels began to resist our advance. All the way was through timber, mostly pine, and a good part of the time we marched through this, in line of battle. As we neared the large and beautiful prairie called Prairie De Anne, the opposition of the rebels increased.[19] Their main body was posted on the prairie, under command of Price himself, and numbered several thousand.[20] Our own force now, as we sup-posed, must have comprised between ten and twelve thousand men.

At about 4:45 P. M., as we came upon the edge of the prairie, the continuous skirmishing merged into a battle, and the artillery-firing became quite heavy. Our regiment advanced in column by division. At one time we marched in this close formation for several minutes, in the direct range of a rebel battery, whose shot and shell came nearer than we deemed imperatively necessary. A piece of shell struck Private Wm. P. Funk, of Company I, wounding him on the head so that he died in a few hours.[21] There was no other casu-alty in our regiment during the battle. Marching steadily forward to the edge of the prairie, we were ordered to support the 9th Wisconsin Battery, which was done, as ordered, by lying down flat on our faces, in line of battle, while the battery continued its vigor-ous and well-directed fire.[22] The rebels responded actively; but their guns were of an old and inferior pattern, and their shot and shell, though very destructive to the trees in the rear, did not come very near us. For a while the cannonade was brisk and lively; but it gradually grew weaker, as the rebels retreated, and before sun-down, had almost ceased.

Now began a slow and cautious advance over the prairie, in line of battle, with skirmishers deployed, and interrupted by frequent orders to halt and lie down. The prairie was at intervals intersected by small brooks, fringed with dense and some times very thorny

Brig. Gen. John M. Thayer. Thayer commanded the
Frontier Division from Fort Smith, Arkansas, which ren-
dezvoused with Steele south of Arkadelphia on April 9,
1864. *Photo courtesy of Massachusetts Commandery
Military Order of the Loyal Legion and U.S. Army
Military History Institute.*

Anonymous Privates, 18th Iowa Infantry. These two members of
Thayer's Frontier Division wear the crescent-and-star badge
adopted by the VII Army Corps after the Camden expedition.
Photo courtesy of Roger Davis.

thickets; but we advanced now, in scarcely broken line, through places where, in peaceful times, we would not think of forcing passage. As it grew too dark to go any farther, the line was ordered back a little, to one of these thickets, where we stacked arms for camp. The night was clear and cold, and our wagons had been left a mile or two behind us, which two facts caused the hearts of the officers to sink considerably, for their blankets, mess-chests, &c., were with the train. The men had all their possessions with them, of course, and could therefore eat hard-tack and drink coffee, and tumble down to sleep about as usual; but the officers had to get along as best they could. Many of them were compelled to stay awake and shiver all night, and that without their accustomed supper. It should not be understood that the men refused to share with the officers, but there was not enough of either food or clothing for all.[23]

During the night the rebels kept up an occasional artillery-fire, aimed at us, but doing its only damage among the trees far in the rear. Those of us who were out on picket, could see not only the flash of their guns, and the light of the shells as they rose in the air, but the very blaze of the old-fashioned matches they used, instead of the improved locks or primers of more modern construction.[24] So near were our picket-lines to those of the rebels, that much ill-humored conversation passed between them, the "Jonnies" being particularly severe on us for being all Dutchmen.[25]

Some time before mid-night, we were suddenly waked by the fierce firing of small arms near us. The rebels were making a bold sortie, to capture one of our guns; but they were repulsed before we could even move toward them.[26] Our sleep that night was too much interrupted to prove refreshing. Next morning, details of men were sent back to the wagons, to make coffee at fires kindled behind some thickets, which hid them from rebel view. The more fastidious also had their pork fried, and some went so far as to stew up crackers in grease and water, as a luxury; but the majority of the line had to take the "hard-tack and sow-belly" in a raw state, and be thankful to have their coffee warm. The remainder of the forenoon, we merely laid there, waiting orders. It was a beautiful day; and the singing of the birds in the thicket near us, contrasted oddly with the occasional booming of the cannon and the continued skirmishing on some part of the line. As for us, we hunted rabbits, played euchre, read old novels, wrote away at letters, slept, and so on, as though there were no thoughts of battle in the world.

At 2:25 in the afternoon, a forward movement commenced.[27] The whole of our little army was drawn up in battle array, in such a disposition that it looked even to ourselves like a large force, and to the rebels in our front, must have seemed an utterly overwhelming array of infantry, cavalry and artillery. We heard afterward, that when General Price saw us thus advancing, he threw up his hands and exclaimed "My God! they are coming in clouds," and immediately ordered a retreat. Certainly it was to us, and must have been more to them, a magnificent spectacle. The vast prairie, with its beautiful diversity of groves and undulations, was just the ground for such a display; and we can not easily forget the enthusiasm awakened by the martial scene.

> "To warrior bound for battle strife,
>   Or bard of martial lay,
> 'Twere worth ten years of peaceful life—
>   One glance at their array."

Toward evening we halted for some time, on the high prairie. There was considerable skirmishing in front. Captain Comstock, in command of our skirmish-line, advanced so near the rebels, that he was confident he could have captured one of their guns, if he had been allowed to go farther.[28] Their old smooth-bore field-pieces threw shot so awkwardly, that some would plunge into the ground far in front of us, and others would come so closely down in our rear, that we began to have some fears of being shot in the back, through fairly fronting the enemy. Meanwhile, as if for relief from the monotony of lying still to be shot at, an old cow, with a bell on, started up near us, and was immediately pursued by some thing less than a hundred shouting and laughing soldiers, but finally succeeded in making a fair escape. It was but a very little matter to write about, yet it made more fun than ten times as great an event could have caused at another time.

That night we marched back to our previous camp; and before six next morning, our whole force was again in battle array, and advancing toward the enemy. The skirmishing was at times, quite lively. Our batteries would open on the rebels, and speedily silence and scatter them. At about 9 o'clock, we reached the edge of the woods, and entered the rebel camp, which their rear-guard had just evacuated. Over a mile of very passable breast-works, alternated with places for cannon, of such a range that they could have literally mowed us down in a direct assault, were now, with a choice of routes from there, in our possession, with hardly any loss; and we were much pleased at this result of a flanking movement.[29]

Halting here but a little while, the column moved off across the prairie, to the Camden road,[30] and soon after reaching that, passed through a town called Moscow, consisting of three houses, one of which had been in use as a temporary rebel hospital, and then contained a member of the 1st Iowa Cavalry, who had been severely wounded, and taken prisoner, a few days before.[31] The orders against foraging were now very strict, and some of the officers—not of our own regiment—were very strict in enforcing them; but men on half-rations, scant half at that, will have some thing more than that amount of food to eat, if they can get it. Sugar, pork, chickens, pigs, &c., fell a frequent prey. Not always to the victor came the spoils. On one occasion, a boy of our regiment had shot a fine pig, by the side of the road, and was just skinning it, when the officer of the day rode up, and made him go off and leave it. During the confab, while the officer's back was turned, another of our boys, quietly walked off with the pig. So the only harm done, was that one mess had an extra camp-kettle full of unauthorized pig.

At one place in the woods, where a short halt was ordered, there was heard a low, continuous sound, like distant thunder, or a mighty water-fall. Attention was at once arrested, but no cause for the sound was visible. The matter bade fair to remain a mystery, when suddenly some one discovered that a large and hollow oak tree, a little distance from the road, had been fired at the bottom, and the sound was produced by the current of heated air passing through it, and escaping by a large knot-hole at the top. It was in fact, a natural chimney, with the best draft in the world.

At frequent intervals on Wednesday, the 13th, we could hear cannonading in the rear, where Thayer's Division marched. In camp that night, there were all sorts of reports concerning the losses of the day. Slightly exaggerated statements represented that one of the colored regiments had lost eleven hundred men and two colonels; but not many believed so much. Finally, all the reports settled down into the fact, that the rebels had followed us, and tried to annoy us all they could.[32] Next day, the route lay through some of the worst swamp that ever was traversed by mortal man.[33] Marching was out of the question, and wading through the mud and water, was the rule instead. The portly figure of the Major, rode at the head of the column, on an old raw-boned white horse, that waded with a mechanical regularity of splashing, until one unlucky moment, in the very worst place in the whole series of swamps, the poor beast stumbled and fell, and the Major went sliding over his head, with all due and perpendicular gravity, plump into the mud and mire. The performance had a tendency to damage fine clothes, but it did the regiment more good than a little; for it roused a freshness and jolliness of feeling that lasted till we struck dry land again.

On the afternoon of the 14th, General Rice was ordered to proceed with our brigade, with all speed, leaving knapsacks behind, to a cross-road, between us and Camden, which the rebels were endeavoring to reach before us. It was a forced march, and we traveled as fast as possible, actually drawing and distributing rations while on the move. We had expected to march all night, or nearly so; but as darkness came on, an unusual fatigue began to overpower us, and word was circulated that we would camp before long. Every mile grew longer than the rest, and still the march went on, with no sign of stopping. We were worn out, hungry, and longing for the brief repose of camp; but our regiment was some where toward the rear, and would not come in till most of the others had got there. "How far is it to camp?" was the question in every one's mind, but no one could answer; and so we jogged wearily on, in silence. At last a cavalry-man came galloping toward the rear, and as he neared us, he shouted "Three miles to camp! three miles to camp!" Seldom were words more welcome. We marched on with renewed vigor, and soon found rest for the night; but the shout of the cavalry-man made so strong an impression on the mind of one of our regiment, that he penned some lines in remembrance of it, which I may be pardoned for introducing here.

"THREE MILES TO CAMP"

APRIL 14TH, 1864.

Onward marching, ever onward, through the forest, lone and drear,
Now fatigue almost o'ercomes us, scarce our limbs their burden bear.

Still the evening shadows deepen, yet no sign of rest appears,
But a horseman comes to meet us, and his glad shout greets our ears:
        "Three miles to camp! three miles to camp!"
        Pass the word along the column,
        Cheer the weary, cheer the solemn;
Soon will rest come now, it's only "three miles to camp!"

Now with strength renewed, our footsteps measure off the weary way,
Till before us "rest and supper," bright the shining camp-fires say.
Stretched at ease, we then remember how the day dragged slowly by,
And how sudden changed our feelings, as we heard that cheering cry,
        "Three miles to camp! three miles to camp!"
        How the word ran down the column,
        Cheering up the sad and solemn;
Soon came rest, for quickly passed the three miles to camp.

So, though gloomy all around us, now the war-clouds seem to lower,
Peace may not be so far distant: this may be the darkest hour.
If a message from the future, like that horseman, could but come,
It might cheer us now with promise of but three months yet to home,
        Three months to home! three months to home!
        Pass the word along the column,
        Cheering up the sad and solemn;
Hardships some time will be o'er, and we'll be at home.

That night we camped at about 9 o'clock, and the night was too cold to let us sleep any; but there were plenty of rails, and we made them keep us warm, instead of the blankets left behind. Next morning, April 15th, reveille came at 4:30; and scarcely time enough was allowed us to boil our coffee, to say nothing of drinking it, before we were again on the move. By 8 o'clock, there began to be some resistance from a party of rebels in front; and from that time till about four in the afternoon, there was almost ceaseless skirmishing.

At 9 o'clock, our regiment being at the head of the column, and having come pretty close upon the advance-guard of cavalry, we suddenly found ourselves in direct range of a rebel battery, which at once opened upon us. Instantly there was an uproar. The shells came tearing through the trees; and there were hasty and contradictory orders, from the front and rear, to advance, and to clear the way for the artillery. For an instant there was confusion; and then the voice of the Major commanding, was heard amid the roar. "Left file," he shouted; and we left filed—that is to say, we turned off hastily to the left from the road, and attempted to find shelter behind a slight ridge of land, from the more direct and point-blank range of the masked battery.

In a few minutes we were ordered across to the other side of the road, and posted behind the same ridge, but at the right and front of the battery, we were to support.[34] From this movement arose, for a day or two, a faint report that "the 33d Iowa ran at Poison Springs;" but the lie was so utterly baseless, it never spread much beyond the few cowardly skulkers from other regiments, who tried to set it going. The 33d Iowa did not run, did not retreat, did not break in confusion, and did not do any more nor less, than any sensible regiment would do, under similar circumstances.

For about an hour and a half there was a very brisk artillery combat; but the rebel shells went either to our left, or through the tree-tops above us. Meanwhile our skirmishers were deployed on the right front, and were gradually advancing across the open field where, behind a thicket, the rebel battery was masked.[35] General Rice had ordered the cavalry to flank the rebels on our right, but for some cause they failed to come up. Had they executed the movement properly, or even had our line of skirmishers been doubled and pushed forward, the battery must have been captured. As it was, our main line lay there and waited, while the artillery-fire grew heavier, then gradually diminished, and finally ceased. The only casualty in our regiment was one man shot through the hand, by the accidental discharge of his gun.[36]

At 10:30 A. M. the rebels had retreated, and we resumed the advance.[37] Our regiment remained at the head of the column. A small squad of cavalry preceded us, but whenever there was any particular danger ahead, they regularly fell to the rear. No blame could attach to the men themselves for this, for they were the same who fought gloriously on greater fields; but their commander on this expedition seemed to us to be contemptibly worthless.[38]

The day wore slowly on. Most of the time our way led through heavy timber. The skirmishing in front was so incessant that a ten-minute's silence, as once in a while occurred, seemed more noticeable and significant than the accustomed popping of the musketry. At frequent intervals the regiment was obliged to change formation, and march through the woods alternately in column, line of battle, column by company or platoons, or otherwise, as the circumstances seemed to demand. This made the advance additionally fatiguing.[39] Having no object but to hinder and annoy us as much as possible, the rebels were very bold. At one time, while General Rice was riding with his staff at the head of our regiment, a rebel on horseback dashed down toward us, into plain view, and sent a bullet so close to the General that he and all his staff involuntarily "bobbed," and then the daring horseman dashed away again. As we neared Camden, the rebels made less and less resistance, and finally none at all. About a mile and a half from town we were ordered into camp, while other regiments went on; but in a few minutes the order was changed, and we marched into town.

Now was the glory of the cavalry. All along the way, so far, they had been willing to go in the rear occasionally; now they came rushing valiantly past us, rich with the forage of a country where no Union troops had ever been before, and charging furiously on as if they were taking the city—though the fact was that two companies of Infantry had been there some time before them.[40] From their performances on this 15th of April, arose most of our opinion derogatory to the name of cavalry.[41]

At about 6:30 P. M., we began to enter the town, in the western suburbs. The neat white houses, and the general air of the place rather pleased us; and there seemed to be a lurking impression that we would stay there a while. Rumors had been in circulation, given with all the usual definiteness and authority, that General Rice with our brigade was to remain as garrison of the place, and that this was why we, and not others, were sent on in advance of the main column. It was a long and uncomfortable walk, fatigued as we were, to wind through the streets and past the frowning fort—which made us glad the rebels had concluded to evacuate—and then out to a desolate, barren place, a half-mile or more from town, where neither wood nor water was convenient; but we struggled through it at last, and long after dark tumbled down to sleep, as best we might after the fatigues of such a day.[42]

There are always some who, weak and tired as they may be during the day's march, even compelled to "give out" and wait for an ambulance to carry them, no sooner reach camp than they seem to have strength and life enough to ransack all the neighboring country in search of forage; and these now found means before morning to gather many a ham and pound of sugar, and pone of corn-bread, in most cases bought at a very small expenditure of legal tender.[43] Never having seen any "green-backs" before, the people were totally ignorant of the relation they bore to customary prices, and some were quite dubious about receiving them at all; but small was the difference to us, whether they took them or not, if only we got what eatables we wanted.[44] So here we were now in Camden, after a march much harder than any other we had experienced, with the exception of one or two days of the march from Helena; and if nothing worse had followed, we should long have looked back with feelings of pleasant remembrance to this part of our Camden expedition.

CHAPTER XI.

___

THE RETREAT FROM CAMDEN.

Arrived in Camden, the march was nominally suspended; but there came little rest for us. We had to move camp some where nearly every day we were there; but in justice to our commander it should be remarked that we got a better camp each time. Since leaving Little Rock there had been no soap issued to the men, and therefore there had been almost no chance for properly washing clothes. Soap even for faces and hands, had been of unparalleled scarcity. Of course, as soon as we had rest now, and soap issued, there came unwonted activity in the laundry department. Every brook was a tub, every bush a clothes-horse, and almost every man a washer-woman. On the 18th, from some whim of the Major, or some high officer, we had parade for the first time since the expedition commenced; and a ragged affair it was. The dresscoats had been left behind, with the sashes and other extra paraphernalia of camp; and the blouses and pants we wore were almost fluttering to the wind in rags.[1] Our band had dwindled down to two or three ragged drummers, and as many fifers who had lost their fifes; and the principal musician had a sore heel, so he paraded up and down the line with one bare foot and one shoe on. Altogether, it was a very ragged affair, and came probably as near an *un*-dress parade as the army regulations ever contemplated. Fine feathers may make fine birds, but a hard march is "death on style."[2]

A forage-train of about a hundred wagons, with but a small escort, was sent out west from town on the morning of the 18th.[3] It had gone out about as far as Poison Springs, or Washington Cross-Roads—the place where the artillery-duel occurred on the 15th—when it was attacked by an overwhelming force of the enemy, and after a fierce and bloody resistance was captured. There was a heavy loss of killed and wounded; but both white and black soldiers kept straggling back to town for two or three days afterward, so the total of casualties was not known.[4] It was afterward learned that a number of the Union soldiers killed there, had been scalped by the rebels.[5] Only one or two of our regiment were with the train, and they escaped uninjured.[6] There was loud complaint of the culpable blunder of sending out such a train, under such circumstances, with so small a guard; but opinion varied widely as to the responsibility of the catastrophe.[7]

Because we had been delayed on the march beyond the calculated time, or because the supply-train, under command of Lieutenant-Colonel Mackey, ordered from Little Rock, by another route, after we started, was behind its time for arrival, we were now almost out of rations. Meat could be obtained, but hard-tack grew more rare and valuable, with each succeeding day. A small, steam-mill in town, was kept running at all hours of the day and night, grinding corn, but it was by no means large enough to supply the demand. Portable iron hand-mills were put up, and relays of four hungry men, at a time, kept them constantly in motion. Corn was issued instead of other food, which was not to be had; and one day our regularly-issued ration was four ears of corn per man.[8]

On the evening of the 20th of April, the supply-train came in. We were heartily glad to welcome our colonel,[9] and the recruits who came with him; but the greatest joy was over the "good old mail" which came with the train, and was distributed that evening. It was the first word we had heard from home or civilization, since the march began. Little could the writers of those letters imagine, how eagerly the envelopes were torn open, or how dear and precious the words of love and hope, from home, seemed to us, there in the enemy's country, and so long cut off from even the comforts of a camp. Welcome and prized as letters always were, they had never been so as much so as now; and few of us can look back to those old days, without remembering "the good old mail we got at Camden."

Next day came such a scratching of pens on paper as was never before known in our regiment. There was word that the train would start back to Little Rock in a day or so, and take a mail with it; and so all the long letters we had been gradually writing since the march commenced, were now closed, and new ones written, and a very large amount of mail matter was started for the dear ones at home. Alas! it never arrived! The disaster at Mark's Mills, a few days later, resulted not only in the capture of some of our own comrades, among others, with the train, but in the loss of all that heavy mail.[10] Doubtless the rebels "had a good time" in reading over the words of love and hope, or the expressions of our opinions as to the situation. Well, "turn about is fair play;" and we remembered the Yazoo Pass, where, without any undue foraging on our part, so many old letters and other documents of the "skedaddling" rebel citizens had fallen into our hands.

Company C, of our regiment, was detailed as part of the provost-guard in town. The orders concerning passes were very strict. In fact, a man without shoulder-straps could hardly get a pass at all; and the result of course was that the men went to town without passes, and didn't experience very much difficulty about it either.[11] It is hard for a soldier to yield strict obedience always to the letter and spirit of an order which is plainly unnecessary and unjust, when he knows well enough that he may disregard it with perfect impunity. Some there were, indeed, to whom the mere fact of an order was law and penalty enough, and who made it a point of honor never to transgress it in any way; but we always noticed that these were the very men who could generally get the least favors of any, while the reckless fellows, who cared for orders no further than they feared the consequences, could be out of camp without leave and around town half the time, and be none the worse off for that. At least, if such was not the actual fact, it was certainly the general impression.[12]

Saturday, the 23d, passed with the usual quiet and listlessness, until about a quarter after four in the afternoon, when there was suddenly heard a very brisk cannonading near a bridge, not far from town, which our picket-line was guarding. In a few minutes we were ordered into line. Men were left in camp to pack up the things, and the regiment formed hastily and marched over toward the fort. But by this time the firing had ceased; and in a few minutes we returned to camp, with orders to be ready to leave at a moment's notice. This is no uncommon order in the army, but some times it amounts to one thing, and some times to another. Oftenest, perhaps, it signifies that we would best lay in needful supplies of postage-stamps and tobacco, for we may start to-morrow; but at

Field and Staff Officers, 36th Iowa Infantry. Lt. Col. Francis M. Drake (seated second from left) commanded the Union infantry brigade and 240-wagon supply train that the Confederates captured at Marks' Mills, Arkansas, on March 25. This disaster precipitated Steele's retreat from Camden, although it did not prevent Drake's election as governor of Iowa after the war. *Photo courtesy of Roger Davis.*

this particular time it meant just what it said. We knew that well enough; for there was a general feeling among us that we were "in a tight place," and might have some trouble in getting out. So our personal equipments and possessions were hastily packed and strapped, and the few cooking materials slung together and piled in readiness to be loaded into the wagons; and then came the wearisome, listless sitting around, and waiting for the orders which were all the time expected. None came, however; and we tumbled down to sleep that night, and stood "at arms" after an early reveille next morning, and then settled back into the uncertain rest of camp. The cannonading which had so suddenly come and gone, appeared to be either a disproportionately heavy, though unsuccessful, attack on the small force defending the bridge, or an exaggerated feint to cover the attack on our train at Mark's Mills. Either way, it was a strange little affair; but the latter view seemed most probable.[13]

The arrival of Lieutenant-Colonel Mackey had of course displaced Major Gibson from command of the regiment. Whatever the general opinion of the military capacity he displayed may have been, he was certainly esteemed and respected as a man. Coming to the conclusion that he could serve the country better as a citizen than as a soldier, he had tendered his resignation, which was immediately accepted, and had started for home with the train from Camden. Captured with that, he was taken to Texas, and suffered much hardship before being finally released. One or two private soldiers of our regiment were captured at the same time, and died in a rebel prison.[14]

The night of the 25th came with as much quiet as usual; there were no signs of any movement; but there seemed to be a strange feeling among us—a kind of presentiment—that "some thing was going to happen." Causeless as it might have been, it was so strong that some of us, after going to bed and lying restless for some time, finally got up and packed our things and made ready to move. It was not much too soon. At 11 o'clock the acting-adjutant, Lieutenant Pearce, came round and silently waked the regiment with the order to immediately make ready to leave.[15] Perhaps no order was ever executed more quickly or quietly. In a few moments we were on the march, in the darkness of the Summer night.

Before long the word passed round that the cavalry had been

sent out to Mark's Mills, and we were moving to take their place on guard. Reaching an open place in the brush some two miles south of town, we spread ourselves down to sleep for the rest of the night. At sun-rise next morning without reveille, or any thing else whatever, to waken us, the whole regiment simultaneously rose, shook and rolled up blankets, and prepared for the day. It was a strange coincidence of thought and feeling, springing from a common knowledge of a common danger. Our duty on the 26th was merely to remain near the line of arms. Toward noon there came up word from town that preparations were making for a hasty retreat.[16] Wagons, tents, mess-chests, cooking utensils, hard-tack and meat, were destroyed by the quantity. Box after box of crackers were burned, which would have been better distributed to the soldiers who soon were in need of them. About 2 o'clock a couple of wagons brought up our rations, and their scanty amount was divided among us. Some companies, for some cause, received much more per man than others. Some men drew but just two crackers, with a small amount of meal, some meat, and coffee, for the full supply that was to last them till we reached Little Rock; and many had not more than two crackers and a half-pint of meal. A few were fortunate enough to get their meal baked up into corn-cakes at houses near, before we started, but the rest had to cook it themselves, as best they might, along the road.[17]

It was evidently supposed that the rebels were so near, they would speedily hear of our movements; and the intention was to give them no warning of our retreat. So we had tattoo on the drums that night, with all the noise they could make; and an hour after that, when the bass drum should sound the "taps" at 9 o'clock, the regiment was to silently fall into line, and move off without further orders. This hour of waiting was a long one. Seated on the grassy slope, we speculated upon the strange appearance of circumstances, and forecasted trouble for the future. This was evidently to be a forced retreat, and in no encouraging way; but we could only obey orders, and be cheerful, and so we tried to do. Nine o'clock came at last; the bass drum sounded the "taps" with unearthly noise; and the regiment fell silently into line, and over the soft grass, moved noiselessly away. There was an enforced halt at the pontoon across the river; and here the woolen blankets began to come out of the knapsacks. It would never do to leave them for the rebels, and so most of them were cut up and destroyed; but of those that were then and afterward thrown away, the artillery-men, who came after us, and who, of course, rode most of the time on their guns and caissons, gathered up a great many, which they sold at a big profit, when we reached Little Rock again. So artillery-men, like other folks, make money some times from the calamities of their companions.

For about three miles from the pontoon-crossing, the road lay in such direction, as to be fully commanded by a battery, near where we had camped the night previous; and over this road our commanding-officers passed with us anxiously, fearing lest the rebels, who were known to be marching close upon us, might reach that battery in time to bring a few guns to bear, and so cut off our retreat. Most of the men, however, knew nothing of this, and therefore passed over the ground, as quiet and careless as usual. The event proved that the rebels were farther behind than was supposed, and that they really did not reach the river, till some time the next evening. About two o'clock in the night, the dangerous three miles having been passed over, we overtook that part of the column which had crossed the river before us. Here came a halt; and without any orders, (a most remarkable thing for soldiers), every body tumbled down on the ground to sleep. There was the most perfect equality and democracy, we had ever seen in the army. The officers had no "sleeping utensils" with them, and therefore, had to lie down as they were. General Rice was fortunate enough to have a cloak to lie on. He made a pillow of the bodies of one or two sleepy soldiers, who happened to be near him. One of the men happened to awake about 4 o'clock, and in moving a little, he almost stumbled over our division-commander, stretched upon the bare ground, with his feet to the fire, and looking like any other Dutchman.

The next day, the 27th of April, was clear and warm. Our loads were very heavy, and the march was very hard. No attack was as yet made in the rear, and hence grew rumors that the rebels had got around between us and Little Rock. Signs enough of the precipitation of our retreat appeared in the constant succession of shreds of clothing, pieces of knapsacks, and other fragments, which fatigue compelled our men to throw away.[18] Next morning, Thursday, reveille was sounded with the bugles at five; and in twenty-six minutes from that time—before we could possibly make coffee and drink it—the march re-commenced. Never before had we seen such haste when a whole column was moving. Marching as fast as we could under the circumstances, we reached the well-built and pleasant looking little town of Princeton, about 1 o'clock, and after considerable delay went into camp in an old corn-field.[19]

Rumors so various and contradictory that one could hardly put the least faith in any of them, were now flying thick among us. The most general belief, however, proved in the end to be the correct one—that the train sent out from Camden had been captured, the prisoners sent to Texas, and the wounded taken to Mt. Elba, a settlement not many miles distant, where the inhabitants were treating them kindly, and taking good care of them. One or two men who had fortunately escaped from the disaster at Mark's Mills, and had wandered through the wood for two or three days, living as best they might, now found and joined us.

For a few miles north from Princeton the road lay through the country which reminded us all of Iowa. No similarity of the kind we had ever noticed in the South, was more striking; but for one great difference we were proud and thankful—that the groves and prairies of Iowa had never trembled to the tread of hostile soldiers. About noon of Friday it commenced raining; and before night the mud was very bad.[20] The rebels were now coming close upon us, and occasional cannonading in the rear was heard during the afternoon.[21] Every night since leaving Camden we had camped in a corn-field, and this night was no exception; but the corn-field here was lower, wetter and more comfortless than ever. Nothing dry could be found to lie on, and there was no shelter from the soaking rain. For two or three days and nights we had had little of sleep and less of food; but bad as circumstances seemed, there was yet worse to come.

We contrived some way to find a little hard-tack and beef for supper, but the scanty meal was hardly done when our regiment was ordered back to the rear, where heavy skirmishing was now going on. Gloomily we gathered up our things, and tramped wearily back through the mud and water in the almost utter darkness; but before we could reach the rear out-posts the skirmishing had ceased, and we were then distributed by companies as a kind of extra picket.[22] During the greater part of the night it rained heavily. Even if we had not been on duty, there was no dry place to lie down; and if there had been, the rain was too cold a covering. So, wearily and cheerlessly passed another night, fit prelude for the bloody morrow.

CHAPTER XII.

THE BATTLE OF JENKINS' FERRY.

The morning of April 30, 1864, was a gloomy one for our little army; and the exceedingly unpleasant weather was but an unimportant item among so much else that was disagreeable. Worn down as we were with fatigue, fasting and loss of sleep, we saw ourselves now almost surrounded by an evidently overwhelming force of the enemy, who certainly had good reasons to expect a full and easy triumph. But "the race is not to the swift, nor the battle to the strong."[1]

Early in the morning our regiment came back from the rear outpost where we had passed the preceding night on duty, to a place some half a mile nearer the river than the corn-field previously mentioned.[2] Soon the battle commenced, with a heavy musketry-fire in the rear.[3] The rebels had swung their long lines of regiment after regiment around upon the hights, which described some thing like a semi-circle around that part of the swampy and heavily-timbered river-bottom where we lay; and they were now closing in to press us, unprepared, to the brink of the river, where their overwhelming numbers seemed to insure our total rout and capture.[4] Almost immediately at the commencement of the battle our regiment was ordered back to the thickest of it, and was soon part of that gallant line of defense which for seven mortal hours, by the pure force and energy of courage in desperation, repulsed every charge of the surprised and maddened foe, whose doubled ranks bore heavily down upon the thin line which we only could bring to oppose them.[5]

The conflict was terrible to experience, but brief to tell. Seven mortal hours, with such fierce vigor and determination that the fire of musketry became one undistinguishable and unbroken roar. Charge after charge was made by the yelling rebels, only to be broken upon

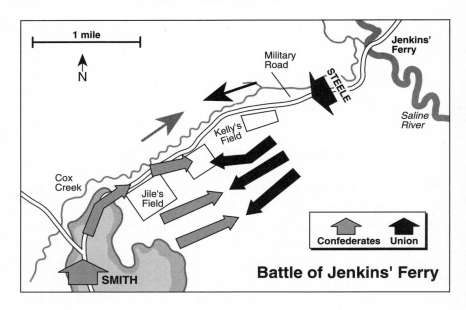

Map by Steve Scallion. *Courtesy Arkansas Historic Preservation Program.*

our line, or if possibly succeeding for a moment, to give way at last
to a charge of still deeper and more deadly determination from our
own brave men. The field presented little of advantage to friend or
foe. A heavily-timbered bottom, swampy at best, and now so covered with water that a foot could not rest on land alone, it would
have been under any other circumstances, deemed impassable.[6]

The battle had not long continued before a dense cloud of powder-
smoke settled so closely down, that at a few feet distant, nothing
was distinguishable. It seemed now almost impossible to fire otherwise than at random. The rebels did, indeed, mostly fire too high or
to low. Had they aimed with any thing like the usual accuracy, few
of us could have escaped. But our men, with that individual
thought and action, which makes the term "thinking bayonets"
more appropriate to Western troops, than to any others, soon
learned to stoop down, and look under the smoke sufficiently to discover the precise position of the rebel masses; and then a horizon-
tal fire at the level of the breast, could not fail to hit its mark,
unless a tree stood in the way.[7] The crowded and more than double
formation of rebel lines, must have suffered a dreadful slaughter.[8]

Maj. Cyrus B. Boydston, 33d Iowa Infantry. When
Colonel Mackey was wounded at Jenkins' Ferry on
April 30, 1864, Boydston, then the captain of Company A,
took command of the 33d Iowa. He was promoted to
major on June 28, 1864. *Photo courtesy of Roger Davis.*

Capt. Paris T. Totten, Company I, 33d Iowa Infantry.
Totten was hit in the thigh at Jenkins' Ferry and died in
the Officers' Hospital at Little Rock twenty days later.
Totten had black hair when he first joined the regiment,
but he grew gray during his year and a half of active service. His remains lie in Grave 5795, Section 12, Little
Rock National Cemetery. *Photo courtesy of Roger Davis.*

Pvt. Benjamin Cruzen, Company E, 33d Iowa Infantry.
Cruzen enlisted on July 24, 1862. He was wounded at
Jenkins' Ferry and taken prisoner. Regimental records
list him as killed in action. *Photo courtesy of
Mark A. Warren.*

Pvt. Levi Shaw, Company E, 33d Iowa Infantry. Shaw, a
resident of Mahaska County, joined the 33d on July 30, 1862.
He suffered a slight hand wound at Jenkins' Ferry.
Photo courtesy of Mark A. Warren.

Our own ranks, too, were badly thinned. Many had already fallen, both officers and men, when Colonel Mackey, riding along the line and urging to continued action, had his arm shattered by a musket-ball, and was compelled to leave the field.[9] Concealing the loss as much as possible from the regiment, Major Boydston assumed command, and gave all his energies to the protracted conflict.[10] Of the more severely wounded, some were borne from the field, but most had to remain unheeded. The living were too busy to attend the dead. It is hard to see a dear friend and comrade shot down by your side, and hear his piteous cries for help, and be unable to stop even to put a canteen of water to his lips, but to leave him like a dog to die as he fell, unheeded in the din and carnage of the battle; yet so it was, then. Thank God! that day is past.[11]

The battle of Jenkins' Ferry, was one of musketry alone. The rebels brought one battery to bear upon us, and fired three or four shots from it; but the 29th Iowa and 2d Kansas colored infantry, charged upon it, and captured its guns.[12] A battery of our own was posted at the corner of the previously mentioned corn-field, to be opened on the rebels, if they should drive our line back too far; but it was not found necessary to fire a single shot from it. While the battle was going on in the rear, our non-combatant forces were not idle. All of the train and stores that could be saved, were sent across the river, on the pontoon that had been laid; and the pontoon-wagons, and large quantities of stores were broken, scattered and destroyed. In this moving of the train, mostly at night, over an almost impassable road, was but another example of the additional power men acquire from sheer desperation.

Such a conflict as this, in the swamps and rain, could not last forever. About two o'clock in the afternoon, the day was won. Desperate courage had conquered numbers and power.[13] The rebels abandoned the field, all their dead and wounded, and as we afterward learned, fell back in such haste and confusion, that one of their own batteries was by accident, turned upon them—the echo of whose suicidal shells was not unwelcome to our ears. Few and exhausted as we were, retreat also, was our only hope of safety.[14] Leaving dead and wounded on the field, but with men to care for them,[15] our forces, victorious, yet sad, withdrew toward the river, and resumed the interrupted march; and as the last straggling company crossed the swollen stream, the pontoon was cut away, and the Saline was a temporary line of separation between us and the foe.[16] The loss of our regiment in the battle was: killed on the field—eight; wounded—one hundred and thirteen; missing—twelve; total—one hundred and twenty-three.[17] The names of killed, wounded and prisoners, will be found appropriately marked in the Roll of the Regiment, in the Appendix.

Surgeon William L. Nicholson, 29th Iowa Infantry.
Nicholson was one of the surgeons who remained to tend
the Union wounded abandoned on the Jenkins' Ferry
battlefield. He operated on some stricken men from the
33d Iowa. *Photo courtesy of Marion Pliner and U.S.
Army Military History Institute.*

Col. Charles E. Salomon, 9th Wisconsin Infantry. A
brother of Gen. Frederick Salomon and Gov. Edward
Salomon of Wisconsin, Charles Salomon took charge of
General Rice's 1st Brigade after the latter was
mortally wounded at Jenkins' Ferry.
*Photo courtesy of Gary D. Remy and U.S. Army
Military History Institute.*

CHAPTER XIII.

LITTLE ROCK AGAIN.

On the south side of the Saline, the mud was as bad as possible; on the north side it was as much worse than that, as that was worse than ordinary. Crossing the river, we found ourselves in a slough, which was in places waist-deep; and in which we waded, rather than walked, for some three miles.[1] Teams stuck, and were abandoned. One wagon contained a half-dozen negro babies, of assorted sizes, belonging to the colored Americans gathered to us since we started, which had been left there, stuck in the slough, drawn there by the feeblest of all possible mules, that was just executing his last drowning kick as we waded by. One negro woman, as was told by many who said they witnessed the incident, having carried her baby as long as she felt able, threw it away and left it, as a soldier would his knapsack. What became of the child can not be told; but probably it was not the only one abandoned.[2]

About three miles from the river we came to land again, and went into camp, in the midst of a steady rain; but before long the clouds turned their dry side toward us, and the rousing camp-fires made a show of comfort. There was rest now, in prospect, but little food. Many of the men's rations were entirely exhausted, and all were nearly so; but there was no help for us till we reached Little Rock.[3] Sleep instead of food will do very well, if one can but get it; and we were weary and exhausted enough to try it. At a little after mid-night, however, the order came, to burn our wagons and most of our equipage, and be ready to march at 4 o'clock in the morning.[4] We privates were not so much interested in the wagons just then, but the officers had all their fine clothes in them; so there came a sudden change of garments, to save the best from burning; and men who had laid down ragged and dirty at dark were seen at day-light finely dressed in glossy coats with shining buttons, but hungry and tired as ever. Mess-chests, company-boxes, &c., made excellent fuel;

and by their blaze the coffee was boiled and the poor pretense of breakfast eaten.[5]

"The 1st of May is moving day."[6] At 4 o'clock in the morning we were moving. Our division was in the front, and our regiment, train-guard. There was a mile or two of marching through mud-holes, and then came the mud in earnest. A pine swamp of four miles' width, in the worst possible condition naturally, and now cut up into almost unfathomable softness by the wagons and artillery that had already crossed it, lay between us and solid land again. Oh! the interminable teams in that dreary swamp! Driven to the last extreme of haste by the imperative necessity for food, and expecting every minute to hear the guns of the once repulsed, but still overwhelming enemy, open upon our rear, there we were compelled to wait and linger, while the long train of wagons would stick in the mud, and the mules would flounder in the mire. One of the most wearisome and vexatious things in the world is compulsory delay; and here we had it under the most disagreeable circumstances. Many as were the wagons that had been destroyed, the train still stretched out apparently two or three miles. Our duty as train-guard that day, was to cut down all the young pine trees near, bring them on our backs to that deepest part of the mire, which was called the road, and so build corduroy across most of the swamp. When a wagon stuck—and all the wagons were constantly sticking —every endeavor was made to raise it out of the mud and get it moving again. If all means failed, the mules were unhitched, and the wagon broken and burned; and so all over the swamp, near the road, were burning wagons and their scattered contents. If the cartridges that were sown that day should bear fruit even sixty-fold, there would never be peace any more. Whenever a wagon was fired, most or all of its contents were thrown into the water bunches and elsewhere; but still the occasional explosions of powder, cartridges, &c., lent variety without beauty to the scene.[7]

At last the four miles wore away, and between one and two P. M. we came to land again. From this time until dark, the march went fast and steadily. All day the weather had been clear and pleasant; but perhaps no one had thought of its being Sunday. Notwithstanding all the rumors and fears, the rebels made no further demonstrations. One good trial had been enough for them; and certainly we were as well pleased as ever Jeff. Davis was to be "let

Anonymous Private, 18th Iowa Infantry. This haggard
survivor of the Camden expedition sports a pair of civilian
corduroy trousers, no doubt "foraged" from an Arkansas
home after his issue trousers wore out on the march.
Photo courtesy of Roger Davis.

alone." Some where near dark there came a halt, with the usual appearances of going into camp. An open field in front of us was aglow along one side with fires that looked like the camp-fires of regiments that had marched in the advance. Worn and weary as we were, and faint from the loss of food and sleep, the idea of camping for the night, seemed as pleasant as coming home might be at some other time. But there was to be no rest. The halt was only caused by another series of mud-holes, and the fires had been kindled as lights along the road.

And all that night the march continued, with no stop but what the mud enforced, till four o'clock next morning. The road was all the way through timber; and details of cavalry kindled and kept up continuous fires, till through the whole forest ran a sinuous line of fitful flames. It was a strange, wild time. We were now almost at the limits of human powers of endurance. Nature will be revenged at last, for there is a point where even her forbearance ceases. All through the night there came frequent little halts of a moment or two, caused by some wagon sticking in a mud-hole; and at every such halt, the instant we ceased moving we were asleep. Many did not feel safe to stop thus, without asking some comrade to be sure and wake them when the start was made; and many actually slept while marching.

Morning came at last, but brought no rest. Having no thing to eat, we did not need to halt for breakfast or dinner; and so we steadily marched on. Still the reports came that the rebels were between us and Little Rock. We had been hungry for some time, but now began to actually suffer for want of food. One man paid a comrade two dollars for a single hard-tack, and another traded a silver watch for two of them.[8] That afternoon, between three and four o'clock, we came out upon the Benton road, and then knew where we were; and in an hour or so we camped, this last night of the march, on the very ground where we had camped the first night of the expedition, more than a month before. How we contrasted the two nights! and how long seemed the times between them!

Kindling fires and making coffee—for this soldier's solace was not yet exhausted—we flung ourselves down to rest. In an hour or two there arose a shout in the advance, which was quickly caught up and passed down the line. The rations had come! Orders had been sent into Little Rock for food; and besides the issues by the

Quarter-master, our comrades left in camp there, had gathered and sent out all they had, to aid us. Never were rations more speedily distributed, or "hard-tack and sow-belly" put inside of blue uniforms with greater haste. The worst was now over.[9] The night was altogether too cold for comfort, but sleep was a necessity and came of course.

Next morning the march was renewed with better hope and vigor. We felt as if almost home. At 10:30 Fort Steele was in sight; and not even the memory of the dreary days of fatigue-duty on its walls could make it seem unwelcome.[10] Halting now to form in better order, the prisoners captured on the march were put between closer files, the ranks all better "dressed," and the "mule brigade"—composed of the sick, weak and wounded who were unable to walk, but who on reporting to the doctor had been supplied with mules—formed in some thing like regular military style. There would undoubtedly have been a good deal of music, but the fifes and drums had been so nearly used up on the campaign, the pounding was hardly as lively as usual.[11]

Marching down through town on the old, familiar streets, and past General Steele's head-quarters, we finally reached our own old camp before noon.[12] Oh! it was joy to be there again! It seemed like home. The welcomes of the comrades who had been left there were warm and cordial; but some thing to eat was the first, and the mail the second, great object of attention. Every thing eatable disappeared like grass before an army of locusts; and it seemed almost strange to be where we could get plenty to eat again. Then came the rest, which took a good while.[13] It seemed almost dream-like to be back there in our old camp—almost too good to be true. We were glad and thankful.[14] Colonel Mackey being disabled, Captain Boydston was temporarily in command of the regiment—a duty of which the chief visible point was to hold parade.

And so was ended the Camden Expedition. Considering the object in primary view, it was a failure; and it narrowly escaped ending in a terrible defeat. But if examples of stern and determined endurance, of desperate courage successfully resisting the force of overwhelming numbers, of faithful attempts to obey orders, and cheerful fortitude in braving disaster, are worthy of remembrance, our memories of the Camden Expedition need not be less proud than terrible.[15]

CHAPTER XIV.

CAMP AND GARRISON.

Soon after our return to Little Rock, Captain Lofland, of Company D, having been promoted to lieutenant-colonel, assumed command of the regiment.[1] Renewed attention was now paid to drill and discipline, and the result was marked improvement. But it was hard for us, after so much soldiering as we had tried, to see the practical benefit of so much daily drill; and the more experience we had, the stronger grew our conviction that half the drilling in the army is of no use so far as fighting is concerned, but that it serves only to make appearances better on reviews and other dress occasions.[2] Drill in loading and firing, and in some of the more common and necessary evolutions, is all we could ever find to be of any use in actual battle. The skirmish-drill, however, we admitted to be valuable and necessary; and more attention was now paid to it. The buglers and other musicians were put through a regular daily drill; and the non-commissioned officers were for some weeks assembled every evening for practice in the bugle signal for skirmishers.[3]

On the 28th of May a flag of truce brought in some letters from our wounded comrades of the battle of Jenkins' Ferry, who were held as prisoners at Mt. Elba, Princeton and Camden; and letters, medicines and clothing were sent out in return. Small as the consolation was of thus hearing from imprisoned and suffering comrades, it was much better than the barbarous treatment of those who fell into rebel hands in other places. And for this amenity in warfare we believe we have to thank the rebel General Price.

Among the other improvements now undertaken in camp, our acting-adjutant, Lieutenant C. H. Sharman, Company G, commenced the preparation of an entire new set of regimental books. They were finished in about a month, and were commended by every Inspecting Officer as peculiarly neat, full and correct.

During the retreat from Camden the most of our regimental- and company-records had been burned among the other luggage, by order of the commanding-general; and it was therefore difficult afterward, to make all the accounts come out square.[4]

The monotony of camp- and garrison-duty, picket and fatigue, picket and fatigue, over and again, and that continually, was interrupted by little more than frequent walks around town.[5] There were of course details occasionally made for guards to accompany boats carrying provisions to Fort Smith, Pine Bluffs and elsewhere; and on some of these trips there were stirring times, when a squad of rebels would attack the boat. Every time a boat went out from Little Rock, before it returned, reports would come of its having been attacked, captured, sunk, &c.; but generally there would be little truth in them. On one occasion, however, one man of our regiment was mortally wounded during an attack on a boat between Little Rock and Fort Smith.[6]

In the afternoon of Monday, June 6th, there was a grand review of our division, before Major-General Sickles, then on his tour as General Inspecting Officer; and on the 20th, our brigade was reviewed by Colonel Marcy, of the Regular Army.[7] Reviews and Inspections seemed now to be about the only occupation of general officers. On these occasions the field-music of the brigade was usually massed at the head of the column, so as to supply the whole four regiments together. One advantage of this was that there was no mixing up of time by different bands; but there was the disadvantage that not even the racket of ten or twenty fifes, fifteen or twenty snare-drums, and two or three bass-drums could all the time be heard by the whole brigade.

Toward the last of June, the ceremony of brigade-guard-mounting was instituted. It was held on the open space, between us and the camp of the 29th, where formerly stood the cabins of the 3d Iowa battery. The bands of the brigade took turns in furnishing the music. On the 3d of July our former Major, H. D. Gibson, who, on his way home from Camden had been captured at Mark's Mills, and had suffered great hardships during his captivity at Tyler, Texas, arrived in camp, clad in a poor suit of butternut homespun, with an old straw hat and not the best foot-gear in the world, and looking very unlike the portly and comfortable Major he was when we last saw him. Having at last succeeded in obtaining a release from the rebels, he had footed it so far toward home, and in a few weeks more he was safe in the North again.[8]

The 4th of July this year passed very quietly. The only celebration of the day in Little Rock was that all the regiments at the post stood in arms on their color-lines, while a national salute was fired from Fort Steele. It was a tame enough affair for us who had "seen the 4th at Helena."[9] For some cause or other, we never knew definitely what, there came now a time when we could send no letters home. The mails would leave camp as usual, but as we afterward learned, they did not leave Duvall's Bluff for a month or more. July 16th there was an alarm of attack on some of our force guarding the railroad from Little Rock to the Bluff, and a thousand men from our brigade, with a day's rations and sixty rounds of ammunition were immediately sent out as re-inforcements; but they came back a little after noon, with orders to hold themselves in readiness, and were never called for again.[10]

Next evening, the 17th, in an almost perfectly clear sky, as some of us were looking dreamily, we perceived a long and very slender line of white cloud, reaching across the sky from north-west to south-east, tracing the side of a shield of very nearly the usual shape. Of course it had to be made an "omen" in some way; and so every man drew his own inferences or forebodings.

On the 21st of July, the news reached us of the death of General Samuel A. Rice, at his residence in Iowa, from wounds received at the battle of Jenkins' Ferry. Half-hour-guns were fired from Fort Steele during the day, in honor of his memory.[11]

The time still passed monotonously in garrison-duty. Occasionally, by way of variety, some of the officers would get up a "grand ratification meeting" by prying up the floors of their tents, upon which whole droves of rats would immediately scatter themselves promiscously over camp, to be captured and killed by the gathered braves, who, armed with sticks, would go through the contest with great military display if not much tactical order.[12] The pay-master arrived on the 15th of August, and paid us for the past six months. On the 19th a recruiting-party, consisting of two line and several non-commissioned officers from the regiment, started for Iowa. How we almost envied them! About this time there began to be

Capt. Levi Carrothers, Company I, 33d Iowa Infantry.
Originally Company I's second lieutenant, Carrothers
was promoted to first lieutenant on June 14, 1864, and to
captain on July 21, replacing the late Paris Totten. *Photo
courtesy of U.S. Army Military History Institute.*

First Lt. James M. Cooper, Company A, 33d Iowa
Infantry. Cooper was promoted from first sergeant to second lieutenant on April 12, 1863. He became Company A's
first lieutenant on July 21, 1864. Broad-brimmed hats like
Cooper's became a common sight in the 33d Iowa soon
after it took up residence at Helena, Arkansas, in the
spring of 1863. *Photo courtesy of Mark A. Warren.*

First Sgt. John S. Morgan, Company G, 33d Iowa
Infantry. A schoolteacher with auburn hair and hazel
eyes, Morgan enlisted as Company G's fourth sergeant on
August 9, 1862. He served in the regiment's color guard
during the Camden campaign and became a first sergeant
on July 21, 1864. He received a second lieutenant's commission on February 20, 1865. Morgan's published diaries
and unpublished journal are important sources on the 33d
Iowa's history. *Photo courtesy of Mark A. Warren.*

rumors that "Mr. Price" was collecting a number of his friends, to
come and pay us a visit; and there was much speculation in camp
as to whether he would be able to come inside of our lines if he
should try it.[13] The garrison of the place was now so reduced, we
felt very doubtful of our ability to withstand a strong attack. On the
24th of the month, by the efforts of Lieutenant-Colonel Lofland, we
drew entirely new arms and equipments, which at least improved
the appearance of the regiment, if not its effective fighting power.

In the first days of September, the rumors of approaching attack
became so strong that the almost invariable order in case of alarm
was received—"Reveille at three, and stand at arms till sun-rise," to
which we were by this time so accustomed that it was obeyed after
the easy interpretation, by stacking arms on the color-line and then
breaking ranks.[14] But the rumors came thick and fast, and lost
no thing as they came. Sunday morning at 3 o'clock our bugle
sounded, and was immediately echoed all over town. The whole
force was in arms and line. That night we went to bed as usual; but
at 10 o'clock the "assembly" called us out, and with arms, canteens
and rubber blankets we marched out to a portion of the defenses,
some two miles west of camp, and then tumbled down and slept till
some time the next forenoon, waiting for Mr. Price.[15]

Monday was hot and cloudless. Tiring of that bare place on the
ground, we moved a little nearer to the wood, and went hard at
work putting up a shade, of posts, poles and boughs, as protection
from the intense rays of the sun. Just as we got it well fixed, and
were ready to rest a while under it, the order came to move back to
camp again; and so regretfully we left our woodland bower.[16]
"Locking the stable after the horse is lost," is hardly considered a
wise rule of action. Now that the danger was apparently over, or so
much so that we need no longer remain under arms and in the line
of defenses, there came very heavy details for fatigue-parties to
throw up earth-works, which, it seemed to us, ordinary common
sense would never have omitted so long.

On the next day, however, these heavy details for unusual hours
of labor were countermanded; the stars and stripes, which for the
past two or three days, had given place to the red hospital-flag,[17]
were again run up to the top of the tall flag-staff, in front of the
general hospital; and things seemed suddenly to have settled back

Capt. Cheney Prouty, Company E, 33d Iowa Infantry.
Originally the first lieutenant of Company E, Prouty
made captain on May 20, 1863. He was sent north on a
recruiting mission on August 16, 1864, rejoining the 33d
Iowa in November. *Photo courtesy of Mark A. Warren.*

to the *statu quo*.[18] This quick transition from one state of affairs to the appearance of another, produced much mystification and distrust; but the facts at the bottom of it, when we learned them, were plain enough: Mr. Price had simply "passed by on the other side," and gone up toward Missouri.[19]

Drills and parades, inspections and reviews, returned now with increased persistence, and took about all the time that picket- and fatigue-duty left unoccupied. Brigade-guard-mounting, was still the daily order. On the 23d of September, an added interest was given it, by the first appearance of our new brigade brass band—usually styled among us "Mein Bender's Band," as General Salomon[20] called it—from Milwaukee, Wisconsin. This band was composed of some fifteen or twenty musicians, nearly all Germans. It discoursed really excellent music, and was a credit to the brigade. No dress occasion was complete without them; and when not on public-duty, they were kept very busy in serenading different officers around town. On the 25th of the month, for the sake of still higher "style," and perhaps, also, for the sake of giving the general and the field officers some thing to attend to, division-guard-mounting was instituted. This was a somewhat imposing display. All the guard-details of our whole division, and all the officers not on duty at the time, had to attend in full uniform; and the whole was a spectacle with much of the "pomp and circumstance" about it.[21] There was usually a large number of spectators, both soldiers and citizens; and even the commanding-general occasionally came out to look on.

News still came some times from the outside world. On the 4th of October, one hundred guns were fired, from the five different forts around town, in honor of Sheridan's great victory in the Shenandoah Valley.[22] On the 8th, further news came of a tremendous victory gained by General Grant, in which he was said to have captured twenty-five hundred prisoners and one hundred guns. This, however, seemed then, as it afterward proved to be, altogether too good to be true. Accompanying all these good reports, but more real than they, Colonel Mackey returned to the regiment, from an absence of three or four months in Iowa, with his wounded arm so nearly well, as to allow of his assuming his command.[23]

Preparations were now commenced toward fitting the camp for Winter. The officers began building new cabins, and the streets

Drummer Thomas W. Cox, Company G, 33d Iowa
Infantry. Gerhard Nollen, a Dutch artist who settled in
Pella, Iowa, in 1854, based this painting, "The Little
Drummer Boy of '62," on a photograph taken shortly
after Cox enlisted in the Union army. According to a
family legend, A. F. Sperry personally recruited the
adventurous thirteen-year-old because of Cox's musical
ability. *Photo courtesy of Pella Historical Society.*

were all changed and cleared.[24] Among the other improvements,
perhaps, the three new brass drums received for the band, are
worth a mention. Company G contributed forty dollars to buy a
brass drum for "Tommy," in whose drumming they had well-
merited pride; and not to be outshone entirely, the drummer of
Company H, and "Johnny" of Company I, bought new drums at
their own expense.[25] These, of course, added much to the noise and
rattle of the "music." There were expectations now of our remaining
in quarters for the Winter; and circumstances certainly seemed to
indicate it. But "all signs fail in a dry time;" and there is no depend-
ance to be placed on them in the army. The monotony was soon broken. Of course, if there was any thing to be done, the 33d was the
regiment to do it; and soon the unwelcome order came for a move.

CHAPTER XV.

TO FORT SMITH AND BACK.

On Sunday, October 30, 1864, our regiment, with a section of the 3d Iowa battery, started out as escort of a train of supplies for Fort Smith.[1] Nothing very special occurred at the commencement of this march. We were used to the business, and knew by this time "how to make the best of it."[2] For the first night we camped in the wood about eight miles from town; the second night, at the Palaime Bayou;[3] the third night, on the Arkansas river, some three miles from the Cadron,[4] where we had to lie over one day to wait for the train to cross the little river.[5] Here some sport and excitement were caused by a chase after half-wild horses on the river bottom. Several of them were finally lassoed.

Not far from noon the 4th of November, we entered Lewisburg, and camped in the outer edge of the little town.[6] The night was cold, with a severe frost; and this made the hard ground a rather cold bed for us. Next day we passed through some country which looked very much like Iowa—a similarity sure to be noticed—but the likeness soon ceased. About five miles from Lewisburg we came upon the Carroll farm—the largest plantation we had ever seen. Thousands of acres of fertile bottom-lands, now in total neglect, and overgrown with weeds, seemed a fit place for the "deserted village" of negro-quarters which stood at a respectful distance from the planter's door. Of course, "the ole man wuz gond, an' the niggers wuz in Texas."[7]

On the night of the 5th, we camped some eleven miles west of Lewisburg. Just in advance of us was a company of colored infantry, and beyond them a part of the 2d Arkansas Infantry, who were to go with us the rest of the way.[8] This camp of the 2d Arkansas was the queerest thing in the military line in all our experience. The members of the regiment had formerly lived some where in this part of the State; and they were now moving all their wives, children, stock, furniture, wagons, and other property, to Fort Smith.

Every thing among them seemed to us to be in promiscuous confusion. We were not accustomed to the sight of soldiers among their families. It must have been hard for women and children to take such a march at such a time, and under those circumstances; but there were many among them who at the hands of the fiends of rebel guerrillas, their own neighbor's family, had suffered wrongs and cruelties compared with which, these hardships were as nothing. After talking some time with them, and with other Southerners who were, and had always been truly loyal, we frequently declared to ourselves that so long as our dear ones at home were safe and comfortable, we would grumble no more—that we knew no thing of the hardships and troubles of the war.[9]

During this halt dispatches were received, announcing the defeat of Price and his rebels in Missouri, and their scattered retreat toward the Arkansas river. Some doubt was entertained of the expediency of our passing very near his flying columns; and a delay of one day in our march was therefore attributed to this cause.[10] On the 7th, starting on again, we made about fourteen miles, and camped for the night around the residence of a Mr. Potts, an arrant old rebel. A large white house, with big barns and granaries, commanding a near view of the abrupt and imposing "Carrion-Crow Mountain," it would have been a good enough home for a much better man.[11] Foraging was prohibited, but not prevented, and the secesh proprietor of the premises unwillingly contributed to the Union army enough to make us two pretty good meals, at least, and very probably suffered the loss of more.

All along the road, the country hereabouts seemed to be good, and well settled. The women and children appeared to be all gathered at the neighbors' houses to look at us, while the men were out in the woods "bushwhacking." There was considerable apprehension among us of trouble with these bushwhackers, and frequent reports came of our having been fired into from the sides of the road; but most or all of these stories, when traced up, were found to start from some wagon-master or train-teamster.

About 1:30 P. M., of November 8th, we camped in a field on the Illinois bayou, three miles from Russellville. In a little while a small wedge-tent was put up, rude tables constructed under it, and the polls opened for election. We felt that on this day the great con-

flict was to be decided, and we did our duty as we could.[12] That
night it rained hard, and did not stop till it turned cold next morning. This made a very uncomfortable time. A warm rain, if followed
by a clear, warm day, is little heeded in the army; but a soaking
flood of water, followed only by clouds, cold and winds, is exceedingly unwelcome. Resuming the march, we found that the bayou,
had risen several inches; and as there was no other means of crossing, we had to wade through it. The cold, raw wind, as well as the
coldness of the water, spoiled all the fun of the thing, and we
marched along about as cheerfully as a poor man goes to jail. That
night, after a march of about fourteen miles over a very rough and
rocky road, we camped in a large field on the Big Piney bayou.

Next day, the 10th, starting at about seven in the morning, as
usual, we entered Clarksville by the covered bridge over Spadra
Creek at about 1:15 P. M.; halted a few minutes, and then turned
back to camp on the bluff. There had been a slight skirmish near
this place, between our advance-cavalry and a small squad of
rebels, and one or two guerrillas were killed.[13] All we regretted was,
that any of the diabolical wretches were left alive. All along the
road of late, we had seen the ruins of houses they had burned
because their occupants were Union men, or were supposed to have
a little money; and there were persons with us who personally
knew, and told us, of the guerrillas entering such and such houses,
whose ruins we passed, and torturing the inmates by burning their
feet over a fire to make them give up their money. At such times, if
we could have got hold of the rebel devils, we would have hewn
them to pieces.[14]

One pathetic incident occurred at Clarksville, of which Sergeant
Hamsick and Commissary-Sergeant Berkey were witnesses.[15] An
old widow living near town stood looking at our little column as it
entered town, and suddenly her eye fell on the countenance of her
son, whom she had not seen or heard of for a long time. He was a
soldier in the 2d Arkansas. After the first surprise and excitement
of the meeting, she told him how the infernal bushwhackers had
been at her house, and had insulted and actually beaten her, and
killed an aged man living near. It is to be hoped the old lady's son
was able to save her from further troubles from them.

At Clarksville we laid over for a day, and sent out a train after forage, which returned without any great supply. The 1st Arkansas Infantry,[16] and the 5th U. S. Colored Infantry[17] arrived from Fort Smith as additional escort for our train; and Colonel Johnson, of the 1st, being the senior officer, assumed command.[18] Starting out again rather early next day, we made some fourteen miles, and a little after noon approached the place that had for some days been dreaded—a narrow canyon called Horsehead Pass, which was represented as the very nest and head-quarters of all the bushwhackers in the country. A fit place for them indeed it was. For a considerable distance the road wound between the almost meeting hills, whose rugged, precipitous and wooded sides gave every opportunity of concealment and safety for a lurking foe. Fifty well-armed men here could have terribly harassed ten thousand. After the pass came the narrows, where the sides of the canyon, though not so high, were nearer together. As we entered the pass, heavy details of flankers were sent out on each side, relieved or reinforced at frequent intervals. Three or four shots were heard as we passed through the defile, but it is not fully certain whether they were fired by bushwhackers or by men of our own force who were camped in advance of us and had gone out foraging. It was of course well to use all possible precaution in such a place, but the danger proved in no wise equal to our expectations.

About 2 o'clock of Tuesday, the 15th, we entered the town of Van Buren, on the Arkansas river, and marched down to camp a mile or two below town, on the river bank.[19] Here we laid over a day, for the train to unload, as the river was so high we could not well cross. Fort Smith was only five miles distant, and we very much wished to go there.[20] Many did foot it the next day, for the sake of seeing the place and going "out of the United States into the Indian Territory." Thursday, the 17th, we turned our faces homeward, as going back to Little Rock then seemed to us. Marching fourteen miles, we camped that night on the ground occupied a few nights before. It rained hard, and was very muddy and disagreeable. One who had never tried it would be astonished to see how much shelter may be made of one common rubber blanket. Suspended by stakes so as to hang in the form of an obtuse-angled roof, about three feet from the ground, it will keep two soldiers passably dry through the rainiest of nights, provided the wind doesn't blow, and the men will lie still and close together. Some shelter for us on this return trip seemed almost necessary, for the rain came down with all persistency.

The boys now seemed to have much better success in foraging than when we went the other way. Tobacco was the great staple. The supply brought with us from Little Rock, having been long ago exhausted, it may be imagined that "natural leaf" and "twist," were doubly welcome. Loads of it were foraged. The cavalry got the most, as usual; but before we reached Lewisburg, all had as much as they wanted to use.

Colonel Bowen and Mr. Gilsoate, two old men from Hempstead County, Representatives in the State Legislature, came with us to Little Rock.[21] They were true Union men, as was apparent in every word and act, and had suffered much for their loyalty. The elder of the two, had lived in Hempstead County, most of his life; and it was intensely amusing to hear him describe and illustrate his utter ignorance of the machinery and improvements of modern civilization. A short visit to the North, a few months previous, had evidently convinced him, that there was no people on earth, like the Yankees, and that the sooner they whipped the South out, and re-settled the country, the better it would be for every body.

Having now been out of the reach of news for some time, we naturally supposed that at least, some thing must have happened in the world, since we started. We had no doubt that Lincoln was re-elected; and many were sure there would be some great news from Richmond. But in this we were disappointed. Reaching Lewisburg, which was connected by telegraph with Little Rock, we heard of Lincoln's triumph, and of Sherman's starting toward Charleston;[22] but from Richmond came nothing remarkable. Long months after this, when the news did finally come, of the overthrow of the rebel strong-hold, it had been, as is usual with so much expected events in life, so heralded and introduced, that the reality, though vast, did not seem equal to the anticipation.

Not far from our camp, three miles west of the Cadron, we noticed a tall cotton-wood stump, about two feet in diameter, hollow, and running down several feet straight into the ground, thus conclusively showing, that the ground there, for at least that depth, was all deposited by the action of water, within the last hundred years or so. The second night of the march out from Little Rock, we had camped in and around a good, old white house, at the bridge across the Palarme. Coming back now, only two or three weeks later, we found the house had been burned; so we camped in the out-buildings and on the vacant lots. Familiar with destruction, we had never yet seen so much house-burning, as had been done on the road from Little Rock to Fort Smith.

Next morning, the 27th of November, we had reveille at three o'clock, and by dint of much hurrying got on the move again before six. There was as yet no trace of day-light, and so we crossed the high bridge over the Palarme, by the glowing light of two large fires. It was a picturesque scene. But starting before day-light, was rather overdoing the matter; and we had to halt and wait half an hour or so for sun-rise, and then went on our way rejoicing, for this was our last day's march. Not far from four o'clock in the afternoon, we found ourselves in sight of town. Our band met us at the pontoon-bridge; and we marched up through town with all the glory of fifes and drums, our ragged and dusty uniforms contrasting shabbily with the bright, new clothes, and paper collars of the city soldiers. But for some cause or other, there was the largest and most enthusiastic crowd gathered to see us, of all qualities and descriptions, military and civilians, that we had ever seen on the streets of Little Rock, since the city fell into our hands.

Arrived in our old camp again, we found our comrades of the last recruiting-party all returned; and the mail that had accumulated during our absence now cheered us all at once. But much inconvenience and some loss had been caused by the stay of the 47th Indiana for several days in our quarters while we were gone.[23] The Fort Smith trip was the longest we were ever on. It had included about 360 miles of consecutive marching, but there was nothing more or worse about it than "mere common soldiering." All had stood it first-rate, and many liked it much better than remaining in camp.[24] The health of the regiment was never better. But the more thoughtful among us noticed, and deplored, the hardening influence a march invariably has upon the finer tastes and sensibilities. It seemed to deaden our better feelings. Remaining quiet in camp for some time, our aesthetic natures seemed to live and grow, but on the march they seemed chilled and stunned by hard realities. Three months of comparative rest would not more than remedy the hardening effect of a month of marching.

CHAPTER XVI.

REST A LITTLE, AND THEN OFF AGAIN.

In camp once more, the usual routine ensued. Fatigue, picket, drill and parade were the standing order of the day, with inspection and review for variation. One evening on parade the solemnity of the occasion was materially interrupted by a couple of little boys who came out among the rest to witness the performances. Tickled most, of course, by the fifes and drums, they followed close behind them; and when the band struck up for the march down and back in front of the line, close behind them tagged the little boys, their short legs wiggling rapidly as they tried to keep up with the music. Down and up the line marched the band as usual, and down and up the line followed the boys, to the intense amusement of the regiment, and the great disgust of the principal musician, who was rallied a good deal over his new recruits.

December 24th, in the morning, a full and distinct rain-bow was visible for some minutes, though the weather was very cold. We could explain it only by supposing the frost in the air had consented to act instead of rain for this particular occasion. Major-General J. J. Reynolds was now in command of the department, and the straightening-up he made there was very perceptible.[1] He inspected our regiment on the 20th of January, and complimented us afterward on our appearance—promising a more general inspection in quarters before many days; from which some inferred quite positively that we were still to remain in town on garrison-duty. But they were soon undeceived.

On the morning of the 21st of January, unexpected orders came for us to be ready to march immediately, with ten days' rations, blankets, and general "heavy-marching order." Most of us believed this to be the beginning of that grand "onward movement" toward Texas which all expected to come in the Spring.[2] Next morning we left our camp again, for another "last time!" A review of the moving force took place in front of the general hospital; and at a quarter after eleven the march commenced. The column consisted of three or four regiments of infantry, with some cavalry and artillery, and was under the command of Brigadier-General Carr.[3] The most utter and unprecedented ignorance prevailed as to our destination, or the probable length of our stay; and all sorts of conjectures were afloat concerning both questions.

The first day's march was but about eight miles, on the Pine Bluff road. Before night it commenced snowing considerably; and the ground became decidedly too cold to sleep on, with comfort.[4] It is very easy for a healthy man to warm up an ordinary bed, by the heat of his body, but it is comparatively difficult thus to warm a whole planet. Next day, marching about ten miles, we camped for the night, on a rather good plantation, then owned by a widow lady, who was naturally very anxious to save her rails and chickens, and therefore discanted considerably upon the fact that her daughters were at school in Indiana; that her husband had been a good Union man; that the rebels had been around there several times and hung him, to punish him for his loyalty; and that at last they had hung him so much that it injured his health, and he finally died. Of course, we respected the chickens and rails.

About noon of the 25th, we entered Pine Bluff, where the Dutch rebel Marmaduke, had been so often and signally repulsed, by the gallant Clayton, and where the condensed and substantial earthworks attested the determined character of the defense, as the buildings in town, showed plainly the fierceness of the onset.[5] Passing through the streets with but little delay, we went into camp about a mile below town.[6] Next day we made some twelve or fourteen miles, without special incident; and on Friday following, traveled sixteen miles, passing a good, white, frame school-house—an exceedingly rare thing in Arkansas.[7] This brought us to the settlement called Mt. Elba, on the Saline river.

Here, camped on an open field, we lay over for two days, while the cavalry pressed on toward Camden, to raise an alarm there, and cause a concentration of the rebel forces.[8] Having nothing to do meanwhile, but to lie still and wait for their return, we sent out a forage-train, which came back well loaded with provisions. This part of the country having never before been occupied by Union troops, except in transit, there was the more left for us; and we lived on the fat of the land. On Monday the cavalry came back, and we turned our faces once more toward the North. A long and tiresome march, through rain and mud, left us for the night, on the place we had occupied the preceding Thursday; and on the next night, after a very fatiguing tramp through the mud, we found ourselves a mile and a half north-west of Pine Bluff, on the road to Little Rock.

Wednesday, February 1st, was another hard day for us, with only mud and rain instead of comfort. It is not easy to march under twenty pounds of knapsack, and twenty or twenty-five pounds of other accoutrements, even on good roads; and mud knee-deep has no tendency to help the matter. But there was no enemy now to hover in our rear, and no prospect of starvation if we did not hurry. Lying over at Rock Springs on Thursday, to wait for our train to come up, we started out again on Friday, and camped that night on the plantation of the widow Campbell, whose husband had been so injuriously hung.

Saturday, the 4th, brought us again to Little Rock, though only for a little while.[9] When we were yet two or three miles out of town, word was brought to us, that we were under immediate orders for New Orleans.[10] Strange as it seemed to us, to be likely to get out of Arkansas, there were many who believed the story, and more who hoped it was true. We had been seeing active service lately; though this last trip had been but easy and ordinary soldiering. All had got along exceedingly well; and the sickness among the regiment had been reduced to the minimum.[11]

There was now for us a short period of complete rest, even the details for fatigue- and guard-duty being remitted; and in consequence, the line of the regiment on parade, had a length which reminded us of the old Camp-Tuttle-days, before sickness and battle had so reduced our numbers.[12] Having before now, repeatedly left Little Rock "for the last time," the parting had become an old story; but this coming time was to be the last indeed. We had no special love for the old place, but having been stationed there for more than half of our term of service, it was but natural for us to feel connected with it by some ties of association. But these were soon parted, and Little Rock became only one more name in the album of our military memories.

CHAPTER XVII.

DOWN SOUTH.

Our Valentine for 1865, came one day too early, in the shape of marching orders for New Orleans.[1] Tuesday, February 14, rose gloomy enough, and it was cloudy and chilly, when not raining, all the rest of the day. If "signs" were to be of any avail, our trip was to be a sad one. At half-past six in the morning, we bade our final adieu to the old camp where so much of our soldier-life had been passed, crossed the river on the wooden pontoon-bridge, and piled ourselves and baggage on the train for Duvall's Bluff. Every moment brought vividly to mind the contrast between our first coming to the city and this last departure from it. When we first arrived at Little Rock, it was amid the smoke of burning buildings, cars and boats. The streets were deserted; the stores were empty; and we looked upon the city as a temporary stopping-place in our march from Helena to Texas. Now it was a busy, bustling town, familiar to us as more than a year's residence could make it. Then, we marched wearily over the prairie, day by day, suffering from heat and thirst, and wondering if we should ever see happier circumstances there. Now, we rode lightly and cheerily along, with no fatigue and comparatively little comfort, passing in a few hours what had taken us toilsome days before. Then, we were in but feeble hope for the end of the rebellion, and looked upon it as a distant and intangible uncertainty. Now, we saw the end approaching, and felt sure that victory could not tarry long. We were bidding farewell to familiar scenes, but with hope brighter than ever, that before many months longer we should greet the still desired and more familiar scenes of home.[2]

Arriving at Duvall's Bluff about noon, we waited a long while for "red tape" to furnish proper transportation, and while climbing and sliding around the muddy hills, had ample time to contrast the past

Brig. Gen. Eugene A. Carr. Carr commanded Steele's
Cavalry Division on the Camden expedition and took
charge of the District of Little Rock afterward. He was
supposed to command the 33d Iowa and five other
infantry regiments detached from the Department of
Arkansas for transfer to New Orleans but was relieved
after a drunken display at De Valls Bluff on February 6,
1865. *Photo courtesy of Massachusetts Commandery
Military Order of the Loyal Legion and U.S. Army
Military History Institute.*

and present appearance of the place.[3] Some time in the afternoon
we embarked on the steamer *Paragon,* and started down the river.[4]
To men who have been either lying in camp, working on fatigue-
duty, or tramping over the heaven-forsaken pine swamps of
Arkansas, so long as we had, there is a pleasing novelty in marching on a steamboat, even with all the discomforts of the manner in
which soldiers are packed and stowed away.

Tying up at night for safety, we went steaming on down the river
next day; and at a little before 1 P. M. came in sight of the noble
Mississippi again, with feelings of gladness and welcome, and soon
afterward rounded to and went ashore to camp at a little huddle of
houses where a small squad of Union troops was stationed.[5] The
gun-boat *Tyler* lay here; and the sight of her brought back to memory
the "bloody 4th" she helped us celebrate at Helena. Next morning,
the 16th, the *Paragon* having gone up the river, we went on board
the large and splendid steamer *Ben Stickney,* and went speeding
southward, rejoicing in the increased room she gave us.[6]

At noon we reached Vicksburg, the historic city. Lying up there
till night, we had time to wander around and see the fortifications,
and note the traces of the mighty contest.[7] And the more we saw,
the more we wondered—not that it took General Grant so long to
take the city, but that it was ever taken. Leaving Vicksburg that
night, we found ourselves on Sunday, floating down the low, luxuri-
ous and orange-laden banks of the lower Mississippi;[8] and at three
o'clock in the afternoon of the 19th, arrived at New Orleans.[9] Some
members of the regiment had been there before; but to most of us
the scenes had all the charm of novelty and of contrast with all we
had left behind. As soon as the boat tied up for a few minutes to
another boat lying at the levee, the fruit-women and juvenile ven-
dors of all sorts of basket-fixings came swarming to us like the
locusts of Egypt. We were all "nearly strapped;" but the oranges
must be had, and in many cases the last cent went for them. The
fact is, human beings in army-blue and under such circumstances,
can't stand more than a certain amount of temptation.[10]

So soon as the necessary reports could be made to head-quarters,
and the necessary orders obtained, we crossed the river and landed
on the Algiers side.[11] There was considerable delay in getting all
our things off the boat; and it was dark and raining when we

reached the flat, open field, not far from the river, which was to be our camp for a few days. All sorts of rumors were current as to our further destination, but most of them tended to Mobile Bay. Every thing now seemed strange and novel. Baggage and transportation were cut down to limits that seemed exceedingly slim, even to us "old soldiers" as we almost thought ourselves. Next day, our extra clothing and other property was packed in boxes, and sent home by express, or stored in the city.[12]

Tuesday night, February 21st, was one of the most uncomfortable times we had experienced. A heavy rain came on, flooding the low, flat ground to the depth of two or three inches, leaving us either to sleep half buried in water, or to get up and wade around till it should fall away. It was a cheerless crowd, that looked like so many drowned rats in camp next morning.[13]

On Thursday, the 23d, marching down to the nearest landing we went on board the *Izetta,* an old side-wheel boat that looked as though she would hardly hold together to cross the river. She did, however, and more too; for she carried us up and down, here and there, forward and backward, seeking the proper landing, for some thing less than half a day.[14] Toward night the rain commenced; and right in the midst of it, between seven and eight in the evening, we took the cars on the Ponchartrain railroad; and after a crowded ride of nearly an hour were unloaded at the wharf on the lake shore. Here was confusion, in almost utter darkness. Only those who have tried it can imagine the bustle and vexation of moving a regiment with all its baggage from the cars to a boat under such circumstances. To make it worse, there was not transportation for all of us. Three companies were put on board the little river-boat *A. G. Brown,* three more on the gulf-steamer *Alabama;* and the remaining four companies had to wait for another boat.[15]

For our first experience on salt-water, between the lake and Navy Cove, we had smooth weather, and met with no difficulty. Some of the weaker stomachs had to settle accounts, but most stood the smell of the brine without a murmur.[16] Passing the little island, of blue-clayey appearance, where once Fort Powell[17] stood, in the neck of the bay, we began to see some of the obstructions which had impeded the advance of the Union fleet some months before. Lines of piles as far as the eye could reach extended across the bay.

Touching for a few minutes at Fort Gaines,[18] which had so oppor-
tunely surrendered in the preceding Fall, and passing the historic
Fort Morgan,[19] which, terrible as we supposed it to be, looked like
nothing more than a long, low sand-bank mounting one or two
guns, we moved on up the bay, and entered the little harbor of Navy
Cove, four miles above the extremity of Mobile Point.

Soon after landing, the advance-companies of the regiment
marched over to the place assigned for our camp, on the gulf side of
the point, and prepared for a stay of several days.[20] Mobile Point is
a strip of land, some four or five miles long, and about a quarter of
a mile wide, extending from the mainland down between the gulf
and the bay. Nearly the whole of it, at any rate, all the lower part,
is a mere bank of sand, on one side washed to a series of low
hillocks, by the endless surf of the gulf, and on the other, smoothed
to a level beach, by the placid waters of the bay. Near Fort Morgan,
at its lower extremity, were camped some regiments which had
been there since the fort was captured. From the fort to the cove,
extended a railroad, with a rolling-stock of a single locomotive, and
a few platform-cars, sufficient to convey supplies from the landing.

Near the cove commenced a kind of swamp in the center of the
point. This was filled with water, grass and alligators.

Around its edges were thickets of thorny bushes, strange weeds,
and a kind of dwarf palmetto. A few straggling old houses stood
near the landing, occupied by the families of pilots and oyster-men.
North of these, and connecting with the bay, was a shallow pond,
almost lined on the bottom with small mud-oysters. Beyond this, a
rather heavy and swampy timber-land commenced, which seemed
to have no limits but the horizon. The whole place seemed strange
and wild, and in no wise like any country to which we had been
accustomed. No description of it could convey a full and proper
impression. Mobile Point was an episode in our military experience;
and if at first, its novelty was pleasing to some, all at last agreed
that it was an excellent place to get away from.

It was glorious fun for us, while the novelty lasted, to go out and
bathe in the surf of the gulf in the hot forenoons; or to walk at night
along the beach, where every step stirred up showers of phospho-
rescent sparkles, that looked as though the very sand were latent
fire; or to wade for oysters in the shallow pond above the cove, and

forget our baked heads and cut and bruised feet, in the tantalizing prospect of fried oysters for supper; or to gather a crowd on the edge of the little swamp, and endeavor to capture an alligator; or to watch the fairy-like sailing craft and war-like steamers, as they glided to and fro, so near us.[21] All these were pleasant at first, but the novelty would not last forever. The discomforts, on the contrary, were present continually. There was endless heat above, and restless sand below,—sand, sand, sand in every thing. Mouths, noses, ears and even eyes were filled with it, and victuals were all seasoned with the everlasting and omnipresent nuisance. To partially balance this, was the strange but grateful fact, that we had only to dig holes a few feet deep in the sand, on the gulf side, to find plenty of the freshest and purest water.

On Monday afternoon, the remaining companies of the regiment arrived. On Wednesday, the 1st of March, Rev. P. P. Ingalls, agent of the Iowa State Orphans' Home, addressed us, and organized subscriptions for the Home; and next day addressed us again. Our regiment contributed four thousand and five hundred dollars.[22] In a day or two after our landing at the cove, shelter-tents were issued to us, and were unanimously considered a very disagreeable novelty. We hated to huddle ourselves into little cloth kennels, hardly big enough for dogs. All despised them, and many savagely prophesied that before two days of marching, they would be all thrown away. Within a month, however, opinions changed; and the men who had so severely derided the dog-tents, were willing enough to carry them for the use they gave. Experience soon showed that they are decidedly better than no tent at all.[23]

Company-drill was commenced on the 6th of March, more perhaps for the sake of exercise than for any other reason. On the 8th there was a brigade-inspection and review, under Major-General Osterhaus, which was a very tiresome affair, in the hot sun and sand.[24] Far south as we were now, and advanced as was the season there, we were by no means beyond the reach of cold. Thursday night, the 9th of March, it was so cold that it was almost impossible to sleep, and we actually shivered, and suffered perhaps more than ever at night before. Saturday, the 11th, most of the gun-boats that were lying at and near the cove, cleared decks for action, and steamed off up the bay. During the day we heard from that direction the sound of heavy cannonading—that low, dull rumble of the gun-boat bolts, which afterward became so familiar.[25]

The next Tuesday was a day of rain and discomfort. The most we could do was to stay in our little dog-tents and exist, in a sort of apathetic sullenness, like so many animals.[26] The Chaplain, poor fellow! who was not so old a soldier as the rest of us, had pitched his dog-tent very carefully, but in a hollow of the sand; and the rain made almost a floating island of his habitation. The poor man got an old cracker-box and put it in the centre of his tent, piled himself on it, on his knees, wrapped in his blankets, and resigned himself to fate with a look of stoical endurance that would have shamed a martyr. To make the situation more uncomfortable, some wretched jokers took turns through the day in going up to the front of his dog-tent, giving him one glance of mischievous commiseration, and then expressing their fellow-feeling by barking like dogs. Words would have been weak in comparison.[27]

So, all the time the weather varied; rain and cold, sunshine and heat, each more intense by contrast. Perhaps we never had more little discomforts at one time, than crowded about us during our stay at Mobile Point; yet the memory of those days will always have a tinge of pleasantness, because every thing was so new and strange.

CHAPTER XVIII.

TO SPANISH FORT.

Short notice was given us of the march from Mobile Point. Our transportation was already cut down to the lowest notch; and there were standing orders, from head-quarters of the military division, that all the troops should hold themselves in readiness to march at a moment's notice. Having been assigned to the 3d Brigade, 3d Division, 13th Army Corps,[1] our brigade-commander was Colonel Conrad Krez, of the 27th Wisconsin;[2] division-commander, Brigadier-General Wm. P. Benton;[3] and corps-commander, Major-General Gordon Granger.[4] This organization was retained until we went to Texas.

Thursday afternoon, March 16th, the order came for us to move next morning, with three days' cooked rations in haversack. We had already on hand the rations that were to last us an additional day.[5] Whatever may be the theoretical view of the case, it is practically certain that for a man to carry, in a sack slung over his shoulder, all he is to eat for four days, and this weight in addition to his knapsack, gun and rigging, is no laughing matter. That night, in the very nick of time, the long-looked-for mail arrived, with news from home about a month old. Next morning at 6:30, the march commenced. The day proved perfectly beautiful. Moving up the beach on the eastern side of the point, we soon entered the wood, left the gulf behind, and after a march of eight or ten miles, pitched camp in a very good place at about 2 P. M.[6]

The next day's march was ten miles, through pine timber, over alternate marsh and sand. In the morning there was a jolly scene, when we waded across a small and shallow arm of the bay. The whole division formed in columns closed in mass; and at the word all proceeded to roll up their pants and prepare to wade. Wade it had to be, for there was no other way of crossing. It was a scene for a comic artist—those heavy columns of blue-coated infantry busily engaged in rolling up the legs of their pants until, like so many boys at play, they struck into the water, and with shouts and laughter waded easily across. Some where about noon, as we were marching through the interminable pine wood, the noise of merriment rose in front again. As we neared the place, the cause was seen. An old negro woman, apparently half-crazed with joy at the sight of the Union army she and hundreds of the race, companions in suffering, had so long prayed for, was standing near the road as the column passed her, shouting, dancing, crying and laughing, almost hysterically, in the vain effort to express her overflowing feelings. "Glory, Hallelujah!" she shouted; "Glory Hallelujah! The Lord's done heard us! Glory! There's eight hundred of us praying for you at Mobile! Go on! Go on! Glory, Hallelujah!" And then the poor creature would dance, and shout and sing, cry and laugh, all at once, while the tears coursed down her worn and wrinkled cheeks as she beheld the army which to so great a portion of her race seemed the harbinger of jubilee, and almost as the coming of the Lord.[7]

It was a pathetic yet ludicrous incident; and the smile mingled with the tear among us as we went marching on. It was no new thing to us, to be hailed by these bondmen as their deliverers; yet if we some times stopped to think of it, there would come a strange question, how much we really deserved their gratitude? But thinking is the very least of a soldier's business; and so the incident and its impressions passed out of mind together, as the important trivialities of the march succeeded. Sunday night our camp was pitched in the midst of the endless forest of tall, straight, almost branchless pines.[8] The ground was flat, smooth, clean and dry; and the camp would have been an excellent one if only wood and water had been near. It may seem odd that in a pine forest should be no wood to burn; but such is very nearly the actual fact. Green pine is abominable fire-wood. Pine knots were scattered around quite plentifully, and we used them for fuel; but they smoke the victuals so in cooking that the soldier will for that purpose, take any other wood in preference. Water was plenty, but not near camp; and what there was, was but a shallow pond where the rain-water had not yet had time to evaporate or become absorbed. A large camp of men and animals will use a great deal of water, and dirty up much more. Men must wash their faces and hands, at least, and to get water for coffee in the center of a little pool, all around whose edges men are washing hands and feet, is not calculated to make the coffee set well on a fastidious stomach.

The next day we lay in camp, waiting, for our place in the train to come along, till about four in the afternoon; and then marched four or five miles. Across the road in one or two places lay the ugly carcasses of alligators, which some of the advance-party had killed and left there; and it was by no means nice to speculate upon the probability of having such an ungainly "insect" some night as a bed-fellow. To explain how alligators came in a dry-pine wood, it should be added that there were occasional ponds and swamps, and these were found near them. Being train-guard, our regiment was divided into two or three squads, and scattered among the train. As night drew on, of course the wagons stuck in the swamps worse than ever. To add to the beauties of the time, a heavy shower came up. It was late in the night when the right wing of the regiment, wet to the bone, chilled and tired, reached the place, where in the middle of a large turpentine-orchard, the camp had been pitched.[9]

The term "turpentine-orchard" may for Northern readers need some explanation. Such an "orchard" in full vigor is a dense, unbroken forest of young pine trees, each of which at a certain age has been tapped by a large chip off one side. The turpentine slowly oozes from the wound, forms a thick coating over the abraded surface, and settles in the hollow at its bottom. Usually the trees are carefully tended, and the turpentine gathered at the proper time; but in this orchard the trees had been neglected, till there was now a thick mass of solidified turpentine on every one. There was warmth for us, and novelty withal; and soon the trees were blazing furiously. Each one would burn fifteen or twenty minutes before its supply of turpentine was exhausted. Whether the process was good for the tree or not, we really did not stop to inquire.

Wednesday was spent in sending back details, taking nearly all the troops by turns, to build corduroys for the last few miles of road, along which the train had "stuck" with remarkable uniformity.[10] At one time, meanwhile, by some accident or carelessness, the forest had been set on fire not far from us; and now the huge volumes of smoke rose black and nearer. The bright, lurid flames played round the trunks of the trees, whose stores of turpentine increased the intensity of the conflagration, till it seemed as if the whole camp must perish, miserable but insignificant, in the growing ruin of surrounding flames. But a certain feeling of terror was the only damage it caused us. Either because the fires of the preceding night had exhausted the combustibility of the trees near camp, or for some other reason, the fire did not come near enough to give us much real discomfort, beyond that vague but deep and "realizing" sense of what would be our own littleness and powerlessness if He who rules the elements had not restrained them.

The wagons having finally got out of the mud, we started on again next morning, moving nearly all the way through the unvarying pine wood, but noting with a real feeling of welcome and joy, the appearance of trees and bushes of a more familiar leaf and living green, as we neared Fish River.[11] This deep and narrow stream we crossed at about half-past two P. M., of the 23d, on a wooden pontoon-bridge which had been laid by men sent around on boats before us. By order from General Benton, every band in our division struck up "Out of the Wilderness" as its regiment crossed the bridge.[12] Moving on up to the high grounds a mile or so from the river, we were marched and counter-marched in various places, and stopped and formed in camp-arrangement here and there, to see how the brigade would fit the ground; and finally settled down to camp.[13]

General A. J. Smith's command, the 16th Army Corps, had arrived here before us.[14] As it was expected we would take some little rest before the whole column moved on farther, the camp was, therefore, laid out with great care and regularity, wells dug, sinks provided,[15] and arrangements made as if we might remain a month. We were now part of the largest army with which we had ever been, and therefore felt "invincible against any force the enemy might send against us."[16] Soon after we had camped, another mail was distributed, strengthening and cheering us with the thought that we were "though absent, not forgotten."

Saturday, the 25th, the column commenced moving in the morning; and by half-past three in the afternoon, it had stretched out so that we took our place in the line of march. We made but about six or eight miles that evening, and then camped so far a head of the wagons, that they did not come up that night. The consequence was, that many a poor officer, whose blankets and provisions were in the train, had to lie down supperless, on the bare and chilling ground, and take what little sleep he could, by the warmth only of the half-tended pine-knot fires.[17] Sunday brought no rest. Rising early, we marched on as usual; and at night camped within two miles of the "Spanish Fort" which was expected to hinder further progress.[18] A change of employment for us, was now to come.

CHAPTER XIX.

THE SIEGE.

Sun-rise of Monday, the 27th of March, saw us in arms, and making ready to move forward. The command was finally formed in column by battalion, properly placed and directed, and at 9:30 the advance commenced. There were frequent stops, mysterious runnings to and fro of officers and orderlies, changes of position by artillery and skirmishers, and all the usual indications of premeditated battle. At 10:20, occasional artillery-firing began, and at a quarter after 11 the first rattle of musketry was heard on our left. The siege had commenced.

Some where within a mile of the rebel fort,[1] our regiment was halted, and lay till nearly dark. Meanwhile a rain came on. Having nothing else to do, we huddled under the trees for shelter, while occasionally some one would go to the front to see what was going on. Early in the evening we were moved forward to our position in the main line of attack which was thrown almost entirely around the land-side of the rebel works, and rested at either extremity upon the bay. Our regiment was the extreme right of the 13th corps; and the 16th corps extended its left around to join us.[2] In the first day of the siege there was much reckless and unpardonable risking of life. Some regiments, for no possible reason but the drunken bravado of general officers, were for hours held in the most exposed positions, in close formation, without shelter of any kind. It was fortunate for the 33d that we were not so ordered.[3] The field-pieces in our main line of attack kept up an occasional firing till some time after dark, but the rebels did not reply very much. This seemed like weakness then; but we afterward learned that they had their guns double-shotted with grape and canister all the time, in readiness for the charge they expected us to make, and from which few of us could have ever returned.

Night at last brought quiet. At day-light next morning, a single bugle sounded reveille; and soon the "ball opened" again. Heavy details were kept on the skirmish-line, and relieved in the day-time. This was all wrong. Several men were wounded while being thus relieved;[4] and soon the details refused to be relieved in the day-time, preferring to remain in their shallow lines, and holes of partial safety, rather than to risk the full exposure of their persons so near the rebel works, for the mere sake of coming back to camp. The time of relieving was therefore changed, and a company or two at a time sent out.[5] The number of casualties was from this time much smaller.[6]

Corporal Haydock, of Company E, describes one or two incidents so vividly as to give a very good picture of the skirmish-line, which was the main scene of action during the siege.[7] The following are very nearly his own words:

"On the night of the 29th of March the enemy charged us and attempted to capture our advanced line. Our company was sent before day-light on the morning of the 29th, to relieve Company K on that portion of the skimish-line directly opposite our regiment. We left camp about three o'clock in the morning, with a day's rations and one hundred rounds of cartridges. Arriving in the vicinity of the rebel fort, we had to march very stealthily to prevent the enemy from hearing and slaughtering us before we reached our ditch. The road was a miserable one to advance over, being covered with fallen trees, whose tops pointed mostly outward. Every now and then a minnie ball[8] would whiz through the air close to our heads, making us dodge, and think it was aimed for no one especially. Once in a while we would come to a deep and narrow pit, containing two or three "bummers"[9] who had let their courage ooze out at their fingers-end before they reached the front ditch. These fellows would lie in their holes all day, and fire at the enemy over the heads of the men in advanced line, making them wonder if they were not in more danger from friends than foes.

Deploying our line, we advanced with a considerable low whistling and other signaling, to the works which had been thrown up the night before by Company K, close to the enemy's line. I was considerably amused at the Dutch (27th Wisconsin) who were on our left. When I came up, I came on them. By that time, the enemy

were firing very briskly. I asked one of the Dutchmen where our
company was. "Get town here, G——tam you!" was all the response
I could get. After blundering and stumbling around for some time,
I got to our ditch. The Dutch were now relieved; but one of them
was left in the ditch asleep. One of our boys shook him, and asked
him if he did not belong to the regiment that was relieved. He
roused himself up, and replied that he did. We told him to go on to
camp, and he started to go; but the flash from the enemy's guns,
accompanied by a warning from some of us to "keep low," so frightened the poor boy that he commenced describing a circle, and performing various other antic feats, which reminded me very much of
a pig with the "blind staggers." "Here, this way, this way," said some
one, pointing with his finger. "Vich vay, vich vay?" replied the poor
frightened boy, as he climbed over our works and was on the point
of running over toward the rebel fort. Some one caught him by the
heels and dragged him back into our ditch; and, after a deal of
crawling and creeping, hither and thither, he started off in the right
direction, and we saw him no more.

By this time it was growing light; and we found ourselves in
front of the rebel fort, so that we could pour our fire directly into
their embrasures. Before it grew too light, we busied ourselves in
improving our ditch, by digging it deeper and throwing the dirt
over in front for protection. Through the day we watched the
enemy's embrasures so closely that they could not use their guns
with any effect. At one embrasure they ran out a huge, grim mon-
ster of a siege-gun, but we kept up such a peppering that they were
glad to withdraw it without firing. About this time the large rebel
fort opened upon our skirmish-line. We would closely watch the
huge pile of yellow dirt seen dimly in the distance; and presently
we would see a dense volume of smoke rising, and "down" would be
our warning. Down we would fall, to the bottom of the ditch. In a
few seconds we would hear a loud explosion, and looking in its
direction would see the smoke curling up in fantastic wreaths from
where the shell had burst.

We were directly between the rebel fort and one of our own batteries, which opened during the day, so that our own shots passed
directly over our heads. One struck very near us, and and bounded
over toward the enemy. Another exploded close to our ditch. By this

time we began to fear our friends. In the afternoon, the enemy appeared very anxious to drive us from our advanced position, and accordingly planted a small mortar so as to bear on us, and fired it at regular intervals. Whenever we heard the report we would watch closely, and could see the huge, round missile slowly ascending, describing a curve like a large foot-ball, and then it would come to the ground with a terrible explosion. In the afternoon I became so fatigued that I went to sleep, with the shells bursting all around me, and the minnie balls whizzing above. I had never before imagined that one could sleep in such circumstances.

The rebels were in the habit of passing before a certain embrasure. J. E. Young,[10] of our company, had his rifle leveled at the place with his finger on the trigger, when a "yellow-coat"[11] passed the opening. He pulled, and down went the Johnny. Another one came along and picked him up. That night, half of us wrapped ourselves in our gum blankets and lay down to sleep; but the rain pelted us so heavily we could not sleep much. At mid-night my relief came on. I sat down in the ditch, with my blanket wrapped around me, thinking how comfortable it would be to be some where else, when suddenly I heard a sharp, heavy rattling of musketry on our left, accompanied by loud cheering. At the same time our vedette gave the warning "The enemy is advancing upon us." Three times he gave the warning, without ever flinching or giving back, although the rebels were close upon him; and then he climbed up into the ditch.

I awakened the boys as quickly as possible; and Sergeant Redpath[12] gave the order "Fix your bayonets, men; and when they come up, punch them back." This order, in his cool, deliberate tone, served to re-assure the men; and in less than a minute every man was loading and firing rapidly. "Buzz, buzz," went the bullets over our heads; but a perfect stream of fire from our ditch kept the enemy at bay. The ditch was too deep for some of us to fire with ease, so we climbed out and gave it to them. Our boys did bravely. We had no chance for retreat, so every man determined to measure bayonets if it were necessary. The enemy had determined to capture our skirmish-line that night, as we had crawled too close for their gunners to work their guns. But our boys convinced them that night that Mobile was a doomed city."[13]

The duty of the main lines of infantry, drawn around the rebel works, was simply to protect themselves, and furnish the tremendous details. Not only the regiments themselves had to be protected by breast-works, but every head-quarters, from brigade on up, must have a heavy line of earth-works in front of it. The artillery-fire of the rebels was not slacked after the first day; and there was great need of protection. Shot and shell occasionally came altogether too close to be convenient. The country immediately around Spanish Fort seemed to have been specially formed for us to lay the siege. Deep gullies, separated of course by ridges or knolls of earth, formed a rough likeness to concentric circles which, connected by the heavy breast-works of logs and dirt, constructed in profusion in an almost incredibly short time, constituted our parallel lines of approach and defense. To aid the fitness of the place, an excellent and copious brook ran at a convenient distance, and good springs gushed from the little hills. Evidently nature had intended Spanish Fort to be besieged.[14]

There was now a certain monotony about the days. Very heavy details were sent out to work on the fortifications; and as their work drew near a close, or became of less importance, they would be relieved by smaller details, or discontinued. One night Lieutenant-Colonel Lofland had been out with a detail of three hundred men; and in the morning a corporal came out with his squad and relieved him. Perhaps that is the only instance where, in due military order, a field officer was relieved by a corporal. The companies out on the skirmish-line, two at a time from each regiment, had occupation enough, having approached so near the opposing line that frequent conversations took place between them and the rebels. A miniature commerce in coffee and tobacco was at least much talked of, if not carried into actual effect; for as there were no sutlers' shops allowed with this expedition, tobacco had now become almost as scarce with us, as coffee among the rebels. Stories were told of a lieutenant leading his men by mistake into the enemy's skirmish-line, and of his learning his error and moving back to his own proper base, with an ease that only the darkness of the night and the nearness of the contestants to each other could account for.

The body of the regiment, as well as of the other parts of the main line, had merely to construct the necessary protections—a work which proved no trifle. The din of reveille dwindled down to a bugle in the early morning; and no sound of bugle or drum was allowed during the day; yet brass bands at the different general head-quarters would make the wood ring with their practice for hours together. We were now for the first time in a regular siege. There was no time in the day when one could feel at all certain that some rebel bullet or shell might not come singing or whistling along especially for him; but it must not be inferred that we considered this uncertainty always as a very serious matter. There were times, indeed, when no one would travel around more than he had good cause for; but much of the time there were men scattered along the brook, washing, or traveling between the line of attack, and the hospitals and trains, which kept themselves at a safe distance in the rear.[15]

Occasionally there were some narrow escapes. One of these was particularly noticeable. In that part of the line which Company D occupied, there was the stump of a tree, which had been cut down for the breast-works. One day a number of men were standing around it, chatting, when a shell came over, and cut in two a musket sticking in the ground near by, struck the stump, and passed on without hitting any person. Those who were there, said that it would seem impossible for any thing to hit the stump, without going through some one of the men, who were gathered so close around it.

Wednesday night, the 29th, the rebels made a bold sortie, and penetrated almost to the main line of our works. There was confusion in camp for a few minutes; but the affair did not last long.[16] The rebels went back more hastily than they came, and gained nothing by their daring. Reports and rumors were now thicker than ever. The rebels at Mobile were doing this, and were going to do that. They were going to surrender, to hold out to the last, to charge on us, and to retreat. In fact, there was nothing they were not going to do, (and we too), except what was really done. On the morning of the 31st, the regiment to the right of us, having moved away, our regiment took a "side step to the right," and occupied their place. They had not only built a heavy breast-work in front of their position, but had constructed bomb-proofs of logs and dirt, partially dug in the ground, enough to shelter themselves entirely. For some cause or other, we had not yet made any protection for ourselves, except the earth-work in front, as ordered, although, nearly or quite all the other troops in the line, had done a great deal of such work; but now upon moving into bomb-proofs already made, we went at work and enlarged and strengthened them. The whole ground was dug in holes, and looked like an oblong of gigantic burrowers. This was by no means useless labor. The firing was of course irregular, and some times almost entirely ceased; but there were spells, as always just before sun-set, when the artillery on both sides would open briskly, and then, when the rebel shot and shell began to whistle closer over us, the bomb-proofs were welcome and crowded; and it was not cowardice but common-sense, which demanded the protection.

About sun-down of the 31st there was a decidedly lively time for a few minutes. The cannonading on both sides was heavier than it been before; and piles of brush lying between the opposing lines were set on fire, either by accident or intentionally, and lit up the scene to almost grandeur.[17] Though the siege had now lasted but four or five days, we felt already well used to it. The regular booming of the half-hour guns was an accustomed sound; and the lively contest of artillery just before sun-down was looked for as a thing of course. Soldiers soon learn to adapt themselves to circumstances. The routine of camp was readily adjusted to the place, and followed with as cheerful carelessness as ever. Laughing and joking abounded.

For several days there had been talk of an issue of tobacco by the quarter-master. It seemed almost too good to be true; but on the 3d of April the tobacco came, almost as welcome as pay-day or a mail. On Wednesday morning, the 5th of the month, the 7th Minnesota came back to their old position, and we had to vacate. A new place was assigned us, about a mile further to the left but in the same main line. It had been occupied by some other regiment, and was almost honey-combed with bomb-proof works; which did not seem to be very effective; and our first business therefore, was to enlarge and improve them, until at last we made them so snug, that many of us would have almost been willing to stay there for the rest of our term of service.[18]

The firing grew all the time heavier. On the evening of the 8th, the gun-boats, which had been taking part but occasionally in the contest, began launching their tremendous bolts in solid earnest. As darkness came on, the scene approached the sublime. The bay was entirely hidden from us by the wooded hills, but the shells from the gun-boats could be distinctly seen as with majestic slowness they described their brilliant arcs, and fell point-blank in the rebel fort almost at the instant of explosion. The gunners seemed to have got the range perfectly. On land, too, the siege-guns which had been so long in coming up, were now in position; and for about an hour on the evening of the 8th there was such a cannonading as we had never heard before. The whole artillery force of our army and gun-boats opened in one terrible storm of fire, so concentrated on the rebel fort that it seemed almost impossible for it to endure a repetition.[19]

That evening we noticed a little circumstance, which seemed odd to us then, and which in earlier days might have hastened exertions on to victory, or been accepted as an omen of defeat. The evening was clear, and the moon shone bright in the southern sky. Some where about 8 o'clock, we saw three very small halos, or circles, of various colors, like the rain-bow, around the moon. The effect was weird and beautiful. Ordinary "rings around the moon" are common enough; but three small rings, brightly and variously colored, in the midst of a cloudless sky, were to us as novel as they were beautiful. There were some who thought the sight portended some thing; and perhaps it did.

That afternoon and evening there was much heavier cannonading some distance up the bay, than we had heard before. General Steele with his negroes was evidently pounding away at Blakely;[20] but there seemed to be nothing new in store for us, and we went to sleep as usual. About mid-night a shout arose. Our forces, pressing closer on the rebel lines, had found the fort just evacuated; and with joy and tumult they rushed in and took possession.[21] The thirteen days of siege at last were ended. We were vexed that the rebels had succeeded in retreating; but to have driven them from their strong-hold was cause enough for joy. Many of our regiment were so eager and excited, that they could not wait till morning, but tumbled out of bed, and went up to see the fort by moon-light.[22]

Sunday morning, the 9th, was rainy and disagreeable. Reveille was sounded on the drums for the first time since the commencement of the siege. Orders soon came for us to be ready to move immediately; but not all of us could restrain the curiosity to see what we had been so long fighting about, and so we had to go up and see the fort. A strange sensation came over us as we climbed, unhindered, over the breast-works and walls, from which a few hours before we would have been swept off with a storm of fire had we attempted to scale them. We were glad enough no "charge" had been ordered; glad, indeed that our position had been on the outside and not inside the fort, the center of such a rain of iron and lead, it showed the marks of conflict every where. There was hardly a square yard of ground in or near the fort which was not torn by shot or shell. Along the top of the inner wall, logs a foot or so in diameter were laid, as protection for the heads of the sharp-shooters stationed behind them; and one of these logs, on the side opposite that part of the line last held by our regiment, was so scarred that not a finger could have been laid on it without covering the mark of a bullet.[23]

The fort—or rather, Battery Huger, as the name of the main work seemed to be—must have been a terribly hot and uncomfortable place during the bombardment.[24] Looking at the traces of ruin and devastation around, one would hardly think it possible that human beings could have lived there and worked the guns, under such a storm of death as beat upon them; and indeed we remember that during the last two days the rebel fire had gently slackened, and finally dwindled to nothing. But the fort evidently had been well supplied with arms and ammunition. Some of the cannon had within the month been cast at the Selma Arsenal. The largest gun, a splendid one-hundred-and-twenty-pound Brook's rifled, had been dismounted by a shot from one of our batteries or gun-boats.[25] The other ordnance was numerous enough, but very various in construction and caliber, though none of them were heavy.[26]

All around the fort, at a suitable distance from the outer walls, the ground was planted with torpedoes set in a double line, such as would be described by the corners of a common rail-fence made with rails a foot or two shorter than usual. The effect of thus planting them, was that no column of men, even so small as four abreast, could have passed over the line without hitting the torpedoes. This same diabolical plan of defense we afterward found in use at Blakely—diabolical, because it was as likely to work destruction after the contest was over, as while it lasted, or even more so; as likely to kill the victor as the enemy.[27] A description of the torpedo may not be useless.

A heavy shell of cast-iron, about the average size of a twenty-four-pound round shot, is perforated with two holes. One of these serves simply to admit or draw out the powder, and is usually secured by a screw cap. Through the other hole runs down a compound substance that communicates the fire to the powder that fills the shell. At the upper part of the substance is a material which will ignite under a sudden pressure of about four pounds. Over this, when the torpedo is in the arsenal, is screwed a thick and solid safety cap; but for actual use, this heavy cap is taken off, and an inner one exposed, consisting of copper so thin that a pressure of four pounds will force it down suddenly upon the explosive compound beneath.[28] The torpedo so prepared, is set in the ground just enough to let the thin cap appear above the surface. Any ordinary foot-step will now cause the explosion, which will in all probability shatter to fragments every thing near it.

The torpedo was an unaccustomed weapon of warfare to us; and it was perhaps for this reason that many, if not most of us, feared them more than bullet or shell. Men, who would have hardly been careful enough of themselves against the missiles of the battle, were very dubious as to torpedoes, and would examine the ground minutely for the little sticks which served to mark the place where a torpedo was buried. At Spanish Fort, as afterward at Blakely, several men were killed by the explosion of torpedoes, after the grounds came into our possession. At Blakely, after the rebel works were captured, squads of the rebel prisoners were set at work, taking up the torpedoes which encircled their lines; but it is probable that many of them were overlooked. Likely enough, the farmer who shall yet plow over the land, where the outer lines of Spanish Fort and Blakely extended, may suddenly strike the cap of one of these terrible shells, and be blown to pieces. Thus the weapon the father prepared, may turn against the son.

For protection from the tremendous fire of our artillery, the rebels in the fort had dug holes and winding ways in the ground, inside the works. It was said that after its evacuation, a number of sick and wounded were found in these holes, and that two or three days afterward, a rebel officer of rather high rank, was found concealed at the extremity of one of the covered ways. But we could not stop to explore much. Another regiment was detailed as guards at the fort, and we were of the number ordered forward.

CHAPTER XX.

HITHER AND THITHER.

Breaking camp on the morning of the 9th, without a thought of its being Sunday, we formed line a little way out in the wood, and drew rations while halting for a few moments. There seemed some thing almost ludicrous in the idea of issuing those two barrels of sour kraut, with the other rations, to men all in line and ready for the march, and whose only means of carrying food was in their haversacks; and in fact the kraut disappeared so fast in other ways that it was not issued.[1] Military discipline and routine are some times so absurdly impossible, that on some occasions harm results from the lack of a reasonable approach to them.

The march of Sunday was of only ten miles' length, but was very tiresome. On the way, the knowledge spread that we were being pushed forward to Blakely to take part in a charge on the rebel works there. Some time before we reached the place, however, the news met us that the charge had been made, and the victory won.[2] We were badly behind-hand, but it was no fault of ours. The charge had been made before the expected time—without orders, we were told—and won by the most recklessly desperate fighting. Had it not been for a sort of Western independence and individuality of action among the troops composing General Steele's command—negroes though many if not most of them were—we should have had part in this last important action of the war.[3]

Next day, the 11th of April,[4] lying in camp about a mile from the rebel works, we had time to rest and look around. A heavy mail, arriving the night before, had given us the latest news from home, and was forthwith answered by one almost as heavy. Many of us spent the forenoon in looking at the prisoners taken, and examin-ing the rebel works. One squad of prisoners, comprising part of an Alabama regiment, was camped near us, in charge of a detail of negroes. We could not but observe that these Alabamians were a very different class of men from those to whom we had been accustomed in Arkansas. More nearly in uniform, with their strong and active physique and hearty bearing, they looked more like "foemen worthy of our steel." Between them and the negroes, however, there seemed to be some old grudge to settle. No display of feeling against the prisoners was allowed to be manifested: there was no sign of "crowing" over a fallen foe, no taunting or insult allowed or attempted; but we could often hear expressions of the deepest hate and vindictiveness from dusky lips when away from the line of guards. Who shall know how many and deep tragedies lay there concealed; what wrongs but partially redressed; what burning sense of injustice and shame that called so grimly for the captive masters' blood![5]

The rebel works at Blakely were extensive, as indeed the rebel works in Alabama always were—always such as would require a force from two to ten times as great as they could ever have, to properly man them. Whose the fault may have been, we could not tell, but its existence was always noticed. Little as we might understand of the theoretical art of war, we had for ourselves fully learned that earth-works, to be effectively available, must not be too extensive for the force likely to defend them. At Pine Bluff, Arkansas, General Clayton had resisted repeated attacks from a force greatly out-numbering his own command; and we could plainly see that his success was partially due to the great concentration of his lines of defense.[6]

The town of Blakely, so far as we could discover, existed almost solely in name.[7] We were told that there had once been a number of fine houses there, and that the town was a well-known watering-place for the beauty and fashion of Mobile. No semblance of such prestige now remained. At the usual landing-place on the bank of the Tensas river, a large crane had apparently been just scared out of the job of mounting a couple of heavy cannon which lay near it, just arrived from the Selma Arsenal. One small frame-building, formerly a grocery, now stood dirty and empty by the street. Several wall-tents, made of the coarse but strong cotton cloth which plainly showed its Southern manufacture, were used as hospitals, and filled with rebel sick and wounded. And a large shed, which had been used as the arsenal, was well stored with torpedoes, shell, shot and other weapons, with the remains of such quarter-master's and ordnance papers as the absconding officials had not taken away. Many of these scraps of paper, of evidently Southern manufacture, were gathered to be sent North; but their interest is now only that which can attach to the millions of similar relics which may be found in the thousands of Northern homes.

The left of the rebel line of defense rested on the deep and narrow Tensas river, of which this bank was a bluff some twenty feet in hight, and the opposite was a low, swampy flat; and its continuation was a series of earth-work, aggregated at every salient point into batteries of varying strength and size, interspersed with palisades and isolated pieces of artillery, and additionally strengthened by the most impregnable abattis we had ever seen, piled high in double, triple, and some times quadruple rows. How men could charge over such lines of defense, we, ourselves not wholly ignorant of warfare, could not imagine; but probably if we had been in the fight we should have known as well as any, and done our share. A negro soldier, who was in the terrible charge, understood the matter in its practical application. As he stood near the works, examining the ground over which his regiment had gone into the rebel lines, the lines of sharp-pointed brush and limbs of trees rose piled up higher than his head. He was a powerful fellow, of the purest African blood, and with all the African fire and fervor. When asked how on earth the men could ever have charged over that most formidable abattis, his eyes glistened, and his quick tongue found the ready though uncouth answer: "Golly, mass'r! Nebber knowed dat ar brush-pile was dar!"

Artillery, ammunitions, rations and all the material of war, seemed to have been abundant among the rebels; and their capture in such quantities, at an early period of the war, would have been considered worthy of conspicuous mention. Now, it was over-shadowed, even among ourselves, by the news of the capture of Richmond. At last, after all the lingering years of uncertainty and effort, Richmond was indeed ours! Often before, in our varied service, we had cheered over reports of its capture; but now, when the news was joyful, and almost undoubted truth, there rose not a cheer. With deep, but quiet thankfulness and joy, we felt that the "backbone of the rebellion" was now indeed broken, and peace must be near. We could endure till the end should come.[8]

There were reports many, and hopes many.[9] Much speculation was hazarded as to the surrender of Mobile. Some man over in the rebel works, early in the morning, looking across the flats and bay, to where the city of Mobile was dimly visible, had discovered some thing there, which seemed to him to be a white flag waving. He called to some one else, and the look was doubled, with the same result. All day long there was a group collected on the spot, continuing the observation; and all arrived at the same belief, though to all it seemed almost impossible, that they could see a white flag floating over Mobile.[10]

Receiving orders on Monday, to be ready to march at a moment's warning, we lay in camp till Tuesday evening, the 11th; and by that time there came news that Mobile was evacuated. The report that reached us, was to the effect that our division-commander had received the news, and, intoxicated with joy, or some thing else, had sworn that his division should be the first to enter Mobile. Some thing of the kind seemed to be in the wind; for at about dark on Tuesday evening, we broke camp again, and turned to retrace our steps toward Spanish Fort. The night was beautifully moon-lit; the report of the evacuation was more than half-credited; and we started out in high spirits, singing and laughing as we marched along. But the tramp proved exceedingly tiresome, before it ended.

Colonel Krez, of the 27th Wisconsin, then commanding our brigade, had managed to acquire the reputation of never getting on the right road. Coming up to Colonel Mackey, at Spanish Fort, one day, he had complained of the bad conduct of some of our boys. "Dey says me Chris," he urges; "dey calls me lose de vay. As I catch 'em, I punish 'em bad." In our ignorance of the occult principles of "military necessity," after the head-quarter's interpretation, we could not feel at all delighted, at being on different occasions put under the command of bloated beer-casks, whose only antecedents were, that they used to keep a saloon. On this mid-night march, when all were tired to the last extreme of unmurmuring endurance, of course the worthy brigade-commander must lose the road. Against the advice of his staff-officers and others, and in default of precautions which ordinary common sense would have provided, he led us off on a wrong track, and had to waste perhaps an hour of marching, before we were finally set right again. The curses of the tired soldiers were loud and deep.[11]

At about two in the morning we reached the bay at Stark's landing, two or three miles south of Spanish Fort. Here we were to take steamers to cross the bay; but were compelled to lie around on the sand, as best we might, and wait for daylight. As early as practicable on the morning of Wednesday, the 12th, we embarked on the fine steamer *General Banks,* used then as the head-quarters of General Granger, whose corps only was moving; and so commenced the crossing for the occupation of Mobile.[12] The morning was foggy; but soon the sun shone out merrily upon the rippling waters, and lit up a scene of military splendor such as we had never beheld. Transports and gun-boats, in single or double lines, with signal-flags rising and falling, and colors proudly flying from the mast-head, moved slowly but majestically across the bay. One or two of the gun-boats were provided with machines for raising the torpedoes with which it was feared the course was strewn; but no trouble occurred.[13] As we neared the western shore there was a greatly-increased display of signal-flags. One gun-boat advanced some distance ahead of the fleet, and threw a single shell as challenge to the shore; but no answer came.[14] Again the signal-flags waved bravely. The gun-boat on which were the head-quarters of the fleet now moved nearer to the *General Banks,* and the portly and bedizened form of Admiral Thatcher appeared majestic on her deck.[15] Turning dignifiedly toward our boat, with a slow and rotund pomposity of manner that words could not convey, he called out "I-propose-to-shell-the-shore." "By———, you'll shell a flag of truce if you do," profanely answered General Granger. The ludicrousness of the situation became apparent when on looking shoreward we saw that all this tremendous array of "fleets, armies and artillery" was thus to be brought to bear against a solitary negro, whose feeble hand waved a white kerchief tremblingly.[16]

It had been the intention to take our regiment to Mobile by boat, but upon further consideration it was not deemed wise to hazard so many lives against the torpedoes which were known to obstruct the channel.[17] The General therefore went on in the boat, and we disembarked over the rotten and broken old wharf at Codfish landing.[18] A

delay of an hour or two ensued, and then we fell in with the column, and marched on toward the city, over the "shell road" of which
we had heard so much, and of which too much could not be said in
praise. Hard as a rock and smooth as a floor, it wound for five miles
along the edge of the bay, shaded by beautiful trees and adorned by
the neat though humble residences of the Creole population. It was
such a delightful change from the rough places where we had usually been, that it must ever hold a place among our bright memories of pleasant scenes.

Still more and better news from the Potomac, drifted through the
higher channels of official information, now came down to us. Not
only was Richmond taken, but Lee's army was captured, and
Petersburg ours. We could believe it now—and nothing seemed too
good to believe. The war must be now virtually ended; and we felt
sure of soon seeing home. Such was our feeling as we went into
camp that night, on a nice, green field, near a part of the main
defenses of Mobile, designated as battery K.[19] Among all the extensive earth-works with which we were now environed, this was the
most elaborate and completely finished we had ever seen; and citizens near there said it was the pride of the rebel engineers.
Artillery abounded along all the works; and had the Johnnies made
a stand they could have given us serious trouble. If they had been
Yankees, or at any rate, if they had been Western men, they would
never have bloodlessly yielded all those elaborate lines of defense
simply because the enemy had captured the works across the bay.
Near this part of the line had been a rebel camp, evidently hastily
abandoned. Numerous relics were obtained here; and many were
the cedar canteens which our boys afterward carried as mementoes
of Mobile.

Next morning there were strict orders to the effect that no man
or officer should leave camp to go to town. The orders were much
more strict than was the obedience to them. Men had not fought
and marched and waited all those weary days before Mobile, to now
quietly be deprived of perhaps their only chance to see the city.[20]
That night there were many men for extra duty, brought to it by
unauthorized absence from camp when the roll was called in the
morning. A little before noon we were called into line; and our division marched on through the city with colors flying, drum-corps
doing their noisy best, and as much display as the ragged and dirty

condition of the uniforms would allow.[21] Every body, except the white folks, turned out to see us.[22] Little delay was allowed. The rebels had retreated up the Mobile and Ohio railroad; and forthwith up the railroad we started after them. At the little town called Whistler, some five miles out from Mobile, were located the manufacturing- and engine-shops of the road; and word had been received that the rear-guard of the rebels had just been committing depredations there.[23]

Marching on a railroad is no pleasant way of traveling. It does very well for a while; but one soon gets tired of straddling from tie to tie, especially if he wears a knapsack. Reaching Whistler at last, we piled all our baggage, except fighting-gear, on the ground, and prepared for a skirmish. Our regiment went forward some distance on the double-quick, but could not come in soon enough. Other regiments, reaching town in advance of us, had done the business. The enemy was only a squad of some two hundred rebel cavalry, as we afterward learned, who had remained behind the main body of the army for the sake of plunder. Had their number been known at the time, there would have seemed some thing ridiculous in rushing to attack them with a whole division of infantry; but they made quite a resistance, as it was, and in the skirmish three of our force and sixteen rebels were killed.[24]

This was the last preparation for battle that we ever saw; and our part of it ended in standing near the railroad for a few hours, and then, toward dark, going into camp, in the wood, in a nice place near town. Next morning, of course, the camp had to be moved again; and then we fixed ourselves up as if to stay for some time, which we really more than half expected. We could not see that there was any further fighting to be done; and the best probabilities seemed to be, that we should remain there in camp, till ordered home for muster-out.[25] But in military matters, as in life generally, the most unexpected thing, is the very one that is sure to happen. The boys were always ready enough to form acquaintances among the ladies of any place, where we might happen to stop; and at Whistler, perhaps on account of our prospective stay there, a peculiarly auspicious commencement for society was made. It seemed too bad to see all these dreams of rest and comfort shattered; but we must be of those to whom "there is no peace."

CHAPTER XXI.

UP THE TOM B.

Wednesday, April 19th, reveille came at 3:30 in the morning; and in two hours we were on the march again. Though only seven or eight miles were accomplished that day, and camp was reached before two o'clock; it was a very hard march, on account of the intense heat, and the length of time we went without stopping.[1] There should be short halts, of perhaps five minutes' duration, made regularly every half-hour, by a column of infantry, on the march; and unless some such precaution is carefully observed, especially in the heat of a Southern climate, there will result much misery, which might be avoided.

There is some thing strange and peculiar in going into camp in the wood at night, as we did on the 20th. When the regiment is near the rear of the column,[2] and all the others get into camp and settled, before we come up, and the gloomy Southern forests are made all the more gloomy and picturesque, by the blazing camp-fires piercing the darkness, every tree and bush, and hollow in the ground, takes on a new aspect as imagination tries to picture the general appearance of the place. Here, you fancy, must be a deep ravine; and off at the left there must be a river—the trees appearing to open, so that you want to walk down to the water's edge to see farther. So one always tries to form some general idea of the ground of camp; but when the morning comes, lo! all is changed. What you thought was the ravine, proves to have been but a couple of logs; the supposed river is only the edge of a prairie, or of a cleared spot in the wood; and the whole scenery, which last night you fancied must be so novel, and pleasant, is now by day-light, as common and prosaic, as the increasing light of age shows most of our youthful illusions to be.

"Reveille at 3 o'clock," was the order again on Friday morning;

and hardly had the drums and fifes ceased their rattle and squeak, when the rain began to patter too. Getting up in the morning, and making fires, and cooking coffee and hard-tack, in the midst of a soaking rain, is very easy to write about, but not the most cheering and comfortable of realities. It has a tendency to make soldiers either very grum, or very jolly; and generally we chose the latter, which proved to be the better way.[3]

Early in the forenoon we passed through the grounds of the United States Arsenal at Mt. Vernon, which was unanimously pronounced to be among the loveliest spots our ennuied eyes had seen. The place appeared now to be deserted, but not much injured.[4] If we had been ordered to stop and garrison the arsenal, we would have obeyed with even more cheerfulness than the army regulations require. But we were not the fortunate ones. The word soon passed round that the 29th Iowa was to remain, and that we were to go on a few miles further, and build a fort.[5]

How reports and conjectures start in the army, we used always to wonder, and shall probably find out when it is discovered "who struck Billy Patterson." Frequently the rumors are far enough from the actual truth; but generally they have some little foundation, though the fact at the bottom is usually so distorted by the accretion of opinions and surmises, that the man who first told the story would never recognize it after the fourth expedition. Some thing of the same kind may have been observed in civil life; but so numerous and definite and positive are the rumors of a camp, or an army, that it became a standing joke to tell that the commanding General was coming down to our quarters, some evening to hear the news and learn what was going to be done.

From the arsenal to our camp that night, the march was not long, but it was a hard one. The rain that had been resting for a while, commenced again with renewed vigor, and soon drenched every thing. Every gully was a creek, and every creek a river. The very road itself, for perhaps a mile or two at a time, on the more level places, was covered with water, through which the splashing column waded drippingly.[6] At half-past 11 our camp was reached, in a pine swamp, near the Tombigbee river.[7] Much difficulty was experienced by our accomplished brigade-commander, in finding the worst possible place for us, and even more than the usual marching and counter-marching in consequence ensued; but finally the ground was chosen so that the whole brigade might rest in line. Military discipline, as interpreted by martinets, may require that in a mere bivouac for a night or two, not less than in regular Winter-quarters, the whole force must be disposed in strict line and order, whatever else may be the result; but Common Sense, if it had ever had the pleasure of commanding a body of soldiers, would, on all such occasions as this, have consented to much irregularity of line for the sake of the comfort the men would gain by having the best ground for camp.[8]

On Sunday, April 23d, the terrible news reached us of the assassination of the President. The blow was so sudden and so strange that we could hardly realize it; but there was left no room for doubt. The feeling with which the terrible event was met in the North will never be forgotten; and to this feeling in all its force we added a certain wrath and vengefulness. We felt as they may feel who see their homes destroyed by Indians. Had we been allowed the privilege of meeting twice our number of rebels then, there would have been no prisoners taken. But we had seen our last enemy in arms; and this rage gradually died away, leaving only that deep grief which the whole loyal nation felt, and must forever feel, over the mighty fallen. Never was man so loved as Abraham Lincoln.[9]

Two days of rest gave us an opportunity of cleaning the mud off our clothes, and part of the rust from our guns. Tuesday morning, the 25th, the left wing of the regiment was sent up the river about ten miles, to McIntosh's Bluff, on the gunboat *Octorora*;[10] and the remainder of the regiment went up on the *Jennie Rogers* in the afternoon.[11] McIntosh's Bluff, dignified by the title of navy-yard, contained one old dwelling-house, three or four new and unpainted frame buildings, a saw-mill and a black-smith's shop. At a little distance from the river there were also several log buildings, which had been used as quarters by the mechanic's who worked at the yard. The place had been one of considerable importance to the rebels, who had repaired and even partially manufactured their steamboat-navy there. Little or no injury appeared to have been done to the works or buildings by the retreating Johnnies; and our soldiers soon set things running again.[12]

Moving up in the wood, half a mile or so from the river, our regiment proceeded to clear off a place for camp, with the rest of the brigade. The shanties were of course appropriated as officers' quarters; but the camping-ground was excellent; and by the help of shades made of boughs and brush, we soon had things fixed quite comfortably for the some what lengthened stay which we expected. This part of the country being comparatively uninjured by the war, there was of course considerable forage to be obtained; and our boys could not justly be accused of neglecting any opportunities, though the strictness of the orders from division head-quarters soon prevented any foraging to amount to any thing.[13]

When soldiers camp in the wood in Summer, and expect to stay some time, as we did here, it is amusing to see what improvements they will make. In a little while our whole camp-ground was nicely cleared off, streets laid out, ample shades put up, wells dug, and preparations made for as much comfort as possible. The band-quarters were even nicer than usual. The boys had set their dog-tents in a row, on light walls of boards and stakes to make them higher; had built a long and heavy booth over the whole of them, dug a well and covered it, made themselves tables and seats in the shade, and even started a barber-shop, with a sign made of a piece of cracker-box badly lettered with shoe-blacking. The impression had now become pretty general that the war was over, and that we would probably stay here until ordered to Mobile for muster-out.[14] Hoping this, and half-believing it, we felt like making the interim endurable as might be. But there were two or three companies who thought they hardly "got the worth of their money," when they kept details laboring faithfully for several days at digging a good, large well, and got it down some twenty or thirty feet, without finding water, when the order came to move. So calculations in the army, as elsewhere, prove very uncertain, though disappointment does not often have as pleasant a flavor as it did in this particular instance.

The colored people seemed to have heard of the "good time coming;" and from all the country round they flocked to our lines. For the first two or three days after our arrival, flat-boat after flat-boat came floating down the river to us, laden with negro-men, women and children, pigs, chickens, bed-clothes, rags and tatters, dirt and all, crowded and piled in promiscuous confusion. These people did not have the air of being as badly treated at home, as those of most other places we had seen; but they still had some idea of freedom and the Yankees, and were willing to risk themselves in trying them. It must be confessed that the reception they met, was not always such as to impress them favorably toward either freedom or the soldiers. Our regiment generally stood among the best in point of civility and kindliness to all; but there were some among us, even mean enough to "take" chickens from these poor creatures, who had thus come among us helpless, and so nearly destitute. The negroes, *en masse,* were provided for, probable as well as the post quarter-master could do under the circumstances; but the unaccustomed roughness of military treatment, though meant in kindness, must have seemed to them in many cases, harder than their accustomed ill-usage at home.

On the 28th, the news reached us of the surrender of Dick Taylor's army—the last organized force of rebels east of the Mississippi.[15] We heard it with joy and thankfulness.[16] The war was now surely over, at least on land, and east of the great river. But the rebel fleet which had gone up the Tombigbee, was still above us, and it was our business to be ready for their coming down.[17] A large fort was planned, on the bank of the river, in such a way as to fully command its passage; and work on it had already been commenced. The saw-mill was pushed to the hardest to get the necessary lumber ready; and heavy fatigue-details were kept at work to build the fort. It was to be an honor to all concerned. But, things did not get ahead fast. The men all believed that the war was over, and the fort would never be of any use; and so they would not work, and could not be made to work. All ways of detailing were tried, from the usual squad from each company, up to a whole regiment, colonel and all; but still the fort would not grow very much. It lacked the pressure of apparent reason. One regiment at Spanish Fort would throw up more dirt in a single night, than all the details did here, in all the time of our stay.

So the days passed—work and rest alternating, but work having greatly the advantage. Saturday morning, the 6th of May, a boat came up the river with a load of paroled prisoners from Lee's army.[18] In a little while, the news spread that the rebel fleet above us, was to come down soon, surrendered, and we were to go with it to Mobile.[19] Great was the cheering and jubilation; for going to Mobile, then seemed to us to be surely the first step for home. Next morning, at a quarter after eight, the first boat of the rebel fleet, came in sight; and as her side swung round so that the name *"Jeff. Davis"* could be read, she was greeted with a cheer from the crowd that gathered on the shore.[20] We would indeed have been very glad to meet the original Jeff. under similar circumstances.

By the next morning, the whole rebel fleet had arrived, with one or two exceptions. Here now was food for curiosity. Here were two of the gun-boats which had thrown "railroad freight-trains" at us, at Spanish Fort; here was the little, black tow-boat-looking craft, yclept the *Diamond,* which had once been rigged out as a gun-boat, by the rebel ladies of Alabama, who had given up even their ear-rings and other jewels for its preparation; and perhaps, even a greater curiosity to us, was the low, rakish-built blockade-runner *Heroine,* with its peculiar wheels, and its alleged powers of running eighteen miles an hour. What scenes had not these boats been through! and what romance might be written of them! They were ours now; and into the hands of our division, this last and most important naval surrender seemed now to be made. Some amuse-ment, by the way, was occasioned by the finding, on one of the boats, of a tin sign, emblazoned in large, gilt letters, with the words "Taylor never surrenders."

The rebel officers commanded much attention, from the portly Commodore Farrand,[21] with the handsome woman in black who was currently reported to be his mistress, down to the youngest and smallest of the grey-backed and gold-laced gentry.[22] The peaceable sight of rebel officers was not then as common to us as it afterward became. Before the boats had all arrived, details for work on the fort had been discontinued by order of the division-commander in person. Spades suddenly stuck fast in the ground, and picks were at a sudden discount. Fort something-or-other, which was to have been an honor to the gallant General, &c., &c., was *mortum in embryo.*[23] The General said there must be wood enough cut to run the boats down to Mobile, and we would go as soon as that was done.[24] In a little while the whole wood rang with the sound of axes; and if ever four-foot-wood was cut and piled up faster, it must have been because there were more men to do it.[25]

At last the welcome order came for the start. Never were knapsacks packed more cheerfully than on this morning of the 9th of
April.[26] We had reveille at half-past three, were ready to move at
five, started about nine, turned back, started again, stacked arms
and waited a long time on the bank of the river; and at last
embarked. Seven companies and head-quarters of the regiment
went on board the *Magnolia;* and the remaining companies on
another boat.[27] At half-past twelve the signal-gun was fired; the
various bands of martial-music, and one brass band belonging to
the division, sent out their most lively strains; and the fleet started
off in due line and order down the river. Good-bye, navy-yard; and
ho! for Mobile.

CHAPTER XXII.

DELAY AND DISAPPOINTMENT.

The trip down the Tombigbee river seemed to us but preparatory to that long-hoped-for one which should take us up the Mississippi to our homes. But we soon found to our sorrow, that "there's many a slip 'twixt the cup and lip;" and many a weary day would roll around ere we could finally turn our faces homeward. Day-light had come, indeed, but the sun-rise was not yet near. We reached Mobile at 8 o'clock on Tuesday evening, and after a delay of two or three hours, marched out north of the city, to find a place for camp. This was by no means a cheerful time. Though the distance was only three miles, it seemed nearer a dozen. The dismal swamp over whose dreary length we had to pass, was resonant with the doleful croak of frogs innumerable, and every one of them, to our imaginative ears, seemed to call the name of our brigade-commander. "K-r-e-e-etz, K-e-e-e-e-tz" they sang, and a hundred or so of voices in the regiment would echo it in a little more intelligible English, but with even more doleful emphasis and drawl, as they thought of the frogs and King Stork in the fable.[1]

Camp was reached at last—a bare and comfortless place, on which we merely tumbled down to sleep as best we could. Next day our regimental-commander found an excellent place for us, near the bank of the river, and within the lines of some old earth-works about three miles above town. Here, under the shade of the noble trees, we cleared off and fixed up a neat, well-arranged and comfortable camp. On the 11th we drew eight months' pay, and settled clothing account for the second year. This made us rich; but our jollity had an off-set in the report that we were to go to Texas. Kirby Smith, it seemed, refused to surrender; and we were to help convince him of the necessities of the case.[2] This was a terrible drawback to our comfort. What reason or justice was there in it? There were plenty of veteran troops in the army; why could they not go, if any had to, and let us go home as we ought? And so the time passed, between hope and fear, till the worst was finally known.

Mobile soon became a familiar place to us. Nominally, there were all the restrictions upon leaving camp, but practically few of the men stopped to ask many questions when they wanted to go. In a day or two, the boys had gathered so many skiffs and canoes from the different wharves in town, that there was a regular fleet of them. Regularly every morning, the whole collection would be manned by soldiers who wanted to go to town. It was but a pleasant row down the river; and for the return-trip the wind generally blew, so that a few leafy boughs, erected as sails, would quickly and easily waft the little fleet home.[3]

The city was now full of rebels, paroled from Dick Taylor's army, who still retained their rebel uniform and opinions, and made no attempt at concealing either. They would talk freely, and with all boldness, generally seeming willing to acknowledge that they were whipped for the present, but confident of a more successful conflict with us in the future. Some were anxious to go over and join Kirby Smith. A few, perhaps, were willing to accept the logic of events, and settle down to quiet citizenship; but certainly, the greater number were rebellious as ever, and wholly unsubdued in thoughts and feelings.[4]

We could not be in town all the time; and as there was now no duty to perform, the time hung slow and idle on our hands. With eight months' pay in their pockets, and nothing to occupy their minds, many of the boys soon got to gambling excessively. "Chuck-a-luck" banks were set up in the wood a few steps from camp, and surrounded all the time by crowds of eager players.[5] The story was the same as in all such cases: the "luck" all gradually centered in a few, and these generally the ones who kept the banks. There were some who gained a considerable amount of money by their gambling, but by far the greater number lost the most of their wages. Starting, of course, among the lower and more ignorant of the soldiers, the excitement soon spread till it involved many who had usually been supposed to hold themselves far above any thing of the kind. Our regiment was not alone in the matter. The practice was universal. Every where, if there was a camp, there was gambling; and every where it was characterized by the same features. Much of the hard-won earnings of many a poor soldier went away from him at the rattling of the dice, while his family at home, hitherto so well remembered, were perhaps suffering for the help it should have given them. But gambling seemed epidemic, and reason in abeyance.

Of course, the mails now had even more than the usual interest for us; and certainly the folks at home, could not accuse us of neglecting them. At one time our regiment sent out five hundred and ninety-six letters, beside papers and parcels, in a mail that had been but three days in gathering. For some cause or other, rations were now better than usual; and they seemed more abundant, because so many of the boys bought their own food. Perhaps our regiment was peculiar in this respect; but most of us seemed determined to have wholesome food, rather than army-rations alone, whenever we could get it; and at ten cents a pound for bread, and sixty cents for butter, with other things in proportion, of course, the money flowed freely away.

These now were days of suspense and doubt; of good news one hour, contradicted by bad the next; of rumors and counter-rumors; of hopes and fears.[6] As to our future, there seemed to be a general state of "don't know." If any of the officers were better informed than the privates about it, they certainly had succeeded in acquiring unprecedented reticence. One day an order would come, such as to immediately start a report that we must soon go home; and the next, another order would give a sadly-contrary impression. We wished to shirk no duty, and never had shrunk from any thing required of us; but this prospect of being ordered to Texas, was one that the most patient could not cheerfully contemplate. We felt that we ought to be at home.[7]

So the days wore on—days of rest, indeed, but weary with suspense and hope deferred. Lying dreaming, under the shady trees, we could look across the bay, in an afternoon, and see the red lines of Spanish Fort, marked distinctly in the sunshine; and as we remembered the long days of fatigue and danger there, and their relation to the present time and circumstances, we could not but wonder whether the next month, witnessing as great a change, should see us safe at home. Home, home! How dear the Northern

Summer seemed to us, with its prairies that blossomed so peaceful and smiling; and how inexpressibly, tenderly dear those loved and loving hearts, that waited patiently and trustingly for our coming, and the fond eyes that would thrill us with their loving gaze, and the gentle fingers that would clasp our own! We had been absent long, in hardship and danger not less than others; had faithfully fulfilled our promises; and now we thought the end should come.

> "The light that shone in the soldiers' eye,
> Was a longing thought of home."

But the monotony of waiting was broken at last, by an event of the most terrible destruction, sudden and fearful to the city, as unexpected and overwhelming battle could have been to soldiers. At 3 o'clock in the afternoon of Thursday, the 25th of May, the warehouse in the northern suburbs of Mobile which was used as a storehouse for ammunition, and then contained many tons of shells, torpedoes, cartridges and powder, exploded, with a noise such as he might hear, who should be shot from a one-hundred-pound cannon. We, who were in camp, were perfectly astonished, but could not imagine the cause of the terrible sound. In a few seconds, the vast and majestic column of smoke that rolled slowly, curling and wreathing upward, told the nature of the explosion. The papers of the time, described the event as well as they could; but no words can convey an adequate idea of the ruin and devastation thus in a single second wrought. Those who saw it will never forget, and those who did not, can never imagine the appearance of the city, after the catastrophe. It is not positively known that any of our regiment were injured by the explosion; but one member was never heard of afterward. Whether he was blown up, or drowned, or whether he took the occasion to desert, was never known.[8]

On the 27th, the official report was received of the surrender of Kirby Smith. The war at last was over.[9] Had the end come suddenly, our joy would have been extreme; but the steps, though so great, had been so gradual and successive that when the first was passed the rest seemed easy. The end had come; and we thanked God. Should we not soon be at home? The suspense had not long to last. Mysterious are the ways of military government. Ignorant of their groundlessness and injustice some times, we obey without a murmur, orders which, if we had more knowledge of the circumstances, would be met with just and indignant disobedience. Had we known at the time, the whys and hows of the order which sent us to Texas, it is possible that some men of the regiment would have been so reckless in their anger, that the General who gave the order, might in five minutes have repented of it to the end of his life.[10]

For a number of days we were under orders to be ready to march at an hour's notice; and on the morning of the 31st the notice came.[11] At two in the afternoon, we were on the move. Knowing it must be a sea-voyage which should take us to Texas, the boys had provided themselves with sacks and boxes of extra provisions, which, had the trip been a march, could not have been carried half a day. But ships will carry a great deal; and the only limit to each man's baggage seemed to be his ability to take care of it. Marching slowly and laboriously down to the city, we rested on a wharf till some time in the night;[12] and then embarked on transports, which took us out to the good ship *Continental,* on which, with a part of another regiment, we stood out to sea.[13] The smell of salt water was no more new to us; but it takes more navigation than we ever tried, to keep a landsman's stomach steady when the ship falls away from under him continually. Sea-sickness is nothing new, and needs no description here. Happy are they who have never known it![14]

With pleasant weather, a comparatively smooth sea, and no remarkable event on the way, except that no lives were lost from thus crowding human beings in a ship, like hogs in a slaughter-pen. The voyage passed quite monotonously;[15] and the 6th of June found us off Brazos Island.[16] Months before, we had heard of this place as one of the worst where soldiers were ever stationed. It was said that they could not even have water to drink, except what was distilled from the sea. We had congratulated ourselves then, that duty had not called us there; yet here it was now before us, and we felt some what as the wicked may feel, who at the end of life have full belief in purgatory.

The channel at Brazos is so shallow that no ships drawing more than nine feet of water can safely pass. The troops were conveyed to the shore by a small steamboat used as lighter, which had to make several trips over the tossing waves to get a single ship unloaded.[17]

On one of these trips, those who were on board had perhaps a nar-
rower escape from death than they had ever known in battle. The
waves ran high; and the frail craft struck bottom several times so
violently that the crew, and others who knew the danger, began to
think their time had come. But here especially ignorance was bliss.
Most of the men on board knew little of the danger until it was
past. Nothing serious actually happened; and after a few more
thumps the little steamer passed the bar, and soon reached the
landing in safety.[18] We were glad enough to set foot on land again,
bare sand though it was; but even the land seemed rolling and tum-
bling occasionally, as bad as the unstable billows; and it was some
time before this feeling wore away. The dangers of the deep were
over for the present, but comfort was no nearer.

CHAPTER XXIII.

THE HOUR IS ALWAYS DARKEST THAT IS JUST BEFORE DAY.

The island which bears the euphoneous Spanish name of Brazos de Santiago, is a low, flat, sandy place, but a few feet out of water; and among its greatest faults is the fact that it is out of water at all.[1] General Taylor's army had gathered here, before the invasion of Mexico; and from the observatory on the flag-staff in front of head-quarters, could be seen with a glass his old battle-fields of Point Isabel and Palo Alto, while Resaca de la Palma was almost in sight. There were men in our regiment who had been here in his army; but the memory of those days was very little help to them now. However, if his army could stand it, we could.[2]

We were here now as part of General Steele's army of occupation, which, hastily thrown together, had not yet been duly subdivided and organized. Our brigade-organization had been partially retained, but beyond that there was little definiteness.[3] Orders for a small detail for fatigue-duty would come some times to the regiment direct from head-quarters of the army. Except the necessary fatigue and guarding of camp, there was no duty to be done; and to merely exist between the blazing sun and an oven of hot sand, with no protection from the one, but the little dog-tents, and no screen from the other, but such bits of boards and wooden boxes as could be gathered and saved among so many men, was the round of the monotonous days. A salt-water bath occasionally lent variety; but there were sharks in those waters, and it was unsafe to venture far from shore.[4]

On the eastern side of the island, where we were now camped, there had for some time been a small military station. A regiment of negroes was now on duty as garrison; and their daily guard-mounting and parade were objects of much attraction to us, their

proficiency in drill being the greatest we had ever seen. The whole
regiment would go through the bayonet-exercise with more uniform accuracy than any single company of white troops in our
knowledge. Whatever else may be affirmed of the negroes, it need
not to us be denied that they made excellent soldiers. As guards,
where white people also are concerned, they are not the most
agreeable, on account of too literal and unreasoning obedience to
orders.[5]

Near the landing, a number of small frame buildings had been
erected by the Government, and were used as head-quarters, ware-
houses, offices, hospital, &c. The condensing apparatus, by which all
the fresh water used there was distilled from the sea, consisted of
four steam engines, located in a building near the water's edge, and
having suitable tanks to hold the nauseous fluid as it was manufactured.[6] As the vile but precious stuff was issued only in scanty
rations, there must of course be a constant guard over the tanks
lest it should be stolen. The negroes were kept on this duty; and
their unreasoning fidelity to the literal words of their orders, with
their inability to read any writing presented to them, were the
cause of much inconvenience, and came near resulting in some
individual collisions.

The ration of water issued to the troops was at first a gallon
daily to each man—the whole allowance, for all purposes.[7] The
amount proved too great for the capacity of the condensers; and on
the 11th, the allowance was cut down to a half-gallon per day to
each. It may be supposed that this was scanty enough; but this
was but a part of the discomfort. The water had to be drawn daily,
like other rations; and there was almost nothing to keep it in.
Canteens, kettles, and every thing else were put to more use than
ever before. Hastily thrown together, in a strange country, and
under strange circumstances, the army had but few conveniences;
and the belief, which had gained ground, that we would not be
retained much longer in the service, had bred a slackness in feeling and discipline that would have greatly impaired the efficiency
of any detail, and which by no means added to the comfort of the
regiment. It was probably the fault of circumstances rather than of
persons.

The scarcity of water was now such as could not long be endured.

On the 14th our regiment, with nearly all the others, was ordered to Clarksville, opposite Bagdad, in Mexico, near the mouth of the Rio Grande, and some nine miles west of Brazos.[8] Here was plenty of fresh water, such as it was. The Rio Grande is a very swift and muddy stream; and its water now looked like very strong coffee into which some generous woman had put the milk and sugar—but it didn't taste that way, to any remarkable extent.[9] If an ordinary bucket was filled with it and left to stand over night, in the morning the water would be found clear and beautiful, with a sediment of mud two inches deep at the bottom. So purified, it was excellent to drink; and even fresh from the river it was better than the distilled water at Brazos, which always had a sickish taste, and was peculiarly calculated to upset the epigastric gravity.

Bagdad would doubtless have been a beautiful city if the site were better, and there had been plenty of nice buildings there.[10] As it is, however, it is a wretched and dirty place; but those who have worn shoulder-straps long enough to know, assert that its like is not to be found, as a place wherein to get some thing good to drink.[11] At first, wonderful bargains were to be had there in goods. Our boys would go over, either with or without a pass, some times by swimming the river, change a few greenbacks for gold with some broker on the street, and buy clothing for the happy days when every man should be a citizen. There were probably few among us who did not thus obtain some memento of Bagdad, and win at the same time the distinction of having been to Mexico.

Between living on a red-hot sand-bar at Brazos, and the same thing at Clarksville—as the place was called, where once a few houses may have stood—the difference, except as to the water, was mostly in name.[12] Existence became more like that of the animals than ever before; for in other places we generally either had some thing to do, or could do some thing. But here, what could be done? The heat was excessive, though there was always a strong breeze.[13] For fuel, the dependence was on the drift-wood which had floated down the river, and been washed on shore by the waves of the gulf. For a day or two, while the novelty lasted, there was much interest in the view of the French fleet and other vessels, lying off the mouth of the river;[14] in aquatic exercises in the surf; and in the strange appearance, desolate as it was, of the country generally;

but this did not last long.[15] A soldier of three years' experience, can exhaust the novelty of a place in a very little while.[16]

Clear down there, almost out of the world, as it seemed to us—and certainly out of the best part of it—we felt as if cut off from civilization. A good, heavy mail from home would have been more than ever welcome—and at last it came. General Weitzel and his corps of Africanos arrived the same day, but that did not seem an event of half so much importance.[17] Yet it was to us the dusky herald of the morning. On the afternoon of Saturday, the 24th of June, unexpected as an angel's visit, and more like that than any thing else, we as soldiers had ever known, came the order that the 33d Iowa Infantry was to be as soon as possible, mustered out of the service.[18] If bad news flies like the wind, good news some times seems to spread instantaneously. When the order was known in camp, there was such joy as only they can guess, who have had a similar experience, and it expressed itself in tumultuous cheers and jubilation.[19]

Tuesday morning, the 27th, we marched down to the landing at the eastern side of the island, to be ready to embark for Galveston. The day was excessively hot; and this last march of ours was one of the hardest we ever had. Many were compelled to lag behind, unable to move so fast over the scorching and yielding sand. But if guns and knapsacks and cartridge-boxes moved heavily, hearts were lighter than ever; for we were going home! But the winds and the sea were against us. A heavy surf had been for some days rolling. The steamer *Louise*,[20] which had been running as a lighter, had gone out just before we reached the landing; and we were therefore compelled to wait, though every minute of delay was hard to bear. Next day at eleven we went on board the *Louise* and started; but the sea was too rough, and we had to turn back again.[21] Thursday was no better. Would we never get started? The order would be countermanded before we could get beyond its reach.[22]

On Friday there was some hope; but in the afternoon a regular "Northeaster" wind and storm arose, which tore up the waves tumultuously, and seemed scarcely likely to leave the land. Lumber-piles tumbled, tents turned summersaults, and valuable papers from the Quarter-master's office were scattered like forest leaves. It was well for us we were not on the gulf. The sand-bank of Brazos was bad enough, but any thing immovable was better than that world of treacherous, tossing waves in such a storm. That night there was a heavy rain. The flat sand of the island was all the time soaked so full of water, that the rain fell almost as on a floor. In the morning, the whole eastern end of Brazos was very nearly an unbroken sheet of water. Thank Providence! it was our last night on the island.

At a quarter after eleven A. M., of Saturday, July 1st, we again went on board the *Louise,* and started, this time for good.[23] "The breaking waves dashed high," but we passed safely through the channel. The boat could not come any where near the ship *Warrior,*[24] on which we were to embark, so a couple of Mexican schooners were used as lighters; and at last, after much difficulty and some danger, we found ourselves and our baggage safely on board the ship, and under way for Galveston.[25] Farewell forever, Brazos de Santiago; and may our worst enemy never see thee!

The *Warrior* was a good, strong ship, sure though slow. We had plenty of room, and nothing to do but hope. Nothing remarkable happened. A sea-voyage at best is monotonous: what must it be, then, to a regiment of soldiers without reading matter, and without any accommodations but those their own ingenuity devised? The sea was not very rough; but the ship rolled considerably. The Chaplain's face became as that of a man who has lost all that makes life desirable; and he was not alone in his misery. There were more pale and sorrowful countenances among us than there would have been on land if we had been going to our own funerals. At about 8 P. M., of Monday, we entered the port of Galveston, and reported for further orders. Compelled to wait for the tide till next morning, we made the best of the opportunities the town afforded, among which were the most excellent water-melons our eyes had ever seen.[26]

The morning of the 4th was clear and beautiful. We were awakened by the lively music of a brass band in town, accompanied by a salute from a battery of field artillery. The 4th of July was being celebrated, even here in Texas, though probably none of the citizens showed any sign of participation. What must have been their feelings, as they reflected that now, for the first time in four years, the

cannon roared in honor of the day, in every State and Territory of
the Union! Our ship moved out at about five in the morning; and as
we passed the U. S. fleet, which guarded the entrance to the bay,
the gun-boats and some of the ships, were gaily decorated with
flags, looking jubilant and patriotic, as a delegation of uniformed
girls, at a Sunday School celebration. As for us, we sped on homeward, and thought of the "4ths" we had seen, and of those yet to
come.

At half past-five of Wednesday afternoon, we entered the Southwest Pass of the Mississippi, and thankfully saw our last of salt
water. It was joy indeed to see again the noble river; and our eyes
rested with delight upon the greenness of the grass and weeds that
fringed its banks. It was now a month since we had seen any vegetation, except the little at Galveston. But there is no rose without
its thorn. With the fresh water came the mosquitos, swarms and
myriads, murdering peace and sleep. At eleven we reached quaran-
tine, and were compelled to lie over till next morning, though the
delay was miserably irksome.

Thursday forenoon, among the new and welcome scenery of the
ever-varying banks of the river, was a school-house—a regular
school-house—strange sight to us in those days! A white lady officiated as teacher, and a whole tribe of little darkey children were
the scholars, the entire crowd of whom rushed out of doors as we
passed, and cheered and shouted welcome. This was the first greeting on our homeward way; and the incident gave cause for
thought. Passing the wreck of the rebel gun-boat *Webb,* which had
so boldly, recklessly run past our fleets and batteries on the way
down from Red river,[27] we came on, slowly but surely, toward the
goal of our immediate hopes; and at half-past twelve we entered
New Orleans.[28] The city seemed familiar, though our acquaintance
with it was so little. We looked across at our former camping-
ground at Algiers, but we cared little for it now; our thoughts were
of home.

By Friday noon a place was found for us to land; but before we
could get to shore the ship had to wander up and down along the
levee, very much as the old *Izetta* did when we were there before.
Disembarking at last, we were marched to the old "Alabama
Cotton-press," on Tchoupitoulas street, at the corner of Robin—one

of a number of large, deserted ware-houses in that vicinity. Here was abundance of room for our regiment, with such accommodations as would have seemed exceedingly comfortable in the earlier part of our soldiering.[29]

Now came days of unavoidable delay, while the papers were being made out for our discharge. Soon there was a scene of more literary activity, than our regiment had ever known. All the tables on the premises were appropriated, and new ones improvised; and pens and ink were in unprecedented demand. All the best penmen in the ranks had to suffer for their skill, by detail to help make out the muster-rolls. In justice to the officers, it must be said that they seemed anxious as any, to hasten the day of discharge. "Many hands make light work;" and so the multitudinous rolls which red-tape requires, before it will say to the waiting soldier "Depart in peace," were prepared with cheerfulness and speed.

But there was sadness among the recruits, whose term of service would not expire soon enough to let them out with the rest. They had the express understanding, when they enlisted, that they were to be mustered out with the regiment; and there was much feeling among them, when the order came now for their transfer to the 34th Iowa. One or two desertions took place among them. The recruits left us on the 13th of July.[30] How much justice there was in their feelings against the officers who recruited them, will not be investigated here. They did not lose as much by the transfer, as was expected, for the 34th was before a great while, mustered out.

As the time drew near for our starting North, our interest in the dry-goods market increased. Citizens' clothing came greatly in fashion; and there were few who did not lay in at least a partial supply. The benefit of new clothes were never more observable. Private soldiers Tom, Dick and Harry, laid aside their ragged uniform, and became Messrs. Thomas, Richard and Henry. And so the change from soldiering to citizenship came gradually. At last the probation ended; the last paper was finished, the arms turned over, the formalities concluded. The discharges which had been all made out, were sent to the mustering-officer, who signed them and returned them, when they were packed with other regimental-documents in a box, and placed in charge of Major Boydston, till we should arrive at the place of final discharge.[31] A little before noon of

Tuesday, July 15th, we left the old press, and marched joyfully down to the levee. Of course, the worst and slowest boat in the city, had been provided for us, and on the old and rickety *"Sunny South"* we embarked, at half-past two in the afternoon.[32] New Orleans was left behind; and we joyfully realized that now indeed, we were homeward bound.

CHAPTER XXIV.

HOME AGAIN.

The steamer *Sunny South* on which we were to ascend the Mississippi, was but a little craft; but we who were mustered out were not a whole regiment. Even if the crowding and discomfort had been manifold worse we should have felt cheerful and jolly; for the end was nigh. Every boat on the river passed us, and vexed us with every new comparison of delay; but still we bore along.[1] At a quarter after nine next morning we reached Baton Rouge, touched Port Hudson at 1:15, rounded to at Morganza Bend at five P. M., and reached Natchez at seven in the evening.[2] Here the old scow had to stop and repair her boilers.[3] Friday, we still lived; and at 5:15 in the afternoon the *Sunny South* tied up at Vicksburg. She was now pronounced unsafe; we were therefore transferred to another boat—the *W. H. Osborne*—which, though not the fastest craft in the world, was roomy, clean and comfortable.[4]

If one would form an idea of the greatness of this country, let him take such a trip as ours, from Brazos to Davenport. Accustomed all our lives to think of New Orleans as down South away toward the tropics, we had found ourselves going some three hundred miles northward to that city, and then commencing a steamboat ride of eighteen hundred miles on a single river to our northern homes. On Sunday evening, before sun-down we reached the mouth of the Yazoo Pass. Every eye was turned with memory's deepest interest to this scene of the beginning of our first expedition. But its appearance was changed since then; and what was deep water when we passed through the channel, was now dry land. It was dark when we touched at Helena, but the outlines of the place, though changed, were still familiar. How the tide of memories rolled over us, as now, homeward bound, our term of service out at last, safe whole and hopeful, we looked back upon the time when these hills and hollows of Helena were a present reality to us, and all the joy we now felt was then but a dream of the uncertain future!

It was but a little thing, yet it seemed a curious coincidence that among the passengers with us on the boat, was a man who had been a rebel Colonel at Fort Pemberton, on the Yazoo, when our forces attacked that position. He was quite talkative and companionable; and conversation with him gave an inside view of the conflict there, to balance the outside one of our own experience. Would all the rebel South prove courteous as he, that vanquished and victors should ever together talk over their battles, and thus in admiration of each other's courage lose the bitterness of the feeling which nerved them to the fight? Would it might be so!

One phenomenon which we noticed, seemed strange to us: On the morning of Tuesday, the 25th, the river where we were appeared to be rather low; and the boat took occasional soundings. By night, however, we found the river high, and frequently out of its banks. This may be nothing remarkable to men of more experience on the Mississippi, but to us it seemed strange. At a little after six P. M. of Tuesday, we reached Columbus, Kentucky, where our first real soldiering occurred; and at half-past nine, the lights of Cairo were before us. It had been our confident expectation, to leave the river here, and take the cars for Davenport; but there was no transportation ready for us, and so we were doomed to boat it the rest of the way. When this was known, there was cursing and gnashing of teeth. Many, who could not endure the prolonged suspense of the steam-boat passage, got off at Cairo, and procured their own transportation by railroad. As every day's travel brought us nearer home, the days and miles seemed to lengthen almost intolerably; and every minute's delay was noticed and irksome.

After reaching Cairo, we felt as though we were on free soil again, for the first time in almost three years. Yet there was little more appearance of welcome, than had greeted us hundreds of miles farther South; for all the way was much the same in this respect. As the boat passed houses along the banks, doors flew open, windows sprang up, kerchiefs fluttered, and the voices of children rang out the shout of greeting. At one place there was an especial expression of enthusiasm: A little crowd of women and children was gathered in front of a house as we passed, and their joy showed

itself even more exuberantly than usual. They waived their bon-
nets, kerchiefs, aprons, or whatever else they happened to have in
hand, and one woman, unable to get hold of any thing else in the
excitement of the moment, enthusiastically waived her baby. The
novel greeting was acknowledged by a shout and much good-
humored laughter.[5]

At 8 o'clock of Thursday morning, we reached St. Louis; and now
came a "realizing sense" that we were indeed, going home. Our
regiment was transferred to the steamer *Muscatine;*[6] and at 4:30
in the afternoon, we were again on the move. The river was much
obstructed by drift-wood, and the boat very heavily loaded.[7] Vexed
as we had been by delays and slowness, every slackening of speed
was noticed. "Making eight hours a mile," the boys would cry. "Who
kicked the boat?" the boys would halloo, when the speed was suddenly accelerated a little. Little Sergeant Crow, would stand on the
bow of the boat, and make piteous appeals to the engineer not to
run so fast and take away his breath.

The repeated soundings vexed the boys. "N-o bot-tom" had been
heard so often, in all the drawling and unearthly tones that could
be imagined, that we were sick of it. "N-o-o bottom—quarter past
twain—no bottom, *scant,*" and so on, with all possible varieties, the
lead-man's calls were echoed. River captains are always careful to
keep their boats trim as possible, by having the weight evenly
adjusted, so that the boat will set right on the water. Soldiers are
always crowding to one side or the other; and thus the officers of
the boats are always in trouble—some times, we thought, too much
so. "Oh! Captain," some one called out to the short but portly
Captain L——, who was standing on the bow, very near the center
of the boat, and looking to one side, "Oh! Captain, turn round; they
want to trim the boat," and some of the boys asserted that the fat
engineer kept walking from side to side, to preserve the balance.

At a little after 9 o'clock on the morning of Saturday, the 29th of
July, our hearts thrilled within us, at the first sight of Iowa. Always
proud as we were of the State, it had never seemed so dear to us as
now. Here were our loved ones, waiting to welcome us. Hail, Iowa!
ever in the van of Freedom, proud among the proudest, young,
beautiful and strong! Three years out of our lives, we had given to
the country's cause; here now was home again, with its peace and

rest. Hail Iowa! As we rounded to at Keokuk, a brass band on a
steamer lying at the levee, struck up its liveliest notes, a lot of
ladies standing near, waved their kerchiefs, and smiled and looked
eloquent welcome, and every body seemed as glad to see us as
though we had all been born and raised in the place. Col. Mackey
called for "Three cheers for old Iowa," and they rang out loud and
hearty, from every blue-coated and true-hearted man of us—three
cheers, and with a will.[8] So our first greeting in the State, though
unheralded and accidental, was hearty and sincere, as the patriotism of the city, that in the beginning of the war, had at a moment's
notice, repeatedly improvised and sent out company after company
to aid the Union cause, when the rebels grew troublesome in North-
East Missouri.[9]

A number of the boys went on shore at Keokuk, and stayed so
long that the boat went off and left them. In some cases, this would
be a very uncomfortable circumstance to the parties concerned; but
it proved of very little consequence to them, for they merely walked
up the railroad track, along the river twelve miles, to Montrose,
waited there till the boat came up, and then came on it again.
Reaching Muscatine next day, we thought the place seemed
remarkably still and lifeless. The stores were closed, and the streets
deserted. What could be the matter? We could hardly buy even a
few apples. It seemed very odd to us; and it was some time before
we happened to remember that the day was Sunday, and we were
now in the North. Down where we had been, Sunday was just like
any other day, "only a little more so;" and the difference now was
very plainly noticed.

At noon that day we reached Davenport. Here our coming was
known. There was quite a little crowd of ladies and gentlemen
gathered on the levee; but the only word or sign of welcome that
greeted us as we touched the landing was the voice of an officer on
shore shouting to our Colonel, "Don't let a man get off! Don't let a
man get off!" If this had been the spirit of the State, we would have
turned our backs on Iowa; and we could not but contrast this greeting with that of Keokuk, and remember that even the negro children in the South, had many times been more glad to see us than
our own fellow-citizens here in a city which expected to receive all
the benefits that could accrue to the place of our muster-out. There

Pvt. James F. Brittain, Company E, 33d Iowa Infantry.
Brittain was eighteen when he enlisted in the 33d Iowa in
July 1862, and he was a corporal when he mustered out
three years later. His brothers, Eli and Harvey, and his
brother-in-law, James H. Bly, served in Company F. Eli
died of disease in Helena, Harvey was disabled by an
injury, and Bly died shortly after his discharge, from a
service-related disease. James Brittain became a Baptist
minister and eventually settled in Oklahoma, dying in
Tulsa in 1920. *Photo courtesy of Renee Brittain.*

was not one of us but remembered it, and will remember it when more important matters are forgotten.

Crossing the river immediately, we landed on the island, and marched up to the camp formerly occupied by rebel prisoners.[10] Here, among the numerous buildings on the north side of the yard, we found comfortable quarters, and taking possession of them, set ourselves to endure the waiting for the pay-master and our discharges. The grounds were beautiful for a camp; and we could have been well content to remain there several months, had the time been taken from the other end of our term of service. As it was, the delay was most irksome and intolerable. It was mere waiting, without occupation, and with one great, absorbing thought and feeling, too prominent to admit any thing else. Discipline was at an end. Even the rations were drawn by voluntary fatigue-parties. Had there been an attempt made to draw a detail from the regiment for any duty, it would have been difficult to gather a dozen men. Fortunately there were no orders given, and scarcely any appearance of authority was continued. The *esprit de corps* was gone, and every one seemed absorbed in his own individual going home.

Previous regiments, upon discharge at Davenport, had made great disturbance, and "played smash" generally; and it was the fear of this from us that sent us over to the Island. But our men roamed free and undisturbed, and no complaint whatever was brought against them. Respecting themselves and others, they behaved like gentlemen, and were complimented therefor in Davenport as well as elsewhere.[11]

If one should have asked us, during the first two or three days of our stay on the Island, what we noticed most in Iowa, the answer most probably would have been different from what he might have expected; for we should have answered, without hesitation, that it was the good looks of the ladies. It is but reasonable to suppose that perhaps we were some what prejudiced in their favor; and some thing is doubtless due to the fact that they did not meet us on the streets with averted eyes, and rebel thoughts and feelings manifest in every feature, as did those to whom we had become most accustomed; but it can not be denied that with at least equal ease and grace of manner, the Northern ladies, in all that the appearance of youth and health, rosy cheeks, sparkling eyes, elastic tread, and cheerful, buoyant intelligence of expression can add to female beauty and attractiveness, have greatly the advantage of the sallow, listless and puny-looking ladies who had been visible to us in the Southern cities; and we could not but frequently notice the difference with admiration. All the ladies we saw now seemed good-looking, and most of them decided beauties.[12]

Seven days we were kept waiting at Davenport for our pay and discharges—seven long, weary days, all the longer and more weary for our being so near home. Had we been a thousand miles away, we could have endured the waiting better; but to be so near home, and hindered so outrageously, as many if not most of us believed, by mere collusion among officials and interested parties, was almost torture. Very likely the officers in charge of the matter may have done the best they could; but there were few of us who thought so.

At last the eventful day came. At 9 o'clock on the morning of Tuesday, the 8th of August, the long expected pay-master came over from town; and our heart thrilled with the feeling that now in a few minutes we should be citizens again, free, and equal. Colonel Mackey called the regiment together *en masse,* without any attempt at military order,[13] and addressed to them the following brief farewell:

"OFFICERS AND SOLDIERS: The time has arrived for the 33d regiment of Iowa Volunteer Infantry to disband. In taking leave of you as your commander, permit me to tender you my kindest regards for the treatment I have received from you during three years of active service. That I have committed errors in the discharge of my duties, I am fully aware; but I trust you will have charity enough to charge them to mistaken judgment. I have endeavored since I have been with you to discharge my duties toward you and our Government as well as I knew how. The best interest of the service, and your own personal welfare, have been my constant aim.

Your courage, industry and patriotism, it is not for me to extol. Of all these you have given ample proof on many well-fought fields; the suffering necessarily incident to three years' campaigning, the impartial historian must give you credit for well enduring; and a grateful people will receive and bless you as their defenders.

You entered the service in the darkest and most gloomy hour of our country's history. You have helped dispel that darkness and gloom, and now return to your homes, with your country at peace with the world, the unholy and unnatural rebellion, that was organized to crush this noble Republic, brought to a final and glorious end, and the integrity and stability of the Government fully vindicated. For all this you have great cause to rejoice and be thankful.

But in your rejoicing do not forget that many of the brave men who went out with us are not here for muster-out. They have sealed their patriotism with their lives, and have been offered up as a sacrifice on the altar of their country. Reserve a place in your hearts to cherish their memories; and let their little ones be your special care.

In retiring to private life, each and every one of you carries with him my warmest wishes for his success. Be as good citizens as you have been soldiers—and I have no doubt you will and your country-men will still have greater cause to be proud of you.

The privations and perils through which we have passed together, have endeared you all to me; and notwithstanding we separate here to join our families and friends, from whom we have been so long absent, the thought that we shall meet no more together, until the Reveille of Eternity shall be sounded, brings with it feelings of sad-ness, feelings which I have not words to express.

Officers and soldiers, as your colonel, and commander, I bid you farewell!"

This parting word was received in respectful silence.[14] It might be supposed that there came now a pathetic scene—that the men who had fought side by side so long, would not disband without some sign of sorrow; but such was not the case. We were to lose our organization, indeed, but would mostly be neighbors still; and even had not the hopes of happy meetings soon, to come with loved ones dearer far, been uppermost in every mind, Western men are made of too stern stuff to show much emotion at such a parting. Practically, the scene was the very reverse of pathetic. Each man, as his name was called, stepped to the window, received his green-backs and discharge, and went forth, free and uncontrolled, whither-soever he pleased, hardly escaping the pleasant banter of those whose turn had not yet come. "How are you, citizen?" "Say, over yonder is Davenport. Do you think you can find the way, now that you have no body to take care of you?" There was much squaring-up of little debts, some hand-shakings and words of parting, from those who did not expect soon to meet again, and then each one, without waiting for the rest, took his individual way westward; and thus unceremoniously, the 33d Iowa Infantry disbanded.[15]

The great majority of the men reached their homes on the night of the 9th—as nearly as could be, three years from the time of their enlisting.[16] Thus had been answered the prayer and prophecy of that dear old song which had so often cheered us in the gloomiest hours:

"God bless you, boys! We'll welcome you home,
    When rebels are in the dust!"

Who shall describe the sacred, sweet emotion of husband and wife, parent and son, so long parted, now met in happiness and home; or that newer, wilder rapture that thrilled the hearts of lovers, faithful still, joined now in an embrace whose exquisite bliss would gild all the past of trial and danger!

Home, home, home!
No more the deep-mouthed cannon's vengeful roar,
Or musket's rattling roll shall come,
    No more, no more

No more the warning cry,
"Halt! who comes there?"—the watchful, straining gaze,
Shall warm the chilling blood with danger nigh,
    In coming days.

No more the dull routine
Of camp, its weary drills and toilsome show—
Muster, parade, review—affect us now:
    These all have been.

No more on burning sand,
Or through the gloomy swamp our course shall lay,
Where lurks the enemy on either hand,
    By night or day.

No more the dreadful scene,
Of battle-field or hospital shall come
The happy dreams of future days between;
    There's peace at home.

The weary night is past,
Oh! who shall tell the heart-felt happiness
Of this dear morning which in joy at last
    Has come to bless?

APPENDIX

―――

ROLL

OF THE

THIRTY-THIRD IOWA INFANTRY

COPIED FROM

REGIMENTAL DESCRIPTIVE BOOK

AT MUSTER-OUT.

FIELD AND STAFF OFFICERS.

MUSTERED IN.

SAMUEL A. RICE, Colonel. Promoted to Brigadier-General, August 4th, 1863.

CYRUS H. MACKEY, Lieut.-Colonel. Promoted to Colonel, April 22d, 1864.

HIRAM D. GIBSON, Major. Resigned, April 22d, 1864.

F. F. BURLOCK, Adjutant. Discharged by promotion to another regiment.

HENRY B. MYERS, Quartermaster. Resigned, March 16th,1864.

ARAD PARKS, Surgeon. Resigned, January 11th, 1864.

JOHN Y. HOPKINS, Assistant Surgeon. Promoted to Surgeon, July 29th, 1864.

WM. N. SCOTT, Assistant Surgeon. Resigned, December 24th,1864.

ROBERT A. MCAYEALLY, Chaplain. Resigned, July 24th,1863.

BARTHOLOMEW FRANKEN, Hospital Steward. Discharged by promotion April 28th, 1864.

EUGENE W. RICE, Quartermaster-Sergeant. Promoted to Quartermaster, April 10th, 1864.

SAMUEL B. EVANS, Commissary-Sergeant. Discharged by promotion, Dec. 30th, 1865.

JOHN F. LACEY, Sergeant-Major. Promoted to Lieutenant, April 16th, 1863.

MUSTERED OUT.

CYRUS H. MACKEY, Colonel. Wounded at Jenkins' Ferry, April 30th, 1864.

JOHN LOFLAND, Lieutenant-Colonel.

CYRUS B. BOYDSTON, Major.

CHARLES H. SHARMAN, Adjutant. Wounded at Helena, July 4th, 1863.

EUGENE W. RICE, Quartermaster.

FRANCIS M. SLUSSER, Chaplain.

JOHN Y. HOPKINS, Surgeon.

JOHN R. CRAWFORD, Sergeant-Major. Wounded and taken prisoner at Jenkins' Ferry, April 30th, 1864.

REUBEN WHITAKER, Hospital Steward.

CHARLES G. BENNETT, Quartermaster-Sergeant.

ALBERT G. BERKEY, Commissary-Sergeant.

A. F. SPERRY, Principal Musician.

CASUALTIES.

COMPANY A.

Josiah F. Curtis, wounded at Helena.

Nathaniel H. Richardson, taken prisoner at Mark's Mills.

James A. Beaver, killed at Helena.

James T. Duncan, wounded and probably killed at Jenkins' Ferry.

David Forst, taken prisoner at Helena.

Alfred Hager, wounded at Jenkins' Ferry.

Hiram P. Henry, taken prisoner at Helena, and wounded at Jenkins' Ferry.

John S. Johnston, wounded at Jenkins' Ferry.

Wm. F. McKern, killed at Helena.

Milton Miner, taken prisoner at Helena.

Peter McKenney, killed at Helena.

John B. Nichols, taken prisoner at Helena.

Henry H. Reaves, wounded at Helena.

Jesse T. Sherwood, killed at Helena.

Jonathan S. Tindall, wounded at Jenkins' Ferry.

James H. Wycoff, killed at Helena.

COMPANY B.

John R. Alsup, taken prisoner at Jenkins' Ferry.

Jas. H. Davis,   "   "   on Yazoo Pass.

Dennis Decker,   "   "   "   "   "

    "   "   wounded and taken prisoner at Jenkins' Ferry.

Francis M. Dyer,   "   "   "   "   "

William Harris, wounded at Spanish Fort.

James B. Herrell, taken prisoner on Yazoo Pass.

John Lee,   "   "   "   "   "

John Manefee, wounded at Helena.

Jacob Newkirk, killed at Helena.

George Payton, jr., taken prisoner on Yazoo Pass.

Hannibal Rogers, wounded and taken prisoner at Jenkins' Ferry.

Jefferson Utterback, taken prisoner on Yazoo Pass.

Francis M. Wertz, wounded at Jenkins' Ferry.

George W. Long, wounded at Spanish Fort.

John E. Nichols, wounded at Jenkins' Ferry.

COMPANY C.

Joshua B. Wells, wounded at Jenkins' Ferry.

John F. Gaunt,   "   "   "   "

George G. Curry, taken prisoner at Helena.

Reuben Coomes, wounded at Helena and taken prisoner at Jenkins'
    Ferry.

Frederick Butler, taken prisoner at Helena.

James Adair, wounded   "   "

Henry Coomes, "   "   "

James E. Chick, taken prisoner   "   "

William Campbell, wounded at Spanish Fort.

Edward Currier, killed at Helena.

Robert W. B. Currey, wounded at Jenkins' Ferry.

John Dove,   "   "   "   "

Joab Fox, killed at Helena.

James H. D. Goodman, taken prisoner at Helena.

Sanford Graham, wounded at Helena.

Thomas G. Gooden, wounded at Spanish Fort.

Edward Graham, killed at Jenkins' Ferry.

William H. Harris, killed at Jenkins' Ferry.

Oliver Johnston, killed at Helena.

George W. Lundy, taken prisoner at Helena.

Henry C. Ludington, killed at Helena.

William Osborn, wounded at Helena, and wounded at Jenkins' Ferry.

John R. Pilgrim, taken prisoner at Helena.

Samuel Ream, wounded at Jenkins' Ferry.

James B. Spain, wounded at Helena.

Robert Talbot,   "   "   "

William Victor, taken prisoner at Helena.

William B. Walker, wounded at Jenkins' Ferry.

John B. Williams, killed at Helena.

Owen Bartlett, wounded at Jenkins' Ferry.

Mortimer Jackson, "   "   "   "

COMPANY D.

Jacob Houser, killed at Helena.

William Hilliard, taken prisoner at Helena.

John W. Jones, wounded and taken prisoner at Jenkins' Ferry.

Moses F. Atwood, wounded at Helena.

Edwin B. Batterson, killed at Helena.

Levi E. Brundage,   "   "   "

William E. Boyer, taken prisoner at Helena.

Samuel H. Doughman, wounded at Jenkins' Ferry.

Samuel L. Deweese,   "   "   "   "

Abraham C. Hopkins, taken prisoner at Helena.

Morris A. Quaintance, wounded and taken prisoner at Jenkins' Ferry.

John H. Ramey, wounded at Helena.

David Adams, wounded at Jenkins' Ferry.

William Trobridge, wounded and taken prisoner at Jenkins' Ferry.

George R. Mitchell, wounded at Jenkins' Ferry.

William Thorp,   "   "   "   "

COMPANY E.

John M. Finney, wounded at Jenkins' Ferry.

Marion Dunbar, taken prisoner at Mark's Mills.

Lewis H. Cochran, wounded at Jenkins' Ferry.

Amos Cornes, killed at   "   "

Benjamin Cruzen, killed at   "   "

Adam Eichelberger, wounded and taken prisoner at Jenkins' Ferry.

John B. Harris, wounded at   "   "

Anthony Hawk, wounded and taken prisoner at   "   "

Thomas H. Hinkle, killed at   "   "

Philander McMullen, wounded and taken prisoner at   "   "

Samuel S. Robertson, wounded at Jenkins' Ferry.

Levi Shaw, wounded at   "   "

John S. Wharton, wounded at Spanish Fort.

David G. Wilson, wounded at Jenkins' Ferry.

Willis S. Bird,   "   "   "   "

John H. Miller,   "   "   "   "

Wheeler Chadwick, wounded and taken prisoner at Jenkins' Ferry.

Joseph Redpath wounded at   "   "

William J. Bowers, wounded at Jenkins' Ferry.

James W. Grover, " " " "

Daniel Bacon,   " " " "

COMPANY F.

Ashley A. Buckner, killed at Helena.

Abraham Day, wounded at Spanish Fort.

Francis M. Gibson, taken prisoner at Jenkins' Ferry.

Walker B. Gibson, wounded and taken prisoner at Jenkins' Ferry.

Samuel B. Montgomery, wounded at   " "

John N. Miner, wounded at Helena.

Daniel McCreary, killed " "

Joseph T. Miller, " " "

Thomas Hillwell, " " "

Jasper Skinner, killed at Jenkins' Ferry.

COMPANY G.

Issac N. Ritner, wounded at Jenkin's Ferry.

Nicholas Schippers, wounded by bushwhackers on Arkansas River, January 28th, 1864.

Lucien Reynolds, wounded and taken prisoner at Jenkins' Ferry.

Klyn de Bruyn, taken prisoner at   " "

Tunis Blockland, killed at Helena.

William H. H. Downing, taken prisoner at Helena.

Joseph W. Dungan, wounded at Spanish Fort.

William O. Downes, wounded at Jenkins' Ferry.

Jacob Miller, killed at Helena.

John Metz, wounded at Spanish Fort.

John Niermeyer, wounded and taken prisoner at Jenkins' Ferry.

William P. Smiley, killed at Helena.

George W. Towne, wounded and taken prisoner at Jenkins' Ferry.

Jacob Taylor, wounded at   " "

Enos M. Woods, wounded near Camden, Ark., April 15th, 1864, and left prisoner at Camden.

Thomas D. Wallace, wounded at Jenkins' Ferry.

Daniel Wiser, taken prisoner at Mark's Mills.

Martin Walraven, wounded at Spanish Fort.

John Henry, wounded and taken prisoner at Jenkins' Ferry.

COMPANY H.

John Wightman, killed at Jenkins' Ferry.
Thomas J. Lawler, wounded at "   "
James Garrett,   "   " "   "
Clark Bevin, wounded and taken prisoner at Jenkins' Ferry.
William T. Dison, wounded at   "   "
Dorman Hiner, wounded at Jenkins' Ferry.
William Goldthwait, wounded at Jenkins' Ferry.
David Holloway, wounded and taken prisoner at Jenkins' Ferry.
William R. Hoyt, wounded at   "   "
Thomas Landry, wounded and taken prisoner at   "   "
Allen A. McNeil, wounded at   "   "
Marvin A. Peck, wounded and taken prisoner at   "   "
William J. Parks,   "   "   "   "   "   "   "
Joseph M. Roland, killed at   "   "
William M. Rodman, wounded and taken prisoner at "   "
Philip Suitor, wounded and taken prisoner at   "   "
Oliver Seaton, left as nurse at Camden.
George W. Shanafelt, killed at Jenkins' Ferry.
John Shoff, wounded at   "   "
James D. Compton, wounded and taken prisoner at Jenkins' Ferry.
Owen McNeal, wounded at   "   "

COMPANY I.

Hans Fergerson, taken prisoner at Jenkins' Ferry.
Oscar L. Jones, wounded at   "   "
Joseph Brobst, wounded and taken prisoner at Jenkins' Ferry.
Peter A. Bonebrake, wounded at   "   "
John Bruett, wounded and taken prisoner at Jenkins' Ferry.
William P. Funk, killed at Prairie de Anne, April 10th, 1864.
William Goff, wounded at Helena.
Eri Goodenough, wounded at Jenkins' Ferry.
John M. Henderson, killed at   "   "
John M. McCleland, wounded at"   "
William H. Parker,   "   " "   "
Thomas Smith, taken prisoner at Helena.
George W. Stanfield, killed at Helena.
James W. Strong, wounded and taken prisoner at Jenkins' Ferry.

John S. Snyder, wounded and taken prisoner at Jenkins' Ferry.
James I. Welch, killed at   "   "
David T. Welch, taken prisoner at   "   "
John Spohn, killed at Helena.
Smith Dunlap, wounded and taken prisoner at Jenkins' Ferry.
William G. Reed, wounded at   "   "

COMPANY K.

Matthew D. Gilchrist, killed at Helena.
William R. Cowan, wounded at Jenkins' Ferry.
David T. Evans,   "   "   "   "
Henry C. Haskell, wounded and taken prisoner at Jenkins' Ferry.
Francis M. Playle,   "   "   "   "   "   "   "
John C. Roberts, wounded at   "   "
George P. Stratton, wounded and taken prisoner at "   "
Alexander Jones,   "   "   "   "   "   "   "
John W. Martin, wounded at   "   "
James Windell, killed at   "   "
William H. Withrow, wounded at Poison Springs, April 15th, 1864.
William H. Anderson, wounded at Poison Springs.
Enoch F. Henderson, wounded at Jenkins' Ferry.
Samuel H Smith, wounded and taken prisoner at Jenkins' Ferry.
William H. Coleburn, "   "   "   "   "   "   "
John Burgess, wounded on Walnut Ridge, April 15th, 1864.
Ephriam Smith, killed at Jenkins' Ferry.

MISCELLANEOUS CASUALTIES.

Colonel Cyrus H. Mackey, wounded at Jenkins' Ferry.
Captain Andrew J. Comstock, Co. C, wounded and taken prisoner at
    Jenkins' Ferry.
Captain L. W. Whipple, Co. G, wounded at Helena.
Captain Paris T. Totten, Co. I, died of wounds received at Jenkins' Ferry.
Second Lieutenant Oliver J. Kindig, Co. C, wounded at Jenkins' Ferry.
Second Lieutenant Charles H. Sharman, Co. G, wounded at Helena.
Second Lieutenant Wilson De Garmo, Co. H, wounded at Jenkins' Ferry.
First Lieutenant Thomas R. Connor, Co. K, killed at Jenkins' Ferry.

ROSTER OF THE REGIMENT.

ROSTER OF THE REGIMENT.

COMPANY A.

CYRUS B. BOYDSTON, *Captain.*
S. S. PIERCE, *First Lieutenant.*
E. R. WOODRUFF, *Second Lieutenant.*

Adams, Edwin M.
Antrim, William
Auten, John B.
Auten, Thomas
Bishop, Abijah W.
Barnhill, Benjamin
Barnhill, James
Brown, George
Brown, Wilson L.
Breese, Issac
Brewster, Henry D.
Bellamy, Samuel W.
Busenburgh, Daniel
Beaver, James A.
Burdick, George L.
Brooks, Peter
Baker, Justus C.
Brown, Francis H.
Brown, William D.
Cooper, James M.
Curtis, Joseph F.
Collins, Lodrick C.
Cooper, Ephraim
Chrisman, William T.
Chrisman, James H.
Chambers, Zephaniah
Chambers, William
Chambers, William R.
Craig, John

Cradick, William W.
Curtis, Francis
Duncan, James F.
Day, Hiram C.
Downing, George S.
Fort, Daniel
Feagins, Leonard B.
Forst, David
Foster, Joseph B.
Grant, John
Gregory, Enoch G.
Gregory, John W.
Gibson, Wm.
Gose, Stephen A.
Harding, John W.
Harned, Michael R.
Hammond, Henry J.
Hammond, Greenville C.
Hager, Alfred
Hunter, Joseph F.
Heaton, Samuel
Hiatt, Lewis
Hodges, Milton J.
Hodges, William W.
Henry, Hiram P.
Hicks, Robert
Hicks, James
Harding, Wm. H.
Inman, John

Ivey, George R.
Johnston, John S.
Jolliffe, Albert
Jeffers, John
Kendrick, Americus
Kendrick, John C.
Kennedy, John
Levan, Jacob
Leach, Vincent
McKinney, John
McGuire, William
McKein, Wm. F.
May, Alexander P.
Miner, Milton
Morrow, William J.
Moltern, Wm. J.
McPheters, Jacob
McElroy, John J.
McKinney, Peter
Miner, Josiah
North, Layton H.
Nichols, Ozias D.
Nichols, John B.
Nichols, Joseph W.
Neal, Charles D. O.
Patterson, Hugh W.
Persons, George E.
Richardson, Nathaniel H.
Roan, Thomas T.

Roan, James M.
Rowland, David W.
Reaves, Henry H.
Reaves, Clark
Richards, Lorenzo D.
Roan, Nat C.
Richards, John
Schee, Oliver
Sherwood, Jesse F.
Smith, Hamilton E.
Smith, George W.
Snyder, John
Shawver, Jacob
Sampson, Levi J.
Stone, Freeman M.

Shilling, John
Sturdefant, Thaddeus
Todd, Jacob P.
Tindall, Jonathan S.
Vandyke, Thomas J.
Vandyke, John H.
Vernon, Elijah.
Vernon, John T.
Vernon, Wm.
Wallace, Thomas J.
Welch, John M.
Wilkenson, James
Wycoff, John W.
Wycoff, James H.
Walker, Simon

Willis, James
Walters, Peter
Walters, Wm. J.
Smith, James
Metcalf, James
Strait, Wm. B.
Wilson, Thomas M.
Millen, Robert A.
Jones, Thomas
Browning, Maxwell H.
Minor, Wm.
Ralston, David C.
Spurgeon, James H.
Booth, Jesse L.

COMPANY B.

JOHN P. YERGER, *Captain.*
WM. S. PARMELEY, *First Lieutenant.*
JOSEPH H. SHAWHAN, *Second Lieutenant.*

Alsup, John R.
Adams, David H.
Allen, John
Bratten, Andrew
Booton, George W.
Butler, Michael
Boegel, Henry H.
Boston, Asa S.
Basey, James A.
Bell, Zephaniah
Bottger, John C.
Bradley, Samuel S.
Baxter, Lewis
Black, Philander

Basil, Jeremiah
Bowman, Henry V.
Crow, John H.
Clarahan, Michael J.
Clemmens, Henry
Connor, Aaron
Cole, Eleazar
Case, James H.
Carlile, Samuel
Courtney, James H.
Cattell, John W.
Case, John H.
Clarahan, Patrick
Case, George C.

Crooks, Jacob V.
Courtney, Howard F.
Carson, Henry S.
Chrisman, John
Davis, James H.
Duree, George W.
Duree, Henry F.
Decker, Dennis
Dyer, Francis M.
Evans, Samuel B.
Evans, Gideon L.
Eastburn, John B.
Fear, James H.
Fowler, David D,

Farmer, John L.

Ford, Jacob

Franklin, Joel

Givan, Henry C.

Gann, Leander O.

Gann, John L.

Griffin, Harlan

Harter, Joseph J.

Howard, John W.

Harris, William

Hax, John

Herrell, James B.

Hardesty, Samuel B.

Jacobs, James B.

Jenner, Thomas A.

Jones, Wm. H.

Keener, John W. C.

Kensler, George

Klett, Godfrey,

Lambert, David

Lee, John

Lowe, James M.

Landers, Henry J.

Leonard, Francis M.

Long, George W.

Matthews, Fenelon B.

Myers, Thomas B.

Mead, Augustus M.

Miles, John

McCalley, Jacob

Miles, Daniel

Moore, Robert

McGonegal, Charles

Moore, Joseph C.

Menefee, John

Morgan, Nathan

McGrew, Leander

Miller, Jacob E.

McAdams, Edwin J.

Malin, Wm.

Malone, James H.

Newkirk, Jacob H.

Nichols, John E.

Nelson, William D.

Nelson, William H.

O'Niel, John S.

Payton, George, jr,

Payton, John

Payton, William,

Payton, George,

Quick, Tennis

Quick, Stheter

Quick, James

Randall, Machron W.

Randall, Charles

Rogers, Hannibal

Shawhan, George W.

Smith, Zelek C.

Shallenberger, Hiram

Stout, George W.

Thompson, Albert J.

Thompson, Thomas J.

Thompson, Albert E,

Trueblood, Elijah,

Utterback, Jefferson

Westcott, Benjamin

Wright, William A.

Wilson, David

Ward, William F.

Ward, Samuel A.

Woolard, James F.

Wertz, Francis M.

Wait, Reuben

Stout, Wm. H.

Moffat, Wm. A.

Long, Edward.

Henderson, Wm.

Tucker, Leander.

Cark, Wm. B.

COMPANY C.

ANDREW J. COMSTOCK, *Captain.*

ROBERT F. BURTON, *First Lieutenant.*

CYRUS H. TALBOT, *Second Lieutenant.*

Armstrong, David

Adair, James

Adair, Marion

Butler, Frederick

Barlean, Samuel

Barlean, Jonas

Butler, Jacob B.

Baker, James W.

Baldwin, Sylvester

Bartlett, Owen P.
Berry, James M.
Currey, George G.
Coomes, Reuben
Crowder, Thomas
Crowder, Charles
Chick, Elijah J.
Castleman, Amanuel
Coomes, Henry
Chick, James E.
Coterell, Wesley
Crayton, James
Campbell, Wm.
Currier, Edward
Curry, Robert W. B.
Chaplain, James M.
Duke, Hamilton
Davis, George R.
Delong, Thomas E.
Dove, George W.
Dove, John
Dodge, Wm.
Eckroate, John
Ellis, Wm. A.
Ellington, Michael W.
Ellington, John D.
Foreman, George
Fox, Joab
Fenn, Deno
Gaunt, John F.
Goodwin, James H. D.
Graham, Sandford
Garey, Frederick
Grant, Cyrus A.
Grace, James R.
Grace, John R.

Gooden, Thomas G.
Graham, Edward
Groves, John H.
Goodwin, Abraham
Graham, Nelson
Hook, Norman R.
Harper, Joseph
Harris, Wm. H.
Harris, Wm.
Holton, Richard W.
Johnston, Oliver
Joy, Solomon
Jones, Alonzo
Jackson, Mortimer
Jones, Wm. R.
Kissick, Robert
Kindig, Allen R.
Kindig, Oliver J.
Kunzman, John George
Kirkpatrick, James W.
Knight, Samuel
Keeser, Rezin
Lundy, Wm.
Lundy, George W.
Ladington, Henry C.
Lincoln, Levi W.
Leatherman, John S.
Mills, Elias
McBride, Harvey C.
Morrow, Wm. W.
Mullen, Isaac A.
McIntosh, Wm.
McIntosh, Jeremiah
Myers, Wm. F.
Nation, James F.
Osborn, Wm.

Pilgrim, John R.
Patten, Wm. H.
Petty, Amos D.
Patten, John M.
Rardin, Jethro
Ryan, Jacob S.
Reaves, James H.
Ryan, Samuel
Scott, James B.
Stroud, Wm. H.
Sharp, George H.
Spain, James B.
Stephens, George W.
Stewart, Joseph P.
Spain, Joshua
Schee, George W.
Talbott, Robert
Talbott, Richard J.
Timbrel, Lot
Vancleve, Samuel G.
Victor, Wm.
Vancleve, Albert
Wells, Joshua B.
Wilson, Wm.
Wilson, Clark
Wilson, Robert
Wright, Joshua
Weense, John
Winn, Robert
Walker, Wm. B.
Williams, John B.
Yeadon, Samuel
Sharp, George
Wright, John
Ream, John T.

COMPANY D.

JOHN LOFLAND, *Captain.*
DENNY M. GUNN, *First Lieutenant.*
RILEY JESSUP, *Second Lieutenant.*

Adams, George
Atwood, Moses F.
Adams, David
Appleton, Clark
Atwood, Stephen
Bennett, Charles G.
Brower, David M. C.
Bass, Andrew J.
Berkey, Albert G.
Brewster, Philander
Batterson, Edwin B.
Brundedge, Levi E.
Boyer, Wm. E.
Brown, Nathaniel H.
Burris, Stacey
Bupp, Frank
Blackstone, Thomas J.
Crawford, John R.
Counsel, Oran
Champ, Thornton
Coe, Alven H.
Cope, Henry
Collins, John C.
Clark, Henry M.
Darrow, James E.
Doughman, Samuel H.
Doughman, Andrew J.
Deweese, Wm. J.
Deweese, Samuel L.
Deweese, John B.

Donelson, Amos W.
Dixon, Harvey M.
Dilley, David M.
Ewing, John N.
Ellis, Adelbert L.
Evans, Wm. L.
Enos, Wm.
Fagan, Wm.
Flanders, Nathan N.
Garden, Thomas J.
Grey, Amos
Hines, Ezra F.
Houser, Jacob
Hughes, Jared
Hilliard, William
Hopkins, Abraham C.
Hiner, Jesse
Hiner, David
Hiner, Wm.
Hiatt, Amos
Hull, Benjamin
Heaverlo, Andrew
Hewson, Samuel
Hull, Ahalial
Jones, John W.
Kindig, Wm. H.
Killough, John H.
Kirkpatrick, George N.
Leighton, Henry C.
Locke, Wm. G.

Lacey, John F.
Likens, Wm.
Lafollett, John W.
Larkins, J.W.
Moore, Eliphaz
Middleton, Jesse H.
Mahaffey, John
McKinsey, David P.
Michener, Henry P.
McNeal, Henry P.
Mitchell, George R.
Needham, David L.
Newton, Henry
Pope, Washington C.
Peckover, Wm.
Peters, Wm. C.
Proctor, Jefferson,
Proctor, Wm.
Packer, Isaac W. D.
Peckover, John
Quaintance, Morris A.
Ramey, John H.
Reeder, Pemberton
Rockwell, Alanson
Reams, Vincent
Randall, Jefferson
Stephens, David
Slater, Elisha W.
Roberts, James M.
Rice, Eugene W.

Schwalm, Albert W.
Stevens, Hugh
Sandiland, Wm. A.
Sandiland, Alexander
Shannon, John A.
Stout, Thomas C.
Shelly, Benjamin F.
Smith, Wm. F.
Tracy, Wm.
Tracy, Marion
Totman, Nathaniel

Thompson, Joseph
Talbot, Wm. H.
Trobridge, Wm.
Thompson, David R.
Vickers, Sandford
Vickroy, Lewis F.
Williams, Thomas J.
Winder, Hugh W.
Widows, James H.
Wood, David J. M.
Warner, James M.

Williams, John D.
White, Wm. L.
Windsor, Joseph
West, Isaac W.
Young, John C.
Zane, Wm. L.
Thorp, Wm.
Mendenhall, Wm.
Barr, Pinckney F.

COMPANY E.

JOHN P. WALKER, *Captain.*
CHENEY PROUTY, *First Lieutenant.*
T. L. SEEVERS, *Second Lieutenant.*

Allen, Elam
Armel, William
Breckenridge, John A.
Blackstone, Wm. M.
Boyer, Richard M.
Brown, Hale B. W.
Brown, John D.
Bones, John
Baughman, Elias
Barnes, William A.
Boswell, Joshua R.
Brittain, James F.
Bird, Willis S.
Bowers, Wm. J.
Burket, Magnus D.
Beal, Nicholas
Bacon, Daniel
Cochran, Lewis H.

Crewder, Robert S.
Cratty, Wm. M.
Capper, Howard
Clammer, David
Church, Alonzo M.
Corns, Amos
Cochran, John D.
Cruzen, Benjamin
Church, Washington
Carson, George S.
Chadwick, Wheeler
Dunbar, Marion
Davis, Clement A.
Dodd, Charles J.
Downing, Wm. H.
Eveland, Linas J.
Eveland, Frank
Eichelbarger, Adam

Finney, John M.
Faucett, George
Glenn, Wm. S.
Glendenning, James E.
Gosnell, Samuel D.
Gosnell, Jesse S.
Grover, James W.
Hines, George
Haleman, James W.
Harris, John B.
Harris, Wm. B.
Howard, Walter
Hawk, Anthony
Hawk, Wm. W.
Himes, Jacob M.
Holloway, John S.
Haney, Jacob D.
Harland, Humphrey M.

Horn, John W.
Haydock, Daniel W.
Hinckle, Thomas H.
Hall, Zachariah T.
Himes, Theodore
Haynes, Robert H.
Haleman, Alexander M.
Kinsman, Theodore S.
Kirkendall, Joseph W.
Lockhart, Isaac M.
Lyster, Asher W.
Miller, Henry T.
McMullen, Philander
McCully, Wm. S.
McLean, John
McLean, Alexander
McCullough, James
Miller, John H.
Nolan, Eugene
Ogden, James
Plumley, James S.

Phillips, John
Perrigo, Ambrose
Redpath, James T.
Ruby, Tilford H.
Roland, George
Ruby, Martin C.
Ross, Wm. A.
Robb, George L.
Reno, Wm. C.
Robertson, Samuel S.
Robertson, William A.
Redpath, Joseph
Redpath, James A.
Snoak, Henry
Sawyer, James H.
Shaver, Levi C.
Shaw, Levi
Shaw, Charles W.
Satchell, James W.
Shelledy, Leander K.
Stoltzer, Stephen

Sumner, Wm. H.
Smith, Marion D.
Stephenson, Charles M.
Slamel, Peter
Tipton, Joshua D.
Whitaker, John
West, John
Wharton, John S.
Wilson, David G.
Whitaker, Reuben
Wells, John W.
Welch, Hiram
Wilson, Abel F.
Williams, Joseph
Young, Jonathan E.
Young, Thomas H.
Kitsmiller, Norman B.
Green, William L.
Likes, Robert B.

COMPANY F.

MEMORIAL W. FORREST, *Captain.*
ANDERSON DAVIS, *First Lieutenant.*
LYCURGUS McCOY, *Second Lieutenant.*

Allison, Wm.
Abrams, Wm.
Abrams, Miles
Allen, Westley
Allison, Thomas J.
Abrams, James
Armstrong, James H.
Bell, James W.
Bell, John
Botkin, Zebedee T.

Braden, Robert C.
Baxter, George F.
Belvel, Samuel
Buckner, Ashley A.
Belvel, Nicholas
Brunt, John M.
Britain, Eli
Britain, Harvey
Bly, James H.
Cushman, Orland D.

Dickerson, James C.
Day, Valentine
Durfey, Orson M.
Day, Charles R.
Day, Abraham
Furgerson, James T.
Furgerson, Russell
Gaston, Wm. J.
Gill, James
Graves, Johnson

Groesbeck, George W.
Glass, Alexander W.
Gibson, Francis M.
Gibson, Walker B.
Golliher, Charles B.
Hillery, Milton
Hart, John S.
Hutton, James K. P.
Hoisington, Wm. V.
Hadley, Joseph H.
Hobson, Joel
Hugh, James A.
Hone, John C.
Hemingher, Henry S.
Hawk, Cornelius
Hagan, Charles M.
Hough, Wm. P.
Hadley, Sidney C.
Hughes, George H.
Jones, John M.
Kawk, Jacob S.
Loomis, Nelson
Lotspeech, Samuel P.
Lynch, Paul A.
Logan, Henry
Larimore, John

McCreary, John
Monohan, Wm.
McPherson, John
Mills, Eli
Miller, Eli
McNies, Wm.
Montgomery, Samuel B.
McConnel, Wm. J.
Monohon, David
Minor, John N.
McConnel, Francis M.
McCreary, Daniel
McNies, John
McNies, Pleasant
Morrison, James
Miller, Joseph T.
Mitchell, Wm. W.
Morgan, John B.
McCreary, James
Nugent, John F.
Nash, Charles W.
Nash, Asa B.
Orndorff, Wm.
Pratt, George A.
Robinson, Wm. S.
Rayburn, John C.

Sechrist, Abraham
Spears, James R.
Sancheztereso, Frederick
Shepherd, Samuel
Street, Samuel F.
Sheets, Leander
Stillwell, Thomas
Spears, Ezra T.
Stillwell, George F.
Skinner, Jasper
Stillwell, George W.
Smith, Marion
Thomas, Gideon
Trent, John
Trent, Josiah
Waugh, Albert F.
Walker, Edwin
Ward, Wm.
Wood, Christopher
Young, James M.
Brenette, George S.
Stewart, Jacob F.
Miller, Asa M.
Miller, John W.
Bennett, Sanford G.
Schank, John Jacob

COMPANY G.

LAURISTON W. WHIPPLE, *Captain.*
GEORGE R. LEDYARD, *First Lieutenant.*
JOHN C. KLIJN, *Second Lieutenant.*

Atkins, Henry D.
Baldwin, Samuel A.
Bauman, Hendrick
Beard, Wm. E.
Black, Jonathan M.

Bowman, Jacob L.
Bousquet, Henry L.
Bruijn, Kryn de
Blockland, Tunis
Cory, Lewis P.

Cox, Thomas W.
Clark, William D.
Canine, Cornelius
Croll, Daniel W.
Campbell, William P.

Davenport, James H.

Dingeman, John W.

Dingeman, Daniel

Downing, William H. H.

Dunaway, Thomas B.

Dungan, Joseph W.

Dunnick, Cornelius

Downs, Wm. O.

Dunnington, Orville R.

Englesma, Martin

Earp, Wm. H.

Fidler, John K.

Ford, James H.

Fisk, Harvey

Griffith, Wm. V.

Garrison, John

Groen, John

Herbert, Henry C.

Henry, John

Hansell, Samuel

Hol, Martinus

Haze, Peter J.

Hamrick, Allen

Hamilton, Wm. H.

Hamilton, Joseph D.

Haven, John Q.

Kock, Stephanus de

Klyne, Cornelius

Lemmons, Jacob

Morgan, John S.

Miller, Jacob

McMichael, David

Metz, John

McCollum, Andrew J.

McCullough, Wm. S.

McLeod, John

Mathes, Valentine

Martin, Larkin

Myers, Holland

Moore, Nathan O.

Moore, Alexander

Martin, Levi

Myers, Delano

Niermeyer, John

Nelson, Frank

Niermyer, John, jr.

Owen, John W.

Pruit, Francis M.

Prouty, Flavius A.

Price, Gilmore

Peters, Julius A. M.

Perkins, Ezra H.

Ritner, Isaac N.

Reynolds, Lucien

Rubertus, Herman D.

Roberts, James P.

Richardson, George R.

Rhynsburger, John J.

Robbins, Charles H.

Sharman, Charles H.

Sleyster, Warnerus

Schippers, Nicholas

Sperry, Andrew F.

Squires, John

Stallard, Luke

Steenwyk, Gerard Van

Steenwyk, John G. Van

Smith, James S.

Smiley, Wm. P.

Sipna, Sjoerd R.

Shull, Richard P.

Shull, Jacob H.

Shull, Charles M.

Steadman, Benjamin T.

Stearman, Robert H.

Templeton, Amaziah

Towne, George W.

Tol, Deik

Thomas, Wm. H.

Thomas, Theodore F.

Taylor, Jacob

Ulsh, Henry J.

Ulsh, Daniel G.

Vanness, Daniel

Versteig, Gyskrt

Vanderkamp, Gerrit

Vandermoelen, Sijtz S. S.

Vandermeer, Isaac R. P.

Vandermaa, Henry J.

Vorhies, Sanford

Vineyard, Thomas

Veenschoten, Evert Van

Vorhies, Wm.

Wheeler, Harman

Woods, Enos M.

Wallace, Thomas D.

Wiser, Daniel

Williamson, Thomas

Watkins, Joseph F.

Walraven, Martin

Ward, Benjamin F.

White, Thomas J.

Wycoff, John W.

Zeenu, Cornelius de

COMPANY H.

JOHN DILLON, *Captain.*
JOSEPH L. SMITH, *First Lieutenant.*
WILLIAM GORE, *Second Lieutenant.*

Adams, Wilson
Allen, William
Ashley, George
Beardsley, Robert B.
Bales, Levi M.
Brown, Stephen J.
Boon, Clark
Brumback, Garrison
Brunson, William D.
Brunson, Newton H.
Cooper, Albert
Campbell, Lewis
Cunningham, John B.
Curby, Abram R.
Cabler, Daniel
Cline, Jacob
Curby, Jeremiah
Campbell, Joseph
Campbell, Wesley
Clark, Thomas J.
Campton, James D.
Campbell, Samuel
Coffman, James A.
Currier, Victor
De Garmo, Wilson
Disor, John W.
Dison, William T.
Doty, Ezra
Dorman, Hiner
Decker, Elisha
Decker, Francis M.

Eaton, John C.
Edmondson, William F.
Eaton, Marcus D.
Ford, Usarius C.
Fry, John
Fry, David
Fish, William J.
Franken, Bartholomew
Garrett, James
Goldthwait, Charles J.
Gow, Daniel A.
Gow, Jefferson
Holland, David O.
Hollingsworth, Ezra
Hayworth, James D.
Holliday, Jerome
Holloway, David
Hermon, James
Heald, Henry
Hardenhook, John
Herr, William
Hoyt, William R.
Hall, Reuben M.
Hildebrand, Samuel M.
Irwin, William
Irons, Charles
Irons, John
Johnson, Frank
Linebarger, Samuel
Lawler, Thomas J.
Lane, John T.

Landreth, Harvey
Landry, Thomas
Lakin, Thomas
Lakin, John W.
Marling, George W.
McCombs, Benjamin M.
Mills, Elwood
McCord, Alfred J.
McNiel, Allen A.
McNeal, Owen P.
Moore, William J.
Nathlich, Adelbert
Nelson, Edward
Nyswanner, David
Newport, Jesse
Peck, Marion A.
Paul, Charles M.
Potts, Sedwick
Parks, William J.
Peterson, Augustus
Riley, Joseph H.
Roland, Joseph M.
Rodman, William M.
Suitor, Joseph L.
Simms, Ellington T.
Stephenson, Thomas
Simpson, Thomas
Shanafelt, John W.
Suitor, Philip
Schoville, William
Smith, John V.

Shanafelt, Owen K.
Smith, William H.
Stokesbury, James H.
Sanders, Samuel R.
Swails, Jacob
Seaton, Oliver
Slate, Lorenzo
Shanafelt, George W.
Shoff, John
Smith, Aaron B.

Smith, Philip S.
Turner, Henry J.
Tracy, Hezekiah W.
Thomas, Milton
Tate, Martin V.
Thompson, Lloyd P.
Thompson, Thomas M.
Ward, Samuel C.
Wightman, John
Wandling, Jacob

Ward, John
Waltze, Benjamin F.
Withrell, Chauncey
Wright, James H.
Wells, Bloomfield E.
Wandling, Jacob A.
Wilson, James M.
Balls, James H.

COMPANY I.

PARIS T. TOTTEN, *Captain.*
JOHN HENDERSON, *First Lieutenant.*
JOHN REICHARD, *Second Lieutenant.*

Allison, John D.
Applegate, George W.
Anderson, John H.
Brobst, Josiah
Brobst, Joseph
Banta, Smith
Bawman, Sylvanus
Bonebrake, Peter A.
Bruett, John
Clark, Joseph M.
Carrothers, Levi
Coura, William P.
Conwell, George
Carder, Henry
Carrothers, William J.
Dennis, Azariah
Dunlap, Smith
De Witt, Henry J.
Fisher, Joseph
Furgerson, Hans

Funk, William P.
Funk, Isaac N.
Farlee, Henry
Gibson, Alpheus W.
Gunter, Henry B.
Gafford, James A.
Godfrey, Thaddeus
Graham, William H.
Goff, William
Goodwin, Nathan D.
Graham, William
Goodenough, Eri
Gaston, James A.
Gaston, Ephraim C.
Gibson, Jacob B.
Hessenflow, John S.
Hessenflow, John F.
Hutchinson, Daniel
Henderson, John M.
Haynes, Clayton T.

Hutchinson, Arnold C.
Hays, James M.
Hornback, Jacob
Horn, Levi P.
Henry, John
Harman, Peter
Henderson, William M.
Hart, James H.
Houghar, George
Irons, William
Jones, Oscar L.
Jacobs, Hubbard
Layton, John
Lemburger, Frederick
Limes, Edgar F.
Long, John W.
McCorkel, John Y.
Mears, John W.
McMillen, Samuel
Manor, Samuel

McCorkel, Joseph L.
McCleland, John M.
Maddy, John W.
McCorkel, John W.
McMillen, Henry
McMillen, Alexander
Newman, James A.
Neal, Solon S.
Parker, William H.
Palmer, Enoch
Pitts, Joseph P.
Pope, William W.
Pearson, Ira A.
Pearson, Young
Penland, Evan B.
Reed, Preston A.
Richards, Josiah

Ream, Walter
Ridgeway, John H.
Rowland, William
Rankin, Andrew M.
Rankin, Harvey
Riddel, Joseph
Reed, William G.
Strong, Samuel L.
Stephens, Drury S.
Smith, David S.
Smith, George J.
Smith, Thomas
Scott, Alexander
Stanfield, George W.
Strong, James W.
Spohn, Hezekiah
Shepherd, John N.

Snyder, John S.
Spohn, John
Schee, James
Teed, George R.
Templin, John
Terry, Dennis
Vandlah, John S.
Willey, Nathaniel D. T.
Willey, Damon W.
Wolf, William W.
Wolf, James M.
Walsh, James J.
Welch, David T.
Woodward, Jacob
Woodward, Calvin
Welcher, Andrew

COMPANY K.

THORNTON MCINTOSH, *Captain.*
GEORGE GILCHRIST, *First Lieutenant.*
JOHN M. BAUGH, *Second Lieutenant.*

Andrews, Thomas R.
Ashmead, James T.
Agnew, James
Allgood, Jefferson
Anderson, William H.
Boswell, John
Blair, Robert
Bell, James M.
Boyd, William
Broyles, Samuel
Buntain, Cary A.
Burgess, Amos
Burgess, Andrew J.

Boyd, Robert F.
Boswell, Levi
Burgess, James S.
Burgess, John
Connor, Thomas R.
Crozier, Thomas S.
Cowan, William R.
Collins, Merrill P.
Crozier, Matthew W.
Carnahan, Francis
Criss, John
Correll, Carey A.
Coleburn, William H.

Drinkle, Henry S.
Dysart, David
Dixon, Matthew
Douglas, John W.
Dixon, Nathan C.
Eastburn, Sanford
Evans, David T.
Emory, William T.
Elwell, Thomas
Foster, Benjamin
Fox, James B.
Furgerson, John
Gilchrist, Matthew D.

Gordon, Jasper H.

Gaston, Cyrus

Gregory, William

Gaston, David

George, Jacob

Heath, Harvey S.

Haskell, Royal

Huff, Charles A.

Higgins, Thomas

Haskell, Daniel

Haskell, Henry C.

Hartman, Robert R.

Howell, William H.

Harris, Augustus A.

Henry, John N.

Henderson, Enoch F.

Hornback, James B.

Jones, Alexander

Jackson, William M.

Kernahan, Thomas A.

Kunnen, Francis

Loughridge, James

Loughridge, William

Lockard, Samuel L.

Musgrove, Benjamin H.

McAllister, William T.

Morgan, John G.

Miller, William G.

McFall, David

McKinney, William

McCune, David

Morgan, Lewis

Myers, David

Mershon, Felix G.

Morris, John A.

Martin, John W.

Myers, Jefferson

Moore, William H.

Nichol, David F.

Porter, John

Playle, Francis M.

Pettichord, Wm. H. H.

Padget, James

Rankin, William A.

Robertson, Darius

Robinson, James

Rea, John B.

Rea, Cyrus

Roberts, John C.

Remington, Sylvester

Ryan, Charles E.

Reed, Andrew R.

Shaw, William H.

Stratton, George B.

Smith, Franklin

Shipley, James B.

Stephenson, James M.

Smith, Samuel H.

Smith, Ephraim S.

Tucker, Leander O.

Todd, Benjamin

Tennis, Samuel M.

Williamson, Stephen A.

Williamson, Solomon

Walker, James A.

Wymore, Robert E.

Wagoner, Lazarus

Williamson, Alburn M.

Withrow, William H.

Windell, James

Wymore, Jasper H.

Jackson, Hugh M.

Jackson, James M.

PROMOTIONS, ETC.

PROMOTIONS, ETC.

The following are the more important changes by promotion, &c., in the companies, as far as can be given from present data:

COMPANY A.

Captain C. B. Boydston, promoted to Major, June 29th, 1864.

Second Lieutenant E. K. Woodruff, resigned, March 3d, 1863.

First Sergeant James M. Cooper, promoted to Second Lieutenant, April 12th, 1863; and to First Lieutenant, July 21st, 1864.

First Sergeant A. W. Bishop, promoted to Second Lieutenant, Dec. 11th, 1864.

First Lieutenant S. S. Pierce, promoted to Captain.

COMPANY B.

Captain John P. Yerger, resigned, May 10th, 1864.

First Lieutenant Joseph H. Shawhan, resigned, March 25th, 1863.

Second Lieutenant Wm. S. Parmeley, promoted to First Lieutenant, May 20th, 1863; and to Captain, June 7th, 1864.

Second Sergeant Joseph J. Harter, promoted to Second Lieutenant, July 1st, 1863; and to First Lieutenant, June 7th, 1864.

COMPANY C.

First Lieutenant Robert F. Burton, resigned, April 8th, 1863.

Second Lieutenant Cyrus H. Talbott, resigned, June 2d, 1863.

Fourth Sergeant Oliver J. Kindig, promoted to Second Lieutenant, Oct. 16th, 1863.

First Sergeant Joshua B. Wells, promoted to First Lieutenant, Sept. 22d, 1864; and to Captain Dec. 8th, 1864.

Second Sergeant Robert Kissick, promoted to Adjutant of 113th A. D., March March 28th, 1864.

Sergeant Norman R. Hook, promoted to Second Lieutenant, Jan. 7th, 1865.

COMPANY D.

Captain John Lofland, promoted to Lieutenant-Colonel, April 23d, 1864.

First Lieutenant Denny M. Gunn, resigned, Oct. 24th, 1864.

Second Lieutenant Riley Jessup, promoted to Captain, May 24th, 1864.

Second Sergeant Henry C. Leighton, promoted to Second Lieutenant, July 21st, 1864; and to First Lieutenant Dec. 22d, 1864.

Private D. J. Woods, promoted to Adjutant of 14th Kansas Cavalry, March, 1863.

Second Sergeant John R. Crawford, promoted to Sergeant-Major, April 16th, 1863.

Fourth Sergeant Charles G. Bennett, promoted to Quarter-Master Sergeant, April 10th, 1864.

Albert G. Berkey, promoted to Commissary Sergeant in 1864.

Amos Hiatt, promoted to Second Lieutenant, Dec. 22d, 1864.

COMPANY E.

Captain John P. Walker, resigned, April 2d, 1863.

First Lieutenant Cheney Prouty, promoted to Captain, May 10th, 1863.

Second Lieutenant T. L. Seevers, promoted to First Lieutenant, May 10th, 1863.

Second Sergeant John A. Breckinridge, promoted to Second Lieutenant, June 2d, 1863; resigned May 26th, 1864.

Private Reuben Whitaker, promoted to Hospital Steward, April 22d, 1864.

Private David Clammer, promoted to Captain in 54th A. D., Aug. 26th, 1863.

Private George Fawcett, promoted to Second Lieutenant in 54th A. D., Sept. 3d, 1863.

COMPANY F.

Captain M. W. Forrest, resigned, March 13th, 1863.

First Lieutenant Anderson Davis resigned, April 24th, 1863.

Second Lieutenant Lycurgus McCoy, resigned, March 13th, 1863.

Corporal John Bell, promoted to Captain, April 16th, 1863.

Second Sergeant Frederick Sancheztereso, promoted to First Lieutenant, June 2d, 1863.

First Sergeant William J. Gaston, promoted to Second Lieutenant,
   March 14th, 1863; resigned Oct., 25th, 1863.
Private Abraham Sechrist, promoted to Second Lieutenant in 54th A. D.,
   Aug. 26th, l863.

COMPANY G.

Captain Lauriston W. Whipple, promoted to Lieutenant-Colonel of 113th
   A. D., June 18th, 1864.
First Lieutenant George R. Ledyard, promoted to Captain, July 21st, 1864.
Second Lieutenant John C. Klijn, resigned, February 24th, 1863.
Fifth Sergeant Charles H. Sharman, promoted to Second Lieutenant,
   March 1st, 1863, to First Lieutenant, July 1st, 1864, and to Adjutant,
   186—.
First Sergeant Lewis P. Cory, promoted to Second Lieutenant, July 21st,
   1864, and to First Lieutenant,———.
First Sergeant Wm. V. Griffith, promoted to Captain in 113th A. D.,
   May 26th, 1864.
First Sergeant John S. Morgan, promoted to Second Lieutenant,
   February 21st, 1865.
A. F. Sperry, promoted to Principal Musician, May 1st, 1863.

COMPANY H.

Captain John Dillon, resigned, July 26th, 1863.
First Lieutenant Joseph L. Smith, resigned, April 8th, 1863.
Second Lieutenant William H. Gore, promoted to First Lieutenant,
   April 9th, 1863, and to Captain, January 1st, 1864.
First Sergeant Wilson DeGarmo, promoted to Second Lieutenant,
   April 9th, 1863, and to First Lieutenant, July 27th, 1864.
First Sergeant David A. Holland, promoted to Second Lieutenant,
   April 22d, 1864.

COMPANY I.

Captain Paris T. Totten, died of wounds received at battle of Jenkins'
   Ferry, May 24th, 1864.
First Lieutenant John Henderson, resigned, March 25th, 1863.

Second Lieutenant John Reichard, promoted to First Lieutenant, March 26th, 1863; resigned, July 26th, 1863.

First Sergeant Joseph M. Clark, promoted to First Lieutenant, November 1st, 1863, resigned, March 30th, 1864.

Second Sergeant Levi Carrothers, promoted to First Lieutenant, June 14th, 1864, and to Captain, July 21st, 1864.

Third Sergeant Samuel L. Strong, promoted to Second Lieutenant, March 26th, 1863; resigned, May 20th, 1864.

Sergeant Oscar L. Jones, promoted to First Lieutenant, July 21st, 1864.

First Sergeant Henry J. Gunter, promoted to Second Lieutenant in 113th A.D., May 27th, 1864.

COMPANY K.

Captain Thornton McIntosh, resigned, March 3d, 1863.

First Lieutenant George Gilchrist, resigned, March 3d, 1863.

Second Lieutenant John M. Baugh, promoted to Captain, March 4th, 1863; resigned, August 16th, 1864.

Fourth Sergeant Thomas R. Connor, promoted to First Lieutenant, March 4th, 1863; killed in battle of Jenkins' Ferry, April 30th, 1864.

Corporal Wm. A. Rankin, promoted to Second Lieutenant, March 4th, 1863, to 1st Lieutenant, July 21st, 1864, and to Captain, September 16th, 1864.

First Sergeant James Loughridge, promoted to First Lieutenant, September 16th, 1864.

Private Royal, promoted to Second Lieutenant in 54th A.D., July 28th, 1863.

Private Sanford Eastburn, promoted to First Lieutenant in 113th A.D., May 8th, 1864.

OFFICIAL REPORTS.

OFFICIAL REPORTS.

DEFENSE OF HELENA, ARKANSAS.

REPORT OF COLONEL S. A. RICE, COMMANDING BRIGADE.

HEAD-QUARTERS 2D BRIGADE, 13TH DIV., 13TH A. C., DEPT. OF THE ⎫
TENN., HELENA, ARK., JULY 7TH, A.D., 1863. ⎰

Captain A. Blocki, A. A. General,

CAPTAIN:—I have the honor to submit the following report of the
part taken by the 2d Brigade in the action of the 4th inst.:

The 33d Missouri Infantry were stationed at Fort Curtis, and at
Batteries A, B, C and D, which covered your entire line of defense. At
all of these points they manned the artillery, and also had a reserve
who acted as sharpshooters.

The 33d Iowa Infantry was ordered to report to Fort Curtis, opposite the center of your line, at day-break, so that in case of an attack
they might readily be thrown to the support of either wing, or the
center of your line. At 4 o'clock, A. M., the enemy, in heavy force, drove
in our pickets, and opened the engagement on Batteries A, C and D.
The 33d Iowa was promptly, in compliance with your orders, moved
into the rifle-pits, in front and flanking Batteries C and D, with a
small portion acting as a reserve, who were posted so as to command
the ravine between these batteries. Three companies of the 36th Iowa
were sent at once to support Battery A and took possession of the
rifle-pits flanking it. The 29th Iowa, with a reserve from the 36th,
was ordered to take possession of the sides of the bluffs, on the east
side, and a short distance in front of Battery A, extending down to the
Sterling road, and drive the enemy from the crests of the hills which
they already had occupied. On batteries C and D the main assault of
the enemy was made. They hurled regiment after regiment, in closed
column, against the works, but were gallantly repulsed at Battery D,
and only after a severe and bloody conflict, took Battery C, driving
our forces before them, but they promptly rallied, and formed at the
bottom of the hill. The artillery from Batteries A, B and D, together
with Fort Curtis, commanding Battery C, was opened upon the

enemy, and after a severe cannonading, assisted by a galling fire from our infantry, they were driven back, with a heavy loss, and the battery retaken. The heavy loss sustained by the 33d Missouri and the 33d Iowa, on this portion of the field, fully attests their undoubted courage.

While the engagement was thus progressing in the center, the enemy were also concentrating a heavy fire on the right wing, which had been assigned to my command. They had planted a battery within four hundred yards of Battery A, but protected from its fire by a point of the hill; from the concentrated fire of the 1st Indiana Battery, (light artillery,) and a section of the 3d Iowa Battery, under Lieutenant Wright, assisted by our sharpshooters and a severe fire along the entire line, the enemy were compelled to withdraw their guns, with a severe loss. On this portion of our line the enemy had, besides their artillery, a brigade of four regiments of infantry, and a brigade of cavalry, under General Marmaduke, and at all points outnumbered us, at least four to one, according to their own estimates.

The officers and soldiers of the 29th Iowa acted with the utmost coolness and bravery, and steadily gained ground from the first onset. The 36th Iowa behaved in a manner worthy of all commendation. They were promptly moved to the relief of the 29th Iowa, and drove, by their well directed fire, the enemy before them, occupying the crests of the hills. The enemy could repeatedly be heard trying to rally their columns for the purpose of charging on our line, and were only prevented by the continuous fire of our line, assisted by a heavy and well directed cross fire from our artillery and the rifle-pits.

The 33d Missouri, manning the guns in the various batteries along the entire line, was at all points exposed to the hottest fire of the enemy, and deserve the highest praise for their bravery and efficiency. The heavy loss sustained by the enemy fully attests the bravery, the discipline, and efficiency of your entire command. There was taken by my command several hundred prisoners. We have buried one hundred and fifty-six of the enemy. There were also taken three stands of colors and several hundred stands of arms. The route of the enemy was complete at all points.

The loss in my command was forty-five killed, ninety-six wounded, and thirty missing. A full report of the above from each regiment, I append hereto. As a portion of my brigade, the 33d Iowa and part of the 33d Missouri, were in another part of the field from that assigned

to my command, and acted more immediately under your own observation, I trust, in case I have not been able to present fully the part
they took in the action, that you will supply the deficiency in your
official report. A detailed account of the part taken by the various
regiments of the brigade, would involve not only what was done by
them but by other brigades, who bore an equally honorable part in
the entire engagement, and especially that of Colonel Clayton, of the
5th Kansas, who, with the 1st Indiana Battery and his cavalry, bore
an important part in the engagement on the right of the line. When
all did so well, invidious distinction would be out of place. If some
bore more conspicuous parts than others, it was because the position
of their own commands placed them in a more important position. I
take especial pleasure in referring to Colonel Benton, of the 29th
Iowa; Colonel Kittredge, of the 36th Iowa; Lieutenant-Colonel Heath,
commanding 33d Missouri; Lieutenant-Colonel Mackey, commanding
33d Iowa; Lieutenant-Colonel Patterson, 29th Iowa; Majors Gibson,
Van Beck, and Shoemaker, who from their coolness, efficiency, and
daring, are worthy of especial mention. They were at all times at the
post of danger cheering their men. Lieutenant Lacy, my A. A. A.
General, acted as my aid during the engagement, and rode to whatever part of the field required his presence, and afforded me assistance of the most valuable character, and I take especial pleasure in
referring to him.

      I am, Captain, very respectfully, your ob't serv't,

(Signed),   SAMUEL A. RICE,
          Colonel 33d Iowa Infantry, comd'g 2d Brigade.

CAPTURE OF LITTLE ROCK, ARKANSAS.

REPORT OF MAJOR-GENERAL STEELE.

HEAD-QUARTERS ARKANSAS EXPEDITION, ⎫
LITTLE ROCK, ARK., SEPT. 12, 1863. ⎭

General:—I have the honor to submit the following as a summary
of the operations which led to the occupation of the capital by the
expeditionary army under my command.

On the 31st day of July I arrived at Helena, and pursuant to instructions from Major-General Grant, reported by letter to the commander of the 16th Army Corps for instructions relative to the fitting out of an expedition against Little Rock. General Hurlbut placed under my command all the troops at Helena, and the cavalry division under Brigadier-General Davidson, then operating in Arkansas. The garrison at Helena had been reinforced by two brigades of Kimball's division, which had just arrived from Snyder's Bluff, and were suffering severely from the malarious influences of the Yazoo country. The proportion of sick among the Helena troops was also very large. Three regiments were designated to remain at Helena, and these, with the sick and convalescents of the whole command were to constitute the garrison of that place. The troops at Helena designated for the expedition amounted to about six thousand (6,000) of all arms. There were three 6-gun and one 4-gun batteries, including six 10-pounder Parrott's. The cavalry, 1st Indiana, and 5th Kansas, amounted to less than (500) five hundred for duty. The 1st Indiana had three small rifled guns.

Davidson reported something less than (6,000) six thousand present for duty in his cavalry division, and (18) eighteen pieces of artillery—showing an aggregate of about (12,000) twelve thousand for duty. Brigadier-Generals Kimball and Salomon obtained leave of absence, and the resignation of General Ross was accepted, which left me with but one general officer, Davidson.

The resignation of my A. A. General was accepted just at this time, and there were no officers of the quartermaster or subsistence department at Helena, except Captain Allen, A. C. S., and Captain Noble, A. Q. M., who were in charge of the stores in the depot. I ordered the establishment of camps for the sick and convalescents, and organized the command in the best manner possible. Davidson pushed on to Clarendon and established a ferry for crossing troops, corduroying two miles of bottom and laying down the pontoon bridges across the Rock Rae bayou. On the 10th of August the Helena troops, organized into a division under Colonel, now Brigadier-General, S. A. Rice, marched toward Clarendon, with orders to reconstruct the bridges which had been destroyed by the rebels and to make all necessary repairs on the road, which was in bad condition.

Kimball's division, under Colonel McLean, followed next day. The whole command was at Clarendon and commenced crossing the river on the 17th of August. Before the crossing was effected I found my operations encumbered by over (1,000) one thousand sick. To have established a hospital and depot at this point would have involved the necessity of occupying both sides of the river. Duvall's Bluff was a more healthy location, and the route from there to Little Rock possessed many advantages over the other as a line of operations. I therefore ordered all the stores and sick to be sent to Duvall's Bluff by water. The enemy had constructed rifle-pits in a commanding position fronting the crossing on Rock Rae bayou, but, on the approach of Davidson's division, had fallen back, leaving only a picket. This position could easily have been turned by the road leading up from Harris's ferry.

On the 22d Davidson was directed to move with his division to Deadman's lake and reconnoiter the enemy's position at Brownsville. On the 23d the rest of the command moved to Duvall's Bluff, the transports carrying the sick and stores under convoy of the gun-boats. An advantageous site was selected on the bluff for a hospital and depot, and details immediately ordered to throw up intrenchments, cut away the timber on the flanks to give the gun-boats clear view and range, to erect sheds, &c.

On the 24th Davidson advanced to Two Prairie bayou, and on the 25th continued the march, skirmishing with Marmaduke's cavalry up to Brownsville, dislodging him at that place, and driving him into his intrenchments at bayou Metoe on the 20th. The attack was renewed on the 27th, and the enemy driven from his works on the bayou, and fired the bridge as he retreated. Davidson was unable to save the bridge, everything having been prepared for the destruction before hand. The bayou was deep and miry, and the pursuit of the rebels being thus checked, Davidson withdrew to his camp at Brownsville, leaving pickets at the crossings on the bayou. I received information that True's brigade from Memphis would arrive at Clarendon on the 20th, and immediately sent a party to construct a bridge across Rock Rae bayou, and a ferry-boat to cross the troops over White river. True crossed on the 30th of August, and on the 1st of September moved up to Deadman's lake. The advance from Duvall's Bluff also commenced on the 1st, the place having been put in such a state of defense that the convalescents and a small detail left there were deemed sufficient to hold it against any force the enemy would be likely to send against it. On the 2d instant all my available force was concentrated at

Brownsville. It had been ascertained that the military road on the south side of Bayou Metoe passed through a section impracticable for any military operations—swamp, timber, and entanglements of vines and undergrowth, and was commanded by the enemy's works. I therefore directed Davidson to make a reconnoissance in force around the enemy's left by way of Austin, and, if practicable, to penetrate his lines and ascertain both his strength and position. Rice's division was ordered forward to make a diversion in Davidson's favor on Bayou Metoe. Rice drove in the enemy's pickets, shelled the woods on the south side of the bayou for several hours, and encamped for the night. In the meantime, Davidson pushed his reconnoissance until the numerous roads on his flanks and rear rendered it dangerous for him to proceed any further. The great length to which it would increase our line of communication with our base rendered it impracticable for us to attack the enemy on his left flank. This reconnoissance occupied two days.

By this time I had collected information in regard to the road leading by Shallow Ford and Ashley's Mills to the Arkansas and the right of the enemy's works, which determined me to take that route. The march to the front was resumed on the 6th. Here we found ourselves again encumbered with a large number of sick—near 700. True's brigade and Ritter's brigade of cavalry were left to guard the supply train and the sick. On the 7th we reached the Arkansas near Ashley's Mills. At this point, Davidson's cavalry, in advance, had a sharp skirmish with the enemy. The 8th and 9th were employed in reconnoissance, repairing the road back to Bayou Metoe, and in bringing up the sick and the supply train, with the two brigades left at Brownsville.

I had now definitely determined upon a plan of attack. Davidson was directed to lay the pontoon bridge at an eligible point, throw his division across the Arkansas river, and move directly on Little Rock, threatening the enemy's right flank and rear, while I moved with the rest of the force on the north flank and assailed the right of his works. During the night of the 9th Davidson made his dispositions for crossing the Arkansas, and on the morning of the 10th had the pontoon bridge laid. The second division was ordered to report to him at day-light to assist in covering his crossing. The bridge was placed in a bend of the river, and the ground on the south side was so completely swept by Davidson's artillery that the enemy could not plant a battery in any position from which he could interrupt the crossing.

Two regiments of infantry passed over the river to drive the enemy's skirmishers out of the woods, and the cavalry division passed on without serious interruption until they reached Bayou Fourche, where the enemy were drawn up in line to receive them. The rebels held their position obstinately until our artillery on the opposite side of the river was opened upon their flank and rear, when they gave way and were steadily pushed back by Davidson, the artillery constantly playing upon them from the other side of the river. Our two columns marched nearly abreast on either side of the Arkansas. Volumes of smoke in the direction of Little Rock indicated to us that the rebels had evacuated their works on the north side of the river, and were burning their pontoon bridges. Heavy clouds of dust moving down toward Davidson on the other side of the river made me apprehensive that the enemy contemplated falling upon him with his entire force. He was instructed in such an event to form on the beach, where his flanks could be protected by our artillery on the other side, and where aid might be sent to him by a ford. But they were in full retreat. Marmaduke's cavalry only were disputing Davidson's entry of the city. The rebels had fired three pontoon bridges laid across the Arkansas at the city, and several railroad cars. Two locomotives were also on fire, but were saved by us; part of the pontoons were also saved. Six steamboats were entirely destroyed by fire, and we are informed that Price intended to have blown up the arsenal, but was pressed so close that he failed in this.

Our cavalry was too much exhausted to pursue the enemy's retreating columns far, on the evening of the 10th. Next morning Merrill's and Clayton's brigades renewed the chase and followed them twenty miles, taking a number of prisoners and causing the enemy to destroy a part of his train. Little Rock was formally surrendered by the municipal authorities on the evening of the 10th. Price had undoubtedly intended to give us battle in his intrenchments, but was entirely surprised by our movement across the Arkansas, and did not suspect it until after the pontoon bridge was laid. When it was reported to him that our infantry were crossing, he took it for granted that our whole force was moving to cut off his retreat to Arkadelphia. I have been assured by citizens that General Cabell, with about (4,000) four thousand troops from Fort Smith, had joined Price on his retreat, he having failed to reach here in time to assist in the defense of the place. I marched from Ashley's Mills on the morning of the 10th with not more than (7,000) seven thousand troops, having parked the trains and left a strong guard to defend them and the sick.

The operation of the army from the time that I commenced organizing it at Helena have occupied exactly forty days.

Our entire loss in killed, wounded, and prisoners, will not exceed (100) one hundred. The enemy's is much greater, especially in prisoners—at least (1,000) one thousand.

I shall reserve the list of casualties and my special recommendations for a future communication. However, I will say that Davidson and his cavalry division deserve the highest commendation.

I enclose Brigadier-General Davidson's report.

Very respectfully, your ob't serv't,

FRED. STEELE,
Major-General commanding.

Major-General SCHOFIELD, *Commanding Department of the Missouri.*

MARCH TO CAMDEN, ARKANSAS.

HEAD-QUARTERS 33D IOWA INFANTRY VOLUNTEERS,}
CAMDEN, ARK., APRIL 20, 1864.}

John F. Lacy, A. A. A. General, 1st Brig., 3d Div., 7th Army Corps, and Army of Arkansas,

LIEUTENANT: In compliance with general orders from head-quarters 1st brigade, I herewith transmit you the following report pertaining to the 33d Regiment Iowa Infantry Volunteers, during the recent campaign, including lists of casualities, etc., etc.

Prior to the arrival of our forces at Prairie d'Anne, the part taken in any engagement by my regiment was entirely unimportant. On arriving at Prairie d'Anne, I was ordered to form line of battle and move to the left of the 50th Indiana, which was done. I was then ordered to form column by division, and in that order I moved forward on to the prairie. While crossing a slough in the timber joining the prairie, a shell from the enemy's gun exploded near the regiment, killing one man and breaking several guns. On reaching the open ground, I again deployed, sending forward two companies as skirmishers, with instructions to move steadily forward, which they did, driving the enemy before them, the regiment moving to their support. In this order I moved forward till the regiment rested where the enemy's artillery first opened fire. It then being dark, the skirmishers were ordered to rest in place, and the regiment retired two hundred yards to unexposed grounds, and bivouacked. At 11 o'clock P. M., the enemy dashed upon the skirmish line, but was repulsed without injury to us. The transactions of the following day are unimportant.

On the morning of the 13th of April, we moved, in connection with the entire forces, through and to the west of Prairie d'Anne, our skirmishers steadily driving the enemy before them. On approaching their works on the Camden and Washington road, the enemy hastily withdrew. From this time till the morning of the 15th, nothing worthy of note transpired.

On the 15th day of April, my regiment was the advance infantry. Two companies were deployed as skirmishers on either side of the road, and, having moved forward two miles, were fired upon by the enemy. The skirmishers moved forward, driving them, assisted by a howitzer, until they came within range of the enemy's artillery, which was opened upon us, wounding four men. My regiment supported the 2d Missouri Battery on the right. Having taken this position, I sent forward three sharpshooters from each company to assist the skirmishers and annoy the enemy's gunners. After an engagement of two hours, the enemy withdrew from his position, after which the march was resumed. At about two miles distance, we were again fired on. While awaiting orders a shell from the enemy's gun burst near my regiment, dangerously wounding one man. A sharp skirmish was kept up for two and a half miles, when the enemy withdrew from our front.

Our entire loss in killed and wounded when we reached Camden amounted to one killed and four wounded.

I was relieved of my command on the 19th of April, while in camp at Camden, Colonel Mackey having arrived at the regiment.

H. D. GIBSON,
Major commanding regiment.

RETURN TO LITTLE ROCK.

HEAD-QUARTERS 33D IOWA INFANTRY VOLUNTEERS,⎫
LITTLE ROCK, ARK., MAY 6TH, 1864.⎭

John F. Lacy, A. A. A. General, 1st Brig., 3d Div., 7th Army Corps,

LIEUTENANT: I have the honor herewith to transmit you the following report of the engagement in which the 33d Regiment Iowa Infantry took part from the time of my taking command at Camden, Ark., until its arrival at Little Rock, including a list of casualties, etc.

I arrived at Camden on the 19th day of April, and immediately took command of my regiment, at this time six hundred strong. Nothing of particular interest took place from the time of the evacuation of Camden until my arrival at Saline river. On the evening of the 29th, at 6 1/2 o'clock P. M., I was ordered to the rear on the Camden road to support Colonel Inglemann's brigade, an attack being anticipated during the night. I stood at arms during the entire night, the enemy making no particular demonstration, although in speaking distance. Night very dark and raining most of the time.

About 4 o'clock A. M. on the 30th, I received orders that, as soon as the 43d Illinois Infantry on my left was withdrawn, I should retire about three-fourths of a mile towards the river, and take position covering the passage of the troops while crossing. This movement I executed without being discovered by the enemy. This position I occupied half an hour when the enemy made his appearance. The skirmishers immediately engaged them, holding them in check for half an hour. When I was relieved by the 27th Wisconsin Infantry, I marched my command to a new position, one mile in the direction of the crossing. In twenty minutes the engagement became general, and I was ordered to the support of the 50th Indiana Infantry on the left. From this time until the close of the battle, the regiment was almost continually engaged.

As to the conduct of both officers and men of my command, I can not speak in terms too high. To attempt distinction would be injustice to my command, as all did their duty nobly. A short time before the close of the action, I received a wound in my right arm, which compelled me to quit the field, the command of the regiment devolving upon Captain Boydston, Company A, who, at the close of the engagement, marched the regiment off in good order.

The regiment arrived in camp at Little Rock, Ark., on the 3d day of May, 1864. Nothing of importance transpired during the remainder of our march.

It would be doing great injustice to the enlisted men of my command to fail to notice the manner in which they endured the fatigue and privations of the march, the rations being exhausted on the 29th of April.

For the operations of the regiment prior to my command, reference is made to the report of Major H. D. Gibson, herewith transmitted.

With the highest respect,

Your obedient servant,

C. H. MACKEY, Colonel comd'g.

EXTENT OF CASUALTIES

Killed—enlisted men, 8. Wounded—commissioned officers, 6; enlisted men, 96. Missing—enlisted men, 13. Total loss, 123.

CASUALTIES IN ARKANSAS.

List of Casualties in 33d regiment Iowa Infantry Volunteers, while in the field, from March 23d, 1864, to April 26th, 1864—Major H. D. Gibson, commanding.

KILLED.—William P. Funk, April 10th, struck in head by piece of shell.

WOUNDED, APRIL 15TH.—Enos M. Woods, leg, by piece of shell; Wm. H. Anderson, thigh, while skirmishing; John Burgess, leg, while skirmishing; William H. Withrow, hand, while skirmishing; all severely.

RECAPITULATION.—Total, killed, 1; wounded, 4; entire loss, 5.

List of Casualties in 33d regiment Iowa Infantry Volunteers, while in the field, from April 26th, 1864, to May 3d, 1864, time of the return of the command to Little Rock.

COMMISSIONED OFFICERS (ALL WOUNDED).—Colonel Cyrus H. Mackey, arm, severe; Captains A. J. Comstock, Co. C, thigh, severely, prisoner; Paris T. Totten, Co. I, thigh, severely, since died; 1st Lieuts. Thos. R. Conner, Co. K, neck, mortal, died in hands of enemy; Wilson DeGarmo, Co. H, hip, slight; 2d Lieut. Oliver I. Kindig, Co. C, leg, slight.

ENLISTED MEN, KILLED.—2d Sergt. John N. Ewing, Co. D, left on the field; Privates Thomas H. Hinckle, Co. E, left on the field; G. W. Shanafelt, Co. H, left on the field; J. M. Rowland, Co. H, left on the field; Smith Banta, Co. I, left on the field; John M. Henderson, Co. I, left on the field; Sergt. Jasper Skinner, Co. F; Private Wm. A. Towbridge, Co. D.

WOUNDED.—Sergeant-Major John R. Crawford, thigh, severe, prisoner.

COMPANY A.—Corp'l John S. Johnston, leg, severe; Privates James T. Duncan, thigh, severe; Jonathan S. Tindall, hip, severe; Hiram P. Henry, thigh, severe; Alfred Hagar, shoulder, slight.

COMPANY B.—Dennis Decker, thigh, severe, prisoner; John E. Nichols, arm, severe; Francis M. Wertz, hand, slight.

COMPANY C.—1st Sergeant Joshua B. Wells, thigh, slight; Sergt. John T. Gaunt, shoulder, severe; Corp'l Reuben Coomes, arm, slight; Privates Mortimer Jackson, hip, slight, prisoner; John Dove, breast, severe, prisoner; Wm. B. Walker, thigh, slight, prisoner; Owen Bartlett, ankle, slight; Wm. Osborn, thigh, severe, prisoner; R. W. B. Curry, thigh, severe, prisoner; Edward Graham, groin, severe, prisoner.

COMPANY D.—Corp'ls John W. Jones, leg, severe, prisoner; Samuel Doughman, face, slight; Privates Samuel L. Deweese, arm, severe; Riley Mitchell, arm, severe, prisoner; David Adams, leg, severe, prisoner; Wm. Thorp, breast, severe, prisoner; Morris A. Quaintance, back, severe, prisoner.

COMPANY E.—2d Serg't John M. Finney, arm, slight; Corp'l David G. Wilson, shoulder, severe, prisoner; Privates Willis S. Bird, leg, slight; Wm. J. Bowers, breast, slight; Amos Corns, abdomen, severe, prisoner; Wheeler Chadwick, ankle, severe, prisoner; Benjamin Cruzen, hip, severe, prisoner; Lewis H. Cochran, back, slight; Adam Eichelbarger, thigh, severe, prisoner; James W. Grover, leg, slight, prisoner; John B. Harris, thigh, slight; Anthony Hawk, knee, severe, prisoner; Philander M. Miller, abdomen, slight, prisoner; John H. Miller, leg, severe, prisoner; Samuel S. Robertson, breast, slight; Joseph Redpath, arm, slight; Levi Shaw, head, slight; Daniel Baun, leg, slight.

COMPANY F.—Corp'l S. B Montgomery, thigh, slightly; Private W. Gibson, leg, severely, prisoner.

COMPANY G.—Corp'ls John K. Fidler, knees, severely, prisoner; Lucien Reynolds, arm, severely, prisoner; Privates William O. Downs, neck, severely; John Henry, leg, severely, prisoner; John Nurmeyer, sr., leg, severely, prisoner; Issac N. Ritner, thigh, slightly; Jacob Taylor, neck, severely, prisoner; George W. Towne, face and thigh, severely, prisoner; Thomas D. Wallace, leg, slightly; Stephanus Dekock, arm, severely.

COMPANY H.—2d Sergt. Philip L. Suiter, shoulder, severely, prisoner; 5th Sergt. John Wightman, abdomen, mortally, prisoner; Corp'ls T. J. Lawler, hand, severely; James Garret, leg, slightly; C. J. Goldthwaite, arm, severely; David Holloway, leg, severely, prisoner; Privates Hiner Dorman, neck, severely; John Shoff, leg, slightly; William M. Rodman, groin, severely, prisoner; William T. Disor, abdomen, slightly; James D. Compton, ankle, severely, prisoner; Thomas Lantry, thigh, severely, prisoner; William J Parke, neck, mortally, prisoner; M. A. Peck, legs, severely, prisoner; A. A. McNeil, side, severely; William R. Hoyt, hand, slightly; O. P. McNeil, neck, slightly.

COMPANY I.—Sergeants Oscar L. Jones, arm, slightly; Peter K. Bonebrake, shoulder, slightly; Corporal James W. Strong, leg, severely, prisoner; Privates Joseph Brobst, breast, severely, prisoner; Smith Dunlap, leg, severely, prisoner; John M. McClelland, hip, slightly; Eri Goodenough, arm, slightly; Enoch Palmer, head, slightly; William G. Reed, leg, slightly; John S. Snyder, leg, severely, prisoner; James I. Welch, abdomen, severely, prisoner; John Bruett, arm, severely, prisoner.

COMPANY K.—Corporals George B. Stratton, thigh, severely, prisoner; William R. Cowan, leg, slightly; Privates D. T. Evans, head, slightly; E. F. Henderson, back, severely; J. C. Roberts, leg, slightly; John M. Martin, arm, slightly; F. M. Playel, leg, severely, prisoner; William H. Coulburn, leg, severely, prisoner; Samuel Smith, ankle, severely, prisoner; Alexander Jones, head, severely, prisoner; H. C. Haskell, leg, severely, prisoner; Ephriam S. Smith, side, severely, prisoner.

MISSING.—Privates John R. Allsup, Co. B; Francis M. Dyer, Co. B; Clark Boon, Co. H; James Wendell, Co. K; Hannibal Rogers, Co. B; Reuben Coomes, Co. C; F. M. Gibson, Co. F; Kryn De Bruyn, Co. G;

John Nurmeyer, jr., Co. G; Hans Ferguson, Co. I; David T. Welch Co. I; George S. Carson, Co. E, April 23. These men have all since been accounted for. Nathaniel H. Richardson, Co. A, David Dunbar, Co. E, Daniel A. Wisir, Co. G, and Samuel M. Tennis, Co. H, were taken prisoners with train near Mark's Mills, April 23d, 1864.

All the above casualties, except when another time is given, occurred on the 30th of April.

RECAPITULATION.—Killed—enlisted men, 8. Wounded—commissioned officers, 6; enlisted men, 97. Missing, 12. Total, 123.

Lost under Major Gibson, 5; prisoners, 4; entire loss on expedition, 133.

PARTIAL HISTORY OF THE REGIMENT

HEAD-QUARTERS 33D IOWA INFANTRY VOLUNTEERS,
MCINTOSH'S BLUFF, ALA., MAY 1, 1865.

GEN. N. B. BAKER, *Adjutant-General of Iowa:*

GENERAL:—I have the honor to make the following report of operations of the 33d Iowa Infantry from October 30, 1864. We left Little Rock, Ark., to escort a supply train of two hundred wagons to Fort Smith, Ark., a distance of 180 miles. We marched to Fort Smith, and returned with the train in twenty-nine days. Number of days marched, twenty-six; entire distance traveled three hundred and sixty miles, all of which was accomplished without the loss of a single team or soldier. This march was made at the time of Gen. Price's retreat from Missouri, and we captured two officers and thirty-eight men belonging to his command.

On the 21st day of January, 1865, the regiment started on an expedition from Little Rock to Mt. Elba, Ark., on the Saline river, and returned on the 4th day of February, 1865, to Little Rock. Distance traveled one hundred and sixty miles.

On our return to Little Rock we were ordered to report to Major-General Canby at New Orleans.

Left Little Rock for New Orleans on the 14th day of February, 1865, and arrived at the latter place, February 19th, 1865. From

Little Rock to Duvall's Bluffs, we were transported by railroad; from the latter place to New Orleans, by steamboat. On the 23d day of February, 1865, we left New Orleans, on Ponchartrain Railroad, and from the terminus of this road—Lakeport—took transports for Navy Cove, Ala. It was at this place that the army was organized for the expedition against the city of Mobile. By this organization we were transferred from the 7th Army Corps to the 13th.

On the 17th day of March, 1865, the movement against Mobile commenced, the 13th Army Corps moving by land around Mobile Bay, east side. The country through which we moved is generally known among citizens as "The Wilderness." We were compelled to make miles of corduroy in order to get our trains and artillery through. The distance through "The Wilderness" we considered ourselves through when we crossed Fish river is forty-five miles; time occupied seven days. The 16th Army Corps arrived at the mouth of Fish river one day in advance of the 13th. On the 25th day of March, 1865, the two army corps took up their line of march for Spanish Fort, twenty-five miles north of the mouth of Fish river, and nearly opposite the city of Mobile, where we arrived on the evening of the 27th of March, 1865. The enemy's works were completely invested the following morning. On the night of the 8th of April, 1865, the enemy evacuated the place, leaving all their artillery and munitions of war. They evacuated by water, the navy having been unable to cut off this way of retreat.

I append herewith a list of the casualties of the regiment during the siege. The little damage we sustained from the enemy's fire is accounted for in this way: During the first night after we invested the place, we succeeded in pushing our skirmishers so close to the enemy's works that their gunners and sharpshooters could not do us much damage. The gunners could not work their guns, and the sharp-shooters of the enemy were compelled to keep inside the main works. On the 9th of April, 1865, we left Spanish Fort for Blakely, twelve miles north, which place had been invested by a portion of our forces under command of Major-General Steele. We arrived there in the evening, just as the place had been carried by assault. We lay at this place until 6 o'clock P. M., April 11th, when we were ordered to retrace our steps to Stark's Landing, (near Spanish Fort,) where we arrived at 4 o'clock the following morning, and immediately embarked on transports and crossed to the opposite side of the bay. That evening we arrived in Mobile, the rebels having evacuated the place.

The following day our division (the 3d) marched from the city of Mobile to Whistler Station, twelve miles; had a slight skirmish with the enemy, and captured a considerable amount of rolling stock of the Mobile & Ohio Railroad.

On the 19th day of April, 1865, we left that place and marched to our present camp, forty miles.

During this campaign we were allowed one six-mule team for every two hundred and fifty men. The men carried in their knapsacks a complete change of underclothing, an extra pair of shoes, one blanket, one poncho, and one shelter tent to every two men, fifty rounds of ammunition each, one spade and one ax to every twelve men, and rations were issued every five days. The average number of men for duty in the regiment during the campaign was five hundred and fifty. The health of the command has been very good during the campaign.

I have the honor to be, Colonel, your obedient servant,

C. H. MACKEY, Colonel commanding.

MAY 1st, 1865.

LIST OF CASUALTIES *(all wounded) in Thirty-Third Iowa Infantry Volunteers during the Siege of Spanish Fort, Ala.:*

Wm. S. Parmley, Captain Co. B, breast slightly.

George L. Ledyard,	"	G, face,	"

Abraham Day, Corporal,	"	F, foot,	"

Wm. Dingeman, Private,	"	G, face,	"

Martin Walraven,	"	"	G, right arm, severely.

John Metz,	"	"	left shoulder,	"

Joseph Dungan,	"	"	G, right hip,	"

G. W. Long,	"	"	B, right leg, slightly.

Wm. Campbell, 1st Serg't,	"	C, head,	"

Thos. J. Gooden, Private,	"	C, right eye,	"

William Harris,	"	"	H, head, mortally.

Stephen Wharton,	"	"	E, mouth, severely.

Respectfully submitted,

C. H. MACKEY, Col. 33d Iowa Infantry.

CONCLUSION OF HISTORY OF REGIMENT.

HEAD-QUARTERS 33D REGIMENT IOWA VOL. INFT.,⎫
DAVENPORT, Iowa, Aug. 8th 1865.⎰

N. B. Baker, Adjutant General of Iowa:

GENERAL: I have the honor to make the following report of the movement of my regiment since last report, which left me on McIntosh's Bluff Alabama. On the 1st of June, we received orders to embark on the ocean steamer Continental, for Brazos Santiago, Texas; which order we obeyed, and landed on the Brazos Island on the 7th of July. Remained on the island one week, during which time we were badly supplied with water, the condenser on the island not being able to furnish sufficient water for the number of the troops there. After remaining here one week, we moved on to the Rio Grande opposite the town of Bagdad.

Here we remained until the 26th of July, when we received orders from Major-General Steele to report to Galveston, Texas, for muster-out of the service. We embarked on the steamer Warrior, on the 1st of July, and arrived at Galveston on the 3d, reporting at that place to Major-General Granger, who ordered us to proceed to New Orleans, La., to make out our rolls for muster-out. Left Galveston on the morning of the 4th of July, and arrived at New Orleans on the 7th, reporting to Major-General Sheridan, who transferred us from the 13th Corps to General Canby's command. We proceeded immediately to making out our rolls and completed them on the 17th of July, and on the 18th started for Davenport. Very poor boats were furnished us to come up the river on, by reason of which we did not arrive in Davenport until the 1st of August. The regiment is being paid off to-day, August 8, 1865.

The health of the command has been good. The three-years recruits of my regiment were not mustered out with the old soldiers, but were transferred to the 34th Iowa. I wish to call your attention to the fact, that nearly all the other regiments are allowed to muster out their recruits. Justice to these men of my regiment, requires that they should be mustered out also. There is no excuse for keeping a few, and allowing the most of them to be mustered out.

The number of enlisted men mustered out is 400; officers, 30. Total, 430.

I have the honor to be, General, your obedient servant,

C. H. MACKEY, Col. Commanding regiment.

NOTES

EDITORS' INTRODUCTION

1. "Company Descriptive Book," n.d., "Field and Staff Muster-out Roll," July 17, 1865, both in Military Files of Andrew F. Sperry, Civil War (Union) Compiled Military Service Records, 33d Iowa Infantry, Military Service Branch, Record Group 94, Records of the Adjutant General's Office, 1780s–1917, National Archives, Washington, D.C.; "Declaration for Invalid Pension," June 30, 1904, Pension File of Andrew F. Sperry, Military Service Branch, Record Group 94, Records of the Adjutant General's Office, 1780s–1917, National Archives, Washington, D.C.; Gregory J. W. Urwin, *The United States Infantry: An Illustrated History, 1775–1918* (New York: Sterling, 1991), 104.

2. Gerald F. Linderman, *Embattled Courage: The Experience of Combat in the American Civil War* (New York: Free Press, 1987), 266–70.

3. Reid Mitchell, *The Vacant Chair: The Northern Soldier Leaves Home* (New York: Oxford University Press, 1993); Stephen Z. Starr, "The Grand Old Regiment," *Wisconsin Magazine of History* 48 (1964): 23.

4. Starr, "Grand Old Regiment," 23; Urwin, *United States Infantry*, 93, 96.

5. Michael P. Musick, "The Little Regiment: Civil War Units and Commands," *Prologue: Quarterly of the National Archives* 27 (Summer 1995): 151.

6. Stephen Z. Starr, "The Second Michigan Volunteer Cavalry: Another View," *Michigan History* 60 (1976): 166; Starr, "Grand Old Regiment," 22–23; Musick, "Little Regiment," 153.

7. Starr, "Grand Old Regiment," 22.

8. Starr, "Second Michigan Cavalry," 167.

9. Linderman, *Embattled Courage*, 266–71.

10. Ibid., 275; Starr, "Grand Old Regiment," 23–25.

11. Stephen Z. Starr, "The Third Ohio Volunteer Cavalry: A View from the Inside," *Ohio History* 85 (1976): 308; Starr, "Grand Old Regiment," 24–26; Linderman, *Embattled Courage*, 291–96.

12. Michael Mullins and Rowena Reed, *The Union Bookshelf: A Selected Civil War Bibliography* (Wendell, N.C.: Broadfoot's Bookmark, 1982), iii–iv, 38–60; Allan Nevins, James I. Robertson Jr., and Bell I. Wiley, *Civil War Books: A Critical Bibliography*. 2 vols. (Baton Rouge: Louisiana State University Press, 1970), 1:162. See also Eugene C. Murdock, *The Civil War in the North: A Selective Annotated Bibliography* (New York: Garland, 1987), 209.

13. Some important works that have made good use of Sperry are: Ludwell H. Johnson, *Red River Campaign: Politics and Cotton in the Civil War* (Kent, Ohio: Kent State University Press, 1993); Edwin C. Bearss, *Steele's Retreat from Camden and the Battle of Jenkins' Ferry* (Little Rock: Eagle Press, 1990); Carl H. Moneyhon, *The Impact of the Civil War and Reconstruction on Arkansas: Persistence in the Midst of Ruin* (Baton Rouge: Louisiana State University Press, 1994); Bobby Roberts and Carl Moneyhon, *Portraits of Conflict: A Photographic History of Arkansas in the Civil War* (Fayetteville: University of Arkansas Press, 1987).

14. "Declaration for Invalid Pension," July 30, 1904, "Certificate of Death, District of Columbia," No. 197.795, April 29, 1911, Questionnaire 3-447, Department of the Interior, Bureau of Pensions, August 23, 1904, all in Sperry Pension File, National Archives; K. Van Stigt, *History of Pella, Iowa and Vicinity*, trans. Elisabeth Kempkes (Pella: Scholte House Foundation, 1995), 5–16, 27, 30–63, 73–76.

15. Van Stigt, *Pella, Iowa*, 84–85, 101–4, 112; Rob Dillard to author, July 7, 1998.

16. "Company Muster Roll," October 1–December 31, 1862, Sperry Military Files, National Archives; Bell Irvin Wiley, *The Life of Billy Yank: The Common Soldier of the Union* (Baton Rouge: Louisiana State University Press, 1978), 45–48; Henry Woodhead, ed., *Echoes of Glory: Arms and Equipment of the Union* (Alexandria, Va.: Time-Life Books, 1991), 236–39; For more on the role of music in Civil War armies, see: Kenneth E. Olson, *Music and Musket: Bands and Bandsmen of the American Civil War* (Westport, Conn.: Greenwood Press, 1981); Francis A. Lord and Arthur Wise, *Bands and Drummer Boys of the Civil War* (New York: Da Capo Press, 1979); Robert Garafalo and Mark Elrod, *A Pictorial History of Civil War Era Musical Instruments and Military Bands* (Charleston, W.V.: Pictorial Histories Publishing, 1985); W. J. Hardee, *Rifle and Light Infantry Tactics; For the Exercise and Manoeuvres of Troops When Acting as Light Infantry or Riflemen*, 2 vols. (Westport, Conn.: Greenwood Press, 1971); Dominic J. Dal Bello, *Parade, Inspection and Basic Evolutions of the Infantry Battalion: Being a Manual for Company Officers and Non-Commissioned Officers of Civil War Living History Units on the Movements of a Battalion of Infantry* (Santa Barbara, Calif.: Army of the Pacific, 1994).

17. "Field and Staff Muster-in Roll," October 1, 1862, Undated Form, "Company Muster-Roll," October 1–December 31, 1862, January–February 1863, "Field and Staff Muster-out Roll," July 17, 1865, all in Sperry Military Files, National Archives.

18. "Field and Staff Muster Roll," May-June 1863 through November-December 1864, "Field and Staff Muster-out Roll," July 17, 1865, "Company Muster-out Roll," May–June 1863, all in Sperry Military Files, National Archives; John N. Shepherd, "Autobiography," Guthrie, Okla., 1908, 40. Photostat copy of a book-length manuscript in the possession of Shepherd descendant Richard S. Warner, Tulsa, Okla.

19. "Certificate of Marriage Record, State of Iowa, Marion County," March 27, 1911, Questionnaire 3-389, Department of the Interior, Bureau of Pensions, August 23, 1904, Paul Sperry Deposition, March 22, 1911, all in Sperry Pension File, National Archives.

20. Questionnaire 3-389, Department of the Interior, Bureau of Pensions, August 23, 1904, Paul Sperry Deposition, March 22, 1911, "Copy of Will of Andrew F. Sperry," July 26, 1907, all in Sperry Pension File, National Archives.

21. "Declaration for Invalid Pension," July 30, 1904, Sperry Pension File, National Archives.

22. Ibid., Questionnaire 3-447, Department of the Interior, Bureau of Pensions, August 23, 1904, "Declaration for Pension," February 27, 1907, all in Sperry Pension File, National Archives.

23. "Declaration for Pension," February 27, 1907, "Drop Order and Report, Department of the Interior, Bureau of Pensions, Finance Division, Washington, D.C.," March 24, 1911, both in Sperry Pension File, National Archives.

24. "Copy of Will of Andrew F. Sperry," July 26, 1907, Sperry Pension File, National Archives.

25. "Certificate of Death, District of Columbia," No. 197.795, April 29, 1911, "Declaration for Widow's Pension," March 16, 1911, "Drop Report—Pensioner," June 20, 1923, all in Sperry Pension File, National Archives.

26. Hubert H. Wubben, *Civil War Iowa and the Copperhead Movement* (Ames: Iowa State University Press, 1980), 3, 11; Robert R. Dykstra, *Bright Radical Star: Black Freedom and White Supremacy on the Hawkeye Frontier* (Cambridge, Mass.: Harvard University Press, 1993), 63.

27. Charles E. Payne, *Josiah Bushnell Grinnell* (Iowa City: State Historical Society of Iowa, 1938), 50–51, 63–66; Kenneth L. Lyftogt, *From Blue Mills to Columbia: Cedar Falls and the Civil War* (Ames: Iowa State University Press, 1993), 18; Wubben, *Civil War*

Iowa, 3; Dykstra, *Bright Radical Star,* vii, 23, 26–27, 36, 46–47, 61–63, 105, 110–13, 134, 136–46; Van Stigt, *Pella, Iowa,* 115.

28. John E. Briggs, "The Enlistment of Iowa Troops during the Civil War," *Iowa Journal of History and Politics* 15 (July 1917): 324, 329, 333–38; Jacob A. Swisher, *Iowa in Times of War* (Iowa City: State Historical Society of Iowa, 1943), 42–44, 46–47, 77, 113, 154–55; H. H. Rood, "Iowa's Record: A Sketch of Iowa's Record during the War for the Preservation of the Union—1861–1865," in *War Sketches and Incidents as Related by Companions of the Iowa Commandery Military Order of the Loyal Legion of the United States,* vol. 1 (Des Moines: Press of P. C. Kenyon, 1893), 370–71; *The History of Mahaska County, Iowa, Containing a History of the County, Its Cities, Towns, &c.* (Des Moines: Union Historical Co., 1878), 385; Steve Meyer, *Iowans Called to Valor: The Story of Iowa's Entry into the Civil War* (Garrison, Iowa: Meyer Publishing, 1993), 21–22.

29. William F. Fox, *Regimental Losses in the American Civil War 1861–1865* (Albany, N.Y.: Brandow Printing Co., 1898), 515–16; Mildred Throne, "The Iowa Regiments," *Palimpsest* 50 (February 1969): 65–66; Julie E. Nelson and Alan M. Schroder, "Iowa and the Civil War: A Military Review," *Palimpsest* 63 (July/August 1982): 100; Meyer, *Iowans Called to Valor,* 9; Dykstra, *Bright Radical Star,* 196; Rood, "Iowa's Record," 378; Briggs, "Enlistment of Iowa Troops," 373; *History of Mahaska County,* 183.

30. Throne, "Iowa Regiments," 65; Meyer, *Iowans Called to Valor,* 9; Dykstra, *Bright Radical Star,* 196; Nelson and Schroder, "Iowa and the Civil War," 105; Rood, "Iowa's Record," 378.

31. Shepherd, "Autobiography," 32.

32. Urwin, *United States Infantry,* 102, 104; Briggs, "Enlistment of Iowa Troops," 354; *Keokuk (Iowa) Daily Gate City,* July 14, 1862.

33. U.S. War Department, *The War of the Rebellion: A Compilation of the Official Records of the Union and Confederate Armies,* 130 vols. (Washington, D.C.: Government Printing Office, 1880–1901), 3d ser., vol. 2, p. 206 (hereafter cited as *OR*); Urwin, *United States Infantry,* 104; Briggs, "Enlistment of Iowa Troops," 353–54.

34. Urwin, *United States Infantry,* 104; *OR,* 3d ser., vol. 2, p. 417; Briggs, "Enlistment of Iowa Troops," 354; Lyftogt, *From Blue Mills to Columbia,* 63; Swisher, *Iowa in Times of War,* 87; *History of Mahaska County,* 412.

35. Allan McNeal to "Dear Father," January 15, 1863, Allan McNeal Letters, 1862–63, in the possession of Larry Pearson, Anchorage, Alaska; Shepherd, "Autobiography," 37–38, 45–46; J. A. Newman, *The Autobiography of an Old Fashioned Boy* (El Reno, Okla.: Privately printed, 1923), 26; For a more detailed examination of religious affairs in the 33d Iowa, see Gregory J. W. Urwin, "'The Lord Has Not Forsaken Me and I Won't Forsake Him': Religion in Frederick Steele's Union Army, 1863–1864," *Arkansas Historical Quarterly* 52 (Autumn 1993): 318–40.

36. Military Files of Robert A. McAyeal, Civil War (Union) Compiled Military Service Records, 33d Iowa Infantry, Record Group 94, National Archives; Military Files of Francis M. Slusser, Civil War (Union) Compiled Military Service Records, 33d Iowa Infantry, Record Group 94, National Archives; *History of Mahaska County,* 483, 487, 581.

37. Samuel A. Rice to N. B. Baker, September 23, 1862, W. M. Scott, "Medical Certificate," June 9, 1863, Robert A. McAyeal to John A. Rawlins, June 28, 1863, all in McAyeal Military Files, National Archives.

38. Shepherd, "Autobiography," 41–42; Newman, *Autobiography,* 21; Charles O. Musser to "Dear Sister Hester," June 6, 1863, in Barry Popchock, ed., *Soldier Boy: The Civil War Letters of Charles O. Musser, 29th Iowa* (Iowa City: University of Iowa Press, 1995), 55.

39. Newman, *Autobiography,* 16; George W. Towne to "Dear Sister," January 2, 1864, George Washington Towne Letters, State Historical Society of Iowa, Des Moines.

40. Two standard sources, Dyer's *Compendium* and Fox's *Regimental Losses,* fix the 33d

Iowa's death toll at 284—68 officers and men killed or mortally wounded and 216 more dead from non-battlefield causes. The figures cited in the text come from two postwar histories of Mahaska and Marion Counties, which offer a much more detailed breakdown on the 33d's casualties than either Dyer or Fox. Military Files of George W. Towne, Civil War (Union) Compiled Military Service Records, 33d Iowa Infantry, Record Group 94, National Archives; *History of Mahaska County*, 183–87; Lurton Dunham Ingersoll, *Iowa and the Rebellion: A History of the Troops Furnished by the State of Iowa to the Volunteer Armies of the Union, Which Conquered the Great Southern Rebellion of 1861–65* (Philadelphia: J. B. Lippincott & Co., 1866), 623; *The History of Marion County, Iowa, Containing a History of the County, Its Cities, Towns, &c.* (Des Moines: Union Historical Co., 1881), 489; Frederick H. Dyer, comp., *A Compendium of the War of the Rebellion: Compiled and Arranged from Official Records of the Federal and Confederate Armies, Reports of the Adjutant Generals of the Several States, the Army Registers and Other Reliable Documents and Sources*, 2 vols. (Dayton, Ohio: Morningside Bookshop, 1978), 2:1179; Fox, *Regimental Losses*, 516.

CHAPTER ONE: FROM HOME TO ST. LOUIS

1. Samuel Jordan Kirkwood (1813–1894) was born in Harford County, Maryland, and educated in Washington, D.C., where he briefly worked as a drugstore clerk and a schoolteacher. His family moved to Ohio in 1835, where he pursued a variety of occupations and studied law. He entered politics as a Democrat, and Richmond County voters elected him their prosecuting attorney in 1845. Kirkwood broke with the Democrats over the passage of the Kansas-Nebraska Act in 1854. In 1855, Kirkwood moved to Iowa and was instrumental in founding the state's branch of the Republican Party. A year later, he won a race for the Iowa state senate. The Republicans nominated him for governor in 1859, and he defeated Augustus Caesar Dodge on October 11 by a majority of 3,170 votes. He was reelected in 1861 by a 17,000-vote margin. Though unversed in military affairs, Kirkwood proved himself an energetic and effective war governor and became an early advocate of emancipation. Dan Elbert Clark, *Samuel Jordan Kirkwood* (Iowa City: State Historical Society of Iowa, 1917), 1, 37, 39–40, 76–79, 86–91, 123–27, 135–36, 143, 155–62, 205, 224–26; John T. Hubbell and James W. Geary, eds., *Biographical Dictionary of the Union: Northern Leaders of the Civil War* (Westport, Conn.: Greenwood Press, 1995), 290–91.

2. The life of Samuel A. Rice (1828–1864) reads like something concocted by Horatio Alger. He was born in Cattaraugus County, New York. He spent most of his boyhood in western Pennsylvania and Belmont County, Ohio, where he received a common school education. The premature death of his father left young Samuel his family's chief support, and he worked on flatboats on the Ohio and Mississippi Rivers, making several trips to New Orleans. Not content with a life of manual labor, Rice decided to work his way through college. He took the preparatory course at Athens Academy (today Ohio University) and then enrolled in Union College at Schenectady, New York, in 1844 or 1845. After earning his baccalaureate degree in 1849, Rice studied for a year in the college's Law Department. He moved to Iowa in 1851, settling at Fairfield in Jefferson County. He helped edit a Whig newspaper for a brief while and then moved to Oskaloosa, in Mahaska County, where he launched a brilliant legal career. Developing a taste for politics, he ran successfully in 1853 for county prosecuting attorney. In the spring of 1856, Rice assisted in organizing the Republican Party in Mahaska County. Later that year, he received his party's nomination as state attorney general. Rice won that race and was reelected two years later.

In 1861, Rice was roundly defeated when he tried to wrest the Republican gubernatorial nomination from Samuel Kirkwood. He made a bid to become his party's standard bearer in the 1862 congressional contest in Iowa's Fifth District but failed once again.

By then, Rice realized that the Civil War would not end soon, and he decided to join
the Union army. Thanks to his statewide popularity and many friends in the Republican
power structure, he was assured high rank. On August 13, 1862, a newspaper reported
that Rice had been offered a lieutenant colonel's commission in a new regiment being
organized by Capt. Ezekiel S. Sampson, a veteran officer from the 5th Iowa Infantry. "That
Mr. Rice will 'acquit himself a man,'" the paper commented, "if not distinguish himself, any
one who knows anything about him cannot for a moment doubt." The story turned out to
be untrue, and Rice ended up accepting a full colonelcy in the 33d Iowa Infantry on August
10, 1862. The thirty-two-year-old attorney had blue eyes, light hair, a fair complexion, and
stood five feet eleven inches tall. His military career flourished from the start, and he
would be promoted to brigadier general after less than a year in uniform. His younger
brother, Elliott (1835–1887), was another natural soldier who ended the war a brevet major
general.
     Capt. A. A. Stuart of the 17th Iowa Infantry knew Rice before the war and described
him in complimentary terms: "The general was kind-hearted and unassuming. I never saw
him without a smile upon his face, and no one could be embarrassed in his presence. Few
promised him the success he met in the service. He was as successful with the sword as he
had been in his civil profession. He was a noble exemplar of our Free State Chivalry."
Military Files of Samuel A. Rice, Civil War (Union) Compiled Military Service Records,
33d Iowa Infantry, Record Group 94, National Archives; A. A. Stuart, *Iowa Colonels and
Regiments: Being a History of Iowa Regiments in the War of the Rebellion; and
Containing a Description of the Battles in Which They Have Fought* (Des Moines: Mills &
Co., 1865), 487–88, 495–96; Ingersoll, *Iowa and the Rebellion*, 613; *History of Mahaska
County*, 322, 340–41, 460; James Harlan to Samuel A. Rice, July 23, 1856, "Election
Certificate," September 4, 1856, both in Samuel A. Rice Papers, State Historical Society of
Iowa; Clark, *Kirkwood*, 197, 422; Payne, *Grinnell*, 148; *Keokuk (Iowa) Daily Gate City*,
August 13, 1862; Ezra J. Warner, *Generals in Blue: The Lives of the Union Commanders*
(Baton Rouge: Louisiana State University Press, 1964), 399–402.
     3. These three counties formed a tier in southeast Iowa, with Mahaska County in the
middle, bounded by Keokuk on the east and Marion on the west. All three counties were
organized in 1844. The 1860 census reported Keokuk's population as 13,271, Mahaska's as
14,816, and Marion's as 16,813. Despite a significant population of Peace Democrats
(called "Copperheads" by their Republican opponents), these three counties contributed
more than their share to the Union war effort. Mahaska County alone would send
1,274 of its sons to the Union Army. Lake Prairie Township in Marion County (which
contained Sperry's hometown of Pella) supplied 260 soldiers all by itself. *History of
Mahaska County*, 189, 257, 384; Wubben, *Civil War Iowa*, 93; Van Stigt, *Pella, Iowa*,
117–20.
     4. Officer elections were common in both Union and Confederate regiments, although
political patronage also played a major role in the distribution of commissions.
On July 22, 1861, the Union Congress announced that each volunteer infantry regiment
was to have: "1 colonel, 1 lieutenant colonel, 1 major, 1 adjutant (a lieutenant), 1 quartermaster (a lieutenant), 1 surgeon and 1 assistant surgeon, 1 sergeant major, 1 regimental
quartermaster sergeant, 1 regimental commissary sergeant, 1 hospital steward, 2 principal
musicians, and 24 musicians for a [brass] band, and shall be composed of 10 companies,
each company to consist of 1 captain, 1 first lieutenant, 1 second lieutenant, 1 first sergeant,
4 sergeants, 8 corporals, 2 musicians, 1 wagoner, and from 64 to 82 privates." By
September 6, 1862, this structure was enlarged with the addition of one chaplain and a second assistant surgeon, but regimental bands were forbidden. Urwin, *United States
Infantry*, 93, 96.
     5. Oskaloosa was the seat of Mahaska County. It was supposedly named after a Creek
Indian princess, who was kidnapped by the Seminoles and married the famed war chief

Osceola. According to local lore, Osceola named his wife Ouscaloosa, meaning the "Last of the Beautiful." *History of Mahaska County*, 269.

6. James Madison Tuttle (1823–1892) was one of Iowa's first war heroes. This Ohio native led the 2d Iowa Infantry at Fort Donelson in February 1862. Elevated to brigade command, Colonel Tuttle succeeded his slain division commander at Shiloh on April 6, 1862, where he helped absorb the force of the Confederate surprise attack at the "Hornet's Nest." Tuttle's tenacity was instrumental in saving Maj. Gen. Ulysses S. Grant's Army of the Tennessee. Rewarded with promotion to brigadier general on June 9, 1862, he commanded the 3d Division in Maj. Gen. William Tecumseh Sherman's XV Corps during the Vicksburg campaign. He would run for governor of Iowa on the Democratic ticket in 1863. Warner, *Generals in Blue*, 513; Hubbell and Geary, *Biographical Dictionary*, 542–43; Stuart, *Iowa Colonels and Regiments*, 51–58.

7. Not having barracks ready for immediate occupation caused the 33d's recruits considerable hardship. It was raining when Company I from Knoxville reached Camp Tuttle on September 10. "We got there in the evening and had to lie under an old leaky Shed," recalled Pvt. John Shepherd, "and it rained all night and I lay there in the rain all night." Shepherd contracted a potentially fatal fever as a result of exposure and had to be sworn into federal service several weeks later while lying in a hospital bed. Shepherd, "Autobiography," 32–33.

8. Regimental records and other sources reveal that the 33d Iowa was actually mustered into federal service on October 1, 1862. Janet B. Hewett, ed., *Supplement to the Official Records of the Union and Confederate Armies*, pt. 2, vol. 20, serial no. 32 (Wilmington, N.C.: Broadfoot Publishing Co., 1995), 788, 792 (hereafter cited as *OR Supplement*); Ingersoll, *Iowa and the Rebellion*, 614; *History of Mahaska County*, 412.

9. An Ohioan by birth, Charles J. Ball was appointed as a first lieutenant in the 13th U.S. Infantry Regiment on May 14, 1861. He was dismissed from the service at that rank on January 10, 1864. Francis B. Heitman, *Historical Register and Dictionary of the United States Army, from Its Organization, September 29, 1789, to March 2, 1903*. 2 vols. (Washington, D.C.: Government Printing Office, 1903), 1:187.

10. With his regiment officially mustered, Colonel Rice pressed to have it posted to the front. "Can the Iowa delegation do anything to get the 33d ordered to Memphis?" he asked a political friend. "We want to get away from [Major] Genl [John] Popes dominions." Pope, who had been ignominiously defeated by Robert E. Lee at the second battle of Bull Run, had been lately banished to Minnesota to deal with Indian troubles. Rice apparently wanted an assignment for the 33d Iowa that promised more prominence and glory. Samuel A. Rice to George Carrie, October 10, 1862, Rice Papers.

11. The Union government had to purchase more than one million shoulder arms from foreign sources to equip the hordes of volunteers that rallied to the Stars and Stripes during the first two years of hostilities. By 1863, Northern industry had expanded sufficiently to meet the Union Army's demands for firearms. The 33d Iowa first carried big .72-caliber Model 1839 Prussian smoothbore muskets. These weapons were not very accurate and had an effective range of only about one hundred yards. Some of the regiment's companies drew .577-caliber Model 1853 Enfield rifle muskets at Helena, Arkansas, on January 25, 1863. Developed for the British army, these surplus weapons were much deadlier. Their effective range was five hundred to six hundred yards, and they could kill at one thousand yards. The Enfield proved to be extremely popular with both Northern and Southern troops. Urwin, *United States Infantry*, 85–86, 90–92; Louis A. Garavaglia and Charles G. Worman, *Firearms of the American West, 1803–1865* (Niwot: University Press of Colorado, 1998), 15, 167–73; Cyrus Gaston, "Diary, Private Cyrus Gaston, Company K, 33d Iowa Vol. Infantry," January 25, 1863, State Historical Society of Iowa.

12. A. L. Ellis enlisted as a musician in the 33d Iowa's Company D on September 6, 1862,

and received an appointment as regimental drum major two days later. *History of Mahaska County*, 414, 420.

13. Not everyone in the vicinity of Camp Tuttle wished the 33d Iowa well. On November 10, 1862, Walter Ream of Company I was shot to death while walking the streets of Oskaloosa. A possible victim of Copperheads, Ream was the first man in the regiment to meet a violent death. He had enlisted on July 28. *History of Marion County*, 495.

14. A month before the 33d Iowa left Camp Tuttle, one of Sperry's more sober-minded comrades took the precaution of drafting the following document:

> In the name of God, Amen, I, James Willis of Marion County Iowa and a private in Company "A" of the 33rd. Regiment of Iowa Volunteer Infantry, of the age of 29 years and being of sound mind, do make, publish and declare this my last will and testament in manner following, that is to say:
>
> First, I give and bequeath all my property, both Real and Personal in equal shares to my father Richard Willis of said county and state one sixth part thereof, and to each one of my sisters to wit: Selena Willis, Mary C. Wilson, Margaret E. McCoy, Rachel Bucklew and Cynthia McCullough one sixth part thereof, Said Real property consisting of the undivided one half of about thirty acres of land in Section 34 of Township 95 N of Range 21 West. The other undivided one half of which is assumed by Hiram Willis of said County.
>
> Second: I will and devise and direct that after my decease all my said Real property be sold for cash, and whatever amount of money I may have at interest or otherwise, together with the proceeds of the property is to be equally paid over to the six persons above named, share and share alike, or to each one sixth part thereof.

James Willis, "Will of Real and Personal Estate," October 10, 1862. Photostat copy in the possession of Willis descendant Charles Swanson, Lawton, Michigan.

15. The day after the 33d Iowa passed through Keokuk, the *Daily Gate City* informed its readers: "The Thirty-Third Regiment, from Oskaloosa, came down on the Des Moines [rail]road yesterday, an extra train having been run for the purpose. . . . It is a Regiment of which the Judicial District may well be proud." *Keokuk (Iowa) Daily Gate City*, November 21, 1862.

16. This obscure ship is not to be confused with the 650-ton armed attack transport, also called the *Northerner*, which operated along the East Coast. Charles Dana Gibson and E. Kay Gibson, comps., *Dictionary of Transports and Combatant Vessels, Steam and Sail, Employed by the Union Army, 1861–1868* (Bath, Me.: Ensign Press, 1995), 242.

17. St. Louis was a bustling commercial center with a population of 166,773 in 1860. Nearly two-thirds of the city's residents were foreign born. Retention of the city proved vital to the Union army's operations in Missouri and the Mississippi Valley. William C. Winter, *The Civil War in St. Louis: A Guided Tour* (St. Louis: Missouri Historical Society Press, 1994), 3–4.

18. Samuel Ryan Curtis (1805–1866) was an Ohio native, West Point graduate, and a Mexican War veteran who moved to Keokuk, Iowa, in 1847. In 1856, he won a seat in Congress, but he returned to the army with the outbreak of the Civil War as colonel of the 2d Iowa Infantry. As a brigadier general commanding the Army of the Southwest, Curtis won a stunning victory at Pea Ridge, Arkansas, in early March 1862. He was promoted to major general on March 21 and named military governor of Arkansas in May. He proceeded to march across Arkansas in a campaign that culminated in the capture of Helena, on the Mississippi River, on July 12, 1862. When the 33d Iowa met Curtis, he was commanding the Department of the Missouri. Warner, *Generals in Blue*, 107–8; Hubbell and Geary, *Biographical Dictionary*, 122; *OR*, ser. 1, vol. 13, p. 808. For more on Curtis's campaigns in Arkansas, see William L. Shea and Earl J. Hess, *Pea Ridge: Civil War Campaign in the West* (Chapel Hill: University of North Carolina Press, 1992).

19. During his brief and troubled stint as commander of the Department of the Missouri (July 25–November 2, 1861), Maj. Gen. John Charles Fremont (1813–1890), the famed "Pathfinder of the West" and former Republican presidential candidate, rented the handsome Brant Mansion on the south side of Chouteau Avenue as his residence and headquarters. A walled garden enclosed the palatial, three-story structure, and Fremont paid the scandalous sum of six thousand dollars for the privilege of living amid such opulence. Winter, *Civil War in St. Louis*, 70–73; Warner, *Generals in Blue*, 160–61.

20. Upon arriving at St. Louis, the 33d Iowa was assigned to the District of St. Louis, a subdivision of Curtis's Department of the Missouri. The district commander was Brig. Gen. Eugene A. Carr. Along with Batteries B, E, H, I, and K, 2d Missouri Artillery, the 33d Iowa served within the city, where it was directly answerable to Col. Henry Almstedt. *OR*, ser. 1, vol. 13, p. 808.

21. Like other recruits from rural America, many of the 33d Iowa's personnel had not been previously exposed to such childhood diseases as measles and chicken pox, not to mention more-virulent infections. Having to stand guard for hours on end in the cold and wet without proper rain gear also precipitated an outbreak of respiratory ailments. Of the six 33d Iowa men to die in St. Louis hospitals between December 27, 1862, and January 3, 1863, four succumbed to pneumonia. From a hospital run by Catholic nuns, Pvt. Allan McNeal of Company H wrote his parents about his ailments: "my health is improveing very fast I think considering I am entirely over the measles coug[h] & I think about over the measles I havent gained my strength yet but my apotite is very good & I will be strong in a few days." *Dubuque (Iowa) Daily Times*, January 8, 1863; Allan McNeal to "Dear parents," December 28, 1862, McNeal Letters.

22. An inspection report filed on the 33d at this time observed: "The discipline of the regiment is good and constantly improving. The regiment has never been in action." *OR Supplement*, pt. 2, vol. 20, serial no. 32, p. 792.

CHAPTER TWO: FROM ST. LOUIS TO HELENA

1. The *Rowena* was a sidewheel steamer of 436 tons. Gibson and Gibson, *Dictionary of Transports*, 276.

2. Capt. Thomas N. Stevens came down to Columbus with the 28th Wisconsin Volunteer Infantry from Cairo, Illinois, on December 23, 1862, and sent this description of his new post to his wife: "The principal fortifications are upon a bluff next the river some 200 feet high I should think, and nearly perpendicular. This is just above the town which is on low ground just by the river, the mighty Mississippi, which sweeps alongside. The large number of cannon of all sizes; the large quantities of shot & shell & other military 'traps,' are far beyond what I expected to see. There are lots of 'contrabands' [runaway slaves] here, also, of all sizes, & shades of color." Thomas N. Stevens to Carrie Stevens, December 23, 1862, in George M. Blackburn, ed., *"Dear Carrie. . . .": The Civil War Letters of Thomas N. Stevens* (Mount Pleasant: Clarke Historical Library, Central Michigan University, 1984), 26.

3. Early in Maj. Gen. Ulysses S. Grant's drive on Vicksburg, Mississippi, Confederate general Braxton Bragg ordered Brig. Gen. Nathan Bedford Forrest to stage a diversion by striking at enemy supply lines in Grant's rear. On the night of December 11, 1862, Forrest crossed the Tennessee River and slipped into western Tennessee with a brigade of 2,100 cavalry. Half of Forrest's men were poorly armed, but he was a master both of hit-and-run tactics and of psychological warfare. By December 24, Forrest could boast: "We have made a clean sweep of the Federals and the [rail]roads north of Jackson." His command had

killed or wounded more than 100 enemy troops, nabbed roughly 1,200 prisoners, and captured Union City, Tennessee, where the Mobile & Ohio Railroad crossed the Nashville & Western Railroad and a smaller line that ran to Paducah, Kentucky. He had also picked up 240 reinforcements and had rearmed his brigade with captured Yankee weapons. Forrest then sent a small force north along the Mobile & Ohio as if he intended to attack the important Union outpost at Columbus, Kentucky, with its $13 million in military stores.

Forrest's bluff succeeded in panicking Brig. Gen. Thomas A. Davies, the Union commander at Columbus, who thought his fifteen-hundred-man garrison was about to be devoured by seven thousand Confederates. Fortunately for Davies's rattled nerves, Maj. Gen. Henry Wager Halleck, the general in chief of the Union army, directed General Curtis to see that Columbus was "quickly and strongly reinforced" with units from the Department of the Missouri. Curtis dispatched Brig. Gen. Clinton B. Fisk and a brigade composed of the 29th and 33d Iowa Infantry, the 21st, 33d, and 35th Missouri Infantry, and a battery with four howitzers to Columbus. More reinforcements arrived from Cairo, Illinois, under Brig. Gen. James M. Tuttle. Edwin Cole Bearss, *The Campaign for Vicksburg*, 3 vols. (Dayton, Ohio: Morningside House, 1985–86), 1:231–51; *OR*, ser. 1, vol. 17, pt. 2, pp. 494–95. For more on Forrest's remarkable Civil War career, see Brian Steel Wills, *A Battle from the Start: The Life of Nathan Bedford Forrest* (New York: HarperCollins, 1992).

4. Pvt. James P. Roberts of Company G captured the atmosphere that attended the 33d Iowa's arrival at Columbus in a letter home: "when we came here the rigiment was cold [called] out in line of battle without any breakfast. The report is that the enemy has thirty or forty thousand our men laid on their arms all night at waiting but they didn't attack us we had ten or twelve thousand." James P. Roberts to S. S. Roberts, December 25, 1862, in the possession of Robert C. Burke, Altus, Okla.

5. As a relieved Private Roberts wrote that day: "The rebels has bin bosting that they are going to take dinner in this place it is nearly noon and they hant here yet and I don't think they can take the place for we hav good brest works." James P. Roberts to S. S. Roberts, December 25, 1862.

6. Also known as an "A" tent, the wedge tent was six feet long and stood nearly six feet tall. It housed four to six enlisted men, which made for cramped quarters at night. Troops so situated usually slept facing in the same direction, a practice called "spooning." When one man wanted to roll over, his tentmates had to do likewise. Wedge tents were carried with a regiment's baggage and often failed to keep up with the troops during their frequent moves. Francis A. Lord, *Civil War Collector's Encyclopedia* (Harrisburg, Pa.: Stackpole Books, 1965), 276.

7. William M. Scott of Marion County was the regiment's junior assistant surgeon. He would resign his commission on December 24, 1864. Military Files of William M. Scott, Civil War (Union) Compiled Military Service Records, 33d Iowa Infantry, Record Group 94, National Archives; *History of Marion County*, 489.

8. Perhaps because of these minor problems (and the desertion of two men from Company B on January 5, 1863), the 33d Iowa received mixed marks during its stay at Union City. An inspecting officer observed: "The discipline of the regiment is good; conduct of the men generally excellent. The officers are mainly desirous of doing their duty, but with few exceptions have made no commendable progress." *OR Supplement*, pt. 2, vol. 20, serial no. 32, pp. 789, 796.

9. On January 3, 1863, General Curtis instructed General Fisk to gather all the troops from the Department of the Missouri on temporary duty at Columbus and ship them to Helena, Arkansas. Curtis feared that the Confederate army recently defeated at Prairie Grove in northwest Arkansas would attempt to save face by storming Helena. Three days later, Fisk reported: "I have here and en route to Helena forces as follows: Thirty-third

Missouri Infantry, say, 800; Thirty-fifth Missouri Infantry, say, 700; Twenty-ninth Iowa Infantry, say, 900; Thirty-third Iowa Infantry, say, 800; Fortieth Iowa Infantry, say, 900, and Tenth Missouri Cavalry (detachment), say, 400." *OR*, ser. 1, vol. 22, pt. 2, pp. 9, 20.

10. The *John D. Perry* was a sidewheeler rated at 382 tons. Sperry forgot to mention that the 33d Iowa was detained at Memphis, Tennessee, from Friday, January 9, until Sunday evening, January 11. Gibson and Gibson, *Dictionary of Transports*, 178; George W. Towne to "Dear Sister," January 13, 1863, Towne Letters; Gaston, "Diary," expanded entry under January 4, 1863.

11. Strategically located on the Mississippi River some sixty miles below Memphis, Helena served the Union military as a staging area for sorties into eastern Arkansas and against Vicksburg and other points downstream. The 1860 census placed the town's population at 1,551 individuals: 1,024 white and 527 black. Many of the Northern troops who served there shared Sperry's poor opinion of the place. A major in the Union army that captured Helena reported soon thereafter: "The greater part of Helena is on low, flat ground, subject to overflow. The handsomest portion of the place was burned not long since, and from all accounts, the rest should be sunk." Pvt. Charles O. Musser of the 29th Iowa Infantry, whose regiment accompanied the 33d Iowa to Helena, was even more scathing: "nobody lives here but negroes and soldiers. the citizens have nearly all left. i would not live here if i owned the whole State of Arkansas. . . . it is one of the dirtyest holes on the river. mud is knee deep there all the time." "Evolution of Arkansas Townships, 1870–1920, from U.S. Census Publications Opening the 1920 Census," n.d., 87; Arkansas History Commission, Little Rock, Arkansas; *Keokuk (Iowa) Daily Gate City*, July 28, 1862; Charles O. Musser to "Dear Father," February 3, 1863, in Popchock, *Soldier Boy*, 24.

12. Supported by a large Union fleet of ironclads, rams, and gunboats, Maj. Gen. John A. McClernand and more than thirty-four thousand troops captured Arkansas Post and its three-thousand-man Confederate garrison on January 11, 1863. Helena's security was actually jeopardized by Brig. Gen. Willis A. Gorman, the commander of the District of Eastern Arkansas, who left on January 11 to raid up Arkansas's White River, stripping the garrison of all its troops except for one thousand cavalry and the six hundred-man 36th Iowa Infantry. The 33d Iowa was actually under orders to join Gorman when it was detained at Helena. Gorman penetrated as far as De Valls Bluff and Des Arc, destroying some minor Confederate installations and throwing a scare into the civilian population. Gorman did not return to Helena until January 24. Mark K. Christ, ed., *Rugged and Sublime: The Civil War in Arkansas* (Fayetteville: University of Arkansas Press, 1994), 61–65; Bearss, *Campaign for Vicksburg*, 1:411–14; *OR*, ser. 1, vol. 22, pt. 2, p. 39; *OR Supplement*, pt. 2, vol. 20, serial no. 32, 789, 792.

13. Another Ohioan who settled in Iowa, Cyrus Bussey (1833–1915), was the colonel of the 3d Iowa Cavalry Regiment. Before his assignment to Helena, he fought at the battle of Pea Ridge, Arkansas, March 7–8, 1862. He commanded Helena in Gorman's absence. On January 13, he informed General Curtis at St. Louis: "The Thirty-third Iowa arrived last night, and report the Twenty-first Missouri not on the way. Colonel Rice thinks they are not ordered down the river. I cannot hold this post with the force left, and have detained the Thirty-third Iowa until the Twenty-first Missouri arrives." Warner, *Generals in Blue*, 58–59; *OR*, ser. 1, vol. 22, pt. 2, pp. 39, 65.

14. This uncertainty resulted from jurisdictional conflicts within the Union high command in the Mississippi Valley. General Grant wanted the 33d Iowa and other newly raised regiments from the Midwest added to his Army of the Tennessee for the Vicksburg campaign. From Columbus, Kentucky, on January 2, 1863, General Fisk warned General Curtis: "General Grant has ordered General Davies to move us to Memphis immediately. . . . General Tuttle . . . is very desirous to retain all of your Iowa regiments as a command for himself. I discover that he is hard at work among the colonels to influence them in the

direction of General Grant; complains bitterly that General Grant has been badly treated in the distribution of the new troops from the Northwest." In the end, Grant prevailed. On January 19, 1863, he received control of the Union troops based at Helena. He first thought to attach them to McClernand's XIII Army Corps, but soon changed his mind. *OR*, ser. 1, vol. 22, pt. 2, p. 8; Bearss, *Campaign for Vicksburg*, 1:432; *OR Supplement*, pt. 2, vol. 20, serial no. 32, p. 792.

15. Also known as a "gum" blanket, the rubber blanket was one of the most useful pieces of equipment issued to the Union infantryman. It was made of rubber-coated fabric, had brass grommets set along its hemmed edges, and measured forty-five by seventy-nine inches. The rubber blanket was a multipurpose item. Laid with the rubber side down, it served as a ground cloth, allowing the soldier to sleep dry on wet ground. Thrown over the shoulders, it became a raincoat. Several men could pool their rubber blankets and fasten them together to make a waterproof tent. Cavalrymen received a poncho version of the rubber blanket, which was even more convenient than the infantry version. Lord, *Collector's Encyclopedia*, 195–96; Woodhead, *Echoes of Glory*, 215.

16. Ulysses S. Grant (1822–1885) was born in Ohio and graduated from the U.S. Military Academy in 1843. Although he performed bravely in the Mexican War, a drinking problem caused his forced resignation from the regular army in 1854. With the outbreak of the Civil War, he would emerge from disgrace and obscurity to establish himself as America's greatest soldier of the nineteenth century. Warner, *Generals in Blue*, 183–86.

17. Colonel Rice's strictness paid off. During the 33d Iowa's first tour at Helena, the regiment's acting adjutant, 1st Lt. Samuel S. Pierce, wrote: "The discipline of the regiment is good and it is fast becoming better and more in accordance with the requirements of the Army regulations." *OR Supplement*, pt. 2, vol. 20, serial no. 32, pp. 789, 792.

CHAPTER THREE: CLEARING OUT THE PASS

1. Yazoo Pass actually lay six miles below Helena, and the distance from the Mississippi River to Moon Lake was closer to one mile. Bearss, *Campaign for Vicksburg*, 1:479, 482–83.

2. The levee was built in 1856, and it was an immense affair, nearly one hundred feet thick and eighteen feet high. Bearss, *Campaign for Vicksburg*, 1:482.

3. Grant initially hoped to descend on Vicksburg from the north with forty thousand troops along the Mississippi Central Railroad, while Maj. Gen. William Tecumseh Sherman and an amphibious army of thirty-two thousand assaulted Chickasaw Bluffs, near the Confederate stronghold. Sherman was repulsed on December 29, 1862, with a loss of seventeen hundred. In the meantime, Grant was forced to cancel his main effort after Maj. Gen. Earl Van Dorn seized his advance supply depot at Holly Springs, Mississippi, on December 20, while Forrest raided Union communications in western Tennessee. Desperate to find a new way to transport men and supplies to the dry ground east of Vicksburg, where he could maneuver, Grant decided to reopen Yazoo Pass. As Sperry explained, that route led to the Yazoo River, and the Yazoo led to Vicksburg, roughly 350 miles south of the pass. A successful passage of the Yazoo Pass route would permit the Yankees to turn the right flank of the Rebels blocking the approaches to Vicksburg at Snyder's Bluff. Bruce Catton, *Grant Moves South* (Boston: Little, Brown, 1960), 324–79; Bearss, *Campaign for Vicksburg*, 1:123–40, 214, 482–83.

4. On February 2, 1863, General Gorman sent a five-hundred-man fatigue party drawn from the Helena garrison to assist in breaching the levee at Yazoo Pass. This was accomplished through a combination of digging and blasting. Bearss, *Campaign for Vicksburg*, 1:485–86.

5. The 33d Iowa left Helena accompanied by the 34th Indiana Infantry, making a force of about one thousand men. Six hundred more troops would soon follow. As Private Shepherd of the 33d Iowa's Company I remembered the trip: "we boarded a Gun Boat and Steamed down the Mississippi about seven miles to where the Leevy was cut. we went through the Leevy into Moon Lake, from the lake to the cold water River." According to Professor Craig L. Symonds of the U.S. Naval Academy History Department, a "mosquito boat" was any kind of small vessel adapted for military purposes. The term was commonly applied to the small, shallow-draft tin-clad gunboats that served the Union navy so well on western waterways. Bearss, *Campaign for Vicksburg*, 1:491; Shepherd, "Autobiography," 35; Craig Symonds to author, July 27, 1998; See John D. Milligan, *Gunboats Down the Mississippi* (Annapolis, Md.: United States Naval Institute, 1965).

6. These obstructions were created in three days by a working party of fifty impressed blacks under Lt. Francis E. Shepperd of the Confederate navy. Bearss, *Campaign for Vicksburg*, 1:483–85.

7. James Harrison Wilson (1837–1925) was destined to become one of the "boy generals" of the Civil War. Reared in Illinois, he graduated from West Point in 1860 and joined the Corps of Topographical Engineers. He served on the staff of Maj. Gen. George B. McClellan during the Antietam campaign and then transferred to Ulysses S. Grant's staff. Grant made the young lieutenant colonel his protégé, and Wilson would rise to lead a massive cavalry corps in the latter stages of the war in Tennessee and Alabama. Warner, *Generals in Blue*, 566–68.

8. Private Shepherd commented that some of the logs were three or four feet in diameter, which made them hard to handle. Shepherd, "Autobiography," 35.

9. Cadwallader Colden Washburn (1818–1882) was a Republican congressman from Wisconsin, but when the Civil War erupted he put on a uniform as colonel of the 2d Wisconsin Cavalry. He was promoted to brigadier general on July 16, 1862. E. S. Norris, an Iowa correspondent who interviewed members of Washburn's fatigue party, came to share Sperry's high opinion of the general. "The expedition was under the command of Gen. Washburn," he wrote, "whose praise is on the tongue of every soldier." Warner, *Generals in Blue*, 542–43; *Dubuque (Iowa) Daily Times*, March 5, 1863.

10. "It was a time of high waters," Private Shepherd elaborated, "and the whole country was flooded." Shepherd, "Autobiography," 35.

11. At various times in its career, the steamer *Hamilton Belle* was rated at 200 or 250 tons. Gibson and Gibson, *Dictionary of Transports*, 142.

12. This skirmish occurred on February 16, 1863, and the Confederates captured seven men from Company B. *OR Supplement*, pt. 2, vol. 20, serial no. 32, p. 796; Bearss, *Campaign for Vicksburg*, 1:495.

13. Private Shepherd took a less callous view of such proceedings. He never forgot a Southern family that lived near the 33d Iowa's camp. The same night that Union officers arrested the man of the house, the family's only child, a baby, died. Then some other Northern troops broke into the house and stole every bite of food they could find. "I can almost hear the Screams of that Poor Woman yet," Shepherd wrote. "Robd of evrything, her husband a Prisoner, her only Child dead. Well I said to myself and my God I will never go into a house to take anything out while in this war." Shepherd, "Autobiography," 35.

14. James Lusk Alcorn (1816–1894) served from 1846 to 1860 in the Mississippi state legislature. A reluctant secessionist, he accepted a commission as brigadier general with the Mississippi State Troops. He was captured and paroled in 1862. He would later become governor of Mississippi. His plantation was located near the levee that blocked access to Yazoo Pass. Jon L. Wakelyn, *Biographical Dictionary of the Confederacy* (Westport, Conn.: Greenwood Press, 1977), 69–70. See also Lillian A. Pereyra, *James Lusk Alcorn: Persistent Whig* (Baton Rouge: Louisiana State University Press, 1966).

15. Hardtack was a standard part of the Union soldier's field ration. It was a flat flour-and-water biscuit about half an inch thick. The government called it "hard bread," but the troops referred to it as "hard crackers," "teeth dullers," or "sheet iron crackers." Stored in wooden boxes, hardtack often grew extremely hard or wormy. It was also prone to develop mold. No wonder the troops detested it. Lord, *Collector's Encyclopedia,* 112–13; Wiley, *Life of Billy Yank,* 237–39.

16. In a dispatch from Helena dated February 24, E. S. Norris reported: "The troops detailed to remove the obstructions from the Yazoo Pass, many of them returned to this place last evening with the good news that the work was accomplished. The 24th, 29th and 33d Iowa did most of the work." Pvt. George W. Towne of Company G conveyed the brevity of the 33d Iowa's stay at Helena in a letter to his sister: "I would like to give you a full history of the expedition but cannot for want of time for I just heard the Adjutant say that we would leave in the morning at ten o clock and we just got back this afternoon to our camp." *Dubuque (Iowa) Daily Times,* March 5, 1863; George W. Towne to "Dear Sister," February 23, 1863, Towne Letters.

Chapter Four: The Yazoo Pass Expedition

1. Two diarists in Sperry's regiment, Sgt. John S. Morgan of Company G and Pvt. Cyrus Gaston of Company K, said that the 33d Iowa received its "State pay" (the money owed the men for the time between their enlistment and muster into federal service) on February 24. Gaston identified the paymaster as a Major Mitchell. "Diary of John S. Morgan, Company G, Thirty-Third Iowa Infantry," Part 1, *Annals of Iowa* 13 (January 1923): 484; Gaston, "Diary," February 24, 1863.

2. On February 15, 1863, while the 33d Iowa was helping to clear Yazoo Pass, General Grant directed that a full division drawn from the Helena garrison be sent to the pass to penetrate the Coldwater, Tallahatchie, and Yalobusha Rivers preparatory to a descent of the Yazoo River and an attack on Yazoo City. Six days later, Brig. Gen. Benjamin Prentiss, who had recently relieved General Gorman as commander of the District of Eastern Arkansas, ordered Brig. Gen. Leonard F. Ross to embark his 13th Division, XIII Army Corps, and launch the Yazoo Pass expedition. The 33d Iowa was assigned to Ross's division. *OR,* ser. 1, vol. 24, pt. 3, p. 56; Bearss, *Campaign for Vicksburg,* 1:493, 496, 509; *OR Supplement,* pt. 2, vol. 20, serial no. 32, pp. 789, 792–93, 805.

3. The 33d Iowa boarded its transports at 6:00 P.M. The *Citizen* was a sternwheel steamer of 211 tons. Existing information on the tonnage of the steamer *Lebanon No. 2* is sketchy. Morgan, "Diary," pt. 1, 484; Gibson and Gibson, *Dictionary of Transports,* 60, 197.

4. Clinton Bowen Fisk (1828–1890) was born in New York and grew up in Michigan. When the Panic of 1857 wiped out his business interests, he moved to St. Louis to start again. Commissioned colonel of the 33d Missouri Infantry on September 5, 1862, he soon received authorization to organize a brigade and was promoted to brigadier general in late November. He commanded the regiments that General Curtis hurriedly dispatched from the Department of the Missouri to reinforce Columbus, Kentucky, in December. Fisk was a teetotaler with pronounced religious tendencies, which endeared him to many of his troops. After the war, he founded Fisk University, a black college in Nashville, Tennessee. He also ran for governor of New Jersey as the Prohibition Party candidate in 1886 and garnered nearly 250,000 votes in the presidential election of 1888. Warner, *Generals in Blue,* 154–55; Gaston, "Diary," April 30, 1863; Martin A. Varner, "Diary," February 1, 8, April 30, May 10, 1863, Martin A. Varner Papers, State Historical Society of Iowa.

5. Fisk's command was formally designated the 2d Brigade, 13th Division, XIII Army Corps. It contained five infantry regiments, the 29th, 33d, and 36th Iowa, and the 33d and 35th Missouri. *OR*, ser. 1, vol. 22, pt. 2, pp. 133–34.

6. The hurricane deck was a steamboat's upper deck, the one most exposed to gunfire from shore. The cabin deck was the level containing compartments for the passengers. In addition to the plank breastworks, the *Citizen*'s crew installed log reinforcements to protect the boat's boilers from cannon fire. John V. Noel, *The VNR Dictionary of Ships and the Sea* (New York: Van Nostrand Reinhold, 1981), 54, 172; Morgan, "Diary," pt. 1, 484.

7. "Sow-belly" was the nickname Union soldiers gave to salt pork, the meat they normally received in their rations. Wiley, *Life of Billy Yank*, 239.

8. According to Sergeant Morgan's diary, it took the *Citizen* from February 26 to March 3 to travel fourteen miles. It was not until the latter date that the Federal fleet began descending the Coldwater River. On March 1, it only steamed one and a half miles, and the following day, just a half-mile more. From the *Diana*, another transport in the Yazoo Pass expedition, Capt. Thomas N. Stevens of the 28th Wisconsin Infantry complained: "We make slow progress,—are probably not more than 20 miles, by the course of the stream, from the Mississippi river. The channel through which we are passing will probably average 60 feet in width, and is very crooked, and some of the larger boats find it difficult moving with any speed." Morgan, "Diary," pt. 1, 501; Bearss, *Campaign for Vicksburg*, 1:510–13; Thomas N. Stevens to Carrie Stevens, February 26, 1863, in Blackburn, *Dear Carrie*, 61.

9. Company G had its quarters disrupted in this way on Sunday, March 8, and six men saw their Prussian muskets swept over the side. Morgan, "Diary," pt. 1, 485.

10. The leading ships in the Union fleet entered the Tallahatchie River on March 5. Though crooked, the Tallahatchie was wider than the Coldwater River, which permitted the transports to make quicker progress. Bearss, *Campaign for Vicksburg*, 1:513–18; Morgan, "Diary," pt. 1, 485, 501.

11. As Sergeant Morgan noted on March 9: "Travel more rapid. Stream more crooked, plantations more abundant cotton burning, negros happy." Morgan, "Diary," pt. 1, 485.

12. Sergeant Morgan's diary for March 6 reads: "Passed many plantations; took on board about 100 bales [of] cotton found one pile in cane brake." Morgan, "Diary," pt. 1, 485.

13. This incident occurred on March 10, as confirmed by Sergeant Morgan's diary: "Started early. Plantations more numerous and on a larger scale, houses very fine but small, white folks more plenty. Negro women, no end to them. cotton burning nearly every place. One warehouse about 500 bales burning. After dark, passed boat load cotton burning, fire far as we could see. Raining all day." Continuing the story on the eleventh, Morgan wrote: "Rained all night, and till 8 A. M. Cotton for 10 mile on fire in the water from the burning boat." Morgan, "Diary," pt. 1, 485.

14. The 33d Iowa disembarked at Shell Mound Plantation at 7:00 P.M. Morgan, "Diary," pt. 1, 485.

15. The Confederate high command awoke to the Yazoo Pass threat between February 9 and 17, 1863. As the Northerners made their slow approach, the Rebels erected a fort made of earth and cotton bales spanning the narrow neck separating the Tallahatchie and Yazoo Rivers a few miles from Shell Mound Plantation. This formidable stronghold bore the name Fort Pemberton in honor of Lt. Gen. John C. Pemberton, commander of the Department of Mississippi and Eastern Louisiana, with headquarters at Vicksburg. By March 11, 1863, there were two thousand Texas and Mississippi troops manning Fort Pemberton, and they had eight guns, including a thirty-two-pound rifled gun and a twenty-pound Parrott, emplaced to cover the Tallahatchie and Yazoo. Fort Pemberton's defenders blocked the Tallahatchie by swinging a raft across the channel, and they soon scuttled the captured Union steamer *Star of the West*, right behind that. Bearss, *Campaign for Vicksburg*, 1:497–502, 506–7.

16. This engagement involved the Union ironclads *Chillicothe* and *Baron de Kalb* and the ram *Lioness*. The Confederates inflicted minor damage on the *Chillicothe*, killing four sailors and wounding nine before the Yankees withdrew. Bearss, *Campaign for Vicksburg*, 1:521–22.

17. The *Citizen* was also part of this foraging expedition, but its engines broke down after going three miles up the Tallahatchie. While awaiting repairs, Companies B, E, and K went ashore to gather food from nearby plantations. Morgan, "Diary." 485; Gaston, "Diary," March 11, 1863.

18. While Union warships made more ineffectual attacks on Fort Pemberton, General Ross sent infantry patrols to probe the difficult ground leading to the enemy works. On the night of March 11–12, 1863, the Yankees built a battery out of cotton bales some seven hundred yards from Pemberton, arming it with a thirty-pound Parrott gun borrowed from the Union navy. Pvt. James A. Newman of Company I, 33d Iowa, described the installation as "a big siege gun on a high wheeled cart [in] a cotton fort." A second Parrott was mounted in the battery on the following night. Bearss, *Campaign for Vicksburg*, 1:521–29; Newman, *Autobiography*, 18.

19. On March 5, 1863, General Grant ordered Brig. Gen. Isaac F. Quinby's division from the XVII Army Corps to sail from Grand Lake, Arkansas, to Yazoo Pass. Quinby (1821–1891) and Grant had graduated from West Point together in 1843 and were lifelong friends. Grant wanted Quinby to overtake Ross and assume command of the Yazoo Pass expedition. Quinby's lead transports entered the pass on March 8, but bad weather, a shortage of ships for the entire division, and other problems prevented him from rendezvousing with Ross until March 21. The two generals finally met at noon at a point forty miles below the confluence of the Coldwater and Tallahatchie Rivers. Bearss, *Campaign for Vicksburg*, 1:515–17, 532–37.

20. Sergeant Morgan's diary contains a more precise account of this tragic accident: "Sabbath, March 29. Stormy during the night and Elm tree blown down across a tent of 47th Indiana Killed 4 and seriously wounded the other two, Military burial at 2 P.M." Morgan, "Diary," pt. 1, 486.

21. Like Ross, Quinby decided that the ground in front of Fort Pemberton was too swampy to permit a head-on infantry assault. Undeterred, Quinby placed two new batteries containing four heavy guns apiece within seven hundred yards of the Rebel works. He hoped to use a pontoon bridge to cross the Tallahatchie beyond the reach of Pemberton's guns and storm the fort from the rear. He also decided to send a second column across the Yalobusha River to cut the enemy's communications along the Yazoo. Before Quinby could bring his plans to fruition, however, he received orders from Grant to abort the Yazoo Pass expedition and withdraw. Grant feared that the Confederates might seize the initiative and trap the stalled Union force by positioning men and artillery along the rivers behind it. Bearss, *Campaign for Vicksburg*, 1:542–46; Catton, *Grant Moves South*, 384.

22. Fisk's brigade received notification to strike camp and prepare to move at 10:00 A.M., April 4, 1863. The 33d Iowa embarked on the *Lebanon No. 2* and the two-hundred-ton sternwheel steamer *Charlie Bowen* between 12:00 and 1:30 P.M. Morgan, "Diary," pt. 1, 487; Gaston, "Diary," April 4, 1863; Gibson and Gibson, *Dictionary of Transports*, 56.

23. According to Sergeant Morgan's diary, the frustrated Yankees began burning plantation houses on the night of April 4 before they received any provocation from shore. On the morning of April 5, 1863, Confederate soldiers fired into the transport *Cheeseman*, killing the captain and two Union soldiers and wounding two more men. That afternoon, shots were fired at the *Logan*, wounding three men of the 36th Iowa Infantry. Morgan, "Diary," pt. 1, 487.

24. In three trips logged between April 8 and April 24, 1863, the Union hospital ship *City of Memphis* brought a total of eighteen seriously ill men from the 33d Iowa to St. Louis for treatment in the larger hospitals there. Pvt. George Washington Towne of Company G

probably reflected the prevalent feelings in the regiment when he wrote home: "I am well at present but the health of the company is not so good as it . . . was. There is so much duty to do & the loss of sleep (according to the army phrase) uses men up. A great many are complaining of rhumatism. . . . The fact is this climate is not fit for a white man to live in it ought to be given to the negroes. I am shure if I get out of Dixie I will not want to revisit Helena yazoo pass or any other [indecipherable] places again very soon." *Dubuque (Iowa) Daily Times*, April 11, 1863; George W. Towne to "Dear Sister," May 22, 1863, Towne Letters.

CHAPTER FIVE: AT HELENA

1. That day a delighted Pvt. Cyrus Gaston confided to his diary: "Paid off at Helena, Ark. By Major Burns. I Rec'd $52.00 dollars four months pay." As a sergeant in Company G, John S. Morgan received sixty-eight dollars. Gaston, "Diary," April 16, 1863; Morgan, "Diary," pt. 1, 488.

2. By April 30, Fisk's brigade had been reduced by one regiment to the 29th Iowa, 33d Iowa, 36th Iowa, and 33d Missouri. According to Private Gaston, not only did Fisk's regiments form a brigade line, but also "we formed a hollow square." Gaston, "Diary," April 30, 1863.

3. William Anderson Pile (1829–1889) was a Methodist Episcopal minister who entered the Civil War as the chaplain of the 1st Missouri Light Artillery. Desiring a more active part in battling the rebellion, he eventually became a battery commander. In August 1862, he joined Fisk's new 33d Missouri Infantry as lieutenant colonel and replaced Fisk as colonel on December 23. His promotion to brigadier general occurred a year later, and he went on to command a brigade of black troops at the siege of Mobile in the spring of 1865. Private Gaston may have mistaken Pile for the chaplain of the 33d Missouri when he scribbled in his diary: "General C. B. Fisk Spoke to us & also the Chaplain of the 33d Missouri preached to us." This service was held at 5:00 P.M. Afterward, Sergeant Morgan sat up with his company's sick until 2:00 A.M. Warner, *Generals in Blue*, 371–72; Gaston, "Diary," April 30, 1863; Morgan, "Diary," pt. 1, 488; Newman, *Autobiography*, 18.

4. Archibald S. Dobbins (1827–1870?), a wealthy planter who lived near Helena, was commissioned a colonel in the Confederate army in 1862. Early in the following year, he raised the 1st (Dobbins's) Arkansas Cavalry Regiment to harass Union forces operating in the Helena area. On May 1, 1863, Dobbins and 500 to 600 of his troopers caught a 160-man detachment from the 3d Iowa Cavalry a mile from La Grange, Arkansas. The Iowans were routed with an admitted 41 casualties. The first news of the disaster created a sensation within the Helena garrison, as related by Capt. Thomas N. Stevens, Company C, 28th Wisconsin Infantry: "Two couriers came dashing down the bluff through our camp, into town, just before noon, and reported the facts to head quarters. In a few minutes all was excitement—from the different camps came dashing out along lines of cavalry heading for the scene of the conflict, while the 'assembly' was being beaten in the Infantry camps, and regiment after regiment fell into line, ready and eager to be led against their enemies." The 28th Wisconsin and the 33d Iowa were the first two infantry regiments to respond to the alarm. Bruce S. Allardice, *More Generals in Gray* (Baton Rouge: Louisiana State University Press, 1995), 79–80; *OR*, ser. 1, vol. 22, pt. 1, pp. 316–18; Thomas N. Stevens to Carrie Stevens, May 2, 1863, in Blackburn, *Dear Carrie*, 93–94.

5. The 5th Kansas Cavalry Regiment, the rest of the 3d Iowa Cavalry, and two guns set out for the La Grange vicinity before the 33d Iowa was ready to move. Each enlisted man in the 33d left Helena carrying sixty cartridges for his Prussian musket or Enfield rifle musket. Morgan, "Diary," pt. 1, 488; Gaston, "Diary," May 1, 1863.

6. Rice's command actually consisted of the 33d Iowa (450 men) and 28th Wisconsin Infantry (400 men), a detachment from the 3d Iowa Cavalry (200 men), and two guns from the 3d Iowa Battery. Another 600 Union cavalry joined Rice four days out from Helena. He marched toward Cotton Plant, Arkansas, via Moro. The expedition was really a raid to disperse Dobbins's guerrillas and deny the enemy sustenance. As the 33d's acting adjutant, 1st Lt. Samuel S. Pierce, reported: "We were out eight days without seeing any enemy in arms. Destroyed a great deal of corn by fire and took what surplus provision we could find with us. The health of the regiment is improving." Ingersoll, *Iowa and the Rebellion*, 615; *OR Supplement*, pt. 2, vol. 20, serial no. 32, p. 793; Thomas N. Stevens to Carrie Stevens, May 13, Thomas N. Stevens to Carrie Stevens, May 14, 1863, both in Blackburn, *Dear Carrie*, 97–100.

7. Cyrus H. Mackey was a twenty-five-year-old lawyer practicing in Sigourney, a town in Keokuk County, Iowa, when recruiting began for the 33d Iowa Infantry. He enlisted on August 10, 1862, and was mustered in as its first lieutenant colonel on October 1, with rank to date from August 13. A native of Fulton County, Illinois, Mackey had blue eyes, sandy hair, and a light complexion, and his height was five feet eleven inches. Though a devoted husband, he left a sick wife behind when he decided to enter the army. He was apparently a regular churchgoer and took an interest in the religious welfare of his men. Military Files of Cyrus H. Mackey, Civil War (Union) Compiled Military Service Records, 33d Iowa Infantry, Record Group 94, National Archives; Thomas N. Stevens to Carrie Stevens, January 1, 1865, in Blackburn, *Dear Carrie*, 273; Shepherd, "Autobiography," 47–48.

8. This is a reference to Washington Irving's book, *A Tour on the Prairies*, originally published in 1835 and reprinted in 1859. See Washington Irving, *A Tour on the Prairies*, ed. John Francis McDermott (Norman: University of Oklahoma Press, 1956).

9. According to Sergeant Morgan, these privations began a day earlier: "Out of rations. Live on parched corn." Morgan, "Diary," pt. 1, 489.

10. An elated Captain Stevens of the 28th Wisconsin wrote his wife that day: "Hurrah! A squad of cavalry has just arrived from Helena, who bring news that Richmond is ours, I hope it may be true *this* time. Once more Hurrah!" Thomas N. Stevens to Carrie Stevens, May 13, 1863, in Blackburn, *Dear Carrie*, 99.

11. Pvt. George Washington Towne of Company G confirmed Sperry's comments on this busy period: "I thought I would write you a few lines before drill time for we have enough to keep us busy from morning until night. We drill from 9 [or 7] o clock until 12 in the forenoon & from [indecipherable] in the afternoon & then we have dress parade at 6 & roll call at 8. . . . So you see we have very little time to write read or sleep." Brigade drill was conducted over five consecutive days beginning on May 18. George W. Towne to "Dear Sister," May 22, 1863, Towne Letters; Morgan, "Diary," pt. 1, 489–90.

12. The exercise was all too real for a few of its participants. As Private Gaston reported: "the 3d Iowa Battery & 5th Kansas cavalry fought a Sham battle this evening there was two men mortally wounded & one horse killed." Gaston, "Diary," May 22, 1863.

13. Benjamin M. Prentiss (1819–1901) was born in western Virginia, lived in Missouri from 1835 to 1841, and then moved to Illinois. He was an officer in a militia company formed to pressure the Mormons into leaving the state, and subsequently fought in the Mexican War as a captain in the 1st Illinois Volunteers. Returning to civilian life, he studied law and ran unsuccessfully in 1860 as a Republican for Congress. With the outbreak of the Civil War, he was commissioned a colonel on April 29, 1861, and helped raise the 10th Illinois Infantry. Upgraded to brigadier general on August 9, Prentiss rose to command the 6th Division in Grant's Army of the Tennessee by late March 1862. Surprised in camp near Shiloh Church, Tennessee, on April 6, 1862, Prentiss rallied enough fragments of his shattered division and elements of other commands to conduct a gallant, six-hour defense of the celebrated "Hornet's Nest"—a delaying action that robbed the Confederates of a

major victory. The Rebels captured Prentiss when they overran his position, but he was later exchanged. Grant put him in charge of the District of Eastern Arkansas in February 1863, and he soon received a promotion to major general to date from November 29, 1862. Warner, *Generals in Blue*, 385–86; Hubbell and Geary, *Biographical Dictionary*, 415–16.

14. Captain Stevens took a dim view of these proceedings: "This afternoon was very warm. At 1 o'clock we fell in and marched to the [parade] ground and formed in line. We had two brigades of infantry, 4 regiments of cavalry, and some artillery present. The pageant was quite imposing to green ones who never saw the like before, but it was rather hard on the men to be out three hours in a broiling sun with blankets & knapsacks on their backs—in heavy marching order. . . . Didn't the hot sand burn our feet though?" Thomas N. Stevens to Carrie Stevens, May 23, 1863, in Blackburn, *Dear Carrie*, 104.

15. On May 23, 1863, Confederate secretary of war James A. Seddon, concerned about Grant's success in isolating Pemberton's army at Vicksburg, suggested that Confederate forces in the trans-Mississippi stage a diversion by capturing Helena. It took two weeks for Seddon's telegram to reach the headquarters of Lt. Gen. Edmund Kirby Smith, commander of the Confederacy's Trans-Mississippi Department, at Shreveport, Louisiana. Kirby Smith, in turn, forwarded the message to Lt. Gen. Theophilus H. Holmes, commander of the District of Arkansas, at Little Rock. Thus Holmes was unable to put an army in motion toward Helena until the latter half of June, just as Vicksburg's defenders were reaching the brink of exhaustion.

Most of Helena's Union garrison felt perfectly safe within the city's defenses. On May 22, Private Towne reassured his sister: "We are expecting an attack from the rebel General Price. . . . There are about 6,000 [Union] troops in Helena & about 50 pieces of artillry I do not believe 20,000 rebels could take the place with what force there is here so if they want to get well whipped let them come to Helena." Cpl. Charles O. Musser, Company A, 29th Iowa Infantry, echoed Towne's sentiments in stronger terms: "the town is now strongly fortifyed. There are several distinct forts all connected by rifle pits. fifty thousand men could not take this town by attacking it. in the rear, the batteries command the whole country around. the country is very rough and hilly in the rear of the town, and no artillery can be brought against it." Bearss, *Campaign for Vicksburg*, 3:1207–14; George W. Towne to "Dear Sister," May 22, 1863, Towne Letters; Charles O. Musser to "My Dear Parents," May 8, 1863, in Popchock, *Soldier Boy*, 51.

16. On June 13, 1863, Rice was appointed to command Fisk's old brigade, which had been redesignated as the 2d Brigade, 13th Division, XIII Army Corps, Army of the Tennessee. Lieutenant Colonel Mackey became the 33d Iowa's acting commander. Rice Military Files; Mackey Military Files.

17. Rice was equally popular among all the regiments in his new command. On July 3, 1863, Lt. Col. R. F. Patterson of the 29th Iowa Infantry wrote from Helena: "Our Brigade is commanded by Col. S. A. Rice, of the 33d Iowa, and a braver or better officer has not been sent from the State." *Keokuk (Iowa) Daily Gate City*, July 9, 1863.

18. As noted earlier, some of the 33d Iowa's companies received Enfields on January 25, 1863. Among the companies that drew the new rifle muskets on the date cited by Sperry was Company G. Morgan, "Diary," pt. 1, 491.

CHAPTER SIX: THE BATTLE OF HELENA

1. The Confederate approach to Helena was agonizingly slow, and the Union garrison received ample warning of the impending blow. John F. Lacey, the 33d Iowa's first sergeant major, who had been recently promoted to first lieutenant to serve as Colonel Rice's assist-

ant adjutant general (brigade chief of staff), recalled the atmosphere at headquarters as June gave way to July: "News came in through spies, refugees, and scouts for many days that General Holmes and Price were marching on Helena, and that they were expecting to celebrate the Fourth of July there."

Having been surprised once at Shiloh, General Prentiss was determined to not be caught napping again. "Conceiving that Helena might be attacked sooner or later," he reported, "I omitted no precaution and spared no labor to add to and strengthen its defenses. To this end I caused rifle-pits to be dug, substantial breastworks to be thrown up, and four outlying batteries to be erected in commanding positions on the bluffs west of the town, and designated respectively, from right to left (north and south) by the letters A, B, C, and D." John F. Lacy [Lacey], "A Battle Scene at Helena, Ark., July 4, 1863," In *The War of the 'Sixties*, ed. E. R. Hutchins (New York: Neale Publishing Co., 1912), 194; *OR*, ser. 1, vol. 22, pt. 1, p. 387.

2. Sperry and other enlisted men may not have been worried, but the garrison's officers, who were better informed, took the threat seriously enough. On July 4, 1863, Capt. Edmund L. Joy, Company B, 36th Iowa Infantry, revealed in his diary: "For the Past Ten days reports from the back country and from Memphis tended to show an intention on the part of the rebel forces in Southern Missouri & Arkansas to mass their forces in a grand attack on Helena. . . . It was known at H.Q. that for 4 days before July 4 the enemy had cut us entirely off from all communication with the Country." Around June 29, Capt. Thomas Stevens of the 28th Wisconsin learned that General Prentiss had "rec'd notice from up river that Price & Marmaduke are massing their forces again for an attack upon this place. He thinks they cannot raise more than 9000 to 10,000 men, & that we can hold Helena against that number." Stevens referred to a warning that Maj. Gen. Stephen A. Hurlbut sent Prentiss from Memphis on June 24. By July 3, the suspense had become so strong that Lt. Col. R. F. Patterson of the 29th Iowa wrote an Iowa newspaper that his men and those of the 33d and 36th Iowa "are all 'spiling for a fight.'" Edmund L. Joy, "Diary," July 4, 1863, Old State House Museum, Little Rock, Ark.; Thomas N. Stevens to Carrie Stevens, June 29, 1863, in Blackburn, *Dear Carrie*, 122; Bearss, *Campaign for Vicksburg*, 3:1217; *Keokuk (Iowa) Daily Gate City*, July 9, 1863.

3. It appears that reveille sounded even earlier than Sperry remembered. As Prentiss revealed in his after-action report: "It was, therefore, ordered, a week previous to the battle, that the entire garrison should be up and under arms at 2.30 o'clock each morning." On July 2, Sgt. John Morgan, Company G, 33d Iowa, scribbled in his diary: "Price reported below Marmaduke close at hand Order to stand at arm from 2 A.M. till day break. and every man with box full of carts [cartridges]." The following day, Morgan noted the evacuation by steamboat of many of the women and children living in the town.

It was also on July 3 that Prentiss announced the cancellation of the gala celebration the Helena garrison had been planning for Independence Day. Later that evening, he met with his brigade commanders and instructed them to "strengthen the picket posts and caution the guards to great watchfulness, and to order the picket guards to make good resistance in case of an attack, so that there might be ample time to form the troops for defense." Then he and his chief subordinate, Brig. Gen. Frederick Salomon, personally inspected the city's outposts before retiring. *OR*, ser. 1, vol. 22, pt. 1, p. 388; Morgan, "Diary," pt. 1, 492; Thomas N. Stevens to Carrie Stevens, July 6, 1863, in Blackburn, *Dear Carrie*, 125; Lacy, "Battle Scene," 194; Bearss, *Campaign for Vicksburg*, 3:1219–20.

4. Lieutenant Lacey called Fort Curtis "a formidable control redoubt commanding and protecting the rear of the advanced batteries." It contained nine thirty-two-pound siege guns situated to blast any enemy breakthrough in Helena's exterior lines. The 33d Iowa reported to this central location as a reserve force. From there, the regiment could be sent to any part of the Union line that required reinforcements. Lacy, "Battle Scene," 193; *OR*,

ser. 1, vol. 22, pt. 1, pp. 395, 400; Roberts and Moneyhon, *Portraits of Conflict*, 98–99; *Memphis Bulletin*, July 6, 1863.

5. Second Lt. Charles H. Sharman rose from the ranks. Born in Sligo, Ireland, he enlisted in the 33d Iowa at Pella on August 9, 1862, at the age of twenty-one. He had dark eyes, dark hair, and a dark complexion, and his height was five feet seven inches. Like Andrew Sperry, he was a teacher by trade. He served as the fifth sergeant of Company G and as the regiment's left general guide from October 1862 until February 1863, when he received his commission.

Sergeant Morgan gave a fuller description of the circumstances surrounding Lieutenant Sharman's injury: "At the Hindman house [near Battery D] met Sergt [Henry] Bousquet with Lieut Sharman wounded while on picket on left temple face very bloody. The ball that wounded Charly took the scalp off Bousquet's hat. Lieut told us his wound was not dangerous but that Tunis Blockland was killed while starting from the picket line which they held for 15 minutes after being attacked." Lieutenant Colonel Mackey credited Sharman with "holding the enemy in check until we were fully prepared to receive them." Military Files of Charles H. Sharman, Civil War (Union) Compiled Military Service Records, 33d Iowa Infantry, Record Group 94, National Archives; John S. Morgan, "Journal," July 4, 1863, State Historical Society of Iowa; *OR*, ser. 1, vol. 22, pt. 1, p. 399.

6. Some of Sperry's comrades later heard that Confederate brigadier general Mosby M. Parsons, whose Missouri infantry brigade was so roughly handled while storming Battery C, exclaimed afterward that he was not eager to face the 33d Iowa a second time. "When a dog jumps on another and gets licked," Parsons allegedly quipped, "he is very backward about repeating the experience." This story became a staple at the 33d's postwar reunions. Newman, *Autobiography*, 77.

7. Around 4:00 A.M., as firing from the retiring Union picket line reached its height, General Salomon ordered Colonel Mackey to march the 33d Iowa to the foot of a hill near where the Upper Little Rock Road entered the south side of Helena. The regiment went into action about five hundred strong. As Confederate troops appeared in front of Battery D, Mackey sent Companies B and G to support that position under his second-in-command, Maj. Hiram D. Gibson. At the same time, he dispatched Companies A and F to support Battery C. A little later, he brought up Companies H, E, I, and K to occupy rifle pits along the Upper Little Rock Road, and he deployed Company C in the ravine between Batteries C and D and Company D to the left of Battery C.

An "eleventh" company of the 33d Iowa also fought at Helena that day. As Union artillery opened fire on the advancing Rebels, many sick soldiers left behind in the regiment's camp grabbed their Enfield rifle muskets and donned their accouterments. As officer of the day, Capt. John P. Yerger of Company B had been left in charge of camp. Grabbing his chance to see some action, Yerger formed the sick into an invalid company and marched to the sound of the guns. *OR*, ser. 1, vol. 22, pt. 1, pp. 398–99; Morgan, "Journal," July 4, 1863.

8. Like other Union participants in the fight, Sperry exaggerated the enemy's strength. The Confederate army that attacked Helena numbered 7,646 effectives—nearly twice as many as the Union garrison. Edwin C. Bearss, "The Battle of Helena," *Arkansas Historical Quarterly* 20 (Autumn 1961): 288.

9. Theophilus H. Holmes (1804–1880) was a North Carolinian who graduated from West Point in 1829 as a classmate of Robert E. Lee. He served well in the Mexican War and had risen to the rank of major in the 8th U.S. Infantry when he decided to cast his lot with the Confederacy.

Promotions came rapidly: brigadier general on June 5, 1861; major general on October 7, 1861; and lieutenant general on October 10, 1862. He fought at First Bull Run and in the Peninsular campaign. In August 1862, he arrived at Little Rock to assume command of the Trans-Mississippi Department. Dismissing the troops available to him as a "crude mass of undisciplined material," Holmes adopted a passive posture and tried to hold what Union forces had not already seized. His poor health, inattention to detail, bombastic orders, and lack of activity prompted his soldiers to mock him as "Granny." By the time of the battle of Helena, he had been demoted to command of the District of Arkansas, making way for Lt. Gen. Edmund Kirby Smith to take charge of the Trans-Mississippi Department. Ezra J. Warner, *Generals in Gray: Lives of the Confederate Commanders* (Baton Rouge: Louisiana State University Press, 1959), 141; Christ, *Rugged and Sublime*, 45–46, 60.

10. Sterling Price (1809–1867) moved in 1831 with his parents from Virginia to Missouri, where he built a distinguished career. He served in the state legislature and the U.S. Congress, advanced from colonel to brigadier general while leading volunteer troops in the Mexican War, and was governor of Missouri from 1853 to 1857. As civil war engulfed his beloved state, he ended up siding with the secessionists and found himself commanding the pro-Southern state militia. He played a prominent role in the pivotal battles at Wilson's Creek, Missouri, and Pea Ridge. Commissioned as a major general in the Confederate provisional army, he fought at Iuka and Corinth, Mississippi, and then returned to the trans-Mississippi. In the Helena campaign, he functioned as Holmes's chief subordinate, commanding the infantry division that pressed the main Rebel assault on Batteries C and D. Price's soldierly abilities were open to question, but not his dedication or charisma. To his Missouri troops especially, he was the living embodiment of the "Lost Cause," and they called him "Old Pap" with affection. Warner, *Generals in Gray*, 247; Christ, *Rugged and Sublime*, 74. See also Albert Castel, *General Sterling Price and the Civil War in the West* (Baton Rouge: Louisiana State University Press, 1968) and Robert E. Shalhope, *Sterling Price: Portrait of a Southerner* (Columbia: University of Missouri Press, 1971).

11. John Sappington Marmaduke (1833–1887) was another flamboyant Missourian who made his mark in the Civil War west of the Mississippi. He studied at Yale and Harvard but graduated from West Point in 1857. He resigned from the U.S. army in 1861, and then served, in rapid succession, with battalions from the Missouri militia, Arkansas, and the Confederate regular army. He led a regiment with great bravery at Shiloh, where he was wounded. Promoted to brigadier general as of November 15, 1862, he commanded a cavalry division of three brigades at the battle of Prairie Grove, Arkansas, December 7, 1862. Marmaduke's division attacked the northern end of the Union line at Helena but made little headway. Marmaduke was elected governor of Missouri in 1884, only to die in office three years later. Warner, *Generals in Gray*, 211; Michael E. Banasik, ed., *Missouri Brothers in Gray: The Reminiscences and Letters of William J. Bull and John P. Bull* (Iowa City: Camp Pope Bookshop, 1998), 143, 146.

12. Perhaps because of Colonel Pile's background as a battery commander, the 33d Missouri's personnel had been trained to double as artillerymen, and they handled many of the big guns defending Helena. Company E manned the cannon mounted in Battery C, while Company H supported the position as sharpshooters. Company B supplied the gunners for Battery D, with Companies G, I, and K as sharpshooters. Companies D and F manned the siege guns in Fort Curtis, Company C performed the same duty in Battery B, and Company A did likewise in Battery A. *OR*, ser. 1, vol. 22, pt. 1, p. 400.

13. Trying in vain to keep up with the 33d Iowa's invalid company, Sergeant Morgan of Company G witnessed the start of the fight on the northern end of the Union line: "As we left our Camp could see the hills above town litterally covered with rebs, saw them drive in the pickets. The 29th Iowa were in the rifle pits in that part of the field to check them. The 36th [Iowa] were just starting out to support them and the 5th Kansas [Cavalry] to do service which was most needed." Morgan, "Journal," July 4, 1863.

14. The Confederates fought bravely enough, but their attack was poorly coordinated.

The blame for that falls mainly on General Holmes, who instructed his subordinates to advance on the enemy's works at daybreak instead of at a fixed time. Recently discovered evidence also reveals that some Confederate troops paused in a small settlement erected by runaway slaves just outside the Union lines to kill several unfortunate black civilians, including women and children. In their retreat after the battle, the Rebels took the time to burn down the hastily vacated shanties. Bearss, "Battle of Helena," 266, 269–72, 274–77, 293; *Keokuk (Iowa) Daily Gate City,* August 25, 1863. For more on the murderous hostility Confederate soldiers in Arkansas felt toward former slaves who fled to Union forces or served in the Union army, see Gregory J. W. Urwin, "'We Cannot Treat Negroes . . . as Prisoners of War': Racial Atrocities and Reprisals in Civil War Arkansas," *Civil War History* 42 (September 1996): 193–210.

15. With his companies divided to cover several different strongpoints, Colonel Mackey had no choice but to keep moving. Writing to the *Daily Gate City* in Keokuk, an "Ex-Hawkeye" expressed some irritation over the 33d Iowa's deployment: "Early in the action it became necessary to divide the 33d Iowa to assist in the support of the batteries; thus depriving Col. Mackey and his men of the opportunity of accomplishing what they might have done had they gone into the fight unbroken." *Keokuk (Iowa) Daily Gate City,* August 25, 1863.

16. Around 8:00 A.M., Parsons's Missouri brigade and an Arkansas brigade under Brig. Gen. Dandridge McRae took Battery C at bayonet point. From the vantage point of Battery D, the ubiquitous Sergeant Morgan of the 33d Iowa witnessed this struggle: "The Rebs charged twice and were driven back, on the 3d attempt our men stood to the work until the rebs began to pour over the breastworks and get between them and . . . cut off their retreat. They [the Federals] then retreated from the battery firing as they went. Our heaviest loss was here and my heart sank as I beheld flapping in the breeze the accursed 'Stars and bars' where but a moment before floated our own 'Stars and stripes.'" *OR,* ser. 1, vol. 22, pt. 1, pp. 388, 398; Morgan, "Journal," July 4, 1863.

17. Company C lost more men than any other company in the 33d Iowa. Three days after the fight, Colonel Mackey reported the company's casualties to his state's adjutant general as two killed, eleven wounded, and three missing. Cyrus H. Mackey, "A Report of the Casualties of the 33d Iowa Infantry, in battle at Helena Arkansas on the 4th day of July A.D. 1863—Commanded by Lieut Colonel Cyrus H. Mackey," July 7, 1863, State Historical Society of Iowa.

18. The Confederates were also hampered by the Union gunners from the 33d Missouri. Although nearly thirty men from that regiment were killed, wounded, or captured in the defense of Battery C, the survivors had enough presence of mind to carry off all their friction primers and priming wires as the enemy poured over the walls, which meant the Rebels could not fire their newly captured trophies. *OR,* ser. 1, vol. 22, pt. 1, p. 400.

19. Anticipating a Confederate attack on Helena as early as June 21, Rear Adm. David Dixon Porter, commander of the Union navy's Mississippi River Squadron, took immediate steps to see that the endangered outpost received naval support. Lt. Comdr. S. Ledyard Phelps allocated three gunboats to that mission, but only the *Tyler* was anchored off Helena when the Southerners struck. Commanded by Lt. Comdr. James M. Pritchett, the *Tyler* was a large tin-clad sidewheeler of 575 tons. Its armament originally consisted of one thirty-two-pound gun and six eight-inch guns, although it might have been carrying even heavier armament by July 1863. The gunboat's fearsome broadsides helped save Grant's Union army from disaster at Shiloh on April 6, 1862. Bearss, *Campaign for Vicksburg,* 3:1218–19, 1223; Bearss, "Battle of Helena," 268; *Dictionary of American Naval Fighting Ships.* 8 vols. (Washington, D.C.: Naval Historical Center, Department of the Navy, 1959–1981), 7: 376–77; *Keokuk (Iowa) Daily Gate City,* July 13, 1863.

20. The *Tyler* certainly put out a lot of fire that day. According to some eyewitnesses, it

threw "upward of 500 shells among the enemy's troops." Lt. Lacey testified to the accuracy of this barrage: "The gunboat *Tyler* began to get the range and threw its immense shells over the heads of the Union soldiers into the ranks of the Confederates." Sergeant Morgan also recorded some Rebel testimony on the *Tyler*'s effectiveness: "While the enemy held the battery [C] they undertook to move one of the guns to the other side of the breastworks to open on our men. The prisoners say 25 men had hold of it when a 15 in. shell from the Tyler struck immediately under it bursting and killing & wounding 24 of the 25." *Memphis Bulletin*, July 6, 1863; Lacy, "Battle Scene," 195; Morgan, "Journal," July 4, 1863.

21. Union participants noticed the fog as early as 2:30 or 3:00 A.M. It cloaked Confederate movements until an increasingly hot sun burned it away around 8:00 A.M. *OR*, ser. 1, vol. 22, pt. 1, pp. 392, 398; Gaston, "Diary," July 4, 1863.

22. As a principal musician, Sperry's battle station was with the 33d Iowa's field music— twelve paces behind the regiment's line of battle just to the left rear of the regimental colors. Dal Bello, *Parade, Inspection and Basic Evolutions*, 6.

23. This unfortunate Confederate brigade consisted of the 34th, 35th, and 37th Arkansas Infantry under Brig. Gen. James F. Fagan. In their second attack on Battery D, which began around 9:00 A.M., the Arkansans managed to seize an outer line of rifle pits and a position in a deep ravine to the left out of range of the Union cannon. Yankee riflemen, however, turned that place of refuge into a trap. "We were ordered to fix bayonets," wrote Sergeant Morgan, "then fire as fast as we could but not to fire without taking good aim. I was surprised at the deliberate coolness with which our men picked off the rebs who were now hiding behind logs stumps and in some rifle pits we had not been able to occupy for the lack of numbers."

Elements of the 43d Indiana Infantry, 33d Missouri Infantry, and a section of the 1st Missouri Battery assisted troops from the 33d Iowa in bagging a large number of Confederate prisoners in front of Battery D, including Lt. Col. Jephta Johnson and most of the 37th Arkansas Infantry, along with Johnson's regimental colors. *OR*, ser. 1, vol. 22, pt. 1, pp. 398, 400–1; Charles O. Musser to "Dear Father," July 6, 1863, in Popchock, *Soldier Boy*, 65, Morgan, "Journal," July 4, 1863.

24. The 33d Iowa fired eighty to one hundred rounds per man in more than six hours of continuous fighting. *OR*, ser. 1, vol. 22, pt. 1, p. 399.

25. "Jake" Miller appears to have been something of a favorite in Company G, Sperry's old company. Sperry knew him well, as Miller also came from Pella. Miller enlisted on August 13, 1862, when he was thirty years old. He stood five feet eleven and a half inches tall, had a dark complexion, hazel eyes, and black hair, and had been a farmer.

A bullet smashed through the center of Private Miller's breast at the lower end of his sternum, "burying itself in vital parts beneath." When a friend asked if he was badly wounded, Miller calmly replied: "Twill soon be over." After the battle, a solicitous Sergeant Morgan had Miller conducted to the Hindman House, which Asst. Surgeon William M. Scott had converted into a field hospital. When Scott was unable to extract the bullet, Morgan had Miller conveyed to a larger hospital in the Exchange Hotel, operated by the 33d Iowa's surgeon, John Y. Hopkins. Hopkins described Miller's case as doubtful, and the latter died between 1:00 and 1:30 A.M., July 6. Military Files of Jacob Miller, Civil War (Union) Compiled Military Service Records, 33d Iowa Infantry, Record Group 94, National Archives; Morgan, "Journal," July 4, 6, 1863.

26. The Confederate breakthrough at Battery C was checked by concentrated artillery fire from the *Tyler;* Fort Curtis; Batteries A, B, and D; and six field pieces, as well as a new defensive line composed of troops belonging to the 33d Iowa (Colonel Mackey and Companies A, C, D, F, I, and K), the 33d and 35th Missouri, and the dismounted 1st Indiana Cavalry, who deployed on a low ridge south of Fort Curtis and 250 yards east of Battery C. After the Confederates were contained, Mackey led his section of the line

forward in a counterattack that drove the Rebels from the vicinity of Battery D and helped recapture Battery C. Bearss, *Campaign for Vicksburg*, 3:1231–35; Ingersoll, *Iowa and the Rebellion*, 617; Lacy, "Battle Scene," 195; Thomas N. Stevens to Carrie Stevens, July 6, 1863, in Blackburn, *Dear Carrie*, 126–27; *OR*, ser. 1, vol. 22, pt. 1, pp. 388, 398–400.

27. Sperry not only inflated Confederate numbers, but he underestimated Union strength, though to a lesser degree. At the start of the battle, Helena's Union garrison counted 4,129 officers and men—3,128 infantry, 831 cavalry, and 170 artillery. *OR*, ser. 1, vol. 22, pt. 1, p. 389.

28. As Colonel Rice proudly reported: "The heavy loss sustained by the Thirty-third Missouri and the Thirty-third Iowa on this portion of the field fully attests their undoubted courage." The 33d Iowa sustained the highest losses in the Helena garrison, followed by the 33d Missouri. Nevertheless, there are numerous discrepancies in the 33d Iowa's casualty statistics for the battle of Helena. The official casualty returns of Prentiss's command, as printed in the *OR*, claim the 33d Iowa had nineteen enlisted men killed, fifty wounded, and sixteen missing. This undoubtedly came from a list of names prepared by Lieutenant Lacey, of Rice's staff. Lacey sent a copy of his list (which contained the names of the casualties from every Iowa regiment at Helena) to an Iowa newspaper for publication. On the other hand, Colonel Mackey's after-action report of July 6, 1863 (also to be found in the *OR*), discloses that the 33d Iowa suffered seventeen killed, fifty-two wounded (eight of whom died within two days), and seventeen missing. Finally, there is a handwritten report housed at the State Historical Society of Iowa, dated July 7, 1863, which lists every casualty by rank and name and bears Mackey's signature. This document gives the 33d Iowa's losses as ten killed, fifty-one wounded, and ten missing—a total of seventy-one. Either the statistics in the *OR* contain some typographical errors, or someone at Helena was guilty of careless bookkeeping. Private records do nothing to clarify the issue. Sergeant Morgan believed his regiment sustained a total of eighty-five casualties, including "fifteen killed on the field." All this highlights the fact that any statistics pertaining to Civil War armies should be treated with caution. *OR*, ser. 1, vol. 22, pt. 1, pp. 391, 395, 399; Mackey, "Report of the Casualties"; Morgan, "Journal," July 6, 1863; *Dubuque (Iowa) Daily Times*, July 19, 1863.

29. The 2d Arkansas Regiment of African Descent (later the 54th U.S. Colored Infantry) began recruiting at Helena in the spring of 1863 and had not filled out its ranks when the Confederates struck on July 4. General Prentiss placed his black troops in trenches about a half-mile south of town, between the Levee Road and east of the Lower Little Rock Road. It was supposed to be a fairly safe position, as befitted the 2d Arkansas's inexperience. Despite these precautions, the black soldiers came under fire from their right flank, which was unprotected by any traverses. "[O]ur black boys behaved well," reported 2d Lt. Minos Miller, a former sergeant with the 36th Iowa Infantry. "[T]hey was placed in a position when they could be fired on and no chance to return the fire and if there is anything that will discourage a man it is that but they took it calm and cool." Three of the men were wounded, but the regiment stood its ground throughout the engagement.

In what may have been the first account of the battle to surface in the Northern press, the *Memphis Bulletin* made no mention of the 33d Iowa or any other white regiment, but it did assert: "The negro regiments fought well, fully demonstrating their usefulness as soldiers." Republican and abolitionist newspapers across the North, eager to justify the Lincoln administration's controversial decision to raise black regiments for the Union army, reprinted that excerpt, much to the irritation of Sperry and his neglected white comrades. Ronnie Nichols, "Baptism by Fire," *Arkansas Preservation*, Fall 1991, 12; Bearss, "Battle of Helena," 279; Minos Miller to "Dear Mother," April 18, 1863, Minos Miller to "Dear Mother," June 12, 1863, Minos Miller to "Dear Mother," July 6, 1863, all in Minos Miller Papers, Special Collections Division, University of Arkansas Libraries,

Fayetteville; *Memphis Bulletin,* July 6, 1863; *New York Times,* July 15, 1863; *National Anti-Slavery Standard,* August 8, 1863.

30. Sergeant Morgan claimed that all the Union wounded had been recovered and were receiving care by noon, an hour after the battle ended. As for the Confederate wounded, he saw that the Union "[s]urgeons were taking all the notorious secesh houses for rebel hospitals." Helena citizens with Confederate sympathies did everything they could to make Rebel patients comfortable. Morgan, "Journal," July 4, 1863.

31. Pvt. Nathan O. Moore, a twenty-one-year-old farmer and another Pella boy, enlisted on July 24, 1862. He was a short fellow who stood less than five foot six. He had blue eyes, light hair, and a fair complexion. Despite his valor, he had to wait until May 22, 1864, to make corporal. He became a sergeant two months later. Military Files of Nathan O. Moore, Civil War (Union) Compiled Military Service Records, 33d Iowa Infantry, Record Group 94, National Archives.

32. The condition of the Confederate dead can be attributed to the extreme heat at Helena on that bloody day. As best can be determined, the Confederates sacrificed at least 1,636 men in their botched assault. On July 9, General Prentiss reported that his troops had buried 427 dead Rebels, sent 939 north as prisoners, and paroled 108 seriously wounded found four to five miles from Union lines. In addition, there were seven wounded Confederates and forty-seven unwounded prisoners still at Helena. The Federals also captured two enemy battle flags and two thousand stand of arms.

Prentiss reported his own casualties as 57 killed, 127 wounded, and 36 missing. *OR,* ser. 1, vol. 22, pt. 1, pp. 389–90, 403; Morgan, "Journal," July 4, 1863.

33. This must have been a nightmarish experience, for Union artillery severely mutilated many Rebel corpses. As an anonymous private in the 36th Iowa told his mother: "The battle field is the most horrid place I ever saw; there are men with their heads shot off, and legs and arms in different places, and in fact you can have no idea of how they looked." Lt. Minos Miller commented: "the Rebels was laying thick some of them tore all to pieces with shell and some shought through with sollid shot they had laid there 24 hours when I seen them last and began to smell bad and look tuff." *Keokuk (Iowa) Daily Gate City,* July 15, 1863; Minos Miller to "Dear Mother," July 6, 1863.

CHAPTER SEVEN: THE LITTLE ROCK EXPEDITION

1. Sgt. John Morgan of the 33d Iowa's Company G described the scene when that alarm sounded: "The rebels were reported to have again appeared in force 2 miles below Helena threatening us again. The signal gun at Ft Curtis was fired at a few minutes after 5 P.M. and every soldier able to fight broke double quick for his command." Morgan, "Journal," July 5, 1863.

2. An exuberant Capt. Thomas Stevens, Company C, 28th Wisconsin, wrote his wife that day: "We have news this morning—official—of the fall of Vicksburg. There we have 22,720 prisoners. They surrendered on the 4th too, at 10 A.M. We have an impression here that the '*Fourth* of July' is a great day. Hurrah for the day! Three cheers in honor of its victories!" Thomas N. Stevens to Carrie Stevens, July 6, 1863, in Blackburn, *Dear Carrie,* 128.

3. The day opened with a cannon salute. The celebration described by Sperry began at 9:00 A.M. and lasted three hours. Pvt. Cyrus Gaston, Company K, 33d Iowa, supplied some additional details: "we had a Great Celebration over the Victory of Vicksburg & also over the Victory of Helena, Ark. We had speeches fro Genls Prentiss, Ross, Solomon [Salomon], & Col. Rice and others we met at ft. Curtis and had Cheering and Cannons were firing all day." Morgan, "Diary," pt. 1, 492; Gaston, "Diary," July 8, 1863.

4. Private Gaston revealed that the Helena garrison was needlessly disturbed on July 7 and 9. As he told his diary on the seventh: "there was A false alarm given & our Regt was in line in A very short time but the pickets of the 36th Iowa fired on Some Niggers they wounded one of them in the thigh." Sergeant Morgan's diary confirms that the almost identical incident mentioned by Sperry occurred on July 10. Gaston, "Diary," July 7, 9, 1863; Morgan, "Diary," pt. 1, 492.

5. Sperry quoted a proverb from Horace's "Ars Poetica" ("Art of Poetry"). "*Parturient montes, nascetur ridiculus mus*" can be literally translated as "The mountains are in labor and a ridiculous mouse will be born." Edward Henry Blakeney, ed., *Horace on the Art of Poetry* (Freeport, N.Y.: Books for Libraries, 1970), 27.

6. Sergeant Morgan recorded the history of this inglorious sortie on July 19: "Scouting party of. 35 Mo. 28 Wis. 43. Ind. 117. Ill. inft. regts. and 1st Ind cav. 4 pieces of Dubuque [3d Iowa] battery go out with 3 day. ration in haversacks This party back before night. Inft. Went out 5. mile cav. 15. Saw Dobbs [Dobbins's] pickets" Morgan, "Diary," pt. 1, 493.

7. "I Rec'd two months pay or $26.00 Dols.," Private Gaston wrote. "I bought a Diary." Gaston, "Diary," July 28, 1863.

8. Maj. Gen. Frederick Steele (1819–1868) hailed from New York. He graduated from West Point in 1843 in the same class as his good friend, Ulysses S. Grant. Steele was a major in the regular army when the Civil War began and led a battalion at Wilson's Creek. Transferring to the U.S. Volunteers, he became the colonel of the 8th Iowa Infantry on September 23, 1861. On January 29, 1862, he received his brigadier's star. He joined Curtis's Army of the Southwest after Pea Ridge, and commanded a division in the campaign that resulted in Helena's capture. Promoted to major general on March 17, 1863, he served under Sherman and Grant in operations against Vicksburg. On July 31, Steele arrived at Helena to organize an expedition to capture Little Rock, the capital of Arkansas. With thousands of Union troops freed by the fall of Vicksburg, and Arkansas's Confederate defenders weakened and demoralized by their repulse at Helena, the time seemed ripe to knock another seceded state out of the war.

Miffed at not receiving a more active command, General Prentiss resigned his commission on August 3. Two days later, he held a lavish farewell party for the officers of the Helena garrison. Exhibiting no trace of bitterness, Prentiss announced his imminent departure and introduced Steele to the surprised throng. "Gen Prentiss took him by the arm," testified Captain Stevens, "and led him . . . to the table & proposed that they set us an example, which they immediately did by taking a drink & inviting us all to do the same." Prentiss then led the officers in singing the "Battle Cry of Freedom." His last words to his former subordinates were: "God bless every man who helped me here on the 4th of July!" The 33d Iowa's enlisted men learned they were going to Little Rock on August 6. Warner, *Generals in Blue*, 386, 474–75; Hubbell and Geary, *Biographical Dictionary*, 416; Edmund Frederick Steele Joy, "Major General Frederick Steele and Staff," *Americana* 5 (1910): 349–52; *OR*, ser., 1, vol. 22, pt. 1, pp. 474–75, 479; Leo E. Huff, "The Union Expedition against Little Rock, August–September 1863," *Arkansas Historical Quarterly* 22 (Fall 1963): 224–27; Thomas N. Stevens to Carrie Stevens, Helena, August 6, 1863, in Blackburn, *Dear Carrie*, 146; Morgan, "Diary," pt. 1, 494.

9. Steele assembled more than six thousand troops at Helena for the Little Rock expedition. In addition to seventeen infantry regiments and Colonel Powell Clayton's five-hundred-man cavalry brigade, this column included three six-gun artillery batteries and one four-gun battery. Clayton's 1st Indiana Cavalry hauled along three more small rifled cannon. To assist Steele, Brig. Gen. John W. Davidson marched his six-thousand-man cavalry division and eighteen guns from Pilot Knob, Missouri, through eastern Arkansas to Wittsburg on the St. Francis River. He reached that site on July 28. *OR*, ser. 1, vol. 22, pt. 1, pp. 470–71, 475; *OR*, ser. 1, vol. 22, pt. 2, p. 506; Huff, "Union Expedition," 227, 231.

10. Rice commanded the 3d Division in the "Arkansas Expedition," the smallest in Steele's army. His 1st Brigade, under Col. Charles Kittredge, contained the 43d Indiana, 36th Iowa, and 77th Ohio. The 2d Brigade, under Col. Thomas Hart Benton Jr., included the 29th Iowa, 33d Iowa, and 28th Wisconsin. Except for the 77th Ohio, all of Rice's regiments had participated in the defense of Helena. An Iowa correspondent at Helena said of the 3d Division: "It is not large, but the material is excellent, and those of us who have had an opportunity to observe the character and habits of the Division commander for months past predict for it a gallant career in the South West." Eleven other infantry regiments composed Col. William E. McLean's 2d Division. General Davidson's command of ten cavalry regiments was designated as the expedition's 1st Division. Colonel Clayton's 1st Indiana and 5th Kansas Cavalry began the campaign as an unattached brigade. *OR*, ser. 1, vol. 22, pt. 1, pp. 470–71; *OR*, ser. 1, vol. 22, pt. 2, p. 433; *Keokuk (Iowa) Daily Gate City*, August 25, 1863.

11. Actually, the marching on August 11 went fairly well. It was cloudy and rainy, which kept the heat down, and the 33d Iowa only tramped five to six miles. According to Captain Stevens, conditions became almost unbearable on the twelfth: "This has been a very hot day. The men carry their knapsacks, and it wears hard on them. Several had to give it up. Knapsacks, blankets, portfolios, shirts, clothing of all kinds, bibles & Testaments &c., &c., lie scattered all along the road, thrown away by the soldiers rather than carry them. Unless the [baggage wagon] teams can carry the knapsacks tomorrow, lots more of them will be thrown away." Gaston, "Diary," August 11, 1863; Morgan, "Diary," pt. 1, 494; Thomas N. Stevens, "Diary of March from Helena, Ark., *towards* Little Rock, Ark.," in Blackburn, *Dear Carrie*, 148–49.

12. The dates given here are erroneous. The 33d Iowa did no marching on August 16 and 17. Sperry must have meant August 13 and 14. Of the march on the former date, Sergeant Morgan observed: "Col Rice Sick. Hard march and hot day many give out." Colonel Rice was still ill on August 14, and rested in a house until sundown. As for the 33d Iowa, Private Gaston related: "we had our knapsacks hauled to day & we carried two days Rations in our haverSacks. . . . We marched about 14 miles & camped on a large creek." After reaching camp late that afternoon, Captain Stevens of the 28th Wisconsin condemned Steele's handling of his infantry: "This has been a terrible hard day for us who go on foot—the dust, the hot sun & sweltering heat—it was *rough*. The men fell out by scores. We are marched too far for men in our condition, & at this time of year in Arkansas, half the time without water." Morgan, "Diary," pt. 1, 494; Gaston, "Diary," August 14, 1863; Stevens, "Diary of March," in Blackburn, *Dear Carrie*, 149.

13. Cpl. Charles Musser witnessed much of the same from the ranks of the 29th Iowa: "a great many men give out and had to be hauled. We all got our knapsacks hauled for us, or we would have been the worst used up army that ever marched through an enemy's country." Charles O. Musser to "Dear Father," August 16, 1863, in Popchock, *Soldier Boy*, 79.

14. Sperry got his dates wrong once again. The 33d Iowa reached Clarendon after dark on August 15, not 14. Gaston, "Diary," August 15, 1863; Morgan, "Diary," pt. 1, 494.

15. John W. Davidson (1824–1881) was a Virginian and the scion of a military family. He graduated from West Point in 1845, fought in the Mexican War, and saw extensive frontier service in the 1850s. Remaining loyal to the Union, Davidson was promoted to brigadier general to date from February 3, 1862, and led a brigade in McClellan's peninsular campaign. Late in the summer of 1862, he was transferred to St. Louis and spent the rest of the Civil War in Missouri and Arkansas. Warner, *Generals in Blue*, 112. For more details, see Homer K. Davidson, *Black Jack Davidson, a Cavalry Commander on the Western Frontier: The Life of General John W. Davidson* (Glendale, Calif.: A. H. Clark, 1974).

16. This is a reference to the myth of Minos, king of ancient Crete, who commissioned the craftsman Daedalus to build a labyrinth to imprison the Minotaur at the royal palace of

Knossos. Sinclair Hood, *The Minoans: The Story of Bronze Age Crete* (New York: Praeger, 1971), 14.

17. On August 17, Sergeant Morgan noted: "Col Rice promoted to Brig Gen." The promotion was approved on August 4, 1863, but it took some time for the news to overtake Rice. According to Lieutenant Lacey of the new general's staff, Rice's elevation came as a reward for his conduct in the battle of Helena. Morgan, "Diary," pt. 1, 494; Warner, *Generals in Blue*, 402; Lacy, "Battle Scene," 193.

18. Clarendon sat on the White River about sixty-five miles from Helena and sixty from Little Rock. It had once been a prosperous village, but it was largely deserted when Steele's Arkansas expedition arrived. Since Clarendon was unincorporated, no statistics on its population appear in the 1860 census, but the population of surrounding Cache Township was 1,085: 694 whites and 391 blacks. *Keokuk (Iowa) Daily Gate City*, August 29, 1863; "Evolution of Arkansas Townships," 86.

19. John Lofland, a watchmaker from Oskaloosa, was thirty-two when he was appointed a captain in Company D, 33d Iowa Infantry, on August 7, 1862. A week later, Lofland's men voted to ratify his selection. The Ohio native had gray eyes, brown hair, and a dark complexion. His height was five feet eight and a half inches. His commission as lieutenant colonel was dated August 18, 1863, but he was not mustered in under his new rank until April 23, 1864. John Lofland Military Files, Civil War (Union) Compiled Military Service Records, 33d Iowa Infantry, Record Group 94, National Archives.

20. After the Arkansas expedition reached Clarendon, General Steele reported: "I found my operations encumbered by over 1,000 sick." The 28th Wisconsin alone had 106 men who were no longer fit to march. "A great part of them will probably be able to join us a week or two," commented Captain Stevens. "Some ought to go north & I hope they will." *OR*, ser. 1, vol. 22, pt. 1, p. 475; Thomas N. Stevens to Carrie Stevens, August 20, 1863, in Blackburn, *Dear Carrie*, 157.

21. In reality, medical care was no joking matter in the Arkansas expedition. As Captain Stevens fumed: "Our sick have been treated inhumanely—have suffered extremely, and for several days received no attention such as sick men are entitled to. . . . When so many sick men are sent along to follow up such an expedition they cannot help but suffer,— especially when an entirely inadequate supply of medical stores are taken along, as was the case in this instance, as I am informed." Sufficient medicines and other hospital supplies did not reach Steele's surgeons until September 3. Thomas N. Stevens to Carrie Stevens, September 20, 1863, in Blackburn, *Dear Carrie*, 181; *Dubuque (Iowa) Daily Times*, September 27, 1863; Morgan, "Diary," pt. 1, 497.

22. The 33d Iowa covered only six miles in that hellish night march. "The mud was boot top deep," griped Private Gaston. When mud made roads impassable, troops would corduroy them by laying logs across the roadbed. Gaston, "Diary," August 21, 1863; Paddy Griffith, *Battle in the Civil War: Generalship and Tactics in America 1861–65* (Camberley, Surrey: Fieldbooks, 1986), 8–9.

23. Sergeant Morgan did not enjoy this leg of the march as much as Sperry: "In hot dust deep, hard marching." Morgan, "Diary," pt. 1, 496.

24. "This is a healthy locality; high plateaus, no swamps in the vicinity, and the current in the river rapid," General Steele boasted of his new advanced base. "There is a grist-mill and a saw-mill, about 2 miles distant by a good road and 4 by water, which can be put in order by supplying a few deficiencies." While his infantry marched up from Clarendon, Steele transported his one thousand sick to De Valls Bluff by steamboat and turned the river port into both a hospital town and a military depot. *OR*, ser. 1, vol. 22, pt. 1, pp. 473, 475; Morgan, "Diary," pt. 1, 496; *Dubuque (Iowa) Daily Times*, September 27, 1863.

25. This was a forty-five-mile stretch of the incomplete Memphis-Little Rock Railroad. The line had begun construction in the 1850s, but state politics and financial problems impeded construction. Nevertheless, the existence of this section made possession of De

Valls Bluff important to the Federals, especially if they meant to take and hold Little Rock. The Arkansas River was not navigable year-round, but the White River was more reliable. James M. Woods, *Rebellion and Realignment: Arkansas's Road to Secession* (Fayetteville: University of Arkansas Press, 1987), 92, 116, 122; Michael B. Dougan, *Confederate Arkansas: The People and Policies of a Frontier State in Wartime* (University: University of Alabama Press, 1976), 2–3, 8, 10; Moneyhon, *Impact of the Civil War*, 88–90; Thomas N. Stevens to Carrie Stevens, September 12, 1863, in Blackburn, *Dear Carrie*, 171; See Leo E. Huff, "The Memphis and Little Rock Railroad during the Civil War," *Arkansas Historical Quarterly* 23 (Autumn 1964): 260–70.

26. This damage probably occurred during Gorman's White River expedition, which occupied De Valls Bluff in the latter half of January 1863. Bearss, *Campaign for Vicksburg*, 1:413–14.

27. While Steele rested his exhausted infantry, he sent Davidson's cavalry ranging westward to scout the approaches to Little Rock. The Union troopers clashed with Confederate cavalry near Brownsville, August 25, and Bayou Meto, August 27. *OR*, ser. 1, vol. 22, pt. 1, pp. 475–76; Huff, "Union Expedition," 229–30.

28. Reinforcements were also on the way. On August 29, 1863, Col. James M. True reached Clarendon with a brigade of four infantry regiments of the XVI Army Corps from Memphis. True overtook Steele at Brownsville, Arkansas, by September 2, boosting the Arkansas expedition's strength to about fifteen thousand effectives. *OR*, ser. 1, vol. 22, pt. 1, pp. 471, 476; *OR*, ser. 1, vol. 22, pt. 2, p. 505; Huff, "Union Expedition," 231.

29. Pvt. Allan McNeal, Company H, 33d Iowa, who remained sick at De Valls Bluff for more than a month, opined that only mounted infantry could operate in Arkansas. "Infantry can not stand it to march throug[h] this country," he told his parent, "for water is to scarce in places." Allan McNeal to "Dear parents," September 27, 1863, McNeal Letters.

30. Compounding the 33d Iowa's misery was the fact that it marched with foul water the day before, August 31. "[O]ur water from mud holes thick scum over it," noted Sergeant Morgan, "when the coffee is made, it has the appearance of haveing cream in it." Morgan, "Diary," pt. 1, 496.

31. "Had a hard march across a praire 80 miles wide," Pvt. George Towne, Company G, 33d Iowa, wrote his sister with pardonable exaggeration, "under the scorching rays of a September sun. The consequence was a great many gave out. We started from Duvals bluff with 13 men in our company fit for duty & several have given out since so you see but few of us are along in the expedition after all." "It was a choking march—23 miles with nothing like a supply of water!" raged Captain Stevens. "I hope we will not have to march as far again very soon, on one canteen full." George W. Towne to "Dear Sister," September 5, 1863, Towne Letters; Thomas N. Stevens to Carrie Stevens, September 1, 1863, in Blackburn, *Dear Carrie*, 164.

32. Private Gaston recorded that the 33d Iowa passed through Brownsville at 5:00 P.M. and marched three more miles before bivouacking. Private Towne liked the town: "Brownsville is quite a place it has a fine brick court house situated in it & a great number of stores in fact it approaches the nearest to the memory of a town of any place I have seen in Ark." George W. Towne to "Dear Sister," September 5, 1863, Towne Letters; Gaston, "Diary," September 1, 1863.

33. Bayou Meto was a sluggish stream with steep banks that screened Little Rock from the east. It was probably the best place the Rebels could have chosen to stop Steele's advance. Union cavalry under Davidson engaged in a six-hour fire fight with Confederate cavalry under Marmaduke along the bayou at Reed's Bridge on August 27, after which the blue horsemen fell back toward Brownsville. Thomas Pedeon Clarke, "Diary," August 27, 1863, in the possession of Richard Merritt, Little Rock, Ark.; Huff, "Union Expedition," 230; *OR*, ser. 1, vol. 22, pt. 1, pp. 471, 476.

34. "Our Division approached within 12 miles of Little Rock & drove the rebel pickets . . .

across the byou behind them," boasted Private Towne. "We also passed the rebel camp & rifle pits without opposition & went to the byou & threw a few shells at them." "[W]e dident find any Rebs as was expected," grumbled Private Gaston. "we found two of david-sons Cavalry & Buried them." Towne also spoke of these burials and called the abandoned Rebel camp where the 33d Iowa spent the night "the most beautiful we ever saw." George W. Towne to "Dear Sister," September 5, 1863, Towne Letters; Gaston, "Diary," September 3, 1863.

35. Steele left seven hundred sick at De Valls Bluff on September 6, detailing Colonel True's "Memphis Brigade" and one cavalry brigade to guard the place. *OR*, ser. 1, vol. 22, pt. 1, p. 476.

36. The 33d Iowa marched twelve miles on September 6 as rear guard, which is why it followed Steele's wagons. The regiment camped that night beside Bayou Meto. Gaston, "Diary," September 6, 1863.

37. "In this section of the country there is some very large corn fields and the tallest corn I ever saw," commented Sgt. Thomas P. Clarke of the 10th Illinois Cavalry. "The ear, as a general thing hangs ten feet from the ground and there is no end to the sweet potatoes." Private Gaston did more than admire these crops: "I run across A Sweet potato patch & I got a mess as we went along." Clarke, "Diary," September 8, 1863; Gaston, "Diary," September 7, 1863.

38. Acting in its accustomed role as Steele's spearhead, Davidson's cavalry fought its way through to the Arkansas River near Ashley's Mills on September 7. Huff, "Union Expedition," 232.

CHAPTER EIGHT: LITTLE ROCK

1. The Confederates tried to save Little Rock by constructing a line of fortifications on the high ground overlooking the city from the north bank of the Arkansas River. Rather than sacrifice his troops in a frontal attack, General Steele decided to flank the enemy out of their position. On the morning of September 10, General Davidson finished throwing a pontoon bridge across the Arkansas River near Terry's Ferry. Supported by artillery and the infantry of Steele's 2d Division, the Union cavalry crossed to the south bank and proceeded toward Little Rock's soft underbelly. At the same time, Rice's 3d Division marched west to threaten the right flank of the enemy fortifications. Rather than be trapped like Pemberton at Vicksburg, Sterling Price, who had assumed command of the District of Arkansas from an ailing Theophilus Holmes on July 23, hastily evacuated Arkansas's capital.

Private Gaston of Company K described the day's proceedings from the 33d Iowa's perspective: "We got orders this morning to draw 2 days Rations to be ready to march at 8 A.M. & by 9 the whole force was in motion, marching toward Little Rock. we march to the River & put down A pontoon bridge & the Cav. & a Battery & the 40 Iowa [Infantry] crossed & we marched up on our side & the cav on the other." *OR*, ser. 1, vol. 22, pt. 1, pp. 476–77; Huff, "Union Expedition," 227, 231–36, Gaston, "Diary," September 10, 1863.

2. The Confederates succeeded in completely destroying six steamboats and most of the rolling stock for the Memphis-Little Rock Railroad, but the Yankees were able to save two locomotives and some flatcars, as well as some pontoons from three bridges across the Arkansas that the retreating Rebels had broken up and set on fire. *OR*, ser. 1, vol. 22, pt. 1, p. 477; Thomas N. Stevens to Carrie Stevens, September 11, 1863, in Blackburn, *Dear Carrie*, 170.

3. This "ironclad" was actually the gunboat CSS *Pontchartrain*. Built as a sidewheel steamer and originally named the *Lizzie Simmons* or *Eliza Simmons*, it was purchased by

the Confederate navy at New Orleans on October 12, 1861, and converted into a warship bearing seven guns. The *Pontchartrain* fought at Island No. 10, New Madrid, Missouri, and St. Charles, Arkansas, between March and June 1862. Several sources mistakenly give October 9, 1863, as the date of the *Pontchartrain's* destruction. According to local tradition, a large gun mounted today in front of Little Rock's Old State House Museum was salvaged from the wreck. It is called the "Lady Baxter." Naval History Division, Navy Department, comp., *Civil War Naval Chronology, 1861–1865* (Washington, D.C.: U.S. Government Printing Office, 1971), VI-288.

4. Exhilarated by their own exploits and the Union victories at Vicksburg and Gettysburg, the men who captured Little Rock thought they would soon see the end of the war. "With 6,000 more infantry," Steele pledged to General Halleck on September 23, "I think I could drive Smith and Price into Mexico." Confederate forces in Arkansas seemed to be disintegrating. "From ten to fifty deserters reach Little Rock daily," the *Dubuque Daily Times* crowed six days later. "They take the oath of allegiance and are released." "Old Prices army I judge is about played out," Pvt. Allan McNeal of the 33d Iowa assured his parents. "[D]eserters are stil comeing in by the 1000. . . . The [Union] soldiers are all in fine spirits in regard to the war they think it can not last a great whil. . . . The Southern army is deserting by whole regs, both east & west." *OR,* ser. 1, vol. 22, pt. 1, p. 482; *Keokuk (Iowa) Daily Gate City,* October 5, 1863; *Dubuque (Iowa) Daily Times,* September 29, 1863; Allan McNeal to "Dear parents," September 27, 1863, McNeal Letters.

5. One member of the 33d Iowa who hoped to stay at Little Rock was Private McNeal of Company H, who was still sick in a hospital that General Steele established at De Valls Bluff when the Arkansas capital fell. "I think we wil go in to winter quarters at Little Rock," McNeal wrote his parents, "they have sent back to Helena for our tents. . . . I think we wil have a splendid time this winter if we go in to quarters at Little Rock as all agree it is the best military Post in the west." Allan McNeal to "Dear parents," September 27, 1863, McNeal Letters.

6. The Anthony House was Little Rock's most popular hotel. It stood on the south side of East Markham Street between Main and Scott Streets. William W. O'Donnell, *The Civil War Quadrennium: A Narrative History of Day-to-Day Life in Little Rock, Arkansas, during the American War between the States, 1861–1865* (Little Rock: Civil War Round Table of Arkansas, 1985), iv.

7. Both Arkansas's capital and largest city, Little Rock had 3,727 residents in 1860: 2,874 whites and 853 African Americans. It also contained five private schools, five hotels, six churches, fourteen small manufacturing plants, a penitentiary, and an abandoned federal arsenal. After more than a month of campaigning in hellish heat, many of the city's conquerors considered it a veritable oasis. "Little Rock is the most pleasant place I have yet seen in rebeldom," declared Capt. Thomas Stevens of the 28th Wisconsin. "I am half in love with it, & feel almost like locating here—that is if a nice square in the city can be held under the 'homestead bill.'" Sgt. Thomas Clarke of the 10th Illinois Cavalry surveyed Little Rock with a more objective eye: "It is a very pretty place. The streets are very uneven in some places. The principal buildings are the state house and arsenal. The state house is built of freestone, is two stories high, is enclosed with a good fence and surrounded with shade trees. The arsenal is three stories, built of the same material, and stands in the centre of a twenty acre lot. It is ornamented with all kinds of shade trees and gravel walks. . . . The next best buildings are the Methodist, Baptist, Presbyterian and Christian Churches—all of which are good buildings. There is very few good private residences, but the appearance of the town is greatly improved by the shade trees." O'Donnell, *Civil War Quadrennium,* iii–v; "Evolution of Arkansas Townships," 87; Donald J. Simon, "The Third Minnesota Regiment in Arkansas, 1863–1865," *Minnesota History* 40 (Summer 1967): 286–87; Thomas N. Stevens to Carrie Stevens, September 14, 1863, Thomas M.

Stevens to his sister, September 24, 1863, both in Blackburn, *Dear Carrie*, 175, 182; Clarke, "Diary," September 23, 1863.

8. This site was about half a mile south of Little Rock. Private McNeal commented on its most attractive feature: "our reg is camped close to a splendid spring which afords plenty of water for t[w]o brigades." Gaston, "Diary," September 15–16, 1863; Allan McNeal to "Dear parents," September 27, 1863, McNeal Letters.

9. These logistical problems ended sooner than Sperry remembered. The Memphis-Little Rock Railroad resumed operations under Union control between September 20 and 23. The line's carrying capacity increased dramatically about a week later, when the stern-wheeler *Lady Jackson* dropped off an additional locomotive and six more flatcars at De Valls Bluff. "[I]t is the roughest road i ever saw," marveled Corporal Musser of the 29th Iowa. "[T]his road is the straitest one i ever saw. . . . there are but few bridges [and] only two of any importance: one on Bayou Meto and one on Ink Bayou. . . . All along the road, it is a very wild looking country. . . . Game is plenty, such as deer, turky, bear, opossum, coon, etc." Rough or not, the reopening of the railroad made it easier to obtain both necessities and luxuries at Little Rock, and the Union troops were not slow to celebrate. "Captain J. M. Baugh treated the company to an Oyster Supper to Night," a pleased Private Gaston scratched in his diary on October 2, "& after supper Seagts Burgess & Bell treated to cigars." *Dubuque (Iowa) Daily Times*, September 29, 1863; *Memphis Daily Appeal*, October 19, 28, 1863; *OR*, ser. 1, vol. 22, pt. 1, p. 481; Thomas N. Stevens to Carrie Stevens, September 20, 1863, Thomas N. Stevens to Carrie Stevens, September 24, 1863, Thomas N. Stevens to his sister, September 24, 1863, Thomas N. Stevens to Carrie Stevens, October 21, 1863, all in Blackburn, *Dear Carrie*, 179–84, 193; Allan McNeal to "Dear parents," September 27, 1863, McNeal Letters; Charles O. Musser to "Dear Father," October 6, 1863, in Popchock, *Soldier Boy*, 88; Gaston, "Diary," October 2, 1863.

10. On September 14, a scandalized Captain Stevens wrote home: "I asked the price of milk at a house near camp the other day. The reply was two 'bits' [twenty-five cents] for buttermilk or four 'bits' for sweet milk! A pretty round price. I didn't buy—though have seen the time when I would." Thomas N. Stevens to Carrie Stevens, September 14, 1863, in Blackburn, *Dear Carrie*, 174.

11. The lure of Yankee gold enabled Little Rock's inhabitants to overcome their fear of Steele's occupation forces with remarkable speed. On September 22, Cpl. Charles Musser of the 29th Iowa told his father: "Business is beginning to get quite brisk in the city. Hotells, Shops, stores, and other public houses are being opened again after being closed for many months. Farmers bring in their produce to Sell and get good prices for it." Charles O. Musser to "Dear Father," September 22, 1863, in Popchock, *Soldier Boy*, 85.

12. Private Gaston wrote this entry in his diary on September 23: "Clear and pleasant I was on Company Drille this forenoon at 9 A. M." Gaston, "Diary," September 23, 1863.

13. This "Mr. Scholte" was none other than Dominie Henry P. Scholte, the founder of Pella, Iowa, Sperry's hometown. A strong supporter of the war, Scholte offered every man from Lake Prairie Township who agreed to enlist in the Union army a lot in North Pella. *Dubuque (Iowa) Daily Times*, September 18, 1863; Van Stigt, *Pella, Iowa*, 116.

14. The Democrats scored a major coup when they nominated James M. Tuttle, Iowa's renowned war hero, for governor in 1863. The Republican candidate, William M. Stone (1827–1893), was the former colonel of the 22d Iowa Infantry and had been wounded during the Vicksburg campaign, but he was a dark-horse candidate and his military stature could not begin to compare with Tuttle's. The campaign was a dirty one, but recent Union military victories seemed to vindicate Republican policies. Furthermore, many Iowa soldiers felt betrayed by Tuttle for siding with the antiwar Democrats. The 33d Iowa cast 295 votes for Stone and 45 for Tuttle. When Pvt. George W. Towne of Company G heard the news, the young Republican gloated: "We had a fine time yesterday at the election & give

the copperhead Tuttle a foretaste of what is to come hereafter." Stone received 85 percent of Iowa's soldier vote and 56.4 percent of the civilian vote, beating Tuttle by 85,896 to 56,169. Wubben, *Civil War Iowa*, 141–45; Lyftogt, *From Blue Mills to Columbia*, 105–6; Hubbell and Geary, *Biographical Dictionary*, 509–10; George W. Towne to "Dear Sister," October 14, 1863, Towne Letters; Morgan, "Diary," pt. 1, 499; Gaston, "Diary," October 13, 1863; *Dubuque (Iowa) Daily Times*, October 30, 1863.

15. On October 14, an upbeat Private Towne scribbled these tidings to his sister: "We have vary easy times now & are fixing winter quarters & expect to remain here all winter. There are only three in a tent & we have therefore plenty of room." George W. Towne to "Dear Sister," October 14, 1863, Towne Letters.

CHAPTER NINE: WINTER

1. On October 25, 1863, the irrepressible General Marmaduke stormed Pine Bluff with more than 2,000 dismounted Confederate cavalry and twelve cannon. The post was bravely defended by 550 troopers from the 5th Kansas and 1st Indiana Cavalry under Col. Powell Clayton, one of the best Union officers to serve in Arkansas. Assisted by roughly 300 former slaves who erected cotton-bale barricades, filled water barrels, and doused flames, the Federals beat off several stubborn attacks, and the Rebels finally retired.

Pvt. George Towne of the 33d Iowa's Company G gave another reason for the dispatch of General Rice's division to Benton: "It was reported that they were fighting at Pine Bluff & we had to take the place of the cavalry which left Benton to reinforce the troops at Pine Bluff." Christ, *Rugged and Sublime*, 96–102; George W. Towne to "Dear Sister," November 2, 1863, Towne Letters. See also William H. Burnside, *The Honorable Powell Clayton* (Conway: University of Central Arkansas Press, 1991); James W. Leslie, ed., "Arabella Lanktree Wilson's Civil War Letter," *Arkansas Historical Quarterly* 47 (Autumn 1988): 257–72; and Edwin C. Bearss, "Marmaduke Attacks Pine Bluff," *Arkansas Historical Quarterly* 22 (Winter 1964): 291–313.

2. Private Gaston of Company K gave a slightly different time sequence in his diary: "we got orders last Knight at 12 o'clock M[idnight] to be ready to move in two hours with two days Rations in our haver Sacks we left camp at 3 o'clock A.M. and marched 8 miles before we eat our Breakfast." Gaston, "Diary," October 26, 1863.

3. This should be sunup, not sundown. Gaston, "Diary," October 26, 1863.

4. Private Towne confirmed Sperry's story: "We reached Benton about 4 o clock in the afternoon & found no troops there except the 3d Iowa cavalry. We were as tired a set of men as you ever saw having marched 26 miles in 12 hours over a sandy rocky road." George W. Towne to "Dear Sister," November 2, 1863, Towne Letters.

5. Benton was the seat of Saline County. The 1860 census reported the population of Benton and the surrounding Saline Township as 1,073 whites, with no blacks listed. Due to the momentary demoralization of Confederate forces in Arkansas, there were more people in Benton than usual in late October 1863. As Private Towne recalled the scene: "The little town of Benton was crowded with [Confederate] deserters & refugees who had fled there for protection from the guerrillas. The streets presented quite a curious spectacle the butternuts & soldiers talking & telling yarns Some of the citizens tell some awful tales about how they have been treated by the secesh They were then raising a battalion to fight the guerrillas a great many are also entering the United States service." "Evolution of Arkansas Townships," 88; George W. Towne to "Dear Sister," November 2, 1863, Towne Letters.

6. "Non-commish" is slang for noncommissioned officer.

7. The 33d Iowa did not have Benton all to itself. Rice also left the 61st Illinois Infantry to help guard the town. Gaston, "Diary," October 29–31, 1863; George W. Towne to "Dear Sister," November 2, 1863, Towne Letters.

8. Then as now, soldiers were interested in meeting pretty girls. In an effort to lure the local beauties, some Union cavalrymen who had been sent to Benton to cooperate with Rice's column held a ball at the Saline County Court House on the night of October 27. Gaston, "Diary," October 27, 1863.

9. The rain fell a day earlier than Sperry remembered. On Friday, October 30, a wetter but wiser Private Gaston noted: "Built A temporary Shed for our Company to sleep under." Gaston, "Diary," October 29, 30, 1863.

10. Rice's infantry went only as far as Rockport on the north bank of the Ouachita River, while the cavalry supporting his division proceeded to Arkadelphia. "Marmaduke had been so badly whipped at Pine Bluff he continued his flight and gave no chance for a fight," commented Lt. Col. R. F. Patterson of the 29th Iowa Infantry. "Indeed the enemy have fallen into such a strange habit of running from danger in this State, we have despaired of having another chance at them." *Keokuk (Iowa) Daily Gate City*, December 10, 1863; George W. Towne to "Dear Sister," November 2, 1863, Towne Letters.

11. Private Towne summed up Rice's excursion to Benton in these words: "all the troops except a few cavelry left to hold Benton returned to Little Rock yesterday after an absence of 7 days & having . . . driven Price from the state & as the saying is we are resting on our Laurels." George W. Towne to "Dear Sister," November 2, 1863, Towne Letters.

12. By "Johnson," Sperry probably meant Gen. Joseph E. Johnston, commander of the Confederate Department of the West, who shortly assumed command of the Army of Tennessee. Warner, *Generals in Gray*, 161–62.

13. As of January 31, 1864, the 33d Iowa belonged to the 2d Brigade in the 3d Division, a command assigned to the newly organized VII Army Corps and Department of Arkansas. General Steele functioned as both corps and department commander. Brig. Gen. Frederick Salomon headed the 3d Division, and Col. James M. Lewis was the acting commander of the 2d Brigade in General Rice's absence. *OR*, ser. 1, vol. 34, pt. 2, pp. 200–1; Frank J. Welcher, *The Union Army, 1861–1865: Organization and Operations*. Vol. 2: *The Western Theater* (Bloomington: Indiana University Press, 1993), 7–9, 246.

14. Private Towne announced his move into winter quarters in a letter dated November 22: "This is Sunday morning & I am writing in [Lieutenant] Ledyard's tent & Henry is bakeing flapjack near by. We built bunks yesterday & some of us moved into the cabin last night. Jack McCollum Tom Sinyard & myself have the best place in the cabin. We have our bunks just above the door where we can get plenty of fresh air." George W. Towne to "Dear Sister," November 22, 1863, Towne Letters.

15. "I am learning to sing," Private Towne informed his sister, "& we have many a good sing these long winter evenings." George W. Towne to "Dear Sister," January 2, 1864, Towne Letters.

16. The Christian Commission had more to offer the Little Rock garrison by the summer of 1864, when J. R. Allen, the local agent, began running the following advertisement in the city's Unionist newspapers: "The U.S. Christian Commission, have opened rooms in the Sanitary Building, corner of Main and Mulberry Sts., Little Rock, Ark., in which they keep a constant supply of the various religion papers of the day, tracts, knap-sack books and pamphlets for distribution among the soldiers. The St. Louis and Chicago daily papers are on file for daily reading; writing materials are supplied the soldiers who wish to write their friends, and a good circulating library is open for use—all are free for the use of the soldier." *Little Rock Unconditional Union*, August 11, 18, 25, September 15, 22, 29, November 3, 1864; *Little Rock Daily National Democrat*, November 9, 30, December 5, 29, 1864, January 9, 1865.

17. Captain Lofland and 1st Lt. George R. Ledyard of Company G left Little Rock on November 15 with a recruiting party of ten men—one from each company in the 33d Iowa. Morgan, "Diary," pt. 1, 499; Gaston, "Diary," November 14–15, 1863.

18. Regimental records say that Company H returned from the tannery on March 12, 1864. *OR Supplement*, pt. 2, vol. 20, serial no. 32, p. 806.

19. The onset of mild weather witnessed a marked improvement in the 33d Iowa's health. As Private Towne attested following his return from Benton: "The helth of the company is esecelent & we have about 40 men for duty. There was not a single man of the regiment sick during the whole march. . . . I have esecelent helth & gained 6 pounds since leaving Helena." George W. Towne to "Dear Sister," November 2, 1863, Towne Letters.

20. Contrary to Sperry's recollection, Private Gaston described December 11 as "Cloudy and warm," and December 12 as "Cloudy and cold." In fact, the twelfth ushered in a spell of cold weather that gripped Little Rock for most of the rest of the month. "We have had vary cold weather here for a couple of weeks past," Private Towne explained on January 2, 1864, "& we suffered some from the cold. I have heard a great deal about the sunny south & the warm weather they have but I suffered as much from cold this winter in Dixie as I ever did in Iowa." Gaston, "Diary," December 11–31, 1863; Morgan, "Diary," pt. 1, 500–501; George W. Towne to "Dear Sister," January 2, 1864, Towne Letters.

21. Private Gaston considered Company K's celebration of Christmas too tame: "we had Nothing more agoing to day than Common, any more than Sutler treated to the Cigars. We had [a dance] this evening we danced till 12 oclock I went to floor for the first time." Gaston, "Diary," December 25, 1863.

22. "Snowing and blowing cold," Sergeant Morgan of Company G scribbled in his diary on December 31. He noted the temperature plunged to 14° F. In addition, two inches of snow fell on the 33d Iowa's camp. Morgan, "Diary," pt. 1, 501; Gaston, "Diary," December 31, 1863.

23. David O. Dodd (1846–1864) was born in Texas, but his parents moved back to Arkansas in 1858. Early in the Union occupation of Little Rock, David worked for the sutlers of the 10th Illinois Cavalry, 1st Missouri Cavalry, and the 43d Illinois Infantry, positions that allowed him to become intimately acquainted with the composition of Steele's army. On December 29, 1863, Dodd was detained by Union pickets when he tried to leave the Little Rock area. A search of his person turned up a memoranda book containing a concise description of the strength of the city's garrison in Morse code. Dodd was tried before a court martial (which included Maj. Hiram Gibson of the 33d Iowa) from December 31, 1863, to January 3, 1864, when he was found guilty and sentenced to hang. Because the seventeen-year-old faced death without flinching, he evolved into the foremost folk hero in Arkansas history. Today, Dodd is the focus of neo-Confederate rituals and eulogized as the "boy martyr" of the Confederacy. Each year on the Saturday closest to the anniversary of his death, Confederate reenactors in full uniform gather to salute his grave in Little Rock's Mount Holly Cemetery. LeRoy H. Fischer, "David O. Dodd: Folk Hero of Confederate Arkansas," *Arkansas Historical Quarterly* 37 (Summer 1978): 130–46; O'Donnell, *Civil War Quadrennium*, 62–72; *Arkansas Democrat*, January 7, 1990; *Arkansas Democrat-Gazette*, January 12, 1992.

24. St. John's College, a Masonic military academy and Little Rock's first institution of higher learning, opened in 1859. Woods, *Rebellion and Realignment*, 92.

25. Pvt. James A. Newman of the 33d Iowa's Company I revealed another reason why some Union soldiers admired Dodd: "We were told he could have saved himself by implicating others, but he preferred to suffer alone." This admiration, however, was by no means universal. Espionage did not yet exude the James Bond-glamour associated with it in the twentieth century. At the time of the Civil War, most Americans thought that real men served their country by meeting the enemy openly in battle. Many boys of seventeen

years and younger honored that code by falsifying their ages to enlist, in the Union and the Confederate armies alike. Perhaps that is why the war's most celebrated spies tend to be women. Private Towne reflected these attitudes when he wrote of the Dodd case: "They say that another Spy will be hung next Friday. I don't like to see men hung but I think it is perfectly right to hang spies for they might be the means of killing thousands of brave men." Newman, *Autobiography*, 21; George W. Towne to "Dear Sister," January 2, 1864, Towne Letters. For more on the values of Civil War soldiers, see Linderman, *Embattled Courage*.

26. Some escaped slaves attached themselves to individual Union soldiers. Sgt. Peter A. Bonebrake of Company I picked up such a sidekick, whose name is lost to history. According to Bonebrake's daughter, this young man would go foraging for Bonebrake on the march, "and reached the next camping place early and cooked over a campfire whatever food he had been able to find." Carrie B. Simpson to Robert B. Simpson Jr., November 30, 1958, in "The Bonebrake Letters," *Grassroots: Journal of Grant County Museum Guild* 6 (April 1986): 11–13.

27. "Six recruits came to our Co. [G] last night," Private Towne noted on March 20. George W. Towne to "Dear Sister Tillie," March 20, 1864, Towne Letters.

28. In what may have been a flash of prescience, Private Towne closed the last letter he would write from Little Rock the day after he dated it: "This is Monday [March 21, 1864] & I seat myself to finish this letter. There is all kind of rumors afloat about us leaving but it is hard to tell any thing about *when* we will leave. I understand that we are transferred to the Mississippi Department under Sherman. If so we will likely cooperate with an expedition that is to go up Red River." Towne would soon find himself marching in the direction of the Red River, but it would be his last expedition. George W. Towne to "Dear Sister Tillie," March 20, 1864, Towne Letters.

CHAPTER TEN: THE CAMDEN EXPEDITION

1. Maj. Gen. Nathaniel P. Banks (1816–1894) was one of the North's more notorious "political generals." This former Speaker of the House of Representatives and governor of Massachusetts suffered multiple humiliations at the hands of Maj. Gen. Thomas J. "Stonewall" Jackson in the Shenandoah Valley and at Cedar Mountain. Banks assumed command of the Department of the Gulf in late 1862, with headquarters at New Orleans.

In January 1864, Banks decided to lead an expedition toward Texas along the Red River. General Halleck, still the Union general in chief, desired an invasion of Texas via northwestern Louisiana. Banks embraced the plan because he believed that there were huge quantities of cotton in the Red River country and in southern Arkansas. That cotton could be confiscated to help finance the Union war effort. New England textile interests would also welcome a fresh supply of cotton to keep their mills humming.

Both Halleck and Banks expected General Steele to march through southern Arkansas and join in the Red River campaign. Steele was reluctant to commit himself. Instead of cooperating directly with Banks, he proposed that his VII Army Corps do nothing more than launch a diversion to draw more Confederate troops into Arkansas. On March 15, 1864, Lt. Gen. Ulysses S. Grant, Halleck's successor as general in chief, telegraphed Steele: "Move your force in full cooperation with Gen. N. P. Banks' attack on Shreveport. A mere demonstration will not be sufficient." *OR*, ser. 1, vol. 26, pt. 1, pp. 683, 807, 834–35; *OR*, ser. 1, vol. 34, pt. 2, pp. 46, 133, 246, 267, 448, 516, 519, 547, 576, 616; Johnson, *Red River Campaign*, 3–48, 85–86; Warner, *Generals in Blue*, 17–18.

2. According to returns dated March 31, 1864, Steele left Little Rock with 4,850 infantry

in Brig. Gen. Frederick Salomon's 3d Division and 2,688 troopers in Brig. Gen. Eugene A. Carr's Cavalry Division. The 33d Iowa marched in Salomon's 1st Brigade, along with the 50th Indiana, 29th Iowa, and 9th Wisconsin Infantry. The 33d Iowa's former colonel, General Rice, commanded the 1st Brigade. Steele was also attended by about a dozen staff officers and a personal escort of ninety cavalrymen. *OR*, ser. 1, vol. 34, pt. 1, pp. 657–59, 684, 692.

3. James. A. Campbell, a corporal in the 1st Iowa Cavalry in Carr's Cavalry Division, confirmed Sperry's claim with this entry in his diary: "We are on half rations and have been all the time since We left Little Rock." James A. Campbell, "Diary," April 5, 1864, J. N. Heiskell Historical Collection, H-16, Box 1, File 4, UALR Archives and Special Collections, UALR Library, University of Arkansas at Little Rock.

4. Much of the country through which Steele's troops passed had already been stripped bare by the Confederates, but Union foraging parties were able to ferret out many stores of food hidden by desperate civilians. Pvt. John Shepherd of the 33d Iowa's Company I remembered waking up one night early in the march to find himself surrounded by all sorts of edible plunder: "I saw the Stars Shining above me and a row of guns Stacked with Chickens and things hung on them." Union cavalrymen, who were able to range further from the column on their horses, gathered even more food. A. W. M. Petty, a member of the 3d Missouri Cavalry, related how his comrades fared on March 31, 1864: "The boys lived high after leaving the command, eating nothing but the best of ham. It would have been an insult to offer one of them a piece of regular sow belly; they insisted sow belly was played out." *OR*, ser. 1, vol. 34, pt. 1, p. 680; Shepherd, "Autobiography," 43; A. W. M. Petty, *A History of the Third Missouri Cavalry: From Its Organization at Palmyra, Missouri, 1861, up to November Sixth, 1864: With an Appendix and Recapitulation* (Little Rock: J. William Denby, 1865), 64.

5. Steele's train was an immense affair. Corporal Campbell observed that it contained 700 wagons in all, 250 of them supply wagons. Moving such a convoy through southern Arkansas in March and April was an exercise in frustration. As Lt. Col. Francis M. Drake of the 36th Iowa Infantry put it, Steele's column passed "through a rough and sparsely settled country, over almost impassable roads, and in unpropitious weather." Capt. Charles A. Henry, the expedition's chief quartermaster, added: "The spring rains had already commenced, swelling the streams and putting the roads in a terrible condition." General Steele also complained on March 27 that both the cavalry horses and draft horses assigned to his command were in poor physical shape. Campbell, "Diary," March 26, 1864; F. M. Drake, "Campaign of General Steele," in *War Sketches and Incidents as Related by Companions of the Iowa Commandery, Military Order of the Loyal Legion of the United States.* Vol. 1. (Des Moines: Press of P. C. Kenyon, 1893), 60; *OR*, ser. 1, vol. 34, pt. 1, pp. 659, 679.

6. Because Lt. Col. Mackey was too sick to leave Little Rock on March 23, command of the 33d Iowa reverted to Maj. Hiram D. Gibson. Gibson enlisted in the regiment at Knoxville, Iowa, on September 5, 1862. A forty-three-year-old merchant, he had blue eyes, dark hair, a fair complexion, and his height was five feet eleven inches. Gibson did not get along well with the other officers of the regiment, and to judge from Sperry's remarks, he was not popular with the rank and file. He was a native of Tennessee, and not a Midwesterner like the majority of his comrades. The fact that he was older and heavier than most other officers might have also accounted for this situation. Gibson also had a checkered service career that reduced the time he spent with his regiment. He was reported sick at Helena in January 1863, and he got to leave Arkansas for a thirty-day sick leave on July 31, returning on September 7 when the worst of the Little Rock campaign was over. Twelve days later, he was detailed to serve on a general court martial for an unspecified amount of time. Gibson returned to court-martial duty on November 24, and saw no further service with his regiment until mid-March 1864, when General Rice pointed

out that the 33d Iowa had no other field officer on hand fit to take the field. Hiram D. Gibson Military Files, Civil War (Union) Compiled Military Service Records, 33d Iowa Infantry, Record Group 94, National Archives; Ingersoll, *Iowa and the Rebellion*, 619.

7. "Dutch" meant German in the slang of the Civil War era.

8. Lt. Col. Adolph Dengler, commander of the 43d Illinois Infantry, also noted this abrupt change of scenery as Steele's column approached Arkadelphia: "The sterile lands and deserted farms which we had met thus far on our march gave way to a fertile country and cultivated lands; the marks of war, although visible, were not so legibly written on this portion of the country as on that through which we had passed." *OR*, ser. 1, vol. 34, pt. 1, pp. 731–32.

9. Arkadelphia sat on a bluff overlooking the Ouachita River roughly seventy-five miles south of Little Rock. It had a prewar population of 680 whites and 225 blacks. Colonel Dengler considered Arkadelphia of vital importance to the Confederate war effort in Arkansas: "Here had been their principal army depots; here was a powder mill, different machine-shops, and the valuable saltpeter and salt works from which a great part of Arkansas was drawing this indispensable article. . . . Everything in and around this place indicated its former prosperity, the fine residences a little dilapidated and neglected, perhaps, but still bearing signs of better times; its extensive trade both by river and land, for the steamboats run on the Ouachita up to this place during two-thirds of the year, and it was also the great thoroughfare to Texas." "Evolution of Arkansas Townships," 84; *OR*, ser. 1, vol. 34, pt. 1, p. 731.

10. Pvt. James Newman, Company I, 33d Iowa, described the typical Arkansas home that the Federals observed between Little Rock and Arkadelphia: "The line of march was through wooded country, with isolated cabins occupied by the families of white or colored people and hounds, the necessary adjunct to the backwoods home. Skins from the squirrel to that of the Bruin adorned the outer walls." Newman, *Autobiography*, 22.

11. Private Newman said that he and his comrades paid for some of their "purchases" with Confederate money, "of which we had an abundance, as we found packages of it in one of the abandoned business houses." If the claims of Confederate soldiers and civilians are to be believed, Steele's Union troops did quite a bit of looting in the countryside surrounding Arkadelphia, if not in the town proper. Newman, *Autobiography*, 22; Gerald S. Allen, ed., "Nelson G. Thomas Civil War Documents," *Clark County Historical Journal* (Spring 1986): 80–88; John N. Edwards, *Shelby and His Men; or, the War in the West* (Cincinnati: Miami, 1867), 256.

12. The Arkadelphia Female Institute occupied an entire block bounded by North Ninth and Tenth Streets on the east and west, respectively, and by Pine and Barkman Streets on the north and south. The school was founded by Rev. Samuel Stevenson, a Baptist preacher and educator, sometime between 1850 and 1855. Stevenson reopened the school after the war, but he sold the property in 1869 to Mary Connelly, one of his teachers, who operated the institution as the Arkadelphia Female College. Wendy Richter, ed., *Clark County, Arkansas: Past and Present* (Arkadelphia: Clark County Historical Association, 1992), 237; Joe May, *The Way We Were: A Pictorial History of Clark County* (Arkadelphia: Curtis Media, 1995), 41; Farrar Newberry, "The Yankee Schoolmarm Who 'Captured' Post-War Arkadelphia," *Arkansas Historical Quarterly* 17 (Fall 1958): 266–67.

13. James F. Fagan (1828–1893) served in the Mexican War with the poorly disciplined "Arkansas Regiment of Mounted Gunmen" and was subsequently elected to one term in the Arkansas General Assembly. He went off to the Civil War as colonel of the 1st Arkansas Infantry and saw action at Shiloh. Promoted to brigadier general later in 1862, he was transferred to the Trans-Mississippi Department. He led an infantry brigade in the Confederate reverses at Prairie Grove and Helena. For the Camden campaign, he assumed command of a cavalry division composed of three brigades and was instrumental in administering two stinging defeats that forced Steele to retire on Little Rock.

Gen. Sterling Price commanded the six thousand cavalry left to defend the Confederate District of Arkansas. Kirby Smith had stripped Arkansas of infantry to concentrate a force large enough to check Banks's advance along the Red River. Though outnumbered, Price's command was really a formidable body of mounted infantry. The troopers had exchanged their shotguns, smoothbore carbines, and horse pistols for rifle muskets. The Rebels also possessed better horses than Steele's cavalry. Warner, *Generals in Gray*, 85–86; *OR*, ser. 1, vol. 34, pt. 1, pp. 779–82, 784–85; James L. Skinner III, ed., The *Autobiography of Henry Merrell: Industrial Missionary to the South* (Athens: University of Georgia Press, 1991), 352; Wiley Britton to his wife, "The Camden Expedition," June 1, 1864, p. 7, Wiley Britton Letters, J. N. Heiskell Historical Collection, H-4, 13, UALR Archives and Special Collections; Ralph R. Rea, *Sterling Price: The Lee of the West* (Little Rock: Pioneer Press, 1959), 100; *Washington (Arkansas) Telegraph*, May 25, 1864; Roman J. Zorn, ed., "Campaigning in Southern Arkansas: A Memoir by C. T. Anderson," *Arkansas Historical Quarterly* 8 (Autumn 1949): 241–42. For the best account of Confederate command decisions in the Red River campaign, see T. Michael Parrish, *Richard Taylor: Soldier Prince of Dixie* (Chapel Hill: University of North Carolina Press, 1992).

14. The area just south of Spoonville was thoroughly plundered on April 1 by some of Steele's mounted troops, as the historian of the 3d Missouri Cavalry candidly admitted a year later: "We went into camp three miles beyond our old camp at Spoonville. At this camp the boys procured a plentiful supply of Turkey, chickens, ham and eggs, and some found a quantity of honey. Indeed from the appearance of affairs the boys of the 3d did not suffer with hunger, at least while at this camp, for go where you would through camps they were partaking of some luxury procured from the neighboring rebs." Petty, *Third Missouri Cavalry*, 64.

15. Rice's brigade pulled out of its camp at Witherspoonville, Arkansas, at 8:00 A.M., April 2. As the last brigade in the 3d Division's line of march, Rice's men were entrusted with guarding Steele's supply and pontoon trains. Rice placed the 33d Iowa at intervals among the wagons, "each company being kept intact under its officers." He detailed the 29th Iowa and two guns from Capt. Martin Voegele's Wisconsin Battery to bring up the rear. Brig. Gen. Joseph O. Shelby struck Rice's rear guard as it crossed Terre Noir Creek at noon with fifteen hundred Rebel troopers and three field pieces. Shelby pressed his attacks with such ferocity that Rice was forced to commit a second section of Voegele's battery and his entire brigade to the fight, excepting only the 33d Iowa. Rice repulsed Shelby's final attack at 6:00 P.M. He then marched to Okolona, where the rest of Salomon's division was camped. Rice reached his bivouac area, about twelve miles from where he was first attacked, between 9:30 and 10:00 P.M. Rice's brigade suffered eight killed, thirty-two wounded, and twenty-three missing. Many of Shelby's men had gone into action in captured Union uniforms, which allowed them to get some close shots at Rice's unsuspecting men. A grim Rice directed his brigade to summarily execute any enemy soldiers captured in blue. "Strange to say" Cpl. Charles Musser of the 29th Iowa wrote after the campaign, "none of Shelby's men are to be found among the prisoners." Shelby's men made no apologies for their unorthodox tactics. "People called us rough and Savages," admitted R. P. Marshall of the 1st Missouri Cavalry Battalion. "[W]e had to be we had to lay aside the Golden Rule with the Federals and treat them just like they treat us. and as old David Haram said do it First." *OR*, ser. 1, vol. 34, pt. 1, pp. 684–85, 693–94, 822; Charles O. Musser to "Dear Father," May 11, 1864, in Popchock, *Soldier Boy*, 127; R. P. Marshall to W. L. Skaggs, February 20, 1912, W. L. Skaggs Collection, Folder 11, Item 256, Arkansas History Commission.

16. Rice's running fight from Terre Noir Creek to Okolona ushered in a twelve-day period of almost constant skirmishing. "From that time onward until the fifteenth of April," recounted Pvt. John W. Long, Company I, 33d Iowa, "either our rear or front guard

skirmished with the enemy every day until we arrived at Camden." Pvt. John Shepherd, another Company I man, added this chilling revelation: "I don't think there was a day passed without some one being Shot." John W. Long to "Sir," May 17, 1864, in "A Union Soldier's Personal Account of the Red River Expedition and the Battle of Jenkins Ferry," *Grassroots* 8 (July 1988): 2; Shepherd, "Autobiography," 42.

17. On April 4, General Marmaduke and two Confederate brigades fell on two regiments and a four-gun battery from Col. William E. McLean's Union infantry brigade at Elkin's Ferry. General Rice rushed to the rescue with the 29th Iowa and 9th Wisconsin. As Rice surveyed the situation, a Rebel bullet gashed his scalp, carrying away the crown of his forage cap and bathing his face in blood. "I feel as though the top of my head was gone," Rice exclaimed to another officer, "and will go to the rear, but will have my brigade in position." Rice later encountered the 33d Iowa and joked about his injury. "He said he dident care for his head," recalled Private Shepherd, "if they had not Spoiled his new nine dollar Cap." *OR*, ser. 1, vol. 34, pt. 1, pp. 685–86, 823; Drake, "Campaign of General Steele," 63–64; Stuart, *Iowa Colonels and Regiments*, 490–91; Shepherd, "Autobiography," 42.

18. Brig. Gen. John M. Thayer (1820–1906) was a veteran of Fort Donelson, Shiloh, and Vicksburg. He transferred to Fort Smith, Arkansas, to assume command of the District of the Frontier on February 22, 1864. The 3,961 officers and men he brought to reinforce Steele belonged to a formation called the "Frontier Division," which was organized on March 21, 1864, expressly for this expedition. The Frontier Division actually overtook Steele on April 9. There were no Native American regiments in Thayer's command, but many of his units had campaigned in Indian Territory, and may have picked up some Indian recruits. Although Sperry did not mention them, Thayer had two crack black regiments in his division, the 1st and 2d Kansas Colored Infantry. The appearance of Thayer's troops might have had something to do with the fact that the Frontier Division had a longer distance to travel and passed through rougher country than Steele's main column. Even after the Frontier Division had been purged of its excess vehicles, Steele's train numbered approximately eight hundred government wagons and twelve thousand draft animals. *OR*, ser. 1, vol. 34, pt. 1, pp. 657–58, 680; Johnson, *Red River Campaign*, 171; Wiley Britton to his wife, "The Camden Expedition," June 1, 1864, pp. 1–2; Wiley Britton, *The Union Indian Brigade in the Civil War* (Kansas City: Franklin Hudson, 1922), 346–47.

19. Prairie D'Ane is a circular area more than twenty-five square miles in size. It is located one hundred miles southwest of Little Rock. As Colonel Dengler described it: "Like an oasis lies this beautiful prairie in midst of dense forests and almost impassable swamps, a relief for the eye of the traveler, who has for many days hardly seen anything but rocks crowned by dark pines or the gloomy cypress swamp. The prairie, elevated above the surrounding country, rises gradually toward its center." *OR*, ser. 1, vol. 34, pt. 1, pp. 732–33; J. H. Atkinson, "The Action at Prairie De Ann," *Arkansas Historical Quarterly* 19 (Spring 1960): 40.

20. In the midst of the confrontation at Prairie D'Ane, Price was reinforced by the 655 Texans and 680 Choctaw Indians of Brig. Gen. Samuel B. Maxey's cavalry division from Indian Territory. Maxey's arrival raised Price's strength to 7,000. *OR*, ser. 1, vol. 34, pt. 1, pp. 780, 819, 848–49; Edwards, *Shelby and His Men*, 263; Mary Elizabeth Moore Carrigan, "Diary," April 11, 1864, SMF #479, Southwest Arkansas Regional Archives, Washington, Ark.

21. Pvt. William P. Funk, a native of Crawford County, Indiana, was eighteen when he enlisted in the 33d Iowa at Knoxville, Iowa, on August 9, 1862. He had gray eyes, black hair, a fair complexion, and stood five feet nine and a half inches tall. He suffered several extended bouts of illness that kept him from serving with the regiment for most of a year. Funk was hit as the 33d Iowa crossed a boggy depression at the edge of Prairie D'Ane. Fragments from the shell that wounded him broke several rifle muskets held by the men

around him. Funk lingered for two days, dying on April 12. He was the 33d Iowa's first combat casualty in the Camden campaign. William P. Funk Military Files, Civil War (Union) Compiled Military Service Records, 33d Iowa Infantry, Record Group 94, National Archives; *OR*, ser. 1, vol. 34, pt. 1, p. 701.

22. This was Voegele's Wisconsin Battery, manned by Company F of the 9th Wisconsin Infantry. *OR*, ser. 1, vol. 34, pt. 1, p. 658.

23. "The night was cold," remarked General Salomon, "but the troops, without complaining, lay out on the open prairie with no fires to warm or shelter to protect them." *OR*, ser. 1, vol. 34, pt. 1, p. 687.

24. To prevent the Rebels from learning the exact location of his brigade's camp, General Rice wisely ordered Captain Voegele not to reply to the enemy guns. *OR*, ser. 1, vol. 34, pt. 1, p. 695.

25. "Johnny" was a nickname that Union soldiers commonly used for the enemy. Bell Irvin Wiley, *The Life of Johnny Reb: The Common Soldier of the Confederacy* (Baton Rouge: Louisiana State University Press, 1978), 13.

26. "At 11 P.M. the enemy dashed upon the skirmish line," Major Gibson reported, "but was repulsed without injury to us." *OR*, ser. 1, vol. 34, pt. 1, p. 701.

27. On April 11, the 33d Iowa and the rest of Rice's brigade composed the left of the battle line formed by Salomon's 3d Division. *OR*, ser. 1, vol. 34, pt. 1, p. 695.

28. Andrew J. Comstock was born in Butler County, Ohio, in 1828 and settled in Mahaska County, Iowa, in 1844, where he bought a farm that eventually grew in size to 120 acres. On October 25, 1848, he enlisted as a private in the 14th Tennessee Regiment at Hannibal, Missouri. As the Mexican War had ended, he was mustered out in August 1849. He enlisted in the 33d Iowa on August 10, 1862, and was elected captain of Company C four days later. He had gray eyes, black hair, and a dark complexion. His height was five feet eight inches. Andrew J. Comstock Military Files, Civil War (Union) Compiled Military Service Records, 33d Iowa Infantry, Record Group 94, National Archives; *History of Mahaska County*, 385, 618.

29. Rice's brigade was on the right of Salomon's line when the Union advance resumed on April 12. Within a mile of the Confederate earthworks, Salomon reported, "Rice's brigade was ordered to change front forward, thereby outflanking the enemy, who left his works without any further contest." *OR*, ser. 1, vol. 34, pt. 1, p. 687.

30. This was a crucial moment in the campaign. Instead of continuing south to Washington, the capital of Confederate Arkansas, and on to Louisiana, Steele turned his army east toward Camden. As a gleeful Sterling Price described his opponent's abrupt change of direction: "With his habitual caution he moved but a short distance beyond our line of intrenchments, and on the morning of the 13th I found that he had fallen back during the night, and was retreating rapidly toward Camden." From that point on, the Union troops would be on the defensive. *OR*, ser. 1, vol. 34, pt. 1, p. 661, 780.

31. Moscow was a little larger than Sperry recalled. It contained two stores, a blacksmith's shop, and a church, as well as a few scattered homes. Artie Whiteside Vardy, "The Battle of Moscow, April 13, 1864: As It Was Told to Me by My Grandmother, Martha Holcomb," n.d, 1–3, SMF #191, Southwest Arkansas Regional Archives.

32. This engagement was known as the battle of Moscow, and it pitted elements of Thayer's Frontier Division against the Confederate cavalry divisions of Fagan and Maxey. The fighting lasted from 1:00 to 5:00 P.M. The 2d Indiana Battery fired 210 rounds of solid shot, switching to grapeshot and canister when the Rebels came into close range. Two Union cannon were overrun and then retaken in a counterattack. Total Union losses were seven killed and twenty-four wounded. *OR*, ser. 1, vol. 34, pt. 1, pp. 743, 780–81.

33. Recalling that swamp, Private Newman of the 33d Iowa's Company I quipped, "In some parts of the globe it would be called an inland sea." Newman, *Autobiography*, 22.

34. General Rice described this incident in his report without slighting the 33d Iowa: "Our skirmishers, with those of the cavalry, with occasional firing from the mountain howitzers, drove the enemy some 2 miles, when they opened upon us with five pieces of artillery. Captain [Gustave] Stange immediately brought his battery [Battery E, 2d Missouri Light Artillery] into position. I formed the Thirty-third Iowa on the right, Twenty-ninth Iowa on the left, the other portion of my command in reserve, and sent out sharpshooters to pick off their cannoneers, together with heavy bodies of skirmishers, on the right and left of our line, to feel the enemy's position and draw their fire if possible." *OR*, ser. 1, vol. 34, pt. 1, pp. 695, 701–2.

35. It was at this juncture that Major Gibson sent forward three sharpshooters from each company of the 33d Iowa to assist the skirmishers and kill the enemy gunners. That order set the scene for an act of friendship and selfless bravery. As Private Shepherd of Company I later told the story:

> here Sharp Shooters was wanted they called for volunteers and the Orderly [first] Sargent told us that we might not any of us get back alive. I volunteered for the last one and my Bunk mate James A. Newman from the other end of the company came up and asked what was going on the Sargent told him, and he said who are going I said I am for one. then Newman Said to me John—your not going I said I am he said your too tall you,l be shot (he was Short) he Said Peter [1st Sgt. Peter A. Bonebrake of Company I] let me go I have no Wife or Children at home. So Peter Said Shepherd you'l have to let Jimmy go. If I ever prayed it was during that little Skirmish that the Lord would protect that Boys life How thankful I was when I Saw him back Safe and Sound.

OR, ser. 1, vol. 34, pt. 1, pp. 701–2; Shepherd, "Autobiography," 43.

36. The only casualty from the 33d Iowa reported by Major Gibson was Enos M. Woods of Company G, who was seriously wounded by a shell fragment. *OR*, Ser. 1, vol. 34, pt. 1, p. 702.

37. Private Shepherd, for one, obtained a tangible reward from the 33d Iowa's small victory: "We drove the Rebs away from their Breakfast. I got one of their Journey [Johnny] cakes these are made of corn meals mixed with Salt and water and spread thinly on a Board and placed before the fire close enough to bake." Shepherd, "Autobiography," 43.

38. Brig. Gen. Eugene A. Carr (1830–1910) commanded Steele's cavalry division on the Camden expedition. An 1850 graduate of West Point, he saw extensive Indian fighting both before and after the Civil War. He was at Wilson's Creek and suffered three wounds at Pea Ridge, where his valor earned him the Medal of Honor. He served in the Vicksburg campaign and then returned to Arkansas, where his conduct, both personal and professional, was often erratic. Nevertheless, he remained in the regular army until 1893, and he is chiefly remembered today for his many successes in battling Native Americans. Warner, *Generals in Blue*, 70–71.

39. To move quickly over roads, a Civil War infantry regiment marched by the flank, forming a column with a four-man front. In line of battle, most of the regiment's personnel deployed in two tightly packed ranks, elbow touching elbow. To reduce its front, a regiment could form a column of companies, which consisted of all ten companies in line of battle, the first company leading the other nine. Each company consisted of two platoons. A column of platoons was similar to a column of companies but had twenty subunits in column rather than ten. The evolutions involved in going from one formation to another could be quite taxing, especially on rough ground. Dal Bello, *Parade, Inspection and Basic Evolutions*, 6–9, 16–19, 28–34; Hardee, *Rifle and Light Infantry Tactics*, 2:18–23, 37–66, 87–115, 132–58, 162–72.

40. The diary of John W. Brown, a merchant, provides a vivid picture of the first Union

troops to enter Camden: "The awful day of all days—the dread event feared for years—the fruits of a climax of folly in the corrupt politicians of the age has over taken us. In the early part of the day we heard cannonading and in the evening small arms. About 6 O clock, an enemy infuriated by combat & hunger came rushing down our main street, and diverging into the cross streets Cavalry first—Northern muskets, swords & bayonets glittering with the last rays of the setting sun with fierce imprecations and hideous shouts of exultation." John W. Brown, "Diary," April 15, 1864, Arkansas History Commission.

41. The Rebels also held Steele's troopers in contempt. As an officer in Shelby's brigade put it: "Indeed, so notoriously inefficient and cowardly were his cavalrymen, that their fighting became a by-word and reproach in the Confederate ranks." Edwards, *Shelby and His Men*, 267.

42. "Camden, high on the banks of the Ouachita, is a strongly fortified town," commented Colonel Dengler. "It had been, up to our occupation, the headquarters of General Price. . . . It is, next to Little Rock, the largest and most prosperous town in the State." "This town is well fortified with forts and rifle pits," added Private Long of the 33d Iowa. Camden's prewar population had been 2,219: 1,343 whites and 876 blacks. When the Civil War broke out, however, many of the town's white males and others from surrounding Ouachita County joined the Confederate army. A large number of the area's slaves would attach themselves to Steele's army, though not all of them would live to reach free territory. "Evolution of Arkansas Townships," 87; *OR*, ser. 1, vol. 34, pt. 1, p. 734; John W. Long to "Sir," May 17, 1864, in "Union Soldier's Personal Account," 2; Gregory J. W. Urwin, "Notes on the First Confederate Volunteers from Ouachita County, Arkansas, 1861," *Military Collector & Historian* 49 (Summer 1997): 83–84; Urwin, "'We Cannot Treat Negroes,'" 201, 204–6.

43. "Our men found considerable commissary stores," confirmed Private Long, "such as bacon and sugar in hogsheads. While we remained there our men had plenty of sugar for all of us." Private Newman was too tired to go foraging on the night of April 15–16, 1864, but he was delighted by the results of his comrades' labors: "On awakening in the morning the scene, to a soldier on short rations, was a gratifying one: barrels of sugar and meal, kegs of molasses, hams suspended on bayonets, turkeys and chickens tied out by the legs." John W. Long to "Sir," May 17, 1864, in "Union Soldier's Personal Account," 2; Newman, *Autobiography*, 23.

44. That first night in Camden, Steele's famished troops swarmed through the town like ravenous brutes. "The soldiers dashed to our doors demanding food," declared John Brown. "I soon handed out all the victuals which were on hand, cooked. After dark they brook into the smoke house & commenced carrying off as they wanted." Mrs. Ann James Marshall, a Camden schoolteacher, told a similar story: "They did as they pleased. They bulged in through the garden [of the Green House] without waiting at all for gates, broke open the smokehouse with one blow of the butt-end of their muskets, stuck their bayonets through as many joints of meat as would stick on them, filled seives and boxes with meal, rice, sugar, coffee, flour, etc." "The privates swarmed into our kitchens and negro houses," an anonymous Camdenite later related to the *Washington Telegraph*, the last major Confederate newspaper in Arkansas, "snatching the food even from the very negro children. . . . Milch cows and calves were killed in common with beef cattle." Mrs. Virginia Mc'Collum Stinson, whose smokehouse and storeroom were ransacked by Northern soldiers from 6:00 P.M. until midnight, later exclaimed: "What a night of terror that was." Brown, "Diary," April 15, 1864; Mrs. A. J. Marshall, *Autobiography* (Pine Bluff, Ark.: Privately printed, 1897), 29; *Washington (Arkansas) Telegraph*, May 25, 1864; Virginia Mc'Collum Stinson, "Memories," in *The Garden of Memory: Stories of the Civil War as Told by Veterans and Daughters of the Confederacy*, comp. Mrs. M. A. Elliott (Camden, Ark.: Brown Printing Co., 1911), 29.

CHAPTER ELEVEN: THE RETREAT FROM CAMDEN

1. Union infantrymen were issued long, nine-button frock coats for dress occasions and shorter, four-button sack coats or "fatigue blouses" for active service. Some soldiers wore their frock coats in the field, but the sack coat was lighter and much more comfortable in warm weather. Robin Smith, *American Civil War Union Army.* Brassey's History of Uniforms (London: Brassey's, 1996), 34–63.

2. Displays such as this dress parade enabled Camden residents to assess the strength and character of Steele's army. On April 23, Henry Merrell, a local businessman, jotted in his diary: "Their Cavalry was inferior in Material to the Confederate but their infantry Excellent. The Infantry regiments were generally small. Those returned from late furlogh & called Veterans appeared to be about 600 strong but the old regiments were as weak as say 300 . . . but very fine troops." Henry Merrell, "Receipts" Book ["Diary"], April 23, 1864, Photostat Copy, Henry Merrell Papers, Southwest Arkansas Regional Archives.

3. Capt. Charles A. Henry, Steele's chief quartermaster, explained the origins of this expedition: "The chief commissary of the army had made requisitions on me for corn for the men of the command, as our supplies of breadstuffs were entirely exhausted, and it was thought best to try and procure sufficient corn to furnish half allowance of forage and one-fourth rations of meal to the men. I accordingly made up . . . a forage train consisting of 177 wagons on the 17th of April, and sent them out some 16 miles to a point where I knew of there being some 5,000 bushels of corn. The trains reached the place and found that about 2,500 had been burnt that day." *OR,* ser. 1, vol. 34, pt. 1, p. 680.

4. Beginning its return to Camden at sunrise on April 18, Steele's forage train proceeded four miles east to Poison Spring, where it was attacked by more than 3,600 Confederate cavalry and twelve guns under General Marmaduke. The train's escort consisted of 438 officers and men from the 1st Kansas Colored Infantry; 383 from the 18th Iowa Infantry; 291 from the 2d, 6th, and 14th Kansas Cavalry; and 58 artillerymen manning four guns. James M. Williams, the colonel of the 1st Kansas, also commanded the escort. Williams's outnumbered troops fought bravely, but they were swept from the field, losing all their wagons and 301 casualties. Taking a circuitous route through a swamp north of the battlefield, Williams's survivors straggled back to Camden, the first of the weary fugitives entering Steele's lines around 8:00 P.M. *OR,* ser. 1, vol. 34, pt. 1, pp. 680, 743–46, 751–56, 792, 818–19, 828, 842, 848, 849; *Fort Smith (Arkansas) New Era,* May 7, 21, 1864; Britton, *Union Indian Brigade,* 369, 370–72. For more on this engagement, see Mike Fisher, "The First Kansas Colored—Massacre at Poison Springs," *Kansas History* 2 (Summer 1979): 121–28; and Ira Don Richards, "The Battle of Poison Spring," *Arkansas Historical Quarterly* 18 (Winter 1959): 338–49.

5. The Confederates transformed their victory at Poison Spring into the most infamous war crime in Arkansas history. Enraged at finding ex-slaves among their opponents, Marmaduke's troopers gave no quarter to personnel from the 1st Kansas Colored Infantry, killing any who fell into their hands, including the helpless wounded. During the Civil War, the number of men wounded in an engagement was normally greater than the number killed. At Poison Spring, however, the 1st Kansas suffered 117 killed and 65 wounded. "It will be seen," argued A. W. M. Petty of the Union 3d Missouri Cavalry, "that the number of our killed exceeds the number of our wounded in this engagement, an unusual occurrence in the warfare of the present day, as it is generally found from the reports of the many battles being daily fought in our land, to be just the contrary. This can be accounted for when it is known as we were informed by one of the 2d Kansas Cavalry who made his escape a few minutes prior to the completion of the struggle, that the inhuman and blood thirsty enemy . . . was engaged in killing the wounded wherever found." In addition to testimony from Union survivors, Rebel troops admitted to the atrocities. The *Washington*

Telegraph, the voice of Confederate Arkansas, even justified the Poison Spring massacre as essential to preserving the Southern way of life: "It follows irresistably that we *cannot* treat negroes taken in arms as prisoners of war, without a destruction of the social system for which we contend. In this we must be firm, uncompromising, and unfaltering." Much of the scalping was done by Choctaw Indians belonging to Maxey's cavalry division from Indian Territory. Petty, *Third Missouri Cavalry,* 76; *Washington (Arkansas) Telegraph,* June 8, 1864; Urwin, "'We Cannot Treat Negroes,'" 196–204. See also Anne J. Bailey, "Was There a Massacre at Poison Spring?" *Military History of the Southwest* 20 (Fall 1990): 157–68.

6. Sperry's comrades were luckier than another white soldier captured at Poison Spring. This story was passed on by a resident of Little Rock to the editor of the Unionist newspaper at Fort Smith: "An officer told me he saw a man who was wounded taken out of the ambulance by the rebels and asked what command he belonged to, he told them the 18th Iowa, they called him a damned liar, and said he belonged to the 12th Kansas, brigaded with the negroes and knocked his brain out with the butt of a gun." *Fort Smith (Arkansas) New Era,* May 7, 1864.

7. The troops engaged at Poison Spring came from Thayer's Frontier Division, and the Unionist newspaper in Fort Smith accused Steele of deliberately sacrificing them. A letter attributed to the quartermaster of Thayer's 2d Brigade charged: "It is stated that the firing was heard at Camden but General Steele would not reinforce Col. W. [Williams] although he had 12,000 men at his command. After the fight an officer rode up to Gen. Steele's head-quarters and said, 'Great God, why didn't you send us reinforcements?'" A Little Rock gentleman who interviewed veterans of the campaign also declared: "I saw men who were with Steele at the time, who said that he heard the firing all the time and did not send reinforcements. Thayer had his cavalry saddled and ready to go but Steele did not or would not order it out, there is great blame attached to Steele, and I feel almost certain he is not the right man." One of Steele's staunchest critics was General Salomon, commander of the expedition's 3d Division. The morning after the battle, Salomon fumed to an aide: "Steele knows that he is a West Pointer, and doesn't appear to know anything about Arkansas, where he is or what he is doing. Damn these regulars! They map out battles on paper, draw their salaries and—smoke cigars. The worst of it is they always keep clear of the fire line, which bars the good luck of getting them shot out of the way!" *Fort Smith (Arkansas) New Era,* May 7, 1864; "The Federal Occupation of Camden as Set Forth in the Diary of a Union Officer," *Arkansas Historical Quarterly* 9 (Autumn 1950): 216.

8. "[W]e foraged Some Corn which was isued to us four Ears a day to the man," testified Private Shepherd of Company I. "[W]e Ground Some of it on hand mills Some we parched and Some we boiled." Shepherd, "Autobiography," 43–44.

9. Mackey was equally glad to be reunited with the 33d Iowa. "I arrived at Camden . . . and immediately took command of my regiment, at this time 600 strong," he reported on May 6. Mackey had another reason to celebrate. On April 21, he was mustered out as a lieutenant colonel, and on April 22, he officially became the colonel of the 33d Iowa. He had been waiting for that ever since he signified his willingness to succeed General Rice on September 7, 1863. *OR,* ser. 1, vol. 34, pt. 1, p. 702; Mackey Military Files.

10. The longer Steele remained at Camden, the more severe his logistical problems grew. Even with the arrival of a supply train on April 20, he was forced to put his men on quarter rations. On April 22, he complained to his superiors: "It is useless to talk of obtaining supplies in this country for my command. The country is well nigh exhausted, and the people are threatened with exhaustion." The following day, Steele dispatched 240 wagons to Pine Bluff to pick up supplies. Chastened by the Poison Spring disaster, he detailed the entire 2d Brigade from Salomon's division (1,200 infantry), 240 cavalry, and two artillery sections under Lt. Col. Francis M. Drake to protect the train. On April 25, Generals Fagan and

Shelby hit Drake's command from two directions at once with 4,000 Confederate cavalry. The Rebels captured 1,300 Union troops and all of Drake's wagons. This setback rendered Steele's position at Camden untenable. Merrell, "Diary," April 23, 1864; *OR*, ser. 1, vol. 34, pt. 1, pp. 712–15, 788–99; Ira Don Richards, "The Engagement at Marks' Mills," *Arkansas Historical Quarterly* 19 (Spring 1960): 54–60; Charles H. Lothrop, "The Fight at Marks' Mills," n.d., p. 1, Civil War Manuscripts, State Historical Society of Iowa; Elizabeth Titsworth, ed., "The Civil War Diary of a Logan County Soldier," *Wagon Wheels* 1 (Winter 1981): 19.

11. General Steele restricted access to Camden to protect a desperate citizenry from his troops' ceaseless search for loot and food. John Brown observed Steele's efforts to impose order the day after the Federals arrived: "I see widows, orphans & the wives of our soldiers, moving apace with haggard visages to beseech protection from the Conqueror, Genl. Steele and his authorities, against the pillaging soldiery. They are taking measures for the protection of the Citizens. Patrols are put out and order hoped for. By noon the main part of the City is pretty well protected from pillage by means of patrols in the Streets and special guards to citizens." Stinson, "Memories," 29; Marshall, *Autobiography*, 97–99; Brown, "Diary," April 16, 1864.

12. The reckless types mentioned by Sperry left Camden in an awful state. "One of the most annoying things they did was seizing people's cows and slaughtering them for beef," explained Mrs. A. J. Marshall. "That they did by wholesale. So, that when they left, the town was one vast slaughter-pen, and, as it was hot weather, the stench was so fearful that I thought I could not take up school again in Camden, especially as the soldiers had taken possession of my school-house, ransacked it, broke doors, gates, etc., and ruined the spring by letting droves of horses drink and tramp around it until it was impossible for me to put it in good condition again." A Union officer described a disturbance he witnessed on April 22: "Heard a racket in a house I was passing last evening. . . . I walked in, to find an Irish brute of a cavalryman belonging to some Kansas regiment performing a jig on the top of the piano with the frightened women begging him to leave the house. He was drunk. When he got sight of my officer's cap he jumped and made for the door. I gave him all the assistance I could with a vigorous kick that landed him half-way to the gate." Stinson, "Memories," 30–31; Merrell, "Diary," April 23, 1864; Marshall, *Autobiography*, 101–2; "Federal Occupation of Camden," 216–17.

13. This attack on Steele's picket line convinced one of General Salomon's staff that "the Johnnies were drawing their cordon closer and tighter about us." Sterling Price, however, confirmed Sperry's suspicions: "On the evening of the 23d, to divert attention from this movement, a feint was made upon the city of Camden. The Arkansas and Missouri divisions of infantry were moved up on the Wire road, the enemy's pickets driven in beyond the bridge over Two Bayous, 1 mile from the town, and shell thrown from Lesueur's battery into the woods on the other side with good effect." "Federal Occupation of Camden," 217–18; *OR*, ser. 1, vol. 34, pt. 1, p. 781.

14. Gibson tendered his "immediate and unconditional resignation" on April 21. He justified his decision by revealing his unpopularity: "My reason for so doing is that in my opinion there is not that full cooperation with me on the part of the line officers of my regiment that the good of the service requires." H. D. Gibson to George O. Sokalski, April 21, 1864, in Gibson Military Files.

15. Samuel S. Pierce was an Ohio native who joined the 33d Iowa as the first lieutenant of Company A at Knoxville on August 8, 1862. He was thirty-two years old, had gray eyes, auburn hair, a light complexion, and stood five feet nine inches tall. He became the regiment's acting adjutant on May 28, 1863, and returned to his company on May 1, 1864. His promotion to captain was approved by Governor Stone on July 1, 1864. Samuel S. Pierce Military Files, Civil War (Union) Compiled Military Service Records, 33d Iowa Infantry, Record Group 94, National Archives.

16. It took more than hunger to drive Steele from Camden. Shortly after he captured the town, he began receiving intelligence that Banks had met with defeat on the Red River and was in full retreat. Those reports were confirmed by two couriers from Banks who reached Steele on April 18 and 22, respectively. On the latter date, Steele also learned that Kirby Smith had come up from Louisiana and was near Camden with three divisions of Confederate infantry, a force estimated at eight thousand. That same day, General Fagan organized a strike force of four thousand Confederate cavalry to cross the Ouachita and cut Steele's communications between Camden and the Arkansas River. It was Fagan's command that damaged Steele's army so badly at Marks' Mills. With the loss of an entire infantry brigade and a large wagon train, Steele realized that he would be trapped at Camden if he did not speedily evacuate his army. *OR*, ser. 1, vol. 34, pt. 1, pp. 661–68, 781–82, 788–89.

17. An anonymous Camden resident may have watched the 33d Iowa draw its rations, for he subsequently reported: "The rations of a private soldier for four days in advance, was carefully noted. It consisted of eight hard bread crackers, (two a day,) and a piece of meat the size of your hand." Sperry and his comrades were luckier than the troops in some of Steele's other regiments. The 29th Iowa Infantry, a part of the same brigade, issued its personnel only two hard crackers apiece. The 43d Illinois, on the other hand, received "coffee, three-fourths rations; salt, full rations; sugar, full rations; bacon, one-fourth rations; pilot bread, 129 pounds, and 5 bushels of corn meal," with instructions to make it last until April 30. *Washington (Arkansas) Telegraph*, May 25, 1864; William L. Nicholson, "The Engagement at Jenkins' Ferry," *Annals of Iowa* 11 (October 1914): 505; *OR*, ser. 1, vol. 34, pt. 1, p. 737.

18. Steele's retreating troops also left evidence of their anger and frustration in their wake. As James M. Dawson, a Rebel infantryman in Brig. Gen. Thomas J. Churchill's pursuing Arkansas Division, informed his family: "He [Steele] laid wast the Country when he marched taken all the people had to eat taken their clothing riped open Fether Beds and strown the Feathers all along the Road Burned houses and done every thing els that was mean." Asst. Surgeon Junius Bragg of the 33d Arkansas Infantry recalled what he saw, chasing after the Federals on April 28: "All day we kept up a weary tramp. Not a living animal was to be seen along the wayside—nothing but ruin and desolation! Women and little children sometime stood by the road and watched us pass. They did not seem very glad to see us, for they were too hungry to be demonstrative, and we had nothing to give them." James McCall Dawson to "Dear Father Sister and Brothers," May 5, 1864, in James Reed Eison, ed., "'Stand We in Jeopardy Every Hour': A Confederate Letter, 1864," *Pulaski County Historical Review* 31 (Fall 1993): 53; J. N. Bragg, "The Battle of Jenkins Ferry," in *Letters of a Confederate Surgeon 1861–1865*, ed. Mrs. T. J. Gaughan (Camden, Ark.: Privately printed, 1960), 224.

19. Mrs. Virginia Davis Gray, a Princeton resident, left a vivid account of the Federals' arrival: "They came and kept coming—the infantry was like hungry wolves—they followed the directions given to Peter, 'Stay and eat.' In less than one hour, great old bristly hogs was killed—cooked and eaten—ditto of cows scusing the bristles." The picture was completed by Surgeon Bragg, who reached Princeton several hours after Steele's troops left: "The enemy had camped there the night before and literally sacked the town. They had left nothing for the inhabitants." Carl H. Moneyhon, ed., "Life in Confederate Arkansas: The Diary of Virginia Davis Gray, 1863–1865, Part I," *Arkansas Historical Quarterly* 42 (Spring 1983): 82–83; Bragg, "Jenkins Ferry," 223.

20. This rain went on without a break for eighteen hours. Bearss, *Steele's Retreat from Camden*, 102.

21. Throughout the march on April 29, Steele's rear guard, Col. Adolph Engelmann's infantry brigade, and two companies of the 6th Kansas Cavalry had to fend off repeated thrusts from Col. William L. Jeffers and the Confederate 8th Missouri Cavalry. *OR*, ser. 1, vol. 34, pt. 1, pp. 723–24; Bearss, *Steele's Retreat from Camden*, 104–7.

22. General Rice sent the 33d Iowa back to support Engelmann's brigade at 6:30 P.M. The Iowans relieved the 43d Illinois Infantry as the rear guard for Steele's army, forming behind the crest of a ridge. The exhausted Illinoisans rested behind the Iowans until 3:00 A.M. At that time, the 43d Illinois was ordered a mile to the rear to cook breakfast. Because the 33d Iowa was within talking distance of Confederate pickets, its men had to endure a rainy night without fires or hot food. *OR*, ser. 1, vol. 34, pt. 1, pp. 697, 702, 724, 735; John W. Long to "Sir," May 17, 1864, "Union Soldier's Personal Account," 2.

CHAPTER TWELVE: THE BATTLE OF JENKINS' FERRY

1. Pinned against the swollen Saline River, Steele's army found itself in a precarious position. Steele's pontoon train threw a bridge across the Saline by 3:15 P.M. on April 29, and his cavalry began crossing immediately. The two miles of ground leading to the bridge was waterlogged, and Steele's wagons and artillery got bogged down. Precious hours were lost while the road was corduroyed and fatigue details pulled floundering animals and anything on wheels through the mud. Steele ordered General Salomon's infantry division and all but two infantry regiments from Thayer's Frontier Division to cover the crossing of his impedimenta. These four thousand Union soldiers would face six thousand vengeful Confederate infantry in the coming battle on April 30. *OR*, ser. 1, vol. 34, pt. 1, pp. 669–70; Bearss, *Steele's Retreat from Camden*, 102, 161.

2. Inspecting the placement of the 33d Iowa around 4:00 A.M., General Rice decided the regiment was too far from any support. He told Colonel Mackey to call in his skirmishers and retire half a mile toward the Saline River. Mackey's Iowans executed the order so stealthily that the Confederates did not detect their withdrawal. The 33d Iowa occupied its new position for thirty minutes until enemy skirmishers reappeared along its front. "The enemy advanced [and] commenced firing on us at 5 A.M.," recalled Pvt. John Long of Company I. "We held them in check for three quarters of an hour." *OR*, ser. 1, vol. 34, pt. 1, pp. 689, 697, 702; John W. Long to "Sir," May 17, 1864, in "Union Soldier's Personal Account," 2–3.

3. While the 33d Iowa battled enemy skirmishers, General Rice sent forward the 50th Indiana Infantry, deploying it on his old regiment's left. Next Rice established a second line with the 9th Wisconsin and the 29th Iowa half a mile closer to the Saline River and under the cover of some timber. After checking the Confederates for over thirty minutes, Rice had his first line fall back on his second. He relieved the 33d Iowa with the 27th Wisconsin and sent the Iowans to the rear to get some breakfast. *OR*, ser. 1, vol. 34, pt. 1, pp. 689, 697, 702.

4. Actually, the fast-thinking Rice had chosen a good position. As Pvt. John Long, Company I, 33d Iowa, related: "The ground was level and swampy and water in places from one inch to a foot deep. Our right wing rested on the creek [Cox Creek]. . . . The enemy's right was in the timber, their left in open field. There they suffered terribly because our right was in a grove of timber between two fields." Robert M. Rodgers of the 26th Arkansas Infantry appreciated the strength of Rice's dispositions: "The enemy had taken position just North of a small field along Cox's creek, behind logs and the timber in the river bottom, in such a way that it was extremely difficult for our forces in making the attack to march without considerable exposure to a cross-fire. . . . As it happened a battle had to be fought by the weary Confederate troops in mud and water from shoe-mouth deep to half-leg deep at a shameful disadvantage." John W. Long to "Sir," May 17, 1864, in "Union Soldier's Personal Account," 3; Alama Rodgers, ed., *The Life Story of R. M. Rodgers* (Sheridan, Ark.: Grant County Museum, 1989), 10–11.

5. Recalled to the front before the men had time to boil water for coffee, the 33d Iowa fell in on the left of the 50th Indiana, which put the Iowans on the far left of Rice's line. A determined Rebel assault turned the 33d's exposed flank and pushed it back 250 yards. Rice prolonged his line by throwing the 12th Kansas Infantry into the fray on the 33d's left, and the two regiments drove the enemy nearly 300 yards, retaking all the ground so recently lost. *OR*, ser. 1, vol. 34, pt. 1, pp. 697, 703; John W. Long to "Sir," May 17, 1864, in "Union Soldier's Personal Account," 3.

6. As W. C. Braly of the 34th Arkansas Infantry wrote his mother a week later: "For five hours there was a continual roar of musketry which was far ahead of anything of the kind that I have ever heard before." Lt. Col. Adolph Dengler of the 43d Illinois recalled watching the 33d Iowa "pouring volley after volley in the thick masses of the enemy." Private Long of the 33d called the battle "one of the greatest musketry drills ever recorded in the war." "The enemy would mass his forces first on our right, then the center, then on our left," Long explained, "but wherever he undertook to break our line by his superior numbers he was failed." W. C. Braly to "My Dear Ma," May 7, 1864, in the possession of Frances Thompson, Clarksville, Ark.; *OR*, ser, 1, vol. 34, pt. 1, p. 730; John W. Long to "Sir," May 17, 1864, in "Union Soldier's Personal Account," 3.

7. Colonel Dengler of the 43d Illinois also noted this visibility problem. "After firing had, without intervals, lasted for half an hour," he reported, "the smoke became so dense, waving like a thick mass between the dark trees over the swampy ground, that it was impossible to see anything else at a distance of 20 yards." Dengler's solution was to allow his regiment to advance through the smoke until it obtained a clearer view of the enemy. *OR*, ser. 1, vol. 34, pt. 1, pp. 730–31.

8. Second Lt. John S. Miller, Company K, 29th Iowa Infantry, concurred with Sperry: "It was the most deadly fight of the war considering the amount of force engaged, and was all musketry at short range." Miller decided that the high quality of the opposing troops accounted for the fierceness of the struggle: "Both armies had never been beaten and each fought with the confidence which is only inspired by long continued success." Finally, he noted the large number of Rebels who fell "before Enfield and Springfield rifles in the hands of men used to sharp-shooting from the time they were large enough to load a gun, and men who were all veterans, and would handle them coolly as if on a squirrel hunt." John S. Miller to "Dear Sister Etta," May 24, 1864, Adee Papers, Earl Gregg Swem Library, College of William and Mary, Williamsburg, Va.

9. Mackey was hit in the upper right arm and suffered a compound fracture of the humerus. Mackey Military Files.

10. Cyrus B. Boydston, a thirty-year-old teacher from Pennsylvania, was elected captain of Company A, 33d Iowa, at Knoxville, Iowa, on August 15, 1862. He fell ill on July 12, 1863, while the regiment was at Helena, and went on an extended leave until October. On April 19, 1864, General Rice placed Boydston "on special duty as acting Field Officer." He received his promotion to major on June 28, and was mustered in at that rank the following day. Boydston had black eyes, light hair, a light complexion, and stood six feet tall. Cyrus B. Boydston Military Files, Civil War (Union) Compiled Military Service Records, 33d Iowa Infantry, Record Group 94, National Archives.

11. Pvt. John Shepherd of the 33d Iowa's Company I testified to the intensity of the enemy's fire. "I look back over the battle of Jenkins Ferry," he wrote, "and see the mercy of God in the preservation of my life I had six or seven holes shot in my Blouse and I was not hit men were Shot down all round me and I was Spared." Shepherd, "Autobiography," 44–45.

12. This "battery" was actually Lt. John O. Lockhart's two-gun section from Capt. Samuel T. Ruffner's Missouri Battery. As the men of the 2d Kansas Colored charged Lockhart's position, they raised a chilling cheer: "Poison Springs!" The black soldiers

thrust their bayonets into any Rebel they could reach, including three gunners who raised their hands in surrender. Only the arrival of the 29th Iowa saved Lockhart and his five surviving cannoneers. Pvt. Milton P. Chambers of the 29th described the scene in a letter home: "one of our boys seen a little negro pounding a wounded reb in the head with the but of his gun and asked him what he was doing. the negro replied he is not dead yet! I tel you they won't give them up as long as they can kick if they can just have their way about it. it looks hard but the rebs cannot blame the negroes for it when they are guilty of the same trick both to the whites and negroes." Samuel J. Crawford, *Kansas in the Sixties* (Chicago: A. C. McClurg & Co., 1911), 124–28; William E. McLean, *Forty-Third Regiment of Indiana Volunteers: An Historic Sketch of Its Career and Services* (Terre Haute: C. W. Brown, 1903), 26; *OR*, ser. 1, vol. 34, pt. 1, pp. 697–98, 781, 813; Skinner, *Autobiography of Henry Merrell*, 368; *Little Rock (Arkansas) Unconditional Union*, May 13, 20, 1864; Milton P. Chambers to "Dear Brother," May 7, 1864, Milton P. Chambers Papers, Special Collections Division, University of Arkansas Libraries.

13. The Federals also owed their salvation to poor Confederate generalship. When the Rebel vanguard reached the Jenkins' Ferry area, most of Kirby Smith's army was strung out on muddy roads for miles behind. Fearful lest Steele escape before their entire force could concentrate, Kirby Smith and his generals committed their troops to battle in piece-meal fashion, attacking the Federals with one regiment, one brigade, or one division at a time. Even after the entire Confederate army came up, the narrowness of the battlefield selected by General Rice prevented Kirby Smith from hitting the Union line with all his strength. As R. S. Wilson of the 18th Texas Infantry complained: "They [the Yankees] were on good ground and our army had to fight in water. The location was such that we could not get more than half the army in action at the same time." Christ, *Rugged and Sublime*, 120–23; Bearss, *Steele's Retreat from Camden*, 114–63; R. S. Wilson, "The Battle of Jenkins's Ferry," *Confederate Veteran* 18 (October 1910): 468.

14. The 2d Kansas Colored was detailed to bring up the rear as the bulk of Steele's infantry crossed the Saline. Still seeking vengeance for the Poison Spring massacre, black soldiers ranged the battlefield, shooting or slitting the throats of Confederate wounded. Crawford, *Kansas in the Sixties*, 131–32; Julius N. Bragg to Anna Josephine Goddard Bragg, May 5, 1864, in Gaughan, *Letters*, 230; Edward W. Cade to "My dear Wife," May 6, 1864, Edward and Allie Cade Correspondence, John Q. Anderson Collection, Texas State Archives, Austin; Skinner, *Autobiography of Henry Merrell*, 361; Mamie Yeary, ed., *Reminiscences of the Boys in Gray, 1861–1865* (Dallas: Smith & Lamar, 1912), 390, 437, 799; James M. Dawson to "Dear Father Sister and Brothers," May 5, 1864, in Eison, "Stand We in Jeopardy," 52; *OR*, ser. 1, vol. 34, pt. 1, pp. 759, 817.

15. The Confederates converted the village of Princeton into a hospital for the abandoned Union wounded. Surgeon William L. Nicholson of the 29th Iowa was one Federal doctor left behind to treat these men. He described the cases of five 33d Iowa soldiers in his diary. John H. Miller of Company G was shot in the thigh, and W. B. Gibson had to have a leg amputated on May 3, but both recovered. W. M. Rodman of Company H lost an arm, and John Niermeyer of Company G and J. D. Compton of Company H each lost a leg. Niermeyer died on May 13, Compton on May 14, and Rodman on June 2. Another member of the regiment to die in captivity was Pvt. George W. Towne, the avid letter-writer from Company G. The only personal effects that he had left in storage at Little Rock were two flannel shirts, one winter great coat, and one frock coat. First Sgt. Peter Bonebrake of Company I fell with a nasty shoulder wound and should have been taken prisoner, but his black servant found him on the morning of May 1 and hoisted him onto the back of a loose mule. Later that afternoon, Bonebrake and his companion encountered some Confederate guerrillas. The irregulars killed the young black for sport, but they let Bonebrake go. Half-starved and drifting in and out of consciousness, Bonebrake managed to stay on the mule's

back until the animal overtook Steele's army. Nicholson, "Jenkin's Ferry," 518–19; George W. Towne Military Files, Civil War (Union) Compiled Military Service Records, 33d Iowa Infantry, Record Group 94, National Archives; Carrie B. Simpson to Robert B. Simpson Jr., November 30, 1958, in "Bonebrake Letters," 12.

16. According to Col. Samuel J. Crawford of the 2d Kansas Colored Infantry, his rear-guard regiment did not quit the battlefield and start crossing the Saline until approximately 4:00 P.M. Crawford, *Kansas in the Sixties*, 131–32; Shepherd, "Autobiography," 44.

17. Sperry either missed a typographical error here, or he was off on his math. The casualty figures he gave total 133. On May 6, 1864, Colonel Mackey reported the 33d Iowa's losses as 8 enlisted men killed, 6 officers and 96 men wounded, and 13 men missing—a total of 123. By May 10, when General Salomon tendered his report, the 33d Iowa's casualties for the battle still totaled 123, but apparently some wounded soldiers listed as missing had rejoined the regiment. Salomon credited the 33d with 9 men dead, 6 officers and 99 other ranks wounded, and only 9 missing. Altogether, Steele's army suffered roughly 700 casualties at Jenkins' Ferry, while Confederate losses were close to 1,000. *OR*, ser. 1, vol. 34, pt. 1, pp. 692, 703; Bearss, *Steele's Retreat from Camden*, 161; *Fort Smith (Arkansas) New Era*, June 16, 1864.

CHAPTER THIRTEEN: LITTLE ROCK AGAIN

1. Pvt. John Shepherd of Company I described his condition and that of his comrades in the 33d Iowa as they emerged from the Saline bottom: "when we came out we were as black as niggers and hungry as Hounds." Shepherd, "Autobiography," 44.

2. These instances of child abandonment are horrifying, but Sperry fails to mention the stark terror that possessed the runaway slaves accompanying Steele's army. These people knew that if they were retaken by Confederate soldiers, they were likely to be summarily executed. Three hundred "Contrabands" were with the supply train captured by the Rebels at Marks' Mills on April 25, but the victorious Southerners took only 150 into custody. Most of the rest were gunned down or clubbed to death. "A large number [of] negroes . . . were inhumanly butchered by the enemy," reported Lt. Col. Francis Drake, the defeated Union commander, "and among them my own negro servant." Lt. Benjamin F. Pearson, who was captured with the 36th Iowa at Marks' Mills, confided to his diary the day of the battle: "There was not an armed negro with us & they shot down our Colored servents & temsters & others what ware following to get from bondage, as they would shoot sheep dogs." Pearson beheld more horrors the following day as he wandered the battlefield in search of his missing son: "The number of Negroes I could not get I saw perhaps near 30, & the Rebs pointed out to me a point of woods where they told me they had killed eighty odd negroes men women & children." Maj. John Edwards, the adjutant of Shelby's cavalry brigade, provided a graphic description of this massacre from the Confederate perspective: "The battle-field was sickening to behold. No orders, threats, or commands could restrain the men from vengeance on the negroes, and they were piled in great heaps about the wagons, in tangled brushwood, and upon the muddy and trampled road." *OR*, ser. 1, vol. 34, pt. 1, pp. 714–15; "Benjamin Pearson's War Diary," Part 5, *Annals of Iowa* 15 (October 1926): 441; Edwards, *Shelby and His Men*, 279. For a more thorough discussion of this atrocity, see Urwin, "'We Cannot Treat Negroes.'"

3. It was at this point that Private Shepherd was accosted by a hungry comrade: "one Boy came to me and Said Shepherd have you any hard tack I said I had one he said wont you give it to me I Said Ill give you half of it when I get washed he said where is it I said in my Napsack he held on to my coat till I washed my hands then I took out the cracker and

gave him half it was then nearly two o clock and I had not tasted food that day." Shepherd, "Autobiography," 44.

4. These orders helped prompt the following comment from an anonymous officer of the 2d Kansas Colored Infantry: "This campaign was very destructive to Government property, resulting in the loss of not less than 4,000 mules, 500 wagons, besides a vast amount of camp and garrison equipage, guns, ammunition, &c.—some of it captured by the enemy, and the rest destroyed by our own forces, to prevent its falling into the hands of the enemy." Lonnie J. White, ed., "A Bluecoat's Account of the Camden Expedition," *Arkansas Historical Quarterly* 24 (Spring 1965): 89.

5. The flames that destroyed the 33d Iowa's baggage wagons also consumed the regiment's muster and pay rolls, plus all company books and papers. As these items gave an accurate view of the regiment's strength, they had to be denied to the Rebels. Cyrus H. Mackey to W. D. Green, October 28, 1864, in Sharman Military Files; *OR Supplement*, pt. 2, vol. 20, serial no. 32, p. 795.

6. An officer of the 2d Kansas Colored, who cast a backward glance at the Saline that morning, saw something that gave him cause for thanks: "The next day the river was four miles wide, and two feet deep all over the bottom. Had we started a day later we could not possibly have crossed. Our entire army would have been on the south side of the river and surrounded." White, "A Bluecoat's Account," 88–89.

7. "The first part of the march from Saline River to Little Rock," explained General Salomon, "was through a quicksand bottom; men and animals were completely worn out, and it was impossible to bring through the entire train." *OR*, ser. 1, vol. 34, pt. 1, p. 691.

8. Private Shepherd described the diet he and his "bunkie," Pvt. James Newman, endured from the evening of April 30 to the evening of May 2, 1864: "Newman and I had about a pint of corn meal that we had ground on the hand mill we made mush for our Supper then we had nothing. the next day I found 24 peas. I ate them raw and I pulled a Small bit of fat meat out of a wagon rut and ate it raw we found a piece of an ear of Corn and we ate that raw. then we had nothing but Coffee. I never knew what hunger was before." Shepherd, "Autobigraphy," 44–45.

9. For Private Shepherd, celebration soon turned into discomfort: "The night before we got to Little Rock we were met with Rations I only ate a little but it started the Diarhea on me." Shepherd, "Autobiography," 45.

10. Private Newman, John Shepherd's best friend in Company I, remembered Fort Steele as "a huge mound of earth." The work stood just south of Little Rock's Mount Holly Cemetery and guarded the southwestern approaches to the city. Newman, *Autobiography*, 25; F. Hampton Roy, Charles Witsell Jr., and Cheryl Griffith Nichols, *How We Lived: Little Rock as an American City* (Little Rock: August House, 1984), 97.

11. General Salomon reported that his division reentered Little Rock at noon on May 3, 1864. *OR*, ser. 1, vol. 34, pt. 1, p. 691.

12. General Steele made his headquarters in the stately, pillared mansion of the late U.S. senator Chester Ashley on East Markham Street. Roberts and Moneyhon, *Portraits of Conflict*, 172; O'Donnell, *Civil War Quadrennium*, 61.

13. Private Shepherd met with a disappointing sight when he reentered the cabin where he had been quartered during the winter of 1863–64. "When we got back to our old quarters," he recalled, "I found my Bible had been torn up and part of it had been used for Toilet paper a Cavilry Regiment had ocupied our Cabins." Next, Shepherd went to an abandoned guardhouse that he and religiously minded comrades from the 33d and 29th Iowa had converted into a chapel. "There was a man put in the guard house for Cowardice," Shepherd discovered, "and he wrote Blackgard and Swearing in our Testaments and Hymn Books." Shepherd, "Autobiography," 45.

14. Pvt. William R. Barnes, Company B, 29th Iowa, summed up the ordeal of Steele's

infantry in a letter to his wife probably written immediately after his return to Little Rock: "Well Amanda I have seen and felt more hard times on this trip than I ever Saw in my life I had a heavy load to Pack I threw away my Blanke[t] and Some Paper and envelops I carried your likeness with me all the time. . . . It is a hard Site to See men cut rite in two with a cannon Ball tha [there] was 15 Days that tha [there] was fiting evry Day we had to fight owr way threw going and coming and we would have Been at it yet if we had any thing to eat." Pvt. John Long of the 33d Iowa offered a more concise overview to a friend: "I have seen some pretty trying scenes since I wrote last to you." William R. Barnes to Amanda Barnes, n.d., William R. Barnes Letters, State Historical Society of Iowa; John W. Long to "Sir," May 17, 1864, in "Union Soldier's Personal Account," 2.

15. The 33d Iowa and the rest of Salomon's 3d Division marched three hundred miles in forty-two days, much of it over rough roads and in rainy weather. *OR*, ser. 1, vol. 34, pt. 1, p. 691; *OR Supplement*, pt. 2, vol. 20, serial no. 32, pp. 798, 809.

CHAPTER FOURTEEN: CAMP AND GARRISON

1. Lofland received his lieutenant colonel's commission on October 1, 1863, but he was not mustered in until late April 1864, when Cyrus Mackey assumed the colonelcy of the 33d Iowa.

On May 11, 1864, General Steele's headquarters issued Special Orders No. 100, decreeing a reorganization of the Union forces assigned to the "District of Little Rock" into two divisions and an independent cavalry brigade. Each division consisted of two infantry brigades, one cavalry brigade, and three artillery batteries. The 33d Iowa, along with the 29th Iowa, 9th Wisconsin, 50th Indiana, and 28th Wisconsin, belonged to the 1st Brigade in Brig. Gen. Frederick Salomon's 1st Division. Col. Charles E. Salomon of the 9th Wisconsin (General Salomon's brother) commanded the 1st Brigade. One of the colonel's regiments, the 28th Wisconsin, was on detached duty at Pine Bluff, but the rest of his brigade was at Little Rock. Steele put Brig. Gen. Eugene Carr in charge of the district. Cpl. Charles Musser of the 29th Iowa thought little of his new brigade commander: "Salomon is a perfect old Swill tub and Whisky blout and cant talk but little English." Lofland Military Files; *OR*, ser. 1, vol. 34, pt. 3, pp. 547–48; *OR*, ser. 1, vol. 34, pt. 4, p. 607; Charles O. Musser to "Dear Father," June 12, 1864, in Popchock, *Soldier Boy*, 136.

2. This renewed attention to drill was apparently a brigade phenomenon. On May 23, 1864, 1st Sgt. Ira Seeley of Company H, 29th Iowa Infantry, informed his wife: "This has been a long day to me. I have drilled about three hours and made my report details, studied tactics [the drill manual] some and talked some." Ira Seeley to "Dear Martha," May 22–24, 1864, in Greg Seeley, ed., *Ira Seeley Civil War Letters* (Afton, Iowa: Privately printed, 1981), 48.

3. In skirmish drill, infantry learned to move and fight in open order, the men standing five paces apart, instead of the standard line of battle, where soldiers stood in two ranks, elbow touching elbow. The one drawback to skirmish order was that it left the troops too spread out to hear their officers' voice commands above the din of combat. That was why it was imperative that at least the noncommissioned officers could recognize the twenty-three bugle calls for skirmishers. Hardee, *Rifle and Light Infantry Tactics*, 2:171–240.

4. Lieutenant Sharman became the 33d Iowa's acting adjutant on May 6, 1864, and was formally transferred to the regimental staff on February 4, 1865. His struggle to reconstruct the regiment's books was more difficult than Sperry realized. Late in October 1864, he had to be sent to Davenport, Iowa, to obtain copies of the 33d's destroyed muster and pay rolls. Sharman Military Files.

5. Pvt. William Barnes of the 29th Iowa described the fatigue duty Sperry found so numbing in a letter home: "we are still here at this Place and have Plenty to do we ar throwing up earth works all a round this town and choping the timber all Down for 2 miles around So that if the Rebs comes that we will be redy for them." William R. Barnes to "Dear wife and little children," May 25, 1864, Barnes Letters.

6. This incident occurred on January 17, 1865. Two days earlier, Confederate colonel William Brooks had been repulsed in an attack on Dardanelle, Arkansas, a Union outpost on the Arkansas River. Undaunted, Brooks moved upstream with a single six-pound gun and a brigade of cavalry and mounted infantry to ambush a convoy of four Union supply boats returning from Fort Smith to Little Rock. Brooks succeeded in capturing and looting the steamer *Chippewa*. The others got away, but not without damage. Cpl. Cyrus Gaston, Company K, 33d Iowa, was part of the guard assigned to the sternwheeler *Lotus*, and he left this account in his diary: "at 3 1/2 P. M. we come up with the Chippawa & her Burning & the Anna Jacobs we got about 2 hundred yds of the Jacobs the rebels opened on us with one piece of Artillry & about 400 or 500 small arms they fired 2 shots with the cannon one shot passed through the Pilot house the other missed we had one corpl Shippers mortally wound[ed] a deck hand & a Doctor Severly [wounded] 3 or 4 Niggers Killed & 3 or 4 wounded & 2 Drowned jumped over board." Cpl. Nicholas Schippers, Company G, was the 33d Iowa man mortally wounded in the attack. Jayme Lynne Stone, "Brother against Brother: The Winter Skirmishes along the Arkansas River, 1864–1865," *Military History of the West* 25 (Spring 1995): 32–46; Cyrus Gaston, "Diary for 1865," January 17, 1865, State Historical Society of Iowa.

7. The ever-controversial Daniel E. Sickles (1819–1914) was a New Yorker in the U.S. House of Representatives from 1857 to 1861. He achieved national notoriety in 1859 when he killed his wife's lover and then became the first to win acquittal by pleading temporary insanity. As a War Democrat, Sickles recruited the Excelsior Brigade in New York City and was soon rewarded with the rank of brigadier general. He rose quickly in the Army of the Potomac. By early 1863, he was a major general and a corps commander. At Gettysburg on July 2, 1863, he disregarded orders and advanced his III Corps into the Peach Orchard, creating an inviting salient that the Confederates overran. Sickles lost a good part of his corps, and he also sustained a wound that cost him his right leg. Grateful for an excuse to grant him no new field commands, the Union government awarded Sickles the Medal of Honor. After Sickles recovered from his amputation, President Lincoln sent him on an inspection tour of Union-held territory across the South. Lt. William Blain, Company A, 40th Iowa Infantry, described the reception Sickles received in Little Rock, where the troops admired him as a fighting general: "Yesterday we had a grand review of all the troops here by Maj. Gen. Sickles of New York. Our line was some two miles long. After firing a Salute of 13 guns (Cannon) he, Gen. Sickles galloped along the line, music playing, flags drooping officers & men saluting. It was a grand sight our pleasure a little marred by it raining some. The Gen. is [a] fine looking man. . . . He has done grand service in his country's cause and deserves the thanks of all true patriots."

Col. Randolph B. Marcy (1812–1887) was a West Point graduate, a long-time regular army officer, and the father-in-law of George B. McClellan. He was appointed as one of the regular service's four inspectors general on August 9, 1861, although he served on McClellan's staff until the latter's final removal from command of the Army of the Potomac after Antietam. Warner, *Generals in Blue*, 311, 446–47; Hubbell and Geary, *Historical Dictionary*, 478–79; William Blain to "Dear Wife," June 7, 1864, in Dolly Bottens, comp., *Rouse-Stevens Ancestry & Allied Families* (Carthage, Mo.: Privately printed, 1970), 110B.

8. Gibson returned to Marion County, Iowa, where he was appointed a commissary of subsistence and became part of the vast bureaucracy that purchased food for the Union army. Ingersoll, *Iowa and the Rebellion*, 622.

9. Sergeant Seeley wrote his wife about how the 29th Iowa celebrated Independence Day: "The Fourth went off quietly, except some got a little too much lager beer and perhaps something stronger. In some companies, it was almost universal, but Co. H for once was very civil. . . . Some of the men in other companies are still drinking to day yet, I suppose just to taper off with." Ira Seeley to Martha Seeley, July 5, 1864, in Seeley, *Civil War Letters*, 62.

10. On July 15, 1864, a Confederate raiding force dispatched by Brig. Gen. J. O. Shelby tore up half a mile of track along the Memphis-Little Rock Railroad between Little Rock and De Valls Bluff. Shelby's repeated hit-and-run strikes against the railroad and Union communications along the White River caused an exasperated General Steele to run his cavalry ragged chasing the elusive Confederates. *OR*, ser. 1, vol. 41, pt. 1, pp. 11–13, 28, 221–31.

11. In the final moments of the battle of Jenkins' Ferry, a Confederate musket ball struck General Rice. The bullet hit a spur buckle and drove the twisted piece of metal into Rice's right foot just in front of his ankle. Although the wound was painful, no one thought it was life-threatening. Rice wrote his report of Jenkins' Ferry on May 8, and ten days later he set out for Oskaloosa to convalesce. Unfortunately, infection set in, and it spread throughout his body before the doctors realized what was happening. Rice died on July 6, 1864. The night before, he told a friend: "I am ready. 'Though I walk through the valley of the shadow of death. He is with me. His rod and His staff, they comfort me.'"

Rice's death came as a shock to the Department of Arkansas, where he was credited with saving Steele's army at Jenkins' Ferry. The day after that army hobbled into Little Rock, Corporal Musser of the 29th Iowa wrote of Rice: "he is one of the Bravest men i ever saw. he does not fear anything and he has a Brigade that will fight for him lots. Rice ought to be in command of this army instead of that rebbel encourager, and rebbel guarder, and Army Selling General [Steele]." Col. William E. McLean of the 43d Indiana Infantry called Rice "the ablest officer in Steele's army." Reflecting on Rice's performance at Jenkins' Ferry, McLean asserted: "On that muddy, bloody field he dominated the battle; he was the central figure, the chief spirt, his inspiring example and unflinching bravery will never be forgotten by those who witnessed it."

Steele was cognizant of Rice's popularity, and when he announced the latter's death on July 20, he ordered that the American flag flying over each Union post in Arkansas be displayed the next day "at half mast from sunrise until sunset," and that "half-hour guns" be fired from Little Rock's Fort Steele. As a final gesture of respect, Steele directed: "The colors of the several regiments of Rice's Brigade, will be draped in mourning for a period of thirty days." General Salomon announced that he and his staff would wear mourning bands in Rice's honor for thirty days. The Iowa Supreme Court asked all the state's lawyers to make a similar gesture. Not to be outdone, the men of the two Iowa regiments in Rice's brigade raised eighteen hundred dollars to erect a monument in his honor. That monument stands today in Oskaloosa's Forest Cemetery—a marble shaft twenty-three feet high and five feet four inches square at the base. The upper part of the column bears Rice's battle honors: "CAMDEN," "PRAIRIE D'ANNE," "HELENA," "JENKINS' FERRY," "TERRE NOIR," "ELKINS' FORD," " LITTLE ROCK", and "YAZOO PASS." Down further is the following inscription:

"SAMUEL A. RICE, BRIGADIER GENERAL U.S. VOLUNTEERS,
Born January 27, 1828,
Died July 6, 1864
Of wounds received at the battle of Jenkins' Ferry.

Erected in honor of their gallant leader by the
members of the Twenty-ninth and Thirty-third
Iowa Infantry Regiments of Rice's Brigade."

Stuart, *Iowa Colonels and Regiments*, 490, 493–95; Nicholson, "Jenkins' Ferry," 511; Charles O. Musser to "Dear Father," May 4, 1864, Charles O. Musser to "Dear Father," June 6, 1864, Charles O. Musser to "Dear Father," September 5, 1864, all in Popchock, *Soldier Boy*, 125, 134, 148; McLean, *Forty-Third Indiana*, 25–26; *OR*, ser. 1, vol. 34, pt. 1, pp. 691, 698; Headquarters, Department of Arkansas, General Orders No. 54, July 20, 1864, Headquarters, First Division, Seventh Army Corps, General Orders No. 17, July 20, 1864, Undated Paper signed by Cyrus Bussey, "President," and John F. Lacey, "Secretary," all in Rice Papers; Newman, *Autobiography*, 25, 80; *History of Mahaska County*, 450–51.

12. The 29th Iowa, which was camped near the 33d Iowa, also had quite a rat problem. "What a time the boys have after rats," wrote Sergeant Seeley. "This is the greatest place for rats I ever saw, and such times as the boys have killing them. It is hard to keep any kind of food safe from them." Ira Seeley to "Dear Martha," June 26, 1864, in Seeley, *Civil War Letters*, 60.

13. Captain Blain of the 40th Iowa made note of the increase in enemy activity on July 16:

We have had no news from the North for ten days. The "Rebs" seem determined to make a bold strike somewhere soon. Boats are prevented from passing White River unless under protection of a strong fleet of "gun Boats."

Last night the train on the railroad was fired with fortunately no lives lost. Their determination is to cut off our supplies and starve us out how they will succeed any time will tell.

Day before yesterday eight scouts were sent out through the lines in the direction of Benton they went out some ten miles and turned about to come to camp again when they were fired at—two killed and four wounded. So you see the "Rebs" are getting very bold. I think that this is the darkest hour of our National Existence.

William Blain to "Dear Wife," July 16, 1864, in Bottens, *Rouse-Stevens Ancestry*, 112C.

14. First Lt. Wilson DeGarmo, Company H, 33d Iowa, mentioned some of these precautions in his diary on September 1: "On duty at Fort Steele. . . . A rebel raid anticipated. Guard strengthened tonight." The following day, he wrote, "The guards strengthen tonight again in view of the rebel raid anticipated." On September 3, Sergeant Seeley of the 29th Iowa confided to his wife: "There seems to be some apprehension of an attack on this place. Night before last, nearly half of the Regt were called out and stacked their arms and laid by them, waiting for an attack, but none was made." Wilson DeGarmo, "Diary," September 1, 2, 1864, in the possession of Larry Pearson, Anchorage, Alaska; Ira Seeley to "Dear Wife," September 3, 1864, in Seeley, *Civil War Letters*, 89.

15. Lieutenant DeGarmo described the alarm succinctly: "Our Regt. ordered out to the rifle pits between 10 & 11 O'clock at night—I go with them." DeGarmo, "Diary," September 4, 1864.

16. Lieutenant DeGarmo's diary corroborated Sperry's account. "The Regt. Goes to camp 1[/]2 past 3 P.M.," he jotted. "The weather hot." DeGarmo, "Diary," September 5, 1864.

17. Sperry's reference to a red hospital flag is curious. In 1862, the Union army began marking its hospitals with plain yellow flags. In January 1864, it switched to a yellow flag with a large green *H* in the center. Woodhead, *Echoes of Glory*, 292.

18. On Tuesday, September 6, Lieutenant DeGarmo noted: "The excitement concerning an attack here has greatly subsided." DeGarmo, "Diary," September 6, 1864.

19. On August 4, 1864, Kirby Smith ordered Price to raid Missouri "with the entire cavalry force of your district." Price's mission was to seize the stockpiles of Union military supplies at St. Louis and recruit Missourians into the Confederate army. Privately, Price hoped to win his state for the Confederacy. Price left Camden on August 28 with a column that eventually grew to twelve thousand troopers. After feinting toward Little Rock, he crossed the Arkansas River at Dardanelle on September 6 and 7, and then proceeded to

Pocahontas, where he organized his command into three divisions. Price crossed into Missouri on September 19, launching a campaign that caused a great deal of furor, but accomplished nothing of lasting significance. Castel, *General Sterling Price*, 200–55; Shalhope, *Sterling Price*, 256–79; Stephen B. Oates, *Confederate Cavalry West of the River* (Austin: University of Texas Press, 1992), 140–54; *OR*, ser. 1, vol. 41, pt. 1, pp. 622–48.

20. Frederick Salomon (1826–1897) served as a lieutenant in the Prussian army and was studying architecture in Berlin when the revolutions of 1848 rocked Europe. He and three younger brothers immigrated to the United States. Edward Salomon (1828–1909) was governor of Wisconsin from 1862 to 1863. Frederick fought under Franz Siegel at Wilson's Creek as a captain in a three-month regiment from Missouri. He became the colonel of the 9th Wisconsin Infantry on November 26, 1861, which he led in Missouri and Arkansas until his promotion to brigadier general on July 18, 1862. Salomon was the 33d Iowa's division commander at the battle of Helena, although his role in the fight was eclipsed by that of General Prentiss. The 33d Iowa also served under Salomon in the Camden expedition. Like his brother Charles, General Salomon apparently had trouble making himself understood in spoken English. Pvt. James Newman of the 33d Iowa described the result when Salomon tried to drill his troops at Little Rock: "Gen Solomon being Dutch, his commands were hardly intelligible and caused much hilarity. Many jokes were told. Wishing to give the command, 'Right wheel by company,' and not being able readily to form it in English, said, 'Swing round mit one gate!'" Warner, *Generals in Blue*, 417–18; Hubbell and Geary, *Historical Dictionary*, 451–53; Newman, *Autobiography*, 21.

21. Sperry was right about off-duty officers having to attend division guard mount. As Lieutenant DeGarmo revealed on September 27, "At camp all day—after attending Div. Guard mounting at 8 in the morning." DeGarmo, "Diary," September 27, 1864.

22. "We got a mail this morning & N. [Northern] papers of the 26. with glorious news from Sheridan," a jubilant Lieutenant DeGarmo scratched in his diary on October 3. The next day, he added this information: "Weather cloudy & wet. . . . 100 minute guns were fired here in honor of Sheridan's victory." The cause of this celebration was the third battle of Winchester, Virginia, September 19, 1864, where Maj. Gen. Philip H. Sheridan routed Lt. Gen. Jubal A. Early's outnumbered Confederate army. DeGarmo, "Diary," October 3, 4, 1864.

23. Mackey received a thirty-day leave of absence on June 3, 1864, to convalesce at home in Sigourney, Iowa, but the seriousness of his wound caused him to request several extensions. His return to duty was duly celebrated by his subordinates, as seen in Lieutenant DeGarmo's diary: "Col Mackey and Capt. [William S.] Parmley arrive—both look well. All glad to see them. Brig. band serenades Col. M. about 9 O'clock P.M." Mackey Military Files; DeGarmo, "Diary," October 8, 1864.

24. Lieutenant DeGarmo referred to this construction in his diary: "Work all day on our shanty. The Co. raise their cook house." DeGarmo, "Diary," October 17, 1864.

25. Company G's "Tommy" was Drummer Thomas W. Cox (1849–1909). Born in Fulton County, Ohio, Cox moved to Pella, Iowa, in 1855 with his parents, four brothers, and one sister. He enlisted in the 33d Iowa on September 4, 1862. The plucky thirteen-year-old had a dark complexion, hazel eyes, and auburn hair. He stood only four feet ten inches tall, but his cheerful courage and spirited drumming endeared him to his company. He once declined a furlough in deference to a comrade with a more acute case of homesickness. When the 33d Iowa had to cross flooded river bottoms, the older men would volunteer to carry Tommy on their backs. Following the war, Cox lived in Pella and several other communities in Iowa, Wyoming, and Texas, working much of the time as a telegraph operator. He married in 1869, became a widower in 1880, and remarried a few years later. He returned to Pella for good sometime in the 1890s. In 1900, he and his older brother Murray (a veteran of the 17th Iowa Infantry) became partners and went into the hotel business. Tommy opened a three-story brick hotel called the American House in 1902. Aided by his

wife, he ran that establishment until his death at age fifty-nine. His neighbors mourned him as an "Honored Veteran . . . friendly to everyone . . . a most genial landlord . . . a kind husband and a great favorite among the 'army' boys." James E. McMillan, ed., *Artisans and Musicians, Dutch and American: Pella, Iowa, 1854–1960* (Pella, Iowa: Pella Printing Co., 1997), 7–13, 19–20, 26.

CHAPTER FIFTEEN: TO FORT SMITH AND BACK

1. Special Orders No. 102, issued by Headquarters, District of Little Rock, on October 28, 1864, spelled out the 33d Iowa's mission: "The Thirty-third Iowa Infantry is hereby detailed as escort for a supply train to Fort Smith, Arkansas. The commanding officer of that regiment will have it in readiness and communicate with Col. B. O. Carr, chief quartermaster Department of Arkansas, and when the train is ready will escort it to Fort Smith and return with the wagons as soon as they are unloaded." *OR*, ser. 1, vol. 41, pt. 4, p. 295.

2. Lieutenant DeGarmo of Company H supplied additional details on the trip's start: "Pack up and get all ready to move soon in the morning, but did not get off untill about 1 O'clock. Our Regt. Started with about 350 men Our Co 30—We march 8 miles and Camp after dark Weather nice." DeGarmo, "Diary," October 30, 1864.

3. This is a misprint of Palarm or Palarme. By the 1920s, the stream was known as Palarm Creek. Alex McPherson, *The History of Faulkner County, Arkansas* (Conway, Ark.: Conway Times Plant, 1927), 5.

4. Adverse weather challenged the 33d Iowa's progress on November 1. "[R]ained some before noon," observed Lieutenant DeGarmo, "and rained very hard in the afternoon and pretty near steedy the road got pretty bad—some wagons upset and we camped after traveling 16 miles and it was after 9 O'clock when the train all got in." DeGarmo, "Diary," November 1, 1864.

5. On November 2, the 33d Iowa and the supply train traveled for two and a half miles over a bad road that led through a soggy bottom to Cadron Creek. Most of the troops spent the rest of the day ferrying all but forty-eight of the wagons across the swollen stream. The next day, the rest of the wagons were ferried to the west bank of the Cadron, and the column camped at a spot one and a half miles away. DeGarmo, "Diary," November 2–3, 1864.

6. According to Lieutenant DeGarmo, the 33d Iowa arrived at Lewisburg "sometime before sun down" and "Camped just west of the town." A prosperous shipping and receiving center on the Arkansas River, Lewisburg had a population of 270 whites and 80 blacks in 1860. With the fall of Little Rock, Union forces converted Lewisburg into a garrison town, and it became the headquarters of the locally raised 3d Arkansas Cavalry, commanded by Col. Abraham H. Ryan, a former member of Steele's staff. DeGarmo, "Diary," November 4, 1864; "Evolution of Arkansas Townships," 84; Stone, "Brother against Brother," 26–28; Nina McReynolds, "A Town That Disappeared: Lewisburg, Arkansas" (M.S. thesis, University of Central Arkansas, 1958), 2–5, 14–15.

7. In 1860, George W. Carroll of Welborn Township owned real estate valued at $32,000 and a personal estate of $133,000. He was also the master of 125 slaves. The 1860 census noted that fifteen slave houses stood on Carroll's land. Beginning in 1862, many Arkansas slaveholders moved their slaves to Texas and northern Louisiana to prevent them from running away or being liberated by Union troops. "Page No. 25, Schedule 1.—Free Inhabitants in Welborn Township in the County of Conway, State of Arkansas, Enumerated by Me, on the 14th Day of June, 1860, H. Gordon, Ass't Marshal," in Betty F.

Murray, ed., *1860 U.S. Census: Conway County Arkansas* (Conway, Ark.: Oldbuck Press, 1993); "Population Schedules the Eighth Census of the United States 1860," National Archives Microfilm Publication, Microcopy 653, Roll 53, Arkansas Slave Schedules, Vol. 1 (1–404) (Washington, D.C.: National Archives Records Service, General Services Administration, 1967); Moneyhon, *Impact of the Civil War*, 133–34.

8. The "colored" infantry company came from the 54th U.S. Colored Infantry, which was organized at Helena in 1863 and originally known as the 2d Arkansas Regiment of African Descent. The white 2d Arkansas Infantry was organized at Springfield, Missouri, and Fort Smith, Arkansas, between October 1863 and March 1864. By the time the 33d Iowa linked up with it, the 2d Arkansas belonged to the 2d Brigade, 2d Division, VII Army Corps. These men were mostly "Mountain Feds," inhabitants of the state's hill country who did not own slaves and were longtime political opponents of the slaveowners who led their state into rebellion. A total of 8,789 white men joined Union units raised in Arkansas during the war. DeGarmo, "Diary," November 5, 1864; Dyer, *Compendium*, 2:999–1000; Charles O. Musser to "Dear Father," January 1, 1864, Charles O. Musser to "Dear Sister Hester," August 5, 1864, both in Popchock, *Soldier Boy*, 102, 141–42; Richard Nelson Current, *Lincoln's Loyalists: Union Soldiers from the Confederacy* (New York: Oxford University Press, 1992), 73–87.

9. By March 1865, the families of two hundred soldiers from the 2d Arkansas Infantry— nearly one thousand civilians—were seeking refuge at Fort Smith. The town also contained large numbers of refugees who were related to members of the 1st and 2d Arkansas Cavalry, 1st Arkansas Infantry, and 1st Arkansas Battery. Most of these people were destitute and depended on government aid to survive. Current, *Lincoln's Loyalists*, 153–54. For more on the war of retaliation that both sides waged against Arkansas civilians, see Daniel E. Sutherland, "Guerrillas: The Real War in Arkansas," *Arkansas Historical Quarterly* 52 (Autumn 1993): 257–85; Kenneth C. Barnes, "The Williams Clan: Mountain Farmers and Union Fighters in North Central Arkansas," *Arkansas Historical Quarterly* 52 (Autumn 1993): 286–317. Also most instructive is Michael Fellman, *Inside War: The Guerrilla Conflict in Missouri during the American Civil War* (New York: Oxford University Press, 1989).

10. News of Price's defeat reached Little Rock before the 33d Iowa's departure. At 11:30 A.M., October 28, General Halleck, now the Union army's chief of staff, telegraphed General Steele: "Price has been defeated and driven south of Fort Scott. Our troops will pursue. He will probably retreat on Fort Gibson and Fort Smith. He should be met and cut off. His army can be captured or destroyed." Perhaps it was because of Price's approach that the 33d Iowa was reinforced at Lewisburg with two hundred Union cavalry under Capt. David Hamilton of the 3d Arkansas Cavalry. Hamilton had orders to accompany the train as far as Clarksville. *OR*, ser. 1, vol. 41, pt. 4, p. 294, 910–11.

11. Kirkbridge Potts, a native of New Jersey, settled in the area that became known as Pottsville, Arkansas, in 1828. The house Sperry saw in 1864 was Potts's second, which was completed around 1852 or 1853. It still stands in the middle of Pottsville. In addition to farming a large tract of land, Potts had served as an Indian agent, postmaster, and the proprietor of a station on the famous Butterfield Overland Mail route from Memphis to San Francisco, providing rooms and meals to passengers on the Little Rock-Fort Smith leg. Crow Mountain rose less than a mile from the center of Pottsville. Mace A. Dunn, "A History of Pottsville, Arkansas" (M.S.E. thesis, University of Central Arkansas, 1962), 2–5, 8.

12. The presidential election pitted Abraham Lincoln against his Democratic challenger, George B. McClellan, the faded military hero. Because they knew that most Union soldiers favored the war effort, Republicans pushed hard to get the Northern states to grant their troops the privilege of voting in the field. The day after the election, the newly promoted

NOTES TO PAGES 127–28

Sgt. Charles Musser of the 29th Iowa told his father how some Iowa units in Arkansas
voted: "our regt Polled 493 votes, and out of that number, Little Mac [McClellan] got 51.
33d Iowa polled 431 votes, 42 for McClellan." Counting the 33d Iowa's 389, Iowa soldiers
cast 17,252 votes for Lincoln, but only 1,920 for McClellan. Charles O. Musser to "Dear
Father," November 9, 1864, in Popchock, *Soldier Boy*, 160; David E. Long, *The Jewel of
Liberty: Abraham Lincoln's Re-election and the End of Slavery* (Mechanicsburg, Pa.:
Stackpole Books, 1994), 215–34, 285–86.

13. The two hundred cavalrymen who accompanied the 33d Iowa from Lewisburg to
Clarksville reported several clashes with roving bands of Confederate cavalry. The
Federals claimed to have killed eleven Rebels and captured fifteen, including a lieutenant.
This was not Clarksville's first brush with guerrilla warfare. On September 28, 1864, a
column of 386 Union cavalry out of Little Rock chased some enemy troopers through
Clarksville, killing seven. "Independent companies and rebel conscripting officers are very
numerous and active in this vicinity, having Clarksville for a rendezvous," wrote Maj.
Thomas Derry, 3d Wisconsin Cavalry, the commander of the Union strike force. Derry and
his troopers had to chase the Confederates out of Clarksville again on October 9. *OR*, ser.
1, vol. 41, pt. 1, pp. 819–20, 910–11.

14. This desire to show no quarter to Confederate guerrillas, or "bushwhackers," was
shared by many Union troops in Arkansas and Missouri. On November 9, Sergeant Musser
of the 29th Iowa wrote his father from Little Rock: "All is quiet around here except an
occasional Brush with the *Bushwhackers*, which don't amount to much neither way—only
the *Hanging of a rascal when caught*. you don't often see an account in the newspapers of
the punishment of Bushwhackers. *but that is no sign that it is not done*." Charles O.
Musser to "Dear Father," November 9, 1864, in Popchock, *Soldier Boy*, 161.

15. Allen Hamrick enlisted as a private in Company G, 33d Iowa, at Pella on August 9,
1862, but was appointed a corporal six days later and promoted to sergeant on November
1, 1863. He was the regiment's acting sergeant major from July 1864 to June 1865. Albert
G. Berkey did not become the 33d Iowa's commissary sergeant until January 2, 1865. A
printer who enlisted as a private in Company D, Berkey was appointed regimental postmaster on May 17, 1863. A year later, he was detailed as a clerk at regimental headquarters.
Allen Hamrick Military Files, Albert G. Berkey Military Files, both in Civil War (Union)
Compiled Military Service Records, 33d Iowa Infantry, Record Group 94, National
Archives.

16. The 1st Arkansas Infantry Regiment was organized at Fayetteville and mustered
into Federal service on March 25, 1863. In March 1864, it was assigned to the 1st Brigade,
District of the Frontier, VII Army Corps. The regiment participated in the Camden
expedition and then returned to Fort Smith, where it saw a lot of escort duty. Dyer,
Compendium, 2:999.

17. What Sperry called the "5th U.S. Colored Infantry" was actually the 112th U.S.
Colored Infantry Regiment. Originally known as the 5th Arkansas Colored Infantry, it
began organizing at Little Rock in April 1864 and had trouble attracting sufficient recruits.
By the year's end, the 112th had filled only four of its ten companies. On April 1, 1865, it
was consolidated with troops from two other regiments to form the 113th U.S. Colored
Infantry (New). Dyer, *Compendium*, 2:1000, 1739. For more on this regiment's first year of
existence, see Edward G. Longacre, ed., "Letters from Little Rock of Captain James M.
Bowler, 112th United States Colored Troops," *Arkansas Historical Quarterly* 40 (Autumn
1981): 235–48.

18. James Martin Johnson (1833–1914) was born in Warren County, Tennessee, and settled
with his family in Madison County, Arkansas, in 1836. He studied medicine in St. Louis and
became a physician. True to his Unionist principles, he served General Curtis as a volunteer aide and then became colonel of the 1st Arkansas Infantry. He was elected to the U.S.

House of Representatives in 1864 but was denied his seat by radical Republicans who did not approve of President Lincoln's Reconstruction policies. Johnson was named a brevet brigadier general of U.S. Volunteers as of March 13, 1865, and filled a term as lieutenant governor of Arkansas, 1867–1869.

Colonel Johnson not only assumed command of the train and escort, but he insisted that Captain Hamilton and his two hundred cavalry accompany the column to Fort Smith. Roger D. Hunt and Jack R. Brown, *Brevet Brigadier Generals in Blue* (Gaithersburg, Md.: Olde Soldier Books, 1990), 316; *OR*, ser. 1, vol. 41, pt. 1, p. 911.

19. Van Buren's prewar population was 750 whites and 229 blacks. "Evolution of Arkansas Townships," 84.

20. Long the gateway to Indian Territory, Fort Smith had loomed large in American frontier affairs since the first military post was built there in 1817. The 1860 census gave the city's population as 1,529 whites but only 1 African American and 2 Indians, which is clearly inaccurate. Maj. Gen. James G. Blunt captured Fort Smith for the Union on September 1, 1863, nine days before Steele took Little Rock. Fort Smith became a place of refuge for thousands of Arkansas Unionists, but the difficulty of supplying the garrison and the town's swollen population by water made Northern officials seriously consider evacuating the city in late 1864. "Evolution of Arkansas Townships," 88; Christ, *Rugged and Sublime*, 85–89, 102–3, 143–44; Stone, "Brother against Brother," 28–32.

21. J. Gilcoat served in the lower house of the Arkansas General Assembly from 1864 to 1865. He traveled with the 33d Iowa to attend a special session of the legislature, which was held in Little Rock from November 7, 1864, to January 2, 1865. There seems to be no record of a Colonel Bowen in the General Assembly at this time. Either Sperry or his typesetter misspelled the other legislator's name. Jerry E. Hinshaw, *Call the Roll: The First One Hundred Fifty Years of the Arkansas Legislature* (Little Rock: Rose Publishing Co., 1986), 42, 44, 192.

22. Maj. Gen. William T. Sherman, the conqueror of Atlanta, began his famous "march to the sea" on November 15, 1864. His objective at that time, however, was Savannah, Georgia. His subsequent advance into South Carolina forced the Rebels to abandon Charleston in mid-February 1865. John F. Marszalek, *Sherman: A Soldier's Passion for Order* (New York: Vintage Books, 1994), 293–322.

23. The 47th Indiana Infantry was organized at Anderson and Indianapolis in late 1861. The regiment saw considerable service, including the Yazoo Pass expedition, Grant's Vicksburg campaign, and Banks's Red River campaign. The 47th Indiana participated in several sweeps through eastern Arkansas in the fall of 1864. After a brief stay at Little Rock, it shipped out for Memphis on November 25. Dyer, *Compendium*, 2:1137.

24. The 33d Iowa's toughness was also reflected in the fact that it suffered no deaths from sickness or exposure on this march. *OR Supplement*, pt. 2, vol. 20, serial no. 32, pp. 790–91.

CHAPTER SIXTEEN: REST A LITTLE, AND THEN OFF AGAIN

1. Maj. Gen. Joseph J. Reynolds relieved Steele as commander of the Department of Arkansas on November 29, 1864. A West Point classmate of Ulysses S. Grant, Reynolds saw some service in the Mexican War and then returned to the U.S. Military Academy for eight years as a faculty member. He resigned from the regular army in 1857 to teach at Washington University in St. Louis. With the outbreak of the Civil War, he became colonel of the 10th Indiana Infantry. He was promoted to brigadier general on January 23, 1862, and major general on November 29. He distinguished himself at Chickamauga and Chattanooga.

Many Union soldiers in Arkansas complained of General Steele's gentle treatment of Confederate civilians and his tolerance of debauchery among the Little Rock garrison. As soon as Reynolds took charge of the department, he launched a general housecleaning, which elicited the approval of his more zealous subordinates. A religious man and a strict teetotaler who had brought his wife and two small sons to live with him in Little Rock, Reynolds was determined to reform his command. On December 29, 1864, Sgt. Ira Seeley of the 29th Iowa noted the incident that marked the inauguration of this campaign: "The new Gen. who superseded Steele is here and appears to be straightening them out. He dismissed two officers the other day for being drunk. That is something new for this department." Three days later, Capt. Thomas Stevens of the 28th Wisconsin Infantry confided to his wife: "General Reynolds will not prove such an officer as General Steele, we think here—we hope not. He has commenced by removing from their positions several officers. He saw a couple of officers in the street intoxicated. He immediately dismissed them from the service of the United States. He has also instituted other reforms, and has given 'notice to quit' to several rebel citizens whom General Steele permitted to remain in the city." "Such doings meet the approbation of all good soldiers," commented Sgt. Charles Musser of the 29th Iowa, "and Genl Reynolds is gaining the good will of all loyal men at this place. I have wished long for such a change." On January 5, 1865, Sergeant Morgan of the 33d Iowa noted that yet another officer had fallen victim to Reynolds's purge: "Capt Wright of 3d Iowa Battery, dismissed the Service for drunkenness on the street, subject to the approval of the President." The 33d Iowa soon learned that Reynolds expected proper conduct from noncommissioned officers as well. "Sergt J. M. Bell and Corp. Cyrus Ria was reduced to ranks to day," Cpl. Cyrus Gaston of Company K wrote on January 7, "in compliance of Genl Reynolds order." Warner, *Generals in Blue*, 397–98; Hubbell and Geary, *Biographical Dictionary*, 433–34; Ira Seeley to "Dear Wife," December 29, 1864, in Seeley, *Civil War Letters*, 141; Thomas N. Stevens to Carrie Stevens, January 1, 1865, in Blackburn, *Dear Carrie*, 275; Charles O. Musser to "Dear Father," December 30, 1864, in Popchock, *Soldier Boy*, 171; "Diary of John S. Morgan, Company G, Thirty-Third Iowa Infantry," Part 2. *Annals of Iowa* 13 (April 1923): 570; Gaston, "Diary," January 7, 1865.

2. John S. Morgan, the first sergeant of Company G since July 21, 1864, noted some of the rumors that swept through the 33d Iowa in the wake of these orders: "Lt Seevers brings report of a march for 10 days. No orders until near noon, orders come to be ready by 8 A.M. tomorrow. . . . Evening prevailing opinion that it is good bye Little Rock how are you Shreveport. A cooperating column reported moving up Red River. nearly all the troops cav. & Inft to go." Morgan, "Diary," pt. 2, 571.

3. Carr left Little Rock with a much larger expedition than Sperry remembered. It consisted of the 1st Iowa, 1st Missouri, and 13th Illinois Cavalry, the 33d Iowa, 43d Illinois, 28th Wisconsin, and 50th Indiana Infantry, the 25th Ohio Light Artillery Battery, and a pontoon corps. Sergeant Morgan described the 33d Iowa's departure in terse terms: "Regt to St Johns Square at 9 A.M. All there at 11.30 and start. . . . All light order. Roads rough." *OR*, ser. 1, vol. 48, pt. 1, p. 60; Morgan, "Diary," pt. 2, 571.

4. Sergeant Morgan noted that the snow began falling at 3:30 P.M. Carr's column camped at a mill burned by Rebel guerrillas at 4:00 P.M. Morgan, "Diary," pt. 2, 571.

5. Pine Bluff was the fourth-largest town in Arkansas in 1860, with a population of 1,396. Bearss, "Marmaduke Attacks Pine Bluff," 291.

6. The 33d Iowa marched at the front of Carr's column on January 25, and the expedition covered thirteen miles before it went into camp at 1:30 P.M. The troops received a rations delivery in the evening. Carr's expedition was also reinforced at Pine Bluff with the 106th and 126th Illinois Infantry Regiments and a section of the 1st Arkansas Colored Battery. Morgan, "Diary," pt. 2, 572; *OR*, ser. 1, vol. 8, pt. 1, p. 60.

7. The march may have seemed routine to the Union infantry, but the cavalry, scouting

in advance of Carr's column, made repeated contact with the enemy. On January 26, a Yankee scout spotted a party of twenty-five Confederates, and some blue cavalrymen nabbed a prisoner. On the twenty-seventh, Federal troopers killed one enemy guerrilla and captured fifteen. One trooper of the 1st Missouri Cavalry died in the skirmish. Morgan, "Diary," pt. 2, 572; *OR*, ser. 1, vol. 48, pt. 1, p. 60.

8. The Union cavalry crossed the Saline at 4:00 P.M. on January 27 on the pontoon bridge that Carr had brought along. The troopers carried two days' rations and instructions to ride all night to throw a scare into enemy troops at Camden. *OR*, ser. 1, vol. 48, pt. 1, p. 60.

9. Carr's mud-spattered soldiers arrived at Little Rock at 3:00 P.M., February 4, 1865. Several officers of the 33d Iowa proudly noted that their regiment marched 160 to 180 miles to Mount Elba and back without losing a single man. *OR*, ser. 1, vol. 48, pt. 1, p. 60; Morgan, "Diary," pt. 2, 572–73; *OR Supplement*, pt. 2, vol. 20, serial no. 32, pp. 791, 806–7, 810.

10. On January 31, 1865, General Reynolds directed that the 29th Iowa, 33d Iowa, 27th Wisconsin, 28th Wisconsin, 50th Indiana, and 77th Ohio Infantry Regiments—a total of 3,025 effectives—be detached from the VII Army Corps for service with the Department of the Gulf. General Grant intended these troops to assist in realizing one of his pet schemes, the capture of Mobile, Alabama. On the thirty-first, General Reynolds asserted his compliance with Grant's will in a dispatch addressed to the assistant adjutant general of the Department of the Gulf: "The order for troops to proceed to Department of the Gulf and report to military division headquarters will be executed without delay. The troops now in the field toward Camden will, by their absence, cause some little delay, but troops to fill the call will be placed en route by regiments as fast as they can be disengaged." At the same time, Reynolds ordered the 11th and 57th U.S. Colored Infantry to Little Rock to replace the white regiments he was sending to New Orleans. *OR*, ser. 1, vol. 48, pt. 1, pp. 691–92; Gaston, "Diary," February 4, 1865; Chester G. Hearn, *Mobile Bay and the Mobile Campaign* (Jefferson, N.C.: McFarland & Co., 1993), 146.

11. Apparently, the other units in Carr's Mount Elba expedition were almost as robust as the 33d Iowa. As George R. Weeks, the expedition's chief surgeon, reported: "The health of the troops was remarkably good during the march; but very few were in the ambulances at any time." *OR*, ser. 1, vol. 48, pt. 1, p. 60.

12. On January 31, 1865, General Reynolds reported that the 33d Iowa had 590 officers and men present for duty. *OR*, ser. 1, vol. 48, pt. 1, p. 691.

CHAPTER SEVENTEEN: DOWN SOUTH

1. On February 1, 1865, General Reynolds reorganized the infantry assigned to the VII Corps. The 33d Iowa and the five other regiments selected for transfer to the Department of the Gulf were designated the "Detached Brigade" under Brig. Gen. Eugene Carr. Carr left Little Rock on February 6, supposedly bound for New Orleans to prepare for the arrival of his command, but he made a mistake that nearly wrecked his career. As Reynolds explained: "A party of officers and ladies went to Devall's Bluff the same afternoon to attend an entertainment given on board the steamer Rowena. . . . General Carr was drunk on the railroad going to the Bluff, carried liquor with him from Little Rock, was drunk on the steamboat, and returned to Little Rock drunk. He behaved in a very unbecoming manner going, returning, and while at the Bluff." On February 9, Reynolds relieved Carr and named Brig. Gen. James C. Veatch to replace him. Unable to mask his disgust, Reynolds requested that Carr be transferred from the Department of Arkansas. "His habits, in my opinion," Reynolds seethed, "are bad and his influence detrimental to the best interests of the service."

In the meantime, the 33d Iowa prepared to depart Little Rock. The regiment received a new issue of clothing on February 9, and the men boxed up such surplus items as blankets and overcoats for shipment to Iowa. On the twelfth, the regiment stood for an inspection, which Cpl. Cyrus Gaston called "the Closest Inspection I have been on for Some time." *OR*, ser. 1, vol. 48, pt. 1, p. 788; James T. King, *War Eagle: A Life of General Eugene A. Carr* (Lincoln: University of Nebraska Press, 1963), 70–71; Thomas N. Stevens to Carrie Stevens, February 14, 1865, in Blackburn, *Dear Carrie*, 294; Morgan, "Diary," pt. 2, 573; Gaston, "Diary," February 9, 12, 1865.

2. Some members of the Detached Brigade expected to see Little Rock again in the near future. From a steamer moored at De Valls Bluff, Capt. Thomas Stevens of the 28th Wisconsin wrote his wife: "It was said at Little Rock that we would return to that place in 6 or 8 weeks, but we have no desire to go there again. We all say heartily, 'Good bye, Arkansas!'" Thomas N. Stevens to Carrie Stevens, February 14, 1865, in Blackburn, *Dear Carrie*, 294.

3. It was raining when the 33d Iowa left camp at Little Rock at 6:30 A.M., and it continued to rain throughout the day. The dousing left Sgt. John Morgan of Company G in a sour mood—despite the fact that he had received his commission as second lieutenant a week earlier. "Duvalls Bluffs a perfect mudhole," he grumbled to his diary. Morgan, "Diary," pt. 2, 573.

4. The *Paragon* carried the 33d Iowa about thirty miles down the White River before tying up for the night. Morgan, "Diary," pt. 2, 573; Gaston, "Diary," February 14, 1865.

5. This post was located at the mouth of the White River. The garrison consisted of the 126th Illinois Infantry and a detachment of the 1st Indiana Cavalry. The 33d Iowa camped a half-mile from the river. Morgan, "Diary," pt. 2, 574; Gaston, "Diary," February 15, 1865.

6. The rejoicing must have subsided considerably somewhere above Helena, when Confederate guerrillas fired from shore at the *Ben Stickney*, wounding one of the boat's occupants. Morgan, "Diary," p. 2, 574.

7. "I was all over the Town viewing the fortifications," noted an excited Corporal Gaston. "[W]alked over town," wrote Sergeant Morgan, "was in 20 of the celebrated holes, & on top of the Court house." Gaston, "Diary," February 17, 1865; Morgan, "Diary," pt. 2, 574.

8. Sergeant Morgan was also impressed by this part of Louisiana, calling it "the richest country I ever saw." In his diary, he wrote of "fine plantations splendid houses & villages of negro houses in regular order with streets." Morgan, "Diary," pt. 2, 574.

9. New Orleans was the largest, wealthiest, and most cosmopolitan city in the Confederacy until it surrendered to the Union navy on April 24, 1862. Its prewar populace numbered 149,063 whites, 14,484 slaves, and 10,939 free blacks. New Orleans remained a bustling port and commercial center under Union occupation, as the men of the 33d Iowa bore witness. Sergeant Morgan counted "more than 200 sailing vessels lieing in river here and about 50 to 100 steamboats some 20 gunboats, no end to small craft." Recalling his first sight of New Orleans, Pvt. James Newman of Company I declared: "The masts of ships looking like a forest almost hide the city." Joe Gray Taylor, *Louisiana Reconstructed, 1863–1877* (Baton Rouge: Louisiana State University Press, 1974), 2–3, 7–8; Chester G. Hearn, *The Capture of New Orleans, 1862* (Baton Rouge: Louisiana State University Press, 1995), 1, 7–9; Morgan, "Diary," pt. 2, 574; Newman, *Autobiography*, 27.

10. Then, as now, New Orleans teemed with both culinary and carnal temptations. It was the latter that inspired the pious Cpl. John Shepherd of the 33d Iowa's Company I to call New Orleans "the wickedest City I was ever in." John Morgan entered the "Crescent City" on February 20 to be mustered in as a second lieutenant, and he was struck by its beauty more than anything else. "New Orleans a fine City," he decided, "streets clean all stone. was in the St Charles Hotel." Shepherd, "Autobiography," 50; Morgan, "Diary," pt. 2, 575.

11. Algiers was a shipbuilding center that sat opposite New Orleans on the right bank of the Mississippi River. "Algiers is a small place," observed Lieutenant Morgan, "& dirty." Morgan, "Diary," pt. 2, 575.

12. It was at this juncture that Corporal Shepherd was finally forced to part with his winter overcoat. Shepherd, "Autobiography," 50; Morgan, "Diary," pt. 2, 575.

13. This rainstorm began at 5:00 P.M. and continued into the night. Private Newman complained that it turned the 33d Iowa's camp into "a paradise for ducks." Nevertheless, the weather did not dampen everyone's spirits. Peering from his tent at the end of Company G's company street, Lieutenant Morgan scribbled: "Men all get wet, but make merry." Newman, *Autobiography*, 27; Morgan, "Diary," pt. 2, 575.

14. The *Izetta* was an armed 476-ton sidewheeler. It ferried the 33d Iowa across the Mississippi to New Orleans. There the regiment boarded a train to Lake Pontchartrain, where ships waited to carry the Iowans to Mobile Bay, Alabama. Gibson and Gibson, *Dictionary of Transports*, 162; Morgan, "Diary," pt. 2, 575; Gaston, "Diary," February 23, 1865.

15. The *A. G. Brown* was a sidewheel steamer, as was the 650-ton *Alabama*. Lieutenant Morgan's diary captured the confusion of that dark and rainy embarkation: "at 8 P.M. cos B. G. & K embark on board steam ship Alabama. find it full of mules & about 300 men of some 7 regts. 35 Wis, 7th Vermont, 27th & 28th Wis 1st La. &c." Gibson and Gibson, *Dictionary of Transports*, 3, 9; Morgan, "Diary," pt. 2, 575.

16. Corporal Gaston's diary contradicted Sperry's memories of fair weather and a smooth voyage. "Cloudy Rainy & windy & the water very Ruff," Gaston wrote on February 24. "[W]e passed out of Lake Ponchartrain through the Mississippi Sound. . . . there was a good many of the men sick today. . . . The wind Blew a Perfect Gale all day & all Night." Gaston, "Diary," February 24, 1865.

17. Fort Powell was a Confederate installation erected to block enemy access to Mobile Bay from Mississippi Sound via shallow Grant's Pass. The Confederates abandoned this post on the night of August 5, 1864, after it was bombarded by the four-gun monitor *Chickasaw*. The 33d Iowa entered the bay via Grant's Pass on February 25, 1865. Mark Mayo Boatner, *The Civil War Dictionary* (New York: David McKay Co., 1959), 298; Morgan, "Diary," pt. 2, 575; Gaston, "Diary," February 25, 1865.

18. The U.S. army constructed Fort Gaines in 1822 at the eastern tip of Dauphine Island to defend the western side of the main entrance to Mobile Bay. Alabama troops seized the post in January 1861, and it soon passed into Confederate control. Union troops laid siege to Fort Gaines on August 4, 1864, and it surrendered four days later. Francis Paul Prucha, *A Guide to the Military Posts of the United States, 1789–1895* (Madison: State Historical Society of Wisconsin, 1964), 75; Boatner, *Civil War Dictionary*, 298.

19. Fort Morgan stood on Mobile Point opposite Fort Gaines and guarded the eastern side of the main entrance to Mobile Bay. The U.S. army first garrisoned the post in March 1834. It fell into Confederate hands after Alabama seceded. In the epic battle of Mobile Bay, August 5, 1864, Rear Adm. David G. Farragut ran his fleet past Fort Morgan and battered the Confederate ironclad *Tennessee* into surrender. After sustaining a heavy bombardment from besieging Union troops on August 23, Fort Morgan surrendered the following day. Prucha, *Guide to Military Posts*, 92–93; Boatner, *Civil War Dictionary*, 298, 558–59.

20. The 33d Iowa landed four miles above Fort Morgan and then marched about a mile across Mobile Point to pitch camp within two hundred yards of the Gulf of Mexico. When the 33d Iowa joined the "U.S. Forces Mobile Point," it was assigned to Col. Conrad Krez's 3d Brigade in Brig. Gen. William P. Benton's 3d Division, XIII Army Corps. Benton was then the senior officer at Mobile Point. Morgan, "Diary," pt. 2, 575; Gaston, "Diary," February 25, 1865; *OR*, ser. 1, vol. 48, pt. 1, pp. 1022–23.

21. The memoirs and diaries of 33d Iowa personnel are full of fond references to life at

Mobile Point. As Corporal Shepherd recalled: "here I had my first Salt Water Bath. We fished up Oysters from the Bay. I ate a big lot of them raw I took a case knife and broke the Shells and Scooped them out and Swalowed them." On February 26, Lieutenant Morgan told his diary: "Fine day. hunt shells on the beach, see the porpoises, &c camp on banks of white sand covered with scrub oaks plenty of fresh water by digging in the sand. boys wade in the bay & gather oysters Plenty of them." Corporal Gaston spent hours that same day simply watching the "Surf Roll" and the porpoises frolic. Shepherd, "Autobiography," 51; Morgan, "Diary," pt. 2, 575–76; Gaston, "Diary," February 26, 1865.

22. The Reverend Ingalls made two speeches to the 33d Iowa on this subject, the first on March 1 and the second on the following day. Many of the regiment's members contributed twenty-five dollars apiece, which made them life members in a charity devoted to caring for the orphaned children of their dead comrades. Newman, *Autobiography*, 29; Morgan, "Diary," pt. 2, 576; Gaston, "Diary," March 1–2, 1865.

23. Known in today's military as a "pup tent," the shelter tent was a simple two-man tent, and it saw widespread use in the Union army. It was made of cotton drilling or sturdy cotton duck. Each soldier received half of a tent (known as a "shelter half"), which he could carry in his knapsack or inside his blanket roll. When the time came to pitch camp, two comrades would button their shelter halves together, improvise some tent poles from a wide variety of materials (including their rifle muskets, tree branches, fence rails, or ropes), and erect their shelter. Company G of the 33d Iowa drew its "dog tents" on February 27, 1865. Lord, *Collector's Encyclopedia*, 279–80; John D. Billings, *Hardtack and Coffee: The Unwritten Story of Army Life* (Lincoln: University of Nebraska Press, 1993), 51–54; Morgan, "Diary," pt. 2, 576.

24. Peter J. Osterhaus (1823–1917) was born in Coblenz, Prussia, and received a military education. Because of his involvement in the revolutions of 1848, he was forced to flee to the United States, eventually settling in St. Louis. He cast his lot with the Union when the Civil War broke out, and led a battalion at Wilson's Creek. Promoted to colonel in the 12th Missouri Infantry, he commanded a division in the Union victory at Pea Ridge. In June 1862, Osterhaus became a brigadier general and went on to serve under Grant and Sherman in the Vicksburg campaign. He distinguished himself at Chattanooga and in Sherman's Atlanta campaign and march to the sea. He was upgraded to major general on June 23, 1864, and is generally regarded one of the ablest foreign-born officers to serve the North.

Corporal Gaston got a close look at Osterhaus, and he preserved his impressions in his diary: "Genl Osterhaus is a man about 6 ft high heavy eyebrow, mustach sandy & heavy & heavy Gotie." Warner, *Generals in Blue*, 352–53; Gaston, "Diary," March 8, 1865.

25. "All the Gunboats & Monitors move out early this morning," wrote Lieutenant Morgan, "going up the Bay toward Mobile, A little before 9 A.M. heavy firing. . . . the firing was a good distance off & kept up incessantly all day except from 1.30 to 3 P.M." Morgan, "Diary," pt. 2, 577.

26. Lieutenant Morgan provided this weather report for Tuesday, March 14, 1865: "Commenced raining at, 12 O.clock last night, rained all the balance of night with moon shining brightly took breakfast in our tents, rained until 2 P.M." Corporal Gaston added: "the wind Blew very hard the Gulf was Very Rough to day the waves run very high." Morgan, "Diary," pt. 2, 577–78; Gaston, "Diary," March 14, 1865.

27. On July 1, 1864, Rev. Francis M. Slusser, a forty-year-old preacher at Oskaloosa's First Methodist Church, received a commission as chaplain of the 33d Iowa from Governor Stone. Slusser had been defeated two years earlier in the election for this post by Robert McAyeal. The new chaplain was a regularly ordained elder and member of the Des Moines Annual Conference of the Methodist Church, Iowa. The officers of the 33d Iowa ratified his selection as chaplain by a vote of eight to three on July 30, a decision endorsed by the chap-

lains of the 3d Missouri Cavalry, 77th Ohio Infantry, 40th Iowa Infantry, and 1st Iowa Cavalry. Slusser Military Files; *History of Mahaska County*, 483.

CHAPTER EIGHTEEN: TO SPANISH FORT

1. The XIII Army Corps contained three infantry divisions. Each division had two light artillery batteries, and there were two additional mortar batteries attached to the division. The 3d Division consisted of three infantry brigades, with four regiments apiece. The other regiments brigaded with the 33d Iowa were the 77th Ohio, 27th Wisconsin, and 28th Wisconsin. *OR*, ser. 1, vol. 49, pt. 1, pp. 105–7.

2. Conrad Krez (1828–1897) was another German refugee who fought to preserve the American experiment in self-government. He was born in Bavaria and attended the Universities of Munich and Heidelberg, becoming a lawyer, politician, and poet. On March 26, 1865, Colonel Krez was named a brevet brigadier general of U.S. volunteers "for faithful and meritorious services during the campaign against the city of Mobile and its defenses." Hunt and Brown, *Brevet Brigadier Generals*, 341.

3. William P. Benton (1828–1867) was born in Maryland and grew up in Indiana. He fought in the Mexican War as an enlisted man in the U.S. Regiment of Mounted Rifles (later the 3d U.S. Cavalry). Returning to Indiana to study law, Benton eventually served as a county district attorney and a judge. At the start of the Civil War, Benton was elected to command a company in the 8th Indiana Infantry, a three-month regiment. When the 8th Indiana reenlisted for three years, Benton became its colonel on September 5, 1861. Benton and his regiment fought at Pea Ridge, where he may have been an acting brigade commander. Appointed a brigadier general on April 28, 1862, he served in the Vicksburg campaign. Cpl. Cyrus Gaston of the 33d Iowa described Benton as "a man about 5 ft 10 in high long Dark hair, very heavy whiskers & mustach well built & very Neat." Warner, *Generals in Blue*, 30–31; Gaston, "Diary," March 8, 1865.

4. Gordon Granger (1822–1876) was born in Joy, New York, and graduated from the U.S. Military Academy in 1845. He fought in Mexico and on the American frontier as an officer in the Mounted Rifles. His bravery at Wilson's Creek earned him a colonelcy in the 2d Michigan Cavalry, and he led a brigade in the New Madrid and Island No. 10 campaigns. Promotion to brigadier general came on March 26, 1862. He was next appointed to major general to rank from September 17, 1862. Granger assisted Maj. Gen. George H. Thomas in saving the beaten Army of the Cumberland at Chickamauga on September 20, 1863. He commanded the IV Army Corps at Chattanooga. Corporal Gaston described Granger as "about 5 ft 8 inches high dark eyes Black curly hair Black whiskers & mustach & very heavy forehead high complexion light." Warner, *Generals in Blue*, 181; Gaston, "Diary," March 22, 1865.

5. Corporal Gaston confirmed Sperry's rations story: "we cooked 4 days Rations of meat & had four days Rations of Coffee & hardtack issued to us." Gaston, "Diary," March 16, 1865.

6. Corporal Gaston did not enjoy the day's march as much as Sperry: "I was pretty tired after marching in sand shoe mouth deep." Gaston, "Diary," March 17, 1865.

7. This incident made an indelible impression on Cpl. John Shepherd of Company I. "Some of the Negros came out to meet us," he wrote forty-three years later, "and I Shall never forget one old Woman. I heard her Shouting 1/4 of a mile away. when we came up to where she was She was Jumping up and down and Shouting Glory to God and the Yankees for ever. She Said my ten Chilen all free haliluyah. [First Sgt.] Peter Bonebrake Said to me Shepherd, don't that make your Knapsack feel lighter I Said yes." Lt. John Morgan noted

this joyful encounter with a cryptic diary reference: "We see one happy wench. we were the first yankees she had seen." Shepherd, "Autobiography," 51; Morgan, "Diary," pt. 2, 578.

8. Krez's brigade made only five miles on Sunday, March 19. Capt. Thomas Stevens of the 28th Wisconsin Infantry complained that he and his men were "lying in a swamp nearly all day, while details of men repaired & 'corduroyed' the roads, which now run through low lands, & are cut up long before our train can pass over it." Lieutenant Morgan of the 33d Iowa's Company G described the brigade's campsite: "have now a continued pine swamp with no under brush, but a thick growth of grass a great deal like our prairie grass, this is called the Meadows." Thomas N. Stevens to Carrie Stevens, March 24, 1865, in Blackburn, *Dear Carrie*, 303–4; Morgan, "Diary," pt. 2, 578.

·9. Lieutenant Morgan claimed that the 33d Iowa marched six miles on Monday, March 20. The regiment moved out at 3:40 P.M., escorting a train of twenty wagons. Before the column had gone far, it began to rain. "The train sticks in the mud & is hard to get through," Morgan wrote. The 33d Iowa kept slogging along until 9:00 P.M., when it went into camp. Morgan, "Diary," pt. 2, 578–79.

10. For the 33d Iowa, making the road passable began on Tuesday, March 21. "[H]eavy detail out cording the road & building a bridge washed away by last nights rain," Lieutenant Morgan scribbled in his diary. The next day, he observed: "Fine day; lay in camp all day quite a no of the men out to forage. . . . Men pull the wagons." Morgan, "Diary," pt. 2, 579.

11. Once again, Corporal Gaston found the day's proceedings to be less pleasant than Sperry. "[W]e had the pack up call [the "General"] before we got our Breakfasts," he grumbled. "[W]e marched out early but our progress was Slow." Gaston, "Diary," March 23, 1865.

12. This song was originally written in 1858 by J. Warner as "Down in Alabam." It was also known as "Johnny Stole a Ham." New lyrics were crafted for the catchy tune, the most familiar of which are "Ain't I Glad I've Got Out the Wilderness" and "The Old Gray Mare." In 1860, the Republicans pressed it into service as a presidential campaign song, "Old Abe Lincoln Came Out of the Wilderness."

It is understandable that General Granger should signal his relief as his corps left the pine swamp. Colonel Krez summarized his brigade's journey to the Fish River as "a most fatiguing march through quicksand, swamps, and over the bottomless roads of South Alabama, that afforded no foothold to horses or mules. With the few tools in the command my brigade was engaged in making corduroys over the worst part of the roads and dragging the artillery and trains." Irwin Silber, *Songs of the Civil War* (New York: Columbia University Press, 1960), 90; John W. Work, *American Negro Songs* (New York: Howell, Soskin & Co., 1940), 185; Morgan, "Diary," pt. 2, 579; *OR*, ser. 1, vol. 49, pt. 1, pp. 226–27.

13. According to Lieutenant Morgan, Krez's 3d Brigade had to maneuver for two hours before it received permission to camp. Corporal Gaston noted the brigade's final formation: "Camped in line of battle." Morgan, "Diary," pt. 2, 579; Gaston, "Diary," March 23, 1865.

14. Maj. Gen. Andrew Jackson Smith (1815–1897) was an 1838 West Point graduate who put in twenty-three years of hard, frontier service with the 1st U.S. Dragoons (later the 1st U.S. Cavalry). He was appointed a brigadier general on March 20, 1862, and received his second star on May 14, 1864. A veteran of the Corinth and Vicksburg campaigns, he led elements of the XVI and XVII Army Corps detached from the Army of the Tennessee in the spring of 1864 in the Red River campaign. It was Smith and his "gorillas" who helped save Nathaniel Banks's defeated Union army from complete disaster. Later in the year at Tupelo, Mississippi, Smith earned the distinction of becoming one of the few Union generals to defeat Nathan Bedford Forrest. Smith and his wandering host ended 1864 at Nashville, where Union forces thrashed Gen. John Bell Hood and the Confederate Army of Tennessee. For the Mobile campaign, Smith commanded a reorganized XVI Corps, consist-

ing of three infantry divisions and seven light artillery batteries. A redeemed Gen. Eugene Carr headed Smith's 3d Division. Warner, *Generals in Blue*, 454–55; *OR*, ser. 1, vol. 49, pt. 1, pp. 107–8.

15. "Sinks" was Civil War soldier slang for latrines. Wiley, *Life of Billy Yank*, 126.

16. Maj. Gen. Edward R. S. Canby, the commander of the Military Division of West Mississippi, assembled an army of 45,200 effectives to take Mobile. In addition to Granger's XIII Corps and A. J. Smith's XVI Corps, Canby had Maj. Gen. Frederick Steele's "Column from Pensacola Bay" (which included a division of black infantry), Brig. Gen. T. Kilby Smith's garrison troops from the District of South Alabama, and assorted infantry, cavalry, engineer, and heavy artillery units. Hearn, *Mobile Bay*, 146, 151; *OR*, ser. 1, vol. 49, pt. 1, pp. 105–9.

17. "The train sticks in the mud three miles back & our grub did not get up," groused Lieutenant Morgan, "boarded with the boys." Morgan, "Diary," pt. 2, 580.

18. The 33d Iowa moved out at 6:45 A.M. on March 26, just as its wagons came up. "The troops moved out on 3 roads," noted Lieutenant Morgan. "Bertrams Brigade [2d Division, XIII Army Corps] on the left, Smiths Corps on the right & Grangers corps in the centre. . . . At 12. M. [midday] our advance is fixed on by a Reb picket post, on a hill on which the corps halts & goes into camp at 7, good running water near. We fortify immediately. . . . Expect to invest Spanish Fort tomorrow." Morgan, "Diary," pt. 2, 580.

CHAPTER NINETEEN: THE SIEGE

1. Spanish Fort was a strong network of earthen redoubts, batteries, breastworks, trenches, and rifle pits located at the head of Mobile Bay on the eastern shore. Mobile sat approximately thirteen miles away across the bay. Old Spanish Fort, the heart of the installation, occupied a tall bluff projecting into the Apalachee River. Its armament consisted of eight-inch Columbiads and thirty-pound Parrotts. Fort McDermott anchored the right (or southeastern) flank of Spanish Fort's outer line of landward defenses. That line stretched for one and a half miles from north to south. A corridor of cleared land extended for several hundred yards beyond the outer works, giving Confederate artillery and infantry a good field of fire. Fort McDermott stood in an advanced position some four hundred yards to the right of Old Spanish Fort. A long line of rifle pits ran north from McDermott through a ravine and past a small stream to Battery No. 3. Here began a six-hundred-yard stretch of redans called Red Fort. A nearly impenetrable barrier of slashed timber, underbrush, and vines—the handiwork of impressed black labor—screened the approaches to Spanish Fort. Beyond that lay a ditch five feet deep and eight feet wide. The Confederates dug rifle pits in front of every battery and placed lines of abatis fifteen to twenty feet wide about fifty feet in front of them. Any Federal troops who attempted to storm Spanish Fort's strongpoints would find themselves snagged on obstructions at point-blank range in front of entrenched enemy riflemen. Spanish Fort's left flank terminated in a swamp choked with fallen timber on the southern shore of Minette Bay.

Confederate Brig. Gen. Randall Lee Gibson initially had 3,400 men to hold Spanish Fort and Forts Huger and Tracy, two earthen island batteries erected upstream in marshes fringing the western bank of the Apalachee. There were only 1,810 troops in Spanish Fort itself, and they faced 30,000 Federals in Canby's XIII and XVI Corps. Hearn, *Mobile Bay*, 47, 147, 150, 157, 159, 161, 163, 165.

2. At the conclusion of this movement, Benton's 3d Division found itself opposite Fort McDermott. That work contained ten heavy guns. Colonel Krez described his 3d Brigade's approach to this position: "The whole division then marched out, right in front, in column

by battalion, my brigade in the rear. When the enemy's works came in sight the brigade was deployed, and two regiments, the Thirty-third Iowa and Twenty-seventh Wisconsin, were ordered to support the Twenty-sixth New York battery, holding the Twenty-eighth Wisconsin in reserve. After the battery had taken position opposite the enemy's works on their left, the brigade took position in front of the artillery on the extreme right of the line of the division, connecting with the left of Gen. A. J. Smith's line." Cpl. John Shepherd of the 33d Iowa put the matter much more simply: "We marched on to near the Rebel fortifications when we got within two or three hundred yard of their works we dug Rifle pits and fortified as best we could and begun the Siege." Hearn, *Mobile Bay,* 159; *OR,* ser. 1, vol. 49, pt. 1, p. 227; Shepherd, "Autobiography," 51–52.

3. The main body of the 33d Iowa may have been kept under shelter, but the regiment's skirmishers were quite aggressive in probing the enemy's lines. "The skirmish line pushes up to within 150 yds of the Reb works," reported Lt. John Morgan of Company G, "and keep them [the Rebels] well down behind them." Pvt. James Newman of Company I, one of the skirmishers, explained how he and his comrades operated: "After dark a detail of skirmishers were sent out, armed with picks and shovels and muskets. After approaching as near the rifle pits of the besieged as was prudent, we are deployed out some three yards apart, each man now proceeded to make a hole, in which to protect himself from the random shots which sent bullets whizzing over head, for our position could only be surmised, everything being done as quietly as possible. Soon each had sufficient protection to save his scalp provided he kept down. Morning revealed to each the position of the other." Morgan, "Diary," pt. 2, 581; Newman, *Autobiography,* 29.

4. Colonel Krez sent four companies "in open daylight" from his brigade to relieve an earlier shift of skirmishers and to "push the line as near as possible to the enemy's works." Companies B and G of the 33d Iowa were part of this relief force. "[H]ad to advance 400 yds through fallen timber exposed to the fire of the enemy," complained Lieutenant Morgan. "[G]ain our position within 100 yds of the Fort & throw up earthern works to protect us." Although Krez commended his skirmishers for their "gallant" behavior, he had to admit: "The loss in so advancing the line consisted in 8 wounded in the Thirty-third Iowa, amongst whom were Capt. William S. Parmley and Capt. George R. Ledyard; 6 wounded in the Twenty-eighth Wisconsin; 1 killed and 4 wounded in the Twenty-seventh Wisconsin, making a total of 1 killed and 18 wounded." *OR,* ser. 1, vol. 49, pt. 1, p. 227; Morgan, "Diary," pt. 2, 581.

5. Colonel Krez was slow in recognizing the wisdom of not exposing his troops to unnecessary danger. He sent Company K of the 33d Iowa to relieve Companies B and G at 3:00 P.M., while the sun was still shining brightly. Fortunately, he waited until the dim light of daybreak to relieve Company K, having Company E man the advanced Union rifle pits at 4:00 A.M., March 28. Morgan, "Diary," pt. 2, 581; Gaston, "Diary," March 28, 1865.

6. Altogether, Krez's brigade lost four killed and thirty-four wounded on the skirmish line in front of Spanish Fort from March 27 to April 4, 1865. After adopting the practice of relieving skirmishers at night, the brigade suffered as many casualties in eight days as it did on the first day of the siege. Total losses in the 33d Iowa for the March 27–April 4 period were twelve wounded. *OR,* ser. 1, vol. 49, pt. 1, p. 227.

7. Daniel W. Haydock was eighteen and a schoolteacher when he enlisted as a private in the 33d Iowa at Oskaloosa on July 21, 1862. He had hazel eyes, brown hair, a light complexion, and measured five feet seven in height. He was promoted to corporal on July 14, 1863. Haydock was reported sick in a hospital at Memphis, Tennessee, on July 5, 1863. He deserted from Gayoso Hospital on September 24, but returned on October 12. Despite such irregular conduct, he managed to retain his corporal's chevrons. Daniel W. Haydock Military Files, Civil War (Union) Compiled Military Service Records, 33d Iowa Infantry, Record Group 94, National Archives.

8. The Minié ball was the standard bullet fired by rifle muskets. It was hollow-based, oblong, and cone-shaped. The all-lead version used in the American Civil War was derived from a design perfected in 1848 by Capt. Claude Étienne Minié of the French army. Lord, *Collector's Encyclopedia*, 15.

9. During Sherman's march to the sea, the term "bummer" was applied to Union soldiers who ranged far from the main columns on ruthless foraging expeditions. Corporal Haydock, however, used it to designate skulkers. Joseph T. Glatthaar, *The March to the Sea and Beyond: Sherman's Troops in the Savannah and Carolinas Campaigns* (New York: New York University Press, 1985), 122–23.

10. Pvt. Jonathan E. Young, a thirty-seven-year-old farmer born in Brown County, Ohio, enlisted in the 33d Iowa at Oskaloosa on July 28, 1862. He had blue eyes, dark hair, and a light complexion. He was five feet eight inches tall. In June 1864, Young received a thirty-day furlough to provide care for his wife, who was dangerously ill. Their two remaining sons had just run off and enlisted, leaving Mrs. Young unattended and the family's affairs unsettled. Jonathan E. Young Military Files, Civil War (Union) Compiled Military Service Records, 33d Iowa Infantry, Record Group 94, National Archives.

11. Due to periodic shortages of gray dye, Confederate authorities were forced to color the wool and jeans uniforms issued to their troops with dyes made from walnut hulls and copperas, as well as other home-grown ingredients. The result was a variety of brownish hues ranging from a deep coffee color to the more common yellowish tint that inspired Union troops to call their opponents "butternuts" and "yellow-coats." Wiley, *Life of Johnny Reb*, 111–12.

12. James T. Ridpath, a native of Montgomery County, Virginia, enlisted in Company E at Peoria, Iowa, on July 21, 1862. His eyes were gray, his hair light, his complexion light, and his height five feet ten inches. Appointed a corporal on October 26, 1862, he made sergeant on July 15, 1863. From November 15, 1863, until February 1864, he was absent from the regiment on recruiting duty in Iowa. James T. Ridpath Military Files, Civil War (Union) Compiled Military Service Records, 33d Iowa Infantry, Record Group 94, National Archives.

13. Lieutenant Morgan reported proudly on Company E's performance: "At 12. Last night the Jonnies made a charge out of their forts on the skirmish line. . . . At 3 A.M. co C. relieves Co E. on the skirmish line. They come in all whole & were not drivn back." Serving in the 2d Brigade of Benton's 3d Division, Sgt. Charles Musser of the 29th Iowa provided additional information on this clash: "last night, a squad of rebel Skirmishers made a mistake and got in to the rifle pits of the 33d Iowa and was Bagged and sent to the rear." Morgan, "Diary," pt. 2, 581–82; Charles O. Musser to "Dear Father," April 1, 1865, in Popchock, *Soldier Boy*, 199.

14. Capt. Thomas Stevens of the 28th Wisconsin presented this view of siege life to his wife: "Our rifle pits are some of them within 150 yards or so of the rebel forts & batteries—the men dig, dig, dig, day & night, with accoutrements on, & their trusty rifles by their sides in the trenches. The rebels dig too, and we have to be cautious not to expose ourselves too far, or *whiz* goes a bullet, much too close to one's head to be pleasant for a timid man. Sometimes they rain around us like hail, and I wonder that the casualties are so few." Thomas N. Stevens to Carrie Stevens, April 6, 1865, in Blackburn, *Dear Carrie*, 307.

15. From Private Newman came an additional portrait of siege life in the 33d Iowa: "So a hat raised about the earthline would attract a shower of bullets and fortunate the owner if his head was not in it. Shells from a [Union] mortar boat behind the fort reminded us of the flight of time, as they came at intervals of half hours. The army on the main line could do but little but try to protect themselves from the shells sent over. Some built bomb-proof caves; heavy details were made every twenty-four hours to relieve those in the rifle pits. This was done at night, batteries and siege guns were got in position behind temporary works." Newman, *Autobiography*, 29–30.

16. "[W]e were all Routed out of our beds," Cpl. Cyrus Gaston of Company K griped about that alarm, "& packed our Knapsacks & put on our accoutrements Ready for Action." Gaston, "Diary," March 30, 1865.

17. Lieutenant Morgan penned a diary entry that captured these lively episodes: "The batteries open on the Forts & keep up a vigorous shelling for 3 hours. P.M. the felled timbers front of the forts where our skirmish line is gets on fire. Rebs open on them with shell & small arms. Could not see how the skirmishers could stand the heat & firing but they did it nobly." Corporal Gaston also marveled at the skirmishers' bravery: "there was a fire broke out between our skirmishers & through the Night the Rebels could see our men as plain as in daylight." Morgan, "Diary," pt. 2, 582; Gaston, "Diary," March 31, 1865.

18. The 33d Iowa made this move in two stages that began on April 4 and ended the next day. On Tuesday, April 4, A. J. Smith's XVI Corps extended its line leftward, and the 33d Missouri, 35th Iowa, and 12th Iowa Infantry occupied the camp of Krez's brigade. At 8:00 P.M. Krez had his regiments fall in and march through a sprinkling rain a mile further south. This placed Krez's brigade on the extreme left of Granger's 3d Division and opposite Old Spanish Fort. Krez's left flank now connected with the right of Col. Henry Bertram's 1st Brigade from the 2d Division of the XIII Corps. "[F]ind very poor quarters," complained Lieutenant Morgan, "lie down almost anywhere for the night." At 9:00 A.M. on April 5, Colonel Mackey marked off the areas where he wanted each company in the 33d Iowa to build a bombproof large enough to shelter all its men. The troops worked hard until noon, when orders came down for the regiment to move several dozen yards further to the left. At this, nearly half the regiment buzzed with grumbling, as Lieutenant Morgan explained: "This move cheated the 4 cos on the left out of their forenoon's work; we all went at it with a will to make the best of a bad bargain, worked until 4, P.M. when the men were all so fatigued that I thought it best to suspend active operations although we had no cover yet." Morgan, "Diary," pt. 2, 584; Gaston, "Diary," April 5, 1865; *OR*, ser. 1, vol. 48, pt. 1, p. 227.

19. By April 8, 1865, General Canby had fifty-nine siege guns and mortars and thirty-seven field pieces in position to bombard Spanish Fort. A vast network of parallels and saps had been dug to furnish Union troops with covered approaches to the edge of the Rebel lines. At some places, Union skirmishers were entrenched so close to enemy batteries that the gunners inside could no longer man their cannon without exposing themselves to certain injury or death. At 5:30 P.M., Federal batteries unleashed a thunderous bombardment lasting two hours. Corporal Gaston called it "the most terrific cannonading I Ever heard." Canby also directed his divisions to assault Spanish Fort at 8:00 A.M., April 9. Hearn, *Mobile Bay*, 187–89; Gaston, "Diary," April 8, 1865.

20. Sperry was wrong in depicting Steele's "Column from Pensacola Bay" as an all-black organization. For operations on the eastern shore, Canby attached two white brigades from Brig. Gen. Christopher C. Andrews's 2d Division, XIII Army Corps, to Steele's command. On April 3, Steele was reinforced by two more white divisions, one from the XIII Corps and one from the XVI Corps. *OR*, ser. 1, vol. 49, pt. 1, p. 106; Hearn, *Mobile Bay*, 183.

21. Colonel Krez claimed that skirmishers from his brigade were the first Union troops to occupy Spanish Fort, but they were cheated of their laurels by another brigade. Krez reported:

> In the evening of the 8th instant at about 10 o'clock it became apparent that the enemy was evacuating the fort, and notice to that effect having been sent to me by Maj. C. B. Boydston, Thirty-third Iowa, in charge of the skirmish line, I sent orders to him to take possession of the fort, which he did, placing guards over the magazines and artillery. Having sent to headquarters of the division for instructions, I was ordered not to send any troops in but the skirmishers. Half an hour after I had possession of the fort and all its contents. Part of Colonel Bertram's command on my left entered the fort, and Major Boydston, not considering it a special claim to honor

to keep possession of an evacuated place, allowed his tired guards to be relieved, by guards from the command of Colonel Bertram.

Lieutenant Morgan's diary placed these events closer to midnight. *OR*, ser. 1, vol. 49, pt. 1, pp. 227–28; Morgan, "Diary," pt. 2, 586–87.

22. Corporal Gaston of Company K was apparently one member of the 33d Iowa who toured Spanish Fort that night. He took a special interest in the enemy's artillery. "Cannon spiked with Nails," he told his diary, "52 pieces in all." Gaston, "Diary," April 8, 1865.

23. The relief and awe felt by the 33d Iowa's personnel are evident in Lieutenant Morgan's description of Spanish Fort's interior: "I found it not so strong a position as I had imagined it to be but to assault it would have been an ugly business if resolutely defended. Our shell & shot had handled the inside very rough tearing great holes. . . . found 9. Pieces of artillery in the fort all in position & spiked. 2 of the guns were splendid 64 lbers. There were bomb proofs enough about to hold the gunners required to work the guns but these were not of the strongest kind, out of one came so strong a stench I was willing to pass it others more inquisitive report a no [number] of dead men in it." Morgan, "Diary," pt. 2, 587.

24. Sperry confused Old Spanish Fort with the outlying post of Fort Huger.

25. This weapon was invented by Capt. John Mercer Brooke of the Confederate navy. It resembled the more familiar Parrott rifle in many ways, but the Brooke was banded at the breech with iron rings that were not welded together. According to one Confederate artilleryman, its rifling consisted of "10 groves Saw fashion," or one-sided grooves. The Brooke rifle came in different calibers, including the massive seacoast gun noted by Sperry. Boatner, *Civil War Dictionary*, 88; Warren Ripley, ed., *Siege Train: The Journal of a Confederate Artilleryman in the Defense of Charleston* (Columbia: University of South Carolina Press, 1986), 71–75, 77, 80, 237, 242, 266, 268; Harold L. Peterson, *Round Shot and Rammers* (Harrisburg, Pa.: Stackpole Books, 1969), 93–95, 101–9.

26. In addition to approximately fifty cannon, the exhilarated Union troops nabbed five hundred dispirited prisoners in and around Spanish Fort. They also captured 1,300 artillery projectiles and large quantities of other munitions. Hearn, *Mobile Bay*, 191.

27. These torpedoes or "subterra shells" were developed by Col. Gabriel J. Rains, head of the Confederate Army Torpedo Bureau. Rains's primer contained 50 percent potassium chlorate, 30 percent sulfuret of antimony, and 20 percent pulverized glass. These components were housed in a thin copper cap, which could be crushed by only seven pounds of pressure. At that, the chemicals exploded, igniting a fuse composed of gunpowder dissolved in alcohol. Rains also produced two types of water mines to threaten the Union warships cooperating with Canby's besieging army.

Sperry did not exaggerate the Confederates' heavy reliance on Rains's land mines. After surveying Spanish Fort on April 9, Corporal Gaston scratched in his diary: "Torpedoes were planted thick all around their Fortifications." Hearn, *Mobile Bay*, 35–36, 39; Gaston, "Diary," April 9, 1865.

28. As Lieutenant Morgan learned on April 9, the Confederates neutralized most of the torpedoes planted around Spanish Fort by not removing these safety caps: "Soon as breakfast is over many of the men go out to see the forts. The report on their return the roads & all arond the forts in the very grond we walked over was planted with hundreds of torpedoes & it was a wonder that hundreds of men had not been killed, the reason is the caps over the tops put there to protect them had not been removed." Morgan, "Diary," pt. 2, 587.

CHAPTER TWENTY: HITHER AND THITHER

1. The 33d Iowa moved up a hill near its division headquarters at noon on April 9 to draw four days' rations. By 1:00 P.M., the regiment was on the march toward Fort Blakely,

another huge earthwork installation guarding the Mobile area's eastern shore. Blakely was only five miles away from Spanish Fort, but because Minette Bay lay between the two strongholds, Canby's troops faced a march of more than ten miles. Morgan, "Diary," pt. 2, 587; Hearn, *Mobile Bay*, 150, 178–79; *OR Supplement*, pt. 2, vol. 20, serial no. 32, p. 794.

2. As Lt. John Morgan of Company G revealed, the news of Fort Blakely's fall reached the 33d Iowa in a dramatic fashion: "in the evening we are on a forced march for some purpose, as we near Blakely meet some soldiers who say, you need not run yourselves to death for Blakely is ours." Morgan, "Diary," pt. 2, 587.

3. Late on the afternoon of April 9, the four infantry divisions under General Steele stormed Fort Blakely. Confronted by 16,000 Federals in thirty-five regiments attacking along a three-mile line, Blakely's defenders were quickly overrun. The victorious Federals snapped up 3,700 prisoners, including 3 generals and 197 commissioned officers. It was widely reported in Canby's army that the assault was precipitated by Steele's black regiments. "The negro troops got impatient and charged on the Fort and took it before we got there," explained Cpl. John Shepherd of the 33d Iowa. "[W]e got close enough to hear them." Shepherd, "Autobiography," 52; Hearn, *Mobile Bay*, 192–200; Joseph T. Glatthaar, *Forged in Battle: The Civil War Alliance of Black Solders and White Officers* (New York: Free Press, 1990), 167–68.

4. The day after Fort Blakely's fall was actually April 10.

5. Lieutenant Morgan offered another reason for the hostility that the black soldiers exhibited toward their captives: "The negros in the charge are said to have taken few prisoners on account of one of their men having been shot who was captured, (this is all rumor)." A white officer in one of Steele's USCT regiments confirmed the rumor: "the niggers did not take a prisoner, they killed all they took to a man." W. R. Murphy, a Mississippi artilleryman captured in the assault, testified that afterwards he and his comrades were "guarded by a 'nigger' company, who told us they would have killed us. They also told us that they did not think we would be alive on the morrow." Morgan, "Diary," pt. 2, 588; Glatthaar, *Forged in Battle*, 158; Yeary, ed., *Reminiscences*, 555.

6. The landward defenses of Fort Blakely ran in a semicircular line three miles long. Like Spanish Fort, they consisted of breastworks, redoubts, and rifle pits, screened by slashed tree limbs, abatis, and mine fields. The town of Blakely lay a mile behind the fortification on the Apalachee River directly opposite where that stream joined the Tensas River. Mobile sat ten miles distant to the southwest. Hearn, *Mobile Bay*, 178–79; Morgan, "Diary," pt. 2, 588.

7. Only about one hundred people lived in the little town of Blakely on the eve of the Mobile campaign. Hearn, *Mobile Bay*, 178.

8. Actually, the 33d Iowa heard of Richmond's fall soon after it began marching toward Fort Blakely early in the afternoon of April 9. "We had gone about a mile," related Lieutenant Morgan, "Lt. Rice rides up & tells us the news . . . that Petersburg & Richmond is evacuated & Lee fallen back to Lynchburgh." Morgan, "Diary," pt. 2, 587.

9. On April 11, Lieutenant Morgan recorded: "At 1 P.M. rumors in camp are that Genl Lee has proposed to Genl Grant to surrender the whole so called Southern confederacy with but one condition which is free pardon to all." Morgan, "Diary," pt. 2, 589.

10. With the capture of Fort Blakely, half of the Confederate troops assigned to defend Mobile fell into Union hands. Recognizing the inevitable, Maj. Gen. Dabney H. Maury directed his remaining forces to evacuate the city, which was accomplished mainly on April 10 and 11. Maury himself left Mobile on the morning of the twelfth with a rear guard of three hundred Louisianans. Arthur W. Bergeron Jr., *Confederate Mobile* (Jackson: University Press of Mississippi, 1991), 189–91; Hearn, *Mobile Bay*, 201.

11. Colonel Krez did admit that his brigade made "a most fatiguing night march" which stretched into the early hours of April 12. *OR*, ser. 1, vol. 49, pt. 1, p. 228.

12. A Gulf steamer formerly known as the *Creole*, the *General Banks* was a sidewheeler

rated at 248 tons. The Union army's Quartermaster Department purchased it at New Orleans on December 31, 1863, for forty thousand dollars. Krez's brigade was the last element from Benton's 3d Division to embark at Starke's Landing, and the 33d Iowa was the third and last of Krez's regiments to get aboard ship. The 27th Wisconsin, the fourth regiment in Krez's brigade, had to be left behind for lack of transport. Gibson and Gibson, *Dictionary of Transports*, 124; *OR*, ser. 1, vol. 49, pt. 1, p. 228; Morgan, "Diary," pt. 2, 589.

13. Lieutenant Morgan counted "6 musketo gunboats & about as many transports," plus two larger "men of war" in the flotilla that carried the 1st and 3d Divisions of the XIII Army Corps across Mobile Bay. The ironclad *Cincinnati* was equipped with one of these "torpedo rakes," and it led the way toward the western shore. Morgan, "Diary," pt. 2, 589.

14. According to Lieutenant Morgan, that single cannon shot elicited an immediate nonviolent response: "A man of war run up close & lifted a shell over which . . . caused a display of white rags at every house along the landing. A boat was sent ashore which brought back word that there was no enemy in Mobile & the Mayor would surrender the city at the approach of our army." Morgan, "Diary," pt. 2, 589.

15. Henry Knox Thatcher (1806–1880) was a native of Maine and a grandson of Henry Knox, George Washington's artillery commander in the Revolutionary War and America's first secretary of war. Thatcher attended the U.S. Military Academy for a few months, but then joined the U.S. navy as a midshipman in 1823. He saw the world on a variety of ships and was promoted to lieutenant in 1833, commander in 1855, and commodore in 1862. During the Civil War, he helped protect Union commerce in the Mediterranean and saw a lot of blockade duty. In January 1865, he was appointed acting rear admiral and given command of the West Gulf Blockading Squadron. Thatcher's flagship for the Mobile campaign was the sidewheel steamer *Stockdale*. Clark G. Reynolds, *Famous American Admirals* (New York: Van Nostrand Reinhold, 1978), 354–55.

16. Lieutenant Morgan revealed why Admiral Thatcher was so eager to shell Mobile: "I hear the navy feel very soar about the little work they have done to reduce Mobile." Morgan, "Diary," pt. 2, 590.

17. Despite the danger of striking a torpedo in the uncleared channel, General Granger decided to run the *General Banks* to Mobile to demand the city's unconditional surrender. Colonel Mackey wanted the 33d Iowa to remain on board to furnish the corps commander with an escort, but Granger refused the offer. "I don't want to lose the men," Lieutenant Morgan heard the general exclaim. "But if they blow me up with a torpedo they may blow and be damned." Morgan, "Diary," pt., 590; Gaston, "Diary," April 12, 1865.

18. Eager for even trivial honors, Colonel Krez reported: "Although the last to embark, the first troops of the Third Division landed below Mobile on the west side of the bay did belong to my brigade." *OR*, ser. 1, vol. 49, pt. 1, p. 228.

19. While Granger had elements of his 1st Division occupy Mobile, his 3d Division (containing the 33d Iowa) camped between two lines of fortifications about a mile or two south of the city. Here Sperry and his comrades could fully appreciate General Canby's wisdom in approaching Mobile along the eastern shore. For three years before the Yankee soldiers came, thousands of slaves had toiled to erect three defensive lines on the western shore to guard Mobile from an army advancing from the south and west. As Capt. Thomas Stevens of the 28th Wisconsin testified, the Confederate engineers and their black laborers had done their work well: "The rebel works here are quite extensive, & very strong—our line, complete in itself, is enclosed within another equally strong. Forts, bastions &c. at every angle, & scores of guns, with large quantities of ammunition are there. Many of the guns are large Caliber—several 7 inch 'Blakely' among them." Hearn, *Mobile Bay*, 48; Thomas N. Stevens to Carrie Stevens, April 15, 1865, in Blackburn, *Dear Carrie*, 311; Morgan, "Diary," pt. 2, 590; Gaston, "Diary," April 12, 1865.

20. Once the South's second-most-important cotton port, Mobile was a smaller version of

cosmopolitan New Orleans and well worth seeing. Its population stood at thirty thousand in 1860 and grew to forty-five thousand by 1865.

Pvt. James Newman of Company I was among those headstrong 33d Iowa men who defied orders and entered Mobile to trade surplus coffee and sugar for cornbread. Returning to camp sometime after 11:00 A.M., Newman and some sixty others were surprised to find that the regiment had marched away. "A sergeant was sent back who piloted us to the regiment," Newman recalled. "It was jokingly suggested all would be court martialed and shot. But a reprimand from the colonel, and a little extra duty, settled all." Richard N. Current, ed., *Encyclopedia of the Confederacy*, 4 vols. (New York: Simon & Schuster, 1993), 3:1057; Newman, *Autobiography*, 31.

21. Some companies of the 33d Iowa still had so many men absent without leave in Mobile that they were hardly bigger than squads. "The men had without leave gone to the city so that I had but 14 men when we fell in," complained Lieutenant Morgan of Company G. "[M]arched through town in platoons, colors flying music playing many remarks made by the by standers about our no's [numbers]." Morgan, "Diary," pt. 2, 591.

22. "Streets full of negros & creoles," noted Lieutenant Morgan. "[M]arched through Royal St. the whits did not show themselves much." Morgan, "Diary," pt. 2, 591.

23. Benton's 3d Division rushed to Whistler on April 13, 1865, to drive off about five hundred Confederate cavalry who had come to destroy some locomotives, cars, and other railroad facilities to deny them to the Yankees. The Confederates also set fire to a bridge over Eight Mile Creek. Thomas N. Stevens to Carrie Stevens, April 15, 1865, in Blackburn, *Dear Carrie*, 311; Morgan, "Diary," pt. 2, 591.

24. Cpl. Cyrus Gaston, Company K, 33d Iowa, heard that the three Federals supposedly killed in the skirmish at Whistler belonged to the 91st Illinois Infantry from the 3d Division's 2d Brigade. According to Col. H. M. Day, the 91st's brigade commander, that regiment actually lost one man mortally wounded and two seriously wounded. Gaston, "Diary," April 13, 1865; *OR*, ser. 1, vol. 49, pt. 1, p. 223.

25. In the Mobile campaign, which lasted close to three weeks, Canby's Union army suffered 1,508 casualties—177 killed, 1,295 wounded, and 36 captured or missing. In Granger's XIII Army Corps, the casualty total was 643, with 161 of those losses occurring in the 3d Division, which contained the 33d Iowa. Krez's 3d Brigade alone suffered 4 men dead and 2 officers and 32 other ranks wounded. The 33d Iowa's share in that tally was 2 officers and 10 men wounded. In exchange, the Federals bagged 5,000 prisoners, twelve enemy flags, nearly three hundred pieces of artillery, and vast supplies of military materiel. Hearn, *Mobile Bay*, 200–1; *OR*, ser. 1, vol. 49, pt. 1, pp. 107, 112.

Chapter Twenty-one: Up the Tom B.

1. Lieutenant Morgan agreed with Sperry about the difficulty of the march on April 19, but he thought the regiment covered a greater distance: "Div [division] on the road at 6. . . . Find the marching hard although the regiment was in the advance. We travel about 11. Miles & camp near a large & deep creek." Corporal Gaston gave the same mileage figure in his diary. Morgan, "Diary," pt. 2, 593; Gaston, "Diary," April 19, 1865.

2. As Sperry implied, the 33d Iowa marched as the 3d Division's rear guard on April 20. "[W]e left Camp about 6 A.M. & marched 15 miles," wrote Corporal Gaston. He also characterized the day's march as "very hard." Gaston, "Diary," April 20, 1865; Morgan, "Diary," pt. 2, 593.

3. Lieutenant Morgan called April 21 "an unlucky day." He awoke to "the rain pouring down & no one having breakfast, fortunately our cook had coffee." Corporal Gaston's diary

captured the regiment's glum mood: "commenced Raining at 3 o'clock A.M. & Rained all day we left Camp at 5 A.M. I didn't get any Breakfast. we waded water all day the Roads were Running full of water." Morgan, "Diary," pt. 2, 593; Gaston, "Diary," April 21, 1865.

4. On January 3, 1861, eight days before Alabama seceded, Governor Andrew B. Moore called out four companies of the 1st Alabama State Troops from Mobile to seize the federal arsenal at Mount Vernon. Lieutenant Morgan shared Sperry's enchantment with the place: "We march through the Arsenal at Mt Vernon no town 1/2 doz houses within a mile or so, some of them very fine and nice flower gardens. The Arsenal was deserted is a much finer gronds & buildings than the Little Rock Arsenal & all in good repair, is enclosed by a thick wall of Brick, 10 ft high." Bergeron, *Confederate Mobile*, 7; Morgan, "Diary," pt. 2, 593.

5. First Sgt. Ira Seeley of the 29th Iowa penned a fuller description of the Mount Vernon arsenal after his regiment and an artillery section were detached to guard the installation:

> This Arsenal is about two miles from Tombigbee River and some twenty-five miles above Mobile. It is located in an almost unbroken wilderness. It is a splendid place. Cost the government perhaps two or three million of dollars and has been built about thirty years.
>
> There is a solid brick wall, two feet thick and twelve high. Well cemented, enclosing twenty-one acres of ground on a beautiful rise or mound. Slopes every way from the center, with an observatory or look out attached which is about 75 feet in height. This building was the main machine shop, carpenter and blacksmith shops, officers houses and several buildings that I do not know the use of. Everything has been on a grand scale. There are gardens of flowers and shrub, berries and rows of beautiful trees of various kinds, principally live oak. There are some of them one foot in diameter with very thick tops making splendid shade.

Ira Seeley to "Dear Martha," April 23, 1865, in Seeley, *Civil War Letters*, 184.

6. "[B]egins to rain as hard as I ever experienced as we pass through this Arsenal," commented Lieutenant Morgan, "& keeps it up almost incessantly until 2 P.M. . . . No dry feet in this army." Morgan, "Diary," pt. 2, 593–94.

7. This spot was known as Nanna Hubba Bluffs. It sat near the junction of the Alabama and Tombigbee Rivers, thirty-five miles from Whistler's Station. *OR Supplement*, pt. 2, vol. 20, serial no. 32, pp. 791, 807.

8. Corporal Gaston revealed that the 33d Iowa was not allowed to pitch camp until 1:00 P.M., nearly two hours after it reached its campsite. Gaston, "Diary," April 21, 1865.

9. To judge from Lieutenant Morgan's diary, Sperry did not exaggerate the grief and anger that took hold of the 33d Iowa on April 23: "Lt Hook comes to the Regt with the sad intiligence of the Assassination of President Lincoln & Sec Seward which is published in the Mobile paper. The news quickly spreads & groups of men can be seen all around talking in low tones with a look of sadness never worn by them before, at 10, A.M. the Div Brass Band plays the 'dead march' & is followed by the bands of Regts in order. It is truly a solemn day & the boys one & all vow to take vengance in Southern blood, many who favored peace this morning now favor utter extermination; about noon we are greeted with the arrival of Luit Sharman. . . . he brings an extra which states that it is thought Seward is not mortally wounded & hopes of his recovery is entertained." Morgan, "Diary," pt. 2, 594.

10. The 829-ton *Octorara* (not to be confused with the 237-ton propeller steamer of the same name which served as a transport or supply ship) was a sidewheel steamer launched at the Brooklyn Navy Yard on December 7, 1861. It carried one eighty-pound rifled gun, one nine-inch smoothbore, and four twenty-four-pounders, and boasted a maximum speed of eleven knots. The *Octorara* took seventeen hits during the battle of Mobile Bay,

August 5, 1864, suffering one killed and ten wounded. *American Naval Fighting Ships*, 5: 137–38; Gibson and Gibson, *Dictionary of Transports*, 244.

11. The *Jenny Rogers*, a 346-ton sternwheel steamer, accompanied Banks's ill-fated Red River expedition in the spring of 1864 as a transport. The Quartermaster Department purchased it at New Orleans in May 1864 for twenty-three thousand dollars. Gibson and Gibson, *Dictionary of Transports*, 176.

12. McIntosh's Bluff was situated fifty miles above Mobile on the Tombigbee River. Lieutenant Morgan expanded on Sperry's description of the place in his diary: "Bluffs here are not more than 12 ft high, there are 4 dwellings, 3 families living here." Morgan also noted a building that showed signs of recent conflict: "one story & a half dwelling house through which one of the gunboats fired a shell just a week ago at a Mr Vaugn who shot at a skiff of negroes coming down to the Boat." *OR Supplement*, pt. 2, vol. 20, serial no. 32, p. 800; Morgan, "Diary," pt. 2, 595.

13. As Corporal Gaston observed, the 33d Iowa's rank and file foraged energetically upon their arrival at McIntosh's Bluff. "Disembarked & went to foraging we got pork hams Chickens." Gaston, "Diary," April 25, 1865.

14. On April 26, 1865, official word reached the 33d Iowa of the surrender of General Johnston and the Confederate Army of Tennessee to Sherman in North Carolina. For every accurate report, however, there was some outlandish rumor. On April 14, for instance, word circulated in the 33d's camp that Union troops operating further north had captured and scalped Nathan Bedford Forrest, the notorious Confederate raider. Morgan, "Diary," pt. 2, 591, 595; Gaston, "Diary," April 26, 1865.

15. Richard Taylor (1826–1879) was one of the ablest generals to hold a major Confederate command in the final year of the war. The son of President Zachary Taylor, he studied in Europe and at Harvard but graduated from Yale in 1845. He accompanied his father for a while as a military secretary in the Mexican War and became a prosperous sugar planter in Louisiana in the 1850s. He also held a seat in the state senate from 1856 to 1861. Taylor entered the Civil War as the colonel of the 9th Louisiana Infantry and fought at First Bull Run. Promoted to brigadier general on October 21, 1861, and major general on July 28, 1862, he served under Stonewall Jackson in the Shenandoah Valley and the Seven Days' battles. In August 1862, he returned to his home state to take charge of the District of Western Louisiana, where he was expected to handle a multitude of challenges with precious few resources. Nevertheless, Taylor proved his military genius by engineering the defeat of Banks's Red River expedition. He was cheated of the pleasure of totally destroying his adversary's army by Kirby Smith, who insisted on marching north with Taylor's infantry divisions to attack Frederick Steele at Camden, Arkansas. Strangely, Kirby Smith promoted the infuriated Taylor to lieutenant general on April 16, 1864. Jefferson Davis confirmed Kirby Smith's unofficial order on July 18, and also named Taylor to command the Department of Alabama, Mississippi, and Eastern Louisiana. After the fall of Mobile, Taylor and General Canby agreed to a truce on April 29, 1865. Taylor met with Canby on May 4 at Citronelle, forty miles from Mobile, and formally surrendered all the troops in his department. Emulating Ulysses S. Grant, Canby granted the defeated generous terms. Warner, *Generals in Gray*, 299–300; Parrish, *Richard Taylor*, 10, 15–18, 33–47, 69–442.

16. Sometime that evening, Lieutenant Sharman, the 33d Iowa's adjutant since February 10, 1865, made the following announcement: "The dispatch is just received from General Canby announcing the surrender of General Taylor and all his forces, and that our men should respect him and his officers en route to Mobile." "[A]s this order is published," reported Lieutenant Morgan, "cheer after cheer rends the air." Morgan, "Diary," pt. 2, 573, 596.

17. Flag Officer Ebenezer Farrand led his small Confederate naval squadron to tempo-

rary safety up the Tombigbee River when the Confederate army evacuated Mobile. Farrand's convoy consisted of the gunboats *Nashville*, *Morgan*, and *Baltic*, and the steamers *Black Diamond* and *Southern Republic*. He was accompanied upriver by four former blockade runners, the *Virgin*, *Red Gauntlet*, *Mary*, and *Heroine*, as well as some other vessels. Bergeron, *Confederate Mobile*, 190; Morgan, "Diary," pt. 2, 599.

18. Lieutenant Morgan identified that steamer as the *Crawford*. Morgan, "Diary," pt. 2, 598.

19. It was at around 8:30 A.M. that Lieutenant Morgan heard a boat whistle, followed soon by cheering from the landing that announced that word of Farrand's surrender had reached McIntosh's Bluff. Later that day, he scribbled, "Every one is in high spirits & the opinion is 4 to 1 that we celebrate the 4th of July at home." Morgan, "Diary," pt. 2, 598.

20. At least five different ships were named for the first and last president of the Confederacy. This one was a steamer that had a Union shell burst in its cabin while attempting to support the garrison of Spanish Fort. Morgan, "Diary," pt. 2, 599; Tony Gibbons, *Warships and Naval Battles of the Civil War* (New York: Gallery Books, 1989), 172.

21. Ebenezer Farrand (1803–1873) was a native New Yorker who considered Florida his home state. He became a midshipman in the U.S. navy in 1823. He had worked his way up to commander, when he resigned on January 21, 1861, to cast his lot with the seceding states. Farrand spent much of his career with the Confederate navy ashore supervising shipbuilding activities and shore defenses. Promoted to captain on January 7, 1864, he assumed command of what remained of the Rebel squadron at Mobile after the battle of Mobile Bay. Current, *Encyclopedia of the Confederacy*, 2:567–68; Bergeron, *Confederate Mobile*, 153.

22. Confederate naval officers wore double-breasted frock coats made of steel gray wool. They displayed their rank on gold-bordered shoulder straps and stripes of gold lace on their cuffs. Philip Katcher, *American Civil War Armies (3): Staff, Specialist and Maritime Services* (London: Osprey, 1986), 24, 31, 33–34.

23. This Latin phrase could be translated as "aborted."

24. This wood detail was formed on May 6, soon after the word of Farrand's surrender reached McIntosh's Bluff. "The details at work on the fort have been set to chopping wood for the fleet," testified Lieutenant Morgan. "This Div is ordered to Mobile on the said fleet." Morgan, "Diary," pt. 2, 598.

25. The 33d Iowa spent much of May 8 carrying fuel aboard the *Jeff Davis*, *Magnolia*, and another ship. Morgan, "Diary," pt. 2, 599.

26. Sperry mistook the date. The 33d Iowa embarked on May 9.

27. Companies G, B, and K of the 33d Iowa embarked on the *Robert Watson*, a sternwheel steamer. Morgan, "Diary," pt. 2, 599–600.

Chapter Twenty-two: Delay and Disappointment

1. Lieutenant Morgan reported that the 33d Iowa disembarked at Mobile at 8:30 P.M. and reached camp at 10:00 P.M. Corporal Gaston revealed that the route of the regiment's moonlight march led up the Mobile and Ohio Railroad. Morgan, "Diary," pt. 2, 600; Gaston, "Diary," May 9, 1865.

2. On May 10, Lieutenant Morgan confided to his diary: "news here that Kirby Smith tells his men by a proclamation that he intend to fight." Morgan, "Diary," pt. 2, 600.

3. Lieutenant Morgan made such a trip to Mobile on May 15, but his return to camp was far from pleasurable: "I go to the pier at the river & take a canoe & am rowed to the city

by '99' in the short space of 43 minutes, find the town crowded with Jonnies, plenty of stores open but no stock on yet. . . . I remained but about 3/4 hour, going back to find our canoe it was gone, & I had to foot it to camp 3 1/2 miles which I found no fun . . . especially as the sun was most unsparingly liberal with its heated rays." Morgan, "Diary," pt. 2, 602.

4. Lieutenant Morgan also noted an unrepentant streak among many of the paroled Confederate soldiers crowding the streets of Mobile. On May 13, he confided to his diary: "Yesterday at the dinner table at the Battle House it so happened that a federal officer sat between two confed officers, pie was placed on the table on plates one to each man, one of the Jonnies . . . having eaten all on his plate spoke to the other, 'If you are not going to eat all your pie pass it to me.' The other Mr. Johnnie . . . instead of handing his own pie handed that of the Federal officer, who said not a word at the table of the insult, but dinner over as the Co. was going down stairs the federal officer struck the Reb a blow that laid him out in a state 'Hors du combat,' I guess the Jonnies will learn that the Yankees know which party holds the highest cards. The excellent treatment they receive makes them bold & insolent." First Sgt. Ira Seeley of the 29th Iowa also noticed the defiant attitude of the Confederate rank and file: "I was in Mobile two days ago. . . . It is full of rebel paroled soldiers awaiting transportation to their homes. Most of them seem to be glad their hardships are over, but some of them look wicked as tigers and are doubtless full of malice and will vent it on union men wherever an opportunity occurs. . . . To the spirited ones, it must be very humiliating to come home and acknowledge themselves whipped." Morgan, "Diary," pt. 2, 601; Ira Seeley to "Dear Martha," May 13, 1865, in Seeley, *Civil War Letters*, 193.

5. Chuck-a-luck was a dice game. David Dary, *Cowboy Culture: A Saga of Five Centuries* (New York: Avon Books, 1982), 214.

6. Among the good news was the capture of Jefferson Davis, word of which first reached the 33d Iowa at 8:00 P.M., May 16. Morgan, "Diary," pt. 2, 602.

7. The 29th Iowa Infantry, which had soldiered alongside the 33d Iowa for two years, also faced the prospect of going to Texas, prompting Sergeant Seeley to write his wife: "I have just learned that we are expected to go to Galveston, Texas, no matter whether Kirby Smith surrenders or not. That place to be garrisoned by the nearest troops and we are the ones." Ira Seeley to "Dear Martha," May 19, 1865, in Seeley, *Civil War Letters*, 195.

8. Cpl. Cyrus Gaston of Company K was in the 33d Iowa's camp at the time of this spectacular disaster, and he excitedly recorded his impressions: "at a quarter past 3 P.M. to day there was Magazine Exploded Down in Town the concusion was very heavy to here 3 1/2 miles Nearly every window [and street] light in Town is Jarred out & there is a good many Killed and wounded there was Some two or three Boats burst & the fire continues to burn & the Shells have been bursting ever Since the first Explosion & Still continues at 8 P.M." "The shock was like an earthquake," recalled Pvt. James Newman of Company I, "windows in the city were broken, shells exploding sent their fragments out in the bay." The initial estimate of human casualties ran to one thousand, with three hundred of that total dead soldiers and civilians. Property damage amounted to approximately $10 million, including three steamers, some railroad locomotives and cars, and eight thousand bales of cotton either burned to ashes or blown to bits. The blast also leveled eight city blocks containing mostly warehouses. As soon as it was safe to do so, men from the 33d Iowa and other Union regiments visited the disaster site to survey the carnage. "I went down the next day," recounted Cpl. John Shepherd of Company I, "and the sight beggared description a Street full of dead Mules dead men here and there, about ten acres of the City was torn to Splinters." "We never knew how many lives were lost by the explosion," added Private Newman. "Legs and arms were found in the ruins." Gaston, "Diary," May 25, 26, 1865; Morgan, "Diary." pt. 2, 603; Newman, *Autobiography*, 32; Shepherd, "Autobiography," 53.

9. "At 11. A.M.," reported Lieutenant Morgan, "Lt Cooper rode along line of [our]

Brig[ade] announcing the surrender of Kirby Smith, Men cheered lustily & fired a no of mines &c." Morgan, "Diary," pt. 2, 604.

10. On May 29, the officers of the 33d Iowa received an indication that their regiment was likely to see service in Texas: "an order from War Dept is Recd to muster out Regt. in the Field," wrote a disappointed Lieutenant Morgan. "Genl Steel assigned to an important comd in Texas 6000 men from this Div to go with him." Morgan, "Diary," pt. 2, 604.

11. Benton's 3d Division received these embarkation orders on May 31:

> Brigade commanders will immediately embark their respective brigades on the boats set opposite the regiments. The regiments not mentioned will remain until other boats arrive. Ten days' forage, ten days' rations, and 100 rounds of ammunition to the man will be taken with each regiment. The regimental teams will be taken on the boats with their commands, viz: Seventh Vermont Veteran Infantry, steamer Sedgwick; 300 men, headquarters, and teams of the Twenty-ninth Iowa, steamer Magenta; the remainder of Twenty-ninth Iowa, Belvidere; Thirty-fifth Wisconsin Infantry, Belvidere; Twenty-eighth Wisconsin Infantry and Thirty-third Iowa Infantry, steamer Continental; brigade headquarters Third Brigade, Continental.

OR, ser. 1, vol. 49, pt. 2, p. 942.

12. The 33d Iowa actually spent the entire night of May 31–June 1, on the wharf at Mobile waiting for a steamer to lighter it out to the *Continental*. Morgan, "Diary," pt. 2, 604; Gaston, "Diary," June 1, 1865.

13. The *Continental* was a 1,623-ton screw steamer, and its size and draft complicated the 33d Iowa's departure from Mobile. At 8:00 A.M., June 1, the regiment had to board a 326-ton sidewheel steamer called the *Peerless* and be lightered fifteen miles to the *Continental*, which was stuck in a sandbar in fourteen feet of water. The *Peerless* did not shove off until 10:00 A.M., and arrived alongside the *Continental* at noon. When the *Peerless* and another lighter, the *Iberville*, failed to budge the *Continental*, it was decided to wait for high tide. In the meantime, the *Peerless* carried the regiment down to Fort Morgan, where the 33d Iowa disembarked. The *Continental* finally pulled free at noon on June 2. It immediately steamed to Fort Morgan, where the 33d Iowa came aboard at 2:00 P.M. The *Continental*, in convoy with the *Magenta* and *Belvidere*, exited Mobile Bay at noon on June 3. Gibson and Gibson, *Dictionary of Transports*, 70, 252; *OR*, ser. 1, vol. 49, pt. 2, p. 942; Morgan, "Diary," pt. 2, 604; Gaston, "Diary," June 1, 2, 3, 1865; Thomas N. Stevens to Carrie Stevens, June 1, 1865, in Blackburn, *Dear Carrie*, 324.

14. Rough weather on the evening of June 5 produced an outbreak of seasickness among the *Continental*'s passengers. "The day before we landed . . . there came up a Storm," reminisced Corporal Shepherd, "and I as well as the rest got awful Sea Sick. it Seemed I couldent vomit until I got in the Bough of the Ship then I cast up Jonah I was Sick four days after I got to shore." Shepherd, "Autobiography," 54.

15. Corporal Gaston described the routine instituted on the 33d Iowa's first day at sea: "we had a Canteen full of Water issued to us to day to do us 24 hours we had coffee & meat twice a day cooked for the Regt in large casks we turned our arms & accoutrements over to day & they were Stored away in the Hold we run at the rate of 10 1/2 knots per hour." Gaston, "Diary," June 3, 1865.

16. The *Continental* arrived off Brazos de Santiago Island at 6:00 A.M. on June 6. Capt. Thomas Stevens of the 28th Wisconsin, who also left Mobile on the *Continental*, specified the location of his new post in a letter to his wife. "This point is about 7 miles from the Mouth of the Rio Grande river, at the south end of Padre Island." Gaston, "Diary," June 6, 1865. Thomas N. Stevens to Carrie Stevens, June 9, 1865, in Blackburn, *Dear Carrie*, 325.

17. "[W]e couldent land," complained Corporal Gaston, "for our Boat Drew 16 ft of

water." As Private Newman discovered, boarding a lighter in rough seas was a death-defying feat: "The ship's anchor is dropped, and we are conveyed to shore by a small boat carrying two companies at each trip. Getting from the ship to the boat was much like getting on an elevator as it passed up and down without stopping. One had to jump at the opportune time with knapsack and haversack, until all were piled promiscuously together." Gaston, "Diary," June 6, 1865; Newman, *Autobiography*, 33.

18. Corporal Gaston of Company K was on the lighter during this brush with disaster, and he was fully aware of his danger: "we Disembarked at 5 P.M. we got on the U.S. G.M.D. Hancock & started to shore & we run aground & come very near Shiprecking us She Danced on the Bottom for Some time before we got off the Breaker Rolled over her Deck & Splashed up on the Boiler Deck the Boat crew pulled their Boots for aswimming went back & tried it again & got through." Gaston, "Diary," June 6, 1865.

CHAPTER TWENTY-THREE: THE HOUR IS ALWAYS DARKEST THAT IS JUST BEFORE DAY

1. "[O]f all the places I ever saw," Sgt. Charles Musser of the 29th Iowa wrote of Brazos de Santiago Island, "this is the most detestable and lonely looking. ther is scarcely an herb to be seen on the Island and not a drop of water to drink, only that which is purified and made fresh by Machinery on the Island." Charles O. Musser to "Dear Father," June 9, 1865, in Popchock, *Soldier Boy*, 211.

2. Between February 3 and March 28, 1846, Brig. Gen. Zachary Taylor moved his 3,900-man Army of Occupation to a point on the north bank of the Rio Grande opposite Matamoros. This abrupt seizure of Mexican territory set off the Mexican War. The Mexican government concentrated an army of 5,000 men at Matamoros, which crossed the Rio Grande at the end of April. On May 8, 1846, Taylor led 2,200 of his effectives against 3,709 Mexican troops at Palo Alto. The Mexicans withdrew after suffering 257 casualties to Taylor's 55. The next day, Taylor found the Mexicans deployed in a dried-out riverbed called Resaca de la Palma and attacked them head-on with his infantry. American bayonets and impetuosity carried the day, inflicting 515 losses on the Mexicans and capturing eight guns. Taylor's army suffered 33 killed and 89 wounded. These two lop-sided victories made Taylor a national hero and assured his elevation to the White House two years later. Urwin, *United States Infantry*, 66–69.

3. With the end of the Civil War, General Grant sent his trusted subordinate, Maj. Gen. Philip H. Sheridan, to Texas with fifty-two thousand veteran Union troops. The ostensible purpose of this army was to force the surrender of Kirby Smith and the restoration of Union authority in Texas, but Grant's real concern was Mexico. Like many other Northerners, Grant was infuriated when Napoleon III of France took advantage of the Civil War to flout the Monroe Doctrine, invade Mexico, and establish a puppet government under the Austrian archduke Maximilian. Grant hoped that Sheridan might provoke a war with the forces of Emperor Maximilian and then assist the republicans under Benito Juarez in liberating their country. In accordance with Grant's instructions to "place a strong force on the Rio Grande," General Steele was given a division's worth of troops and sent to Brazos de Santiago Island. Fortunately for the men of the 33d Iowa, Secretary of State William H. Seward insisted that Sheridan behave in a moderate fashion, and American forces avoided direct intervention in Mexico's struggle. Paul Andrew Hutton, *Phil Sheridan and His Army* (Lincoln: University of Nebraska Press, 1985), 20–21; John M. Taylor, *William Henry Seward: Lincoln's Right Hand* (New York: HarperCollins, 1991), 228–30, 251–53; Philip H. Sheridan, *Personal Memoirs of P. H. Sheridan*, 2 vols. (New York: Charles L. Webster & Co., 1888), 2:206–28.

4. On June 12, 1865, Lieutenant Morgan of Company G noted in his diary that he had seen "a young shark" off Brazos de Santiago Island. Morgan, "Diary," pt. 2, 605.

5. The regiment in question may have been the 62d U.S. Colored Infantry, originally organized on March 11, 1864, as the 1st Missouri Colored Infantry. It was sent to Brazos de Santiago in September 1864, and 250 of its men fought in the last battle of the Civil War, at White's Ranch on May 13, 1865. Dyer, *Compendium*, 1:250; Dyer *Compendium*, 2:1733; *OR*, ser. 1, vol. 48, pt. 1, pp. 265–69.

6. Of the water available from the distillation plant, Sergeant Musser commented: "and such water it is: filthy, warm, and not fit to wash with, but it is the best we can do, for ther is no water nearer than 10 miles that is fit to drink." Charles O. Musser to "Dear Father," June 9, 1865, in Popchock, *Soldier Boy*, 211.

7. Capt. Thomas Stevens of the 28th Wisconsin Infantry complained of the inadequacy of this gallon-a-day water ration: "I hope we will soon go where we can get plenty of water, so that we can cook & wash all we want to—it will be a luxury." Thomas N. Stevens to Carrie Stevens, June 9, 1865, in Blackburn, *Dear Carrie*, 325–26.

8. The 33d Iowa actually made this move on June 13, and the officers in charge had the sense to march the men in the cool of the early morning. "[W]e had Roll-Call at 3 A.M.," Cpl. Cyrus Gaston of Company K jotted in his diary, "& a little after Sunrise we fell in line & marched Down the Beach 9 miles to Clarksville on the Rio Grand River." "Pleasant wind," added Lieutenant Morgan, "good traveling, reach Clarksville at 8.30." Gaston, "Diary," June 13, 1865; Morgan, "Diary," pt. 2, 605.

9. Lieutenant Morgan supported Sperry's opinion: "the Riogrande is narrow swift and so muddy cant wash in it." Morgan, "Diary," pt. 2, 605.

10. This was how Pvt. James A. Newman, Company I, 33d Iowa, remembered Bagdad: "One narrow street paralleled the river, with low adobe houses on either side where all manner of tropical fruit and merchandise were exhibited for sale. A few dirty, half-clad men, who we were told were soldiers, paroled the streets with old muskets." Captain Stevens offered his wife an equally unflattering portrait of the town: "Bagdad is a small, dirty little place, built up almost entirely during the rebellion, by the illicit trade with the rebels." Newman, *Autobiography*, 33; Thomas N. Stevens to Carrie Stevens, June 12, 1865, in Blackburn, *Dear Carrie*, 327.

11. The officers of Steele's division wasted no time in frequenting Bagdad's fleshpots. On June 13, the same day the 33d Iowa reached Clarksville, Corporal Gaston confided to his diary: "there was a good many Officer & Sailors from the command went over the River & Came Back Drunk." The enlisted men followed their superiors down the paths of vice at the earliest opportunity. "Visit the Mexican side," Lieutenant Morgan reported on July 14. "About 300 of our soldiers over. Many drunk, drink & everything else cheap." For those not inclined to such pursuits, Bagdad had little to offer. "I was over at Bagdad again yesterday," Captain Stevens informed his wife, "but there is nothing scarcely there to interest one, unless he is a billiard player or a gambler." Gaston, "Diary," June 13, 1865; Morgan, "Diary," pt. 2, 605; Thomas N. Stevens to Carrie Stevens, June 21, 1865, in Blackburn, *Dear Carrie*, 329.

12. "Clarksville is a place—no, *a spot*—immediately opposite Bagdad, Mexico," observed Captain Stevens. "It contains, at present, some half a dozen buildings, such as they are. It had been something more of a settlement, but the buildings have either been removed or destroyed." Thomas N. Stevens to Carrie Stevens, June 21, 1865, in Blackburn, *Dear Carrie*, 327–28.

13. "While up on the Riogrande," recalled Cpl. John Shepherd of Company I, "the Sun was so hot we could hardly Stand it." Captain Stevens captured the desperation of the troops at Clarksville in a letter home: "My mind seems to-day as desolate, and my thoughts as barren of sense, as are the sand banks on which we at present *exist*—not live—of vegetation. Since we came here we have had a sun, burning hot, shining brightly down on us

day after day—and oh, how hot it would be all the time were it not for the sea-breeze which just renders the heat endurable. We have nothing going on to relieve the monotony." Shepherd, "Autobiography," 54; Thomas N. Stevens to Carrie Stevens, June 21, 1865, in Blackburn, *Dear Carrie*, 329.

14. This flotilla of French warships—a response to the American show of force along the Rio Grande—appeared off Clarksville on June 20, 1865. The French displayed their firepower by firing "salutes" on June 20, 21, 22, and 24. Gaston, "Diary," June 20–22, 24, 1865.

15. Private Newman, for one, entertained himself by touring Zachary Taylor's old battlefields, "where rusty cannon balls and other evidences of war were seen." On June 24, Corporal Gaston went upstream to hunt wolves. Newman, *Autobiography*, 33; Gaston, "Diary," June 24, 1865.

16. Some of Sperry's comrades wore out their welcome in Bagdad by getting drunk and attacking Mexican soldiers and policemen. On June 14, Mexican authorities declared Bagdad off limits to American enlisted men, although officers were still permitted to enter the town if in uniform. After that, Mexican merchants would cross the Rio Grande to sell their wares to the banned troops. Gaston, "Diary," June 14, 15, 1865; Thomas N. Stevens to Carrie Stevens, June 15, 1865, in Blackburn, *Dear Carrie*, 328.

17. Godfrey Weitzel (1835–1884) was born in Cincinnati, Ohio, and graduated from West Point in 1855. He served four years in the Engineer Corps and then taught two years at the Military Academy. Weitzel went to New Orleans in 1862 as the chief engineer of the notorious political general, Benjamin F. Butler, who made him second-in-command of the Union occupation forces. Weitzel was elevated to brigadier general on August 29, 1862. He commanded a division in Nathaniel Banks's 1863 siege of Port Hudson and then transferred to Virginia to serve Butler again as the chief engineer of the Army of the James. By November 17, 1864, he was a major general. During the Appomattox campaign, he commanded the all-black XXV Army Corps, which performed with great élan. Within weeks of Lee's surrender, Gen. Henry Halleck, the newly appointed commander of the Department of Virginia, assigned every black unit in his jurisdiction to Weitzel's corps, which he shipped to Texas. Warner, *Generals in Blue*, 548–49; Glatthaar, *Forged in Battle,* 218–20; *OR*, ser. 1, vol. 46, pt. 3, pp. 990, 1062.

18. This order was brought to the 33d Iowa by the steamer *Heroine*, which then proceeded up the Rio Grande to carry Generals Sheridan, Steele, Weitzel, and Granger to Brownsville. Morgan, "Diary," pt. 2, 606; Gaston, "Diary," June 24, 1865.

19. With a slight trace of envy, Captain Stevens of the 28th Wisconsin wrote of the 33d's good fortune: "The 33d Iowa which was mustered in Oct. 1st 1862, twelve days before we were, is instructed to get their Muster-out rolls ready. Am glad *they* can go home, if *we* cannot." Thomas N. Stevens to Carrie Stevens, June 25, 1865, in Blackburn, *Dear Carrie*, 332.

20. The *Louise* was a sidewheel steamer of 1,351 tons. It helped supply Sherman's army after the fall of Savannah, Georgia, and afterwards during Sherman's Carolinas campaign. *Louise* may not have been the name of the ship the 33d Iowa used as a lighter to reach the *Warrior*, as it was nearly as big as the latter. Lieutenant Morgan and Corporal Gaston called the vessel the *Louisa*, and Corporal Gaston called it both *Louisa* and *Louise*. *Louisa* was the nickname for three other vessels operated by the Union army—the *Maria Louisa*, the *Mary Louisa*, and the *Sarah Louisa*. There was also a steamer named the *Louisa Moore*, not to mention the schooners *Louisa*, *Louisa Crockett*, *Louisa Fraser*, *Louisa Reeves*, and *Louisa Spanier*. Gibson and Gibson, *Dictionary of Transports*, 204.

21. Lieutenant Morgan claimed that the 33d Iowa embarked on the *Louise* at 9:00 A.M., and Corporal Gaston thought the time was 10:00 A.M. Both agreed with Sperry on the reason why the regiment did not transfer to the *Warrior*. "[T]he Sea was so Rough we Couldent lay within 50 yds of the Warrior," stated Corporal Gaston. Morgan, "Diary," pt. 2, 606–7; Gaston, "Diary," June 28, 1865.

22. "Last night a little rain a great deal of wind & sand," Lieutenant Morgan scratched on June 29. "Wait all day wind still up." Morgan, "Diary," pt. 2, 607.

23. It was still raining when the 33d Iowa embarked on the *Louise* at 9:00 or 10:00 A.M. on July 1. "Ship rools much," Lieutenant Morgan observed. Morgan, "Diary," pt. 2, 607; Gaston, "Diary," July 1, 1865.

24. The fifteen-hundred-ton *Warrior* was a sidewheeler which had been used to transport horses to Texas for Sheridan's army. Gibson and Gibson, *Dictionary of Transports*, 332.

25. Sperry did not exaggerate when he said that boarding the *Warrior* was dangerous. "[T]he Gulg [Gulf] was very Rough," remarked Corporal Gaston. "I lost my Gun overboard." Gaston, "Diary," July 1, 1865.

26. Galveston was the second-largest city in Texas in 1860, with a population of 7,307, including 2,688 European immigrants, 1,178 slaves, and two free blacks. During the war, the city was a haven for blockade runners, but some merchants and many of the better citizens relocated to Houston to avoid the threat of Union attack.

Corporal Gaston enjoyed the brief time he spent at Galveston. "I had all the water mellon I could for 75 [cents] apiece," he boasted. "I Bought a Mellon to take along with me to eat while out on the Gulf." Lieutenant Morgan mentioned nothing about watermelons in his diary, but penned these impressions of the city: "business part of town dead. Suburbs beautiful, fine residences, with shade trees & flowers in profusion." Current, *Encyclopedia of the Confederacy*, 2:655; Gaston, "Diary," July 3, 1865; Morgan, "Diary," pt. 2, 607.

27. The *Webb* was a sidewheel tug of 655 tons. Its armament consisted of one 130-pound rifle and two 12-pound howitzers. It was run ashore and torched below New Orleans on April 24, 1865, after a hopeless race from the Red River. Gibbons, *Warships and Naval Battles*, 175.

28. According to Lieutenant Morgan, the 33d Iowa reached New Orleans at 1:00 P.M., July 6. That same day, General Sheridan's headquarters issued the following orders: "The Thirty-third Iowa Volunteers is hereby transferred from the Thirteenth Army Corps to the Department of the Gulf. The commanding officer will report without delay to Major-General Canby for orders." Morgan, "Diary," pt. 2, 607; *OR*, ser. 1, vol. 48, pt. 2, p. 1054.

29. Private Newman called the Alabama Cotton Press "a huge structure, with plenty of water for all purposes. Large box tanks furnished good bathing facilities, which we did not fail to use." Newman, *Autobiography*, 35.

30. The 33d Iowa received the unwelcome orders to transfer its "recruits" to the 34th Iowa on July 8. Five days later, these men left at noon for Houston, Texas, to join their new command. The 34th Iowa Infantry Regiment was mustered in at Burlington on October 15, 1862. It took part in the assault on Arkansas Post, the Vicksburg campaign, the Red River campaign, and supported the Union navy during the opening of Mobile Bay. It mustered out on August 15, 1865. Morgan, "Diary," pt. 2, 607–8; Dyer, *Compendium*, 2:1179.

31. Four hundred and thirty officers and men of the 33d Iowa were mustered out at New Orleans on July 17. Morgan, "Diary," pt. 2, 608; *History of Mahaska County*, 414; Shepherd, "Autobiography," 55.

32. The date given here is erroneous. The 33d Iowa departed New Orleans for the last time on Tuesday, July 18, 1865. The *Sunny South* was a 320-ton sidewheel steamer chartered repeatedly by the Union army since the spring of 1862. It was also a veteran of the Yazoo Pass expedition. Morgan, "Diary," pt. 2, 608; Gibson and Gibson, *Dictionary of Transports*, 305.

CHAPTER TWENTY-FOUR: HOME AGAIN

1. An entry in Lieutenant John Morgan's diary dated July 19 reflected his impatience with the *Sunny South*'s modest speed. "Lockport passes us at 9 P.M. with 19th Iowa, several boats pass us we are on a very slow tub." Morgan, "Diary," pt. 2, 608.

2. Natchez was the largest town in Mississippi before the Civil War. It escaped signifi-cant damage by meekly surrendering to the Federals without a fight in 1863. Occupation authorities ruled Natchez in an enlightened fashion, improving sanitation and street light-ing, paying off outstanding public debts, and leaving the city treasury with a balance of $8,501 in May 1865. William C. Harris, *Presidential Reconstruction in Mississippi* (Baton Rouge: Louisiana State University Press, 1967), 20, 62.

3. Despite Sperry's flippant tone, the situation on the *Sunny South* was no laughing matter. "[B]oat boilers in dangerous condition," Lieutenant Morgan wrote on July 20. "Enjineer & firemen run from their places last night for a while fearing an explosion, 3 of the Boilers blistered badly." Taking advantage of the delay, Morgan toured Natchez in both the morning and afternoon. He pronounced its "suburbs fine" and appreciated the many shade trees lining the streets. Morgan, "Diary," pt. 2, 608.

4. The *W. H. Osborne* was a sidewheel steamer of 1,156 tons. A pleased Lieutenant Morgan characterized it as a "large roomy boat & faster to boot." Gibson and Gibson, *Dictionary of Transports*, 329; Morgan, "Diary," pt. 2, 608.

5. Lieutenant Morgan may have referred to this baby-waving incident when he wrote in his diary on July 25: "Humorous incident, woman tossing up her baby to the boys." Morgan, "Diary," pt. 2, 609.

6. The 33d Iowa landed beside the *Muscatine*, a large steamer, at 8:00 A.M., July 27. The regiment transferred to the *Muscatine* at 9:00 A.M. "Our boat crowded," noted Lieutenant Morgan, "about 150 passengers besides the Regt." Morgan, "Diary," pt. 2, 609.

7. In addition to more than six hundred military and civilian passengers, the *Muscatine* stopped at Alton, Illinois, at 9:00 P.M., July 27, to take a barge in tow. Morgan, "Diary," pt. 2, 609.

8. Lieutenant Morgan found nothing special to remark on concerning the 33d Iowa's reception at Keokuk, but Burlington, which the *Muscatine* reached at dusk, was another matter. "[Q]uite a no of citizens at the wharf," he observed. It seems that the 18th Iowa Infantry, which had passed Burlington an hour earlier on the *Silver Wave*, warned the town's populace of the 33d's approach. Morgan, "Diary," pt. 2, 609.

9. Camp Ellsworth at Keokuk was the rendezvous for some of the first regiments that Iowa raised for the Civil War, the 1st, 2d, and 3d Iowa Infantry. On June 13, 1861, Brig. Gen. Nathaniel Lyon ordered these units into northern Missouri to protect railroad lines. Confederate troops briefly menaced Keokuk in early August 1861, but they were checked at Athens by a Union force which included some Keokuk militiamen, including one com-pany known as the Keokuk Gate City Rifles. Three more military camps were established at Keokuk, and several other Iowa regiments rendezvoused there. Steve Meyer, ed., *Iowa Valor: A Compilation of Civil War Combat Experiences from Soldiers of the State Distinguished as Most Patriotic of the Patriotic* (Garrison, Iowa: Meyer Publishing, 1994), 11, 19–24; Swisher, *Iowa in Times of War*, 132–37.

10. The island, as Sperry called it, was famed Rock Island, which sat in the Mississippi River between Davenport and Rock Island, Illinois. It stretched some three miles in length and was about half a mile wide. In 1863, Union authorities constructed a prison there to house captured Confederate soldiers. The installation was designed for a prison population of 10,000. There were eighty-four poorly ventilated and heated barracks sur-rounded by a twelve-foot-high stockade fence. A total of 12,286 Rebels were confined there, and 1,961 died of disease. The last of the prisoners left Rock Island on July 11, and the buildings were turned over to the Ordnance Department on August 7. Patricia L. Faust, ed., *Historical Times Illustrated Encyclopedia of the Civil War* (New York: Harper & Row, Publishers, 1986), 639; Swisher, *Iowa in Times of War*, 279–81.

11. Perhaps one reason why the 33d Iowa's personnel behaved so well in Davenport is that the city's vice district came to them. On August 6, a Sunday, Lieutenant Morgan confided to his diary: "Fancy women thick in the woods of the island." Morgan, "Diary," pt. 2, 610.

12. Sperry's opinion of Southern women was much more charitable than that of another Hawkeye, 1st Sgt. Ira Seeley of the 29th Iowa Infantry, who wrote from Little Rock on September 16, 1864: "There are many men here who seek out female associations, not perhaps with any bad motive in view, but simply to while away the time. But I do not care for the society of any woman except the one I love, and least of all, do I care for the society of Arkansas women. As a general rule, they are filthy and repulsive in their habits." Ira Seeley to "Dear Martha," September 16, 1864, in Seeley, *Civil War Letters*, 98.

13. Sperry may have altered the sequence of events here for a more dramatic effect. According to Lieutenant Morgan, Colonel Mackey made his "short Speech" to the 33d Iowa at 8:00 A.M., an hour before the arrival of the paymaster. Morgan added that it took only until 10:00 A.M. for his company to get paid off. Morgan, "Diary," pt. 2, 610.

14. Pvt. James Newman of Company I recalled the thoughts that filled his mind the day the 33d Iowa disbanded: "Just three years ago, lacking one day, we had enlisted to serve our country, and with some satisfaction of having filled a place in the line of the great Union hosts reaching from the Atlantic to the Pacific and driving the foe to the Gulf of Mexico—and there was no longer an armed foe to demand our service." Newman, *Autobiography*, 37.

15. Several companies of the 33d Iowa received an opportunity to reassemble less than a month after their discharge. Many of the regiment attended a grand reunion of Mahaska County's veterans, hosted by Oskaloosa on August 26, 1865. The 33d Iowa held its first three regimental reunions before 1890. The regiment's fourth reunion, which occurred at Sigourney from September 16–18, 1891, drew 266 veterans. Ninety-seven of the 33d's survivors attended the 1919 reunion in Oskaloosa. The regiment's fourteenth reunion brought 117 old soldiers to Oskaloosa in September 1923. *Mahaska County*, 448–50; Newman, *Autobiography*, 41–42, 77, 79.

16. It took Cpl. John Shepherd of Company I a little longer to reach his home in Marion County, but the delay did not diminish the sweetness of his return: "I arrived home on the morning of the 10th it being the 11th anaversary of our weding. how glad was I to meet my Wife and little ones." Shepherd, "Autobiography," 55.

BIBLIOGRAPHY

PRIMARY SOURCES

Manuscripts In Public Repositories

ARKANSAS HISTORY COMMISSION, LITTLE ROCK

John W. Brown, "Diary."
"Evolution of Arkansas Townships, 1870–1920, from U.S. Census Publications
Opening the 1920 Census." n.d.
W. L. Skaggs Collection.

EARL GREGG SWEM LIBRARY, COLLEGE OF WILLIAM AND MARY,
WILLIAMSBURG, VA.

Adee Papers.

NATIONAL ARCHIVES, WASHINGTON, D.C.

Record Group 94, Records of the Adjutant General's Office, 1780s–1917 (Military
Service Branch)
Civil War (Union) Compiled Military Service Records, 33d Iowa Infantry.
Pension Files.

OLD STATE HOUSE MUSEUM, LITTLE ROCK, ARK.

Edmund L. Joy, "Diary."

SOUTHERN HISTORICAL COLLECTION, MANUSCRIPTS DEPARTMENT,
WILSON LIBRARY, UNIVERSITY OF NORTH CAROLINA, CHAPEL
HILL, N.C.

Edmund Kirby Smith Papers.

SOUTHWEST ARKANSAS REGIONAL ARCHIVES, WASHINGTON, ARK.

Henry Merrell "Receipts" Book (Diary). Photostatic copy.
Mary Elizabeth Moore Carrigan, "Diary," SMF #479.
Artie Whiteside Vardy, "The Battle of Moscow, April 13, 1864: As It Was Told to
Me by My Grandmother, Martha Holcomb," n.d., SMF #191.

SPECIAL COLLECTIONS DIVISION, UNIVERSITY OF ARKANSAS
LIBRARIES, FAYETTEVILLE

Milton P. Chambers Papers.
Minos Miller Papers.

STATE HISTORICAL SOCIETY OF IOWA, DES MOINES

William R. Barnes Letters.

Cyrus Gaston, "Diaries."

Charles H. Lothrop, "The Fight at Marks' Mills," n.d.

Cyrus H. Mackey, "A Report of the Casualties of the 33d Iowa Infantry, in battle at Helena Arkansas on the 4th day of July A.D. 1863—Commanded by Lieut Colonel Cyrus H. Mackey," July 7, 1863.

John S. Morgan, "Journal."

Samuel A. Rice Papers.

George W. Towne Letters.

Martin A. Varner, "Diary."

TEXAS STATE ARCHIVES, AUSTIN

John Q. Anderson Collection
    Edward W. and Allie Cade Correspondence.

UALR ARCHIVES AND SPECIAL COLLECTIONS, UALR LIBRARY, UNIVERSITY OF ARKANSAS AT LITTLE ROCK

J. N. Heiskell Historical Collection
    Wiley Britton Letters.
    James A. Campbell, "Diary."

Manuscripts in Private Hands

W. C. Braly to "My Dear Ma," May 7, 1864. In the possession of Frances Thompson, Clarksville, Ark.

Thomas Pedeon Clarke, "Diary." In the possession of Richard Merritt, Little Rock, Ark.

Wilson DeGarmo, "Diary." In the possession of Larry Pearson, Anchorage, Alaska.

Allan McNeal Letters. In the possession of Larry Pearson, Anchorage, Alaska.

James Polk Roberts to S. S. Roberts, December 25, 1862. In the possession of Robert C. Burke, Altus, Okla.

John N. Shepherd, "Autobiography," Guthrie, Okla., 1908. In the possession of Richard S. Warner, Tulsa, Okla.

William M. Stafford, "Battery Journal, 1864." In the possession of M. D. Hutcheson, Camden, Ark.

James Willis, "Will of Real and Personal Estate," October 10, 1862. Photostatic copy. In the possession of Charles Swanson, Lawton, Mich.

Newspapers

Dubuque (Iowa) Daily Times.
Fort Smith (Ark.) New Era.
Keokuk (Iowa) Gate City.
Logansport (Ind.) Journal.
Little Rock Daily National Democrat.
Little Rock Unconditional Union.
Memphis Bulletin.
Memphis Daily Appeal.
National Anti-Slavery Standard.
New York Times.
Parke County (Ind.) Republican.
Putnam (Ind.) Republican Banner.
Washington (Ark.) Telegraph.

Public Documents

Hewett, Janet B., ed. *Supplement to the Official Records of the Union and Confederate Armies.* Part 2, Volume 20, Serial No. 32. Wilmington, N.C.: Broadfoot Publishing Co., 1995.

"Population Schedules the Eighth Census of the United States 1860." National Archives Microfilm Publication, Microcopy 653, Roll 53, Arkansas Slave Schedules, Volume 1 (1–404). Washington, D.C.: National Archives Records Service, General Services Administration, 1967.

U.S. War Department. *The War of the Rebellion: A Compilation of the Official Records of the Union and Confederate Armies.* 130 vols. Washington, D.C.: Government Printing Office, 1880–1901.

Books and Articles

Allen, Gerald S. "Nelson G. Thomas Civil War Documents." *Clark County Historical Journal* (Spring 1986): 80–88.

Banasik, Michael E., ed. *Missouri Brothers in Gray: The Reminiscences and Letters of William J. Bull and John P. Bull.* Iowa City: Camp Pope Bookshop, 1998.

"Benjamin Pearson's War Diary," Part 5. *Annals of Iowa* 15 (October 1926): 433–63.

Billings, John D. *Hardtack and Coffee: The Unwritten Story of Army Life.* Lincoln: University of Nebraska Press, 1993.

Blackburn, George M., ed. *"Dear Carrie. . . .": The Civil War Letters of Thomas N. Stevens.* Mount Pleasant: Clarke Historical Library, Central Michigan University, 1984.

Blakeney, Edward Henry, ed. *Horace on the Art of Poetry*. Freeport, N.Y.: Books for Libraries, 1970.

"The Bonebrake Letters." *Grassroots: Journal of Grant County Museum Guild* 6 (April 1986): 11–13.

Bottens, Dolly, comp. *Rouse-Stevens Ancestry & Allied Families*. Carthage, Mo.: Privately printed, 1970.

Britton, Wiley. *The Union Indian Brigade in the Civil War*. Kansas City, Mo.: Franklin Hudson, 1922.

Crawford, Samuel J. *Kansas in the Sixties*. Chicago: A . C. McClurg & Co., 1911.

"Diary of John S. Morgan, Company G, Thirty-Third Iowa Infantry," Part 1. *Annals of Iowa* 13 (January 1923): 482–508.

"Diary of John S. Morgan, Company G, Thirty-Third Iowa Infantry," Part 2. *Annals of Iowa* 13 (April 1923): 570–610.

Drake, F. M. "Campaign of General Steele." In *War Sketches and Incidents as Related by Companions of the Iowa Commandery, Military Order of the Loyal Legion of the United States*. Volume 1. Des Moines: Press of P. C. Kenyon, 1893, 60–73.

Edwards, John N. *Shelby and His Men; or, the War in the West*. Cincinnati: Miami, 1867.

Eison, James Reed, ed. "'Stand We in Jeopardy Every Hour': A Confederate Letter, 1864." *Pulaski County Historical Review* 31 (Fall 1993): 50–54.

Ewing, Laura. "The Retreat from Little Rock in 1863." *Pulaski County Historical Society Review* 11 (December 1963): 53–57.

"The Federal Occupation of Camden as Set Forth in the Diary of a Union Officer." *Arkansas Historical Quarterly* 9 (Autumn 1950): 214–19.

Fountain, Sarah M., ed. *Sisters, Seeds, & Cedars: Rediscovering Nineteenth-Century Life through Correspondence from Rural Arkansas and Alabama*. Conway: University of Central Arkansas Press, 1995.

Gaughan, Mrs. T. J., ed. *Letters of a Confederate Surgeon 1861–1865*. Camden, Ark.: Privately printed, 1960.

Hardee, W. J. *Rifle and Light Infantry Tactics; For the Exercise and Manoeuvres of Troops When Acting as Light Infantry or Riflemen*. 2 vols. Westport, Conn.: Greenwood Press, 1971.

Harrell, John M. "Arkansas." In *Confederate Military History*. Volume 10. Edited by Clement A. Evans. Secaucus, N.J.: Blue & Grey Press, 1975.

Ingersoll, Lurton Dunham. *Iowa and the Rebellion: A History of the Troops Furnished by the State of Iowa to the Volunteer Armies of the Union, Which Conquered the Great Southern Rebellion of 1861–65*. Philadelphia: J. B. Lippincott & Co., 1866.

Irving, Washington. *A Tour on the Prairies*. Edited by John Francis McDermott. Norman: University of Oklahoma Press, 1956.

Jones, Steven W., ed. "The Logs of the U.S.S. Tyler." *Phillips County Historical Quarterly* 15 (March 1977): 23–41.

Lacy [Lacey], John F. "A Battle Scene at Helena, Ark., July 4, 1863." In *The War of the 'Sixties*. Edited by E. R. Hutchins. New York: Neale Publishing Co., 1912, 193–96.

Leslie, James W., ed. "Arabella Lanktree Wilson's Civil War Letter." *Arkansas Historical Quarterly* 47 (Autumn 1988): 257–72.

Longacre, Edward G., ed. "Letters from Little Rock of Captain James M. Bowler, 112th United States Colored Troops." *Arkansas Historical Quarterly* 40 (Autumn 1981): 235–48.

Lothrop, Charles H. *A History of the First Regiment Iowa Cavalry Veteran Volunteers, from Its Organization in 1861 to Its Muster Out of the United States Service in 1866.* Lyons, Iowa: Beers & Eaton, 1890.

Marshall, Mrs. A. J. *Autobiography.* Pine Bluff, Ark.: Privately printed, 1897.

McLean, William E. *Forty-Third Regiment of Indiana Volunteers: An Historic Sketch of Its Career and Services.* Terre Haute, Ind.: C. W. Brown, 1903.

Moneyhon, Carl H., ed. "Life in Confederate Arkansas: The Diary of Virginia Davis Gray, 1863–1865, Part I." *Arkansas Historical Quarterly* 42 (Spring 1983): 47–85.

———. "Life in Confederate Arkansas: The Diary of Virginia Davis Gray, 1863–1865, Part II." *Arkansas Historical Quarterly* 42 (Summer 1983): 134–69.

Murray, Betty F., ed. *1860 U.S. Census: Conway County Arkansas.* Conway, Ark.: Oldbuck Press, 1993.

Newman, J. A. *The Autobiography of an Old Fashioned Boy.* El Reno, Okla.: Privately printed, 1923.

Nicholson, William L. "The Engagement at Jenkins' Ferry." *Annals of Iowa* 11 (October 1914): 505–19.

Petty, A. W. M. *A History of the Third Missouri Cavalry: From Its Organization at Palmyra, Missouri, 1861, Up to November Sixth, 1864: With an Appendix and Recapitulation.* Little Rock: J. William Denby, 1865.

Popchock, Barry, ed. *Soldier Boy: The Civil War Letters of Charles O. Musser, 29th Iowa.* Iowa City: University of Iowa Press, 1995.

Rea, Ralph R. "Diary of Private John P. Wright, U.S.A., 1864–1865." *Arkansas Historical Quarterly* 16 (Autumn 1957): 304–18.

Ripley, Warren, ed. *Siege Train: The Journal of a Confederate Artilleryman in the Defense of Charleston.* Columbia: University of South Carolina Press, 1986.

Rodgers, Alama, ed. *The Life Story of R. M. Rodgers.* Sheridan, Ark.: Grant County Museum, 1989.

Rood, H. H. "Iowa's Record: A Sketch of Iowa's Record during the War for the Preservation of the Union—1861–1865." In *War Sketches and Incidents as Related by Companions of the Iowa Commandery Military Order of the Loyal Legion of the United States.* Volume 1. Des Moines: Press of P. C. Kenyon, 1893.

Ross, Frances Mitchell, ed. "Civil War Letters from James Mitchell to His Wife, Sarah Elizabeth Latta Mitchell." *Arkansas Historical Quarterly* 37 (Winter 1978): 306–17.

Seeley, Greg, ed. *Ira Seeley Civil War Letters.* Afton, Iowa: Privately printed, 1981.

Sheridan, Philip H. *Personal Memoirs of P. H. Sheridan.* 2 vols. New York: Charles L. Webster & Co., 1888.

Skinner, James L., III, ed. *The Autobiography of Henry Merrell: Industrial Missionary to the South.* Athens: University of Georgia Press, 1991.

Stillwell, Leander. *The Story of a Common Soldier of Army Life in the Civil War, 1861–1865.* Erie, Kans.: Franklin Hudson, 1920.

Stinson, Virginia Mc'Collum. "Memories." In *The Garden of Memory: Stories of the Civil War as Told by Veterans and Daughters of the Confederacy.* Compiled by Mrs. M. A. Elliott. Camden, Ark.: Brown Printing Co., 1911, 28–35.

Stuart, A. A. *Iowa Colonels and Regiments: Being a History of Iowa Regiments in the War of the Rebellion; and Containing a Description of the Battles in Which They Have Fought.* Des Moines: Mills & Co., 1865.

Titsworth, Elizabeth, ed. "The Civil War Diary of a Logan County Soldier." *Wagon Wheels* 1 (Winter 1981): 16–25.

"A Union Soldier's Personal Account of the Red River Expedition and the Battle of Jenkins Ferry." *Grassroots* 8 (July 1988): 2–4.

United Confederate Veterans, Arkansas Division. *Confederate Women of Arkansas in the Civil War 1861–'65: Memorial Reminiscences.* Little Rock: H. G. Pugh Printing Co., 1907.

White, Lonnie J., ed. "A Bluecoat's Account of the Camden Expedition." *Arkansas Historical Quarterly* 24 (Spring 1965): 82–89.

Whittenmyer, Annie. "Under the Guns: A Woman's Reminiscences of the Civil War." *Phillips County Historical Quarterly* 17 (September 1979): 1–10.

Wilson, R. S. "The Battle of Jenkins's Ferry." *Confederate Veteran* 18 (October 1910): 468.

Yeary, Mamie, ed. *Reminiscences of the Boys in Gray, 1861–1865.* Dallas: Smith & Lamar, 1912.

Zorn, Roman J., ed. "Campaigning in Southern Arkansas: A Memoir by C. T. Anderson." *Arkansas Historical Quarterly* 8 (Autumn 1949): 240–44.

SECONDARY SOURCES

Newspapers

Arkansas Democrat-Gazette.
Arkansas Democrat.

Books and Articles

Allardice, Bruce S. *More Generals in Gray.* Baton Rouge: Louisiana State University Press, 1995.

Atkinson, James Harris, ed. "The Action at Prairie De Ann." *Arkansas Historical Quarterly* 19 (Spring 1960): 40–50.

————, ed. "The Battle of Marks Mill by Edward Atkinson." *Arkansas Historical Quarterly* 14 (Winter 1955): 381–84.

————. *Forty Days of Disaster: The Story of General Frederick Steele's Expedition into Southern Arkansas.* Little Rock: Pulaski County Historical Society, 1955.

Bailey, Anne J. "Was There a Massacre at Poison Spring?" *Military History of the Southwest* 20 (Fall 1990): 157–68.

Barnes, Kenneth C. "The Williams Clan: Mountain Farmers and Union Fighters in North Central Arkansas." *Arkansas Historical Quarterly* 52 (Autumn 1993): 286–317.

Bearss, Edwin C. "The Battle of Helena." *Arkansas Historical Quarterly* 20 (Autumn 1961): 256–97.

————. *The Campaign for Vicksburg.* 3 vols. Dayton, Ohio: Morningside House, 1985–86.

————. "Marmaduke Attacks Pine Bluff." *Arkansas Historical Quarterly* 22 (Winter 1964): 291–313.

————. *Steele's Retreat from Camden and the Battle of Jenkins' Ferry.* Little Rock: Eagle Press, 1990.

Bergeron, Arthur W., Jr. *Confederate Mobile.* Jackson: University Press of Mississippi, 1991.

Boatner, Mark Mayo. *The Civil War Dictionary.* New York: David McKay, 1954.

Bradbury, John F., Jr. "'This War Is Managed Mighty Strange': The Army of Southeastern Missouri, 1862–1863." *Missouri Historical Review* 89 (October 1994): 28–47.

Briggs, John E. "The Enlistment of Iowa Troops during the Civil War." *Iowa Journal of History and Politics* 15 (July 1917): 323–92.

Burnside, William H. *The Honorable Powell Clayton.* Conway: University of Central Arkansas Press, 1991.

Castel, Albert. *General Sterling Price and the Civil War in the West.* Baton Rouge: Louisiana State University Press, 1968.

Catton, Bruce. *Grant Moves South.* Boston: Little, Brown, 1960.

Christ, Mark K., ed. *Rugged and Sublime: The Civil War in Arkansas.* Fayetteville: University of Arkansas Press, 1994.

Clark, Dan Elbert. *Samuel Jordan Kirkwood.* Iowa City: State Historical Society of Iowa, 1917.

Current, Richard N., ed. *Encyclopedia of the Confederacy.* 4 vols. New York: Simon & Schuster, 1993.

————. *Lincoln's Loyalists: Union Soldiers from the Confederacy.* New York: Oxford University Press, 1992.

Dal Bello, Dominic J. *Parade, Inspection and Basic Evolutions of the Infantry Battalion: Being a Manual for Company Officers and Non-Commissioned Officers of Civil War Living History Units on the Movements of a Battalion of Infantry.* Santa Barbara, Calif.: Army of the Pacific, 1994.

Dary, David. *Cowboy Culture: A Saga of Five Centuries.* New York: Avon Books, 1982.

Davidson, Homer K. *Black Jack Davidson, a Cavalry Commander on the Western Frontier: The Life of General John W. Davidson.* Glendale, Calif.: A. H. Clark, 1974.

Dictionary of American Naval Fighting Ships. 8 vols. Washington, D.C.: Naval Historical Center, Department of the Navy, 1959–1981.

Dougan, Michael B. *Confederate Arkansas: The People and Policies of a Frontier State in Wartime.* University: University of Alabama Press, 1976.

Dyer, Frederick H., ed. *A Compendium of the War of the Rebellion: Compiled and Arranged from Official Records of the Federal and Confederate Armies, Reports of the Adjutant Generals of Several States, the Army Registers and Other Reliable Documents and Sources.* 2 vols. Dayton, Ohio: Morningside Bookshop, 1978.

Dykstra, Robert R. *Bright Radical Star: Black Freedom and White Supremacy on the Hawkeye Frontier.* Cambridge, Mass.: Harvard University Press, 1993.

Faust, Patricia L., ed. *Historical Times Illustrated Encyclopedia of the Civil War.* New York: Harper & Row, 1986.

Fellman, Michael. *Inside War: The Guerrilla Conflict in Missouri during the American Civil War.* New York: Oxford University Press, 1989.

Fischer, LeRoy H. "David O. Dodd: Folk Hero of Confederate Arkansas." *Arkansas Historical Quarterly* 37 (Summer 1978): 130–46.

Fisher, Mike. "The First Kansas Colored—Massacre at Poison Springs." *Kansas History* 2 (Summer 1979): 121–28.

———. "Remember Poison Spring." *Missouri Historical Review* 44 (April 1980): 323–42.

Fox, William F. *Regimental Losses in the American Civil War 1861–1865.* Albany, N.Y.: Brandow Printing Co., 1898.

Franzmann, Tom L. "'Peculiarly Situated between Rebellion and Loyalty': Civilized Tribes, Savagery, and the American Civil War." *Chronicles of Oklahoma* 78 (Summer 1998): 140–59.

Garafalo, Robert, and Mark Elrod. *A Pictorial History of Civil War Era Musical Instruments and Military Bands.* Charleston, W.V.: Pictorial Histories Publishing, 1985.

Garavaglia, Louis A., and Charles G. Worman. *Firearms of the American West, 1803–1865.* Niwot: University Press of Colorado, 1998.

Gatewood, Robert L. *Faulkner County, Arkansas, 1778–1964.* Conway, Ark.: Privately printed, 1964.

Gibbons, Tony. *Warships and Naval Battles of the Civil War.* New York: Gallery Books, 1989.

Gibson, Charles Dana, and E. Kay Gibson, comps. *Dictionary of Transports and Combatant Vessels, Steam and Sail, Employed by the Union Army, 1861–1868.* The Army's Navy Series. Camden, Me.: Ensign Press, 1995.

Glatthaar, Joseph T. *Forged in Battle: The Civil War Alliance of Black Soldiers and White Officers.* New York: Free Press, 1990.

————. *The March to the Sea and Beyond: Sherman's Troops in the Savannah and Carolinas Campaigns*. New York: New York University Press, 1985.

Griffith, Paddy. *Battle in the Civil War: Generalship and Tactics in America 1861–65*. Camberley, Surrey: Fieldbooks, 1986.

Harris, William C. *Presidential Reconstruction in Mississippi*. Baton Rouge: Louisiana State University Press, 1967.

Hearn, Chester G. *The Capture of New Orleans, 1862*. Baton Rouge: Louisiana State University Press, 1995.

————. *Mobile Bay and the Mobile Campaign*. Jefferson, N.C.: McFarland & Co., 1993.

Heitman, Francis B. *Historical Register and Dictionary of the United States Army, from Its Organization, September 29, 1789, to March 2, 1903*. 2 vols. Washington, D.C.: Government Printing Office, 1903.

Hinshaw, Jerry E. *Call the Roll: The First One Hundred Fifty Years of the Arkansas Legislature*. Little Rock: Rose Publishing Co., 1986.

The History of Mahaska County, Iowa, Containing a History of the County, Its Cities, Towns, &c. Des Moines: Union Historical Co., 1878.

The History of Marion County, Iowa, Containing a History of the County, Its Cities, Towns, &c. Des Moines: Union Historical Co., 1881.

Hood, Sinclair. *The Minoans: The Story of Bronze Age Crete*. New York: Praeger, 1971.

Horton, Louise. *Samuel Bell Maxey*. Austin: University of Texas Press, 1974.

Hubbell, John T., and James W. Geary, eds. *Biographical Dictionary of the Union: Northern Leaders of the Civil War*. Westport, Conn.: Greenwood Press, 1995.

Huff, Leo E. "The Memphis and Little Rock Railroad during the Civil War." *Arkansas Historical Quarterly* 23 (Autumn 1964): 260–70.

————. "The Union Expedition against Little Rock, August–September 1863." *Arkansas Historical Quarterly* 22 (Fall 1963): 224–37.

Hunt, Roger D., and Jack R. Brown. *Brevet Brigadier Generals in Blue*. Gaithersburg, Md.: Olde Soldier Books, 1990.

Hutton, Paul Andrew. *Phil Sheridan and His Army*. Lincoln: University of Nebraska Press, 1985.

Johansson, M. Jane. *Peculiar Honor: A History of the 28th Texas Cavalry, 1862–1865*. Fayetteville: University of Arkansas Press, 1998.

Johnson, Ludwell H. *Red River Campaign: Politics and Cotton in the Civil War*. Kent, Ohio: Kent State University Press, 1993.

Jones, Allen W., and Virginia Ann Buttry. "Military Events in Arkansas during the Civil War." *Arkansas Historical Quarterly* 22 (Summer 1963): 124–70.

Josephy, Alvin M., Jr. *The Civil War in the American West*. New York: Alfred A. Knopf, 1991.

————. *War on the Frontier: The Trans-Mississippi West*. Alexandria, Va.: Time-Life Books, 1986.

Joy, Edmund Frederick Steele. "Major General Frederick Steele and Staff." *Americana* 5 (1910): 349–52.

Junas, Lil. *Cadron Creek: A Photographic Narrative*. Little Rock: Ozark Society Foundation, 1979.

Katcher, Philip. *American Civil War Armies (3): Staff, Specialist and Maritime Services*. London: Osprey, 1986.

Kelly, Orr, and Mary Davies Kelly. *Dream's End: Two Iowa Brothers in the Civil War*. New York: Kodansha International, 1998.

King, James T. *War Eagle: A Life of General Eugene A. Carr*. Lincoln: University of Nebraska Press, 1963.

Knight, Rena Marie. *Civil War Soldiers Buried in Arkansas National Cemeteries*. Conway, Ark.: Arkansas Research, 1996.

Korn, Jerry. *War on the Mississippi: Grant's Vicksburg Campaign*. Alexandria, Va.: Time-Life Books, 1985.

Linderman, Gerald F. *Embattled Courage: The Experience of Combat in the American Civil War*. New York: Free Press, 1987.

Long, David E. *The Jewel of Liberty: Abraham Lincoln's Re-election and the End of Slavery*. Mechanicsburg, Pa.: Stackpole Books, 1994.

Lord, Francis A. *Civil War Collector's Encyclopedia*. Harrisburg, Pa.: Stackpole Books, 1965.

Lord, Francis A., and Arthur Wise. *Bands and Drummer Boys of the Civil War*. New York: Da Capo Press, 1979.

Lowry, Don. *No Turning Back: The Beginning of the End of the Civil War, March–June 1864*. New York: Hippocrene Books, 1992.

Lyftogt, Kenneth L. *From Blue Mills to Columbia: Cedar Falls and the Civil War*. Ames: Iowa State University Press, 1993.

Marszalek, John F. *Sherman: A Soldier's Passion for Order*. New York: Vintage Books, 1994.

May, Joe. *The Way We Were: A Pictorial History of Clark County*. Arkadelphia, Ark.: Curtis Media, 1995.

McMillan, James E., ed. *Artisans and Musicians, Dutch and American: Pella, Iowa, 1854–1960*. Pella, Ia.: Pella Printing Co., 1997.

McPherson, Alex. *The History of Faulkner County, Arkansas*. Conway, Ark.: Conway Times Plant, 1927.

Meyer, Steve, ed. *Iowa Valor: A Compilation of Civil War Combat Experiences from Soldiers of the State Distinguished as Most Patriotic of the Patriotic*. Garrison, Iowa: Meyer Publishing, 1994.

———. *Iowans Called to Valor: The Story of Iowa's Entry into the Civil War*. Garrison, Iowa: Meyer Publishing, 1993.

Milligan, John D. *Gunboats Down the Mississippi*. Annapolis, Md.: United States Naval Institute, 1965.

Mitchell, Reid. *The Vacant Chair: The Northern Soldier Leaves Home*. New York: Oxford University Press, 1993.

Monaghan, Jay. *Civil War on the Western Border, 1854–1865*. Boston: Little, Brown, 1955.

Moneyhon, Carl H. *The Impact of the Civil War and Reconstruction on*

Arkansas: Persistence in the Midst of Ruin. Baton Rouge: Louisiana State University Press, 1994.

Moneyhon, Carl, and Bobby Roberts. *Portraits of Conflict: A Photographic History of Louisiana in the Civil War.* Fayetteville: University of Arkansas Press, 1990.

Mullins, Michael, and Rowena Reed. *The Union Bookshelf: A Selected Civil War Bibliography.* Wendell, N.C.: Broadfoot's Bookmark, 1982.

Murdock, Eugene C. *The Civil War in the North: A Selective Annotated Bibliography.* New York: Garland, 1987.

Musick, Michael P. "The Little Regiment: Civil War Units and Commands." *Prologue: Quarterly of the National Archives* 27 (Summer 1995): 151–71.

Naval History Division, Navy Department, comp. *Civil War Naval Chronology, 1861–1865.* Washington, D.C.: U.S. Government Printing Office, 1971.

Nelson, Julie E., and Alan M. Schroder. "Iowa and the Civil War: A Military Review." *Palimpsest* 63 (July/August 1982): 98–105.

Nevins, Allan, James I. Robertson Jr., and Bell I. Wiley. *Civil War Books: A Critical Bibliography.* 2 vols. Baton Rouge: Louisiana State University Press, 1970.

Newberry, Farrar. "The Yankee Schoolmarm Who 'Captured' Post-War Arkadelphia." *Arkansas Historical Quarterly* 17 (Fall 1958): 265–71.

Nichols, Ronnie. "Baptism by Fire." *Arkansas Preservation,* Fall 1991, 12.

Noel, John V. *The VNR Dictionary of Ships and the Sea.* New York: Van Nostrand Reinhold, 1981.

Oates, Stephen B. *Confederate Cavalry West of the River.* Austin: University of Texas Press, 1992.

O'Donnell, William W. *The Civil War Quadrennium: A Narrative History of Day-to-Day Life in Little Rock, Arkansas, during the American War between the States, 1861–1865.* Little Rock: Civil War Round Table of Arkansas, 1985.

Olson, Kenneth E. *Music and Musket: Bands and Bandsmen of the American Civil War.* Westport, Conn.: Greenwood Press, 1981.

Parrish, T. Michael. *Richard Taylor: Soldier Prince of Dixie.* Chapel Hill: University of North Carolina Press, 1992.

Payne, Charles E. *Josiah Bushnell Grinnell.* Iowa City: State Historical Society of Iowa, 1938.

Pereyra, Lillian A. *James Lusk Alcorn: Persistent Whig.* Baton Rouge: Louisiana State University Press, 1966.

Perkins, John D. "The Titus Hunters: Company D, 11th Texas Infantry Regiment, Walker's Division." *East Texas Historical Journal* 35, no. 1 (1997): 17–29.

Peterson, Harold L. *Round Shot and Rammers.* Harrisburg, Pa.: Stackpole Books, 1969.

Prucha, Francis Paul. *A Guide to the Military Posts of the United States, 1789–1895.* Madison: State Historical Society of Wisconsin, 1964.

Rea, Ralph R. *Sterling Price: The Lee of the West.* Little Rock: Pioneer Press,
    1959.
Reynolds, Clark G. *Famous American Admirals.* New York: Van Nostrand
    Reinhold, 1978.
Richards, Ira Don. "The Battle of Jenkins' Ferry." *Arkansas Historical
    Quarterly* 20 (Spring 1961): 3–16.
———. "The Battle of Poison Spring." *Arkansas Historical Quarterly* 18
    (Winter 1959): 338–49.
———. "The Engagement at Marks' Mills." *Arkansas Historical Quarterly* 19
    (Spring 1960): 51–60.
———. *Story of a Rivertown, Little Rock in the Nineteenth Century.* Benton,
    Ark.: Privately printed, 1969.
Richter, Wendy, ed. *Clark County, Arkansas: Past and Present.* Arkadelphia:
    Clark County Historical Association, 1992.
Roberts, Bobby, and Carl Moneyhon. *Portraits of Conflict: A Photographic
    History of Arkansas in the Civil War.* Fayetteville: University of Arkansas
    Press, 1987.
Roy, F. Hampton, Charles Witsell Jr., and Cheryl Griffith Nichols. *How We
    Lived: Little Rock as an American City.* Little Rock: August House, 1984.
Rushing, Anthony C. "Rackensacker Raiders: Crawford's First Arkansas
    Cavalry." *Civil War Regiments* 1, no. 2 (1991): 44–69.
Scott, Kim Allen. "A Diminished Landscape: The Life and Death of Major
    Robert Henry Smith." *Missouri Historical Review* 91 (July 1997): 353–72.
Shalhope, Robert E. *Sterling Price: Portrait of a Southerner.* Columbia:
    University of Missouri Press, 1971.
Shea, William L. "The Camden Fortifications." *Arkansas Historical Quarterly*
    41 (Winter 1982): 318–26.
Shea, William L., and Earl J. Hess. *Pea Ridge: Civil War Campaign in the West.*
    Chapel Hill: University of North Carolina Press, 1992.
Silber, Irwin. *Songs of the Civil War.* New York: Columbia University Press,
    1960.
Simon, Donald J. "The Third Minnesota Regiment in Arkansas, 1863–1865."
    Minnesota History 40 (Summer 1967): 281–92.
Smith, Robin. *American Civil War Union Army.* Brassey's History of Uniforms.
    London: Brassey's, 1996.
Starr, Stephen Z. "The Grand Old Regiment." *Wisconsin Magazine of History* 48
    (1964): 21–31.
———. "The Second Michigan Volunteer Cavalry: Another View." *Michigan
    History* 60 (1976): 161–82.
———. "The Third Ohio Volunteer Cavalry: A View from the Inside." *Ohio
    History* 85 (1976): 306–18.
Stone, Jayme Lynne. "Brother against Brother: The Winter Skirmishes along
    the Arkansas River, 1864–1865." *Military History of the West* 25 (Spring
    1995): 32–46.

Sutherland, Daniel E. "Guerrillas: The Real War in Arkansas." *Arkansas Historical Quarterly* 52 (Autumn 1993): 257–85.

Swisher, Jacob A. *Iowa in Times of War.* Iowa City: State Historical Society of Iowa, 1943.

Taylor, Joe Gray. *Louisiana Reconstructed, 1863–1877.* Baton Rouge: Louisiana State University Press, 1974.

Taylor, John M. *William Henry Seward: Lincoln's Right Hand.* New York: HarperCollins, 1991.

Throne, Mildred. "The Iowa Regiments." *Palimpsest* 50 (February 1969): 65–68.

Todd, Frederick P. *American Military Equipage, 1851–1872.* Vol. 2, *State Forces.* New York: Chatham Square Press, 1983.

Urwin, Gregory J. W. "'The Lord Has Not Forsaken Me and I Won't Forsake Him': Religion in Frederick Steele's Union Army, 1863–1864." *Arkansas Historical Quarterly* 52 (Autumn 1993): 318–40.

————. "Notes on the First Confederate Volunteers from Ouachita County, Arkansas, 1861." *Military Collector & Historian* 49 (Summer 1997): 83–84.

————. *The United States Infantry: An Illustrated History, 1775–1918.* New York: Sterling, 1991.

————. "'We Cannot Treat Negroes . . . as Prisoners of War': Racial Atrocities and Reprisals in Civil War Arkansas." *Civil War History* 42 (September 1996): 193–210.

Van Stigt, K. *History of Pella, Iowa and Vicinity.* Translated by Elisabeth Kempkes. Pella, Iowa: Scholte House Foundation, 1995.

Wakelyn, Jon L. *Biographical Dictionary of the Confederacy.* Westport, Conn.: Greenwood Press, 1977.

Warner, Ezra J. *Generals in Blue: The Lives of the Union Commanders.* Baton Rouge: Louisiana State University Press, 1964.

————. *Generals in Gray: Lives of the Confederate Commanders.* Baton Rouge: Louisiana State University Press, 1959.

Welcher, Frank J. *The Union Army, 1861–1865. Organization and Operations.* Vol. 2, *The Western Theater.* Bloomington: Indiana University Press, 1993.

Wiley, Bell Irvin. *The Life of Billy Yank: The Common Soldier of the Union.* Baton Rouge: Louisiana State University Press, 1978.

————. *The Life of Johnny Reb: The Common Soldier of the Confederacy.* Baton Rouge: Louisiana State University Press, 1978.

Wills, Brian Steel. *A Battle from the Start: The Life of Nathan Bedford Forrest.* New York: HarperCollins, 1992.

Winter, William C. *The Civil War in St. Louis: A Guided Tour.* St. Louis: Missouri Historical Society Press, 1994.

Woodhead, Henry, ed. *Echoes of Glory: Arms and Equipment of the Union.* Alexandria, Va.: Time-Life Books, 1991.

Woods, James M. *Rebellion and Realignment: Arkansas's Road to Secession.* Fayetteville: University of Arkansas Press, 1987.

Work, John W. *American Negro Songs.* New York: Howell, Soskin & Co., 1940.

Wubben, Hubert H. *Civil War Iowa and the Copperhead Movement.* Ames: Iowa State University Press, 1980.

Theses

Bellas, Joseph. "The Forgotten Loyalists: Unionism in Arkansas, 1861–1865." M.A. thesis, Ohio State University, 1991.

Dunn, Mace A. "A History of Pottsville, Arkansas." M.S.E. thesis, University of Central Arkansas, 1962.

McReynolds, Nina. "A Town That Disappeared: Lewisburg, Arkansas." M.S. thesis, University of Central Arkansas, 1958.

INDEX